The Art of Creating Self-Organizing Teams

Agile Team Coaching from a Journeyman to an Expert

Roman Lobus

The Art of Creating Self-Organizing Teams: Agile Team Coaching from a Journeyman to an Expert

Roman Lobus
Singapore, Singapore

ISBN-13 (pbk): 979-8-8688-2150-9　　　ISBN-13 (electronic): 979-8-8688-2151-6
https://doi.org/10.1007/979-8-8688-2151-6

Copyright © 2025 by Roman Lobus

This work is subject to copyright. All rights are reserved by the publisher, whether the whole or part of the material is concerned, specifically the rights of translation, reprinting, reuse of illustrations, recitation, broadcasting, reproduction on microfilms or in any other physical way, and transmission or information storage and retrieval, electronic adaptation, computer software, or by similar or dissimilar methodology now known or hereafter developed.

Trademarked names, logos, and images may appear in this book. Rather than use a trademark symbol with every occurrence of a trademarked name, logo, or image we use the names, logos, and images only in an editorial fashion and to the benefit of the trademark owner, with no intention of infringement of the trademark.

The use in this publication of trade names, trademarks, service marks, and similar terms, even if they are not identified as such, is not to be taken as an expression of opinion as to whether or not they are subject to proprietary rights.

While the advice and information in this book are believed to be true and accurate at the date of publication, neither the authors nor the editors nor the publisher can accept any legal responsibility for any errors or omissions that may be made. The publisher makes no warranty, express or implied, with respect to the material contained herein.

>	Managing Director, Apress Media LLC: Welmoed Spahr
>	Acquisitions Editor: Shivangi Ramachandran
>	Development Editor: James Markham
>	Editorial Assistant: Jessica Vakili
>	Copy Editor: April Rondeau

Cover designed by eStudioCalamar

Distributed to the book trade worldwide by Springer Science+Business Media New York, 1 New York Plaza, New York, NY 10004. Phone 1-800-SPRINGER, fax (201) 348-4505, e-mail orders-ny@springer-sbm.com, or visit www.springeronline.com. Apress Media, LLC is a Delaware LLC and the sole member (owner) is Springer Science + Business Media Finance Inc (SSBM Finance Inc). SSBM Finance Inc is a **Delaware** corporation.

For information on translations, please e-mail booktranslations@springernature.com; for reprint, paperback, or audio rights, please e-mail bookpermissions@springernature.com.

Apress titles may be purchased in bulk for academic, corporate, or promotional use. eBook versions and licenses are also available for most titles. For more information, reference our Print and eBook Bulk Sales web page at http://www.apress.com/bulk-sales.

Any source code or other supplementary material referenced by the author in this book is available to readers on GitHub. For more detailed information, please visit https://www.apress.com/gp/services/source-code.

If disposing of this product, please recycle the paper

For
Melissa *— Your unwavering support and
belief in me have meant more than words can say.
and*
Uliana *— Your quiet strength has inspired me
in ways you may never fully know.*

Table of Contents

About the Author xiii

Acknowledgments xvii

Introduction xix

Part I: Team Coaching for Agility 1

Chapter 1: Why Use Team Coaching in the Agile Context 3

The Agile Landscape and the Growing Need for Team Coaching 3
How Team Coaching Differs from Other Practices 5
How Team Coaching Aligns with Agile Principles 7
    Empowering Self-Organizing Teams 7
    Fostering Collaboration and Communication 8
    Driving Continuous Improvement 9
    Navigating Change and Complexity 10
The Evolving Role of the Agile Coach: From Directive to Facilitative 10
Addressing Team Dynamics and Relationships 13
Challenges in Implementing Agile Team Coaching 16
    Balancing Coaching with Directing (When to Coach Versus When to Lead) 16
    Distinguishing the Team Coach Role from the Scrum Master (and Other Roles) 17
    Measuring Impact and ROI of Team Coaching 18
    Overcoming Resistance to Coaching 19
    Investing in Coach Development 20
Conclusion: Unlocking Agile's Full Potential Through Team Coaching 22

TABLE OF CONTENTS

Chapter 2: Mastering the Fundamentals: Essential Competencies for Agile Team Coaches 23

Competency 1: Demonstrates Ethical Practice 24

Competency 2: Embodies a Coaching Mindset 25

Competency 3: Establishes and Maintains Agreements 27

Competency 4: Cultivates Trust and Safety..29

Competency 5: Maintains Presence...31

Competency 6: Listens Actively..33

Competency 7: Evokes Awareness...35

Competency 8: Facilitates Client Growth 37

Team Coaching vs. Agile Facilitation..40

Conclusion 42

Part II: Coaching Techniques and Processes 45

Chapter 3: Sealing the Deal: Effective Contracting............................47

Why Contract...48

Contracting = Alliance Building..52

Meet the Sponsor...55

Contact Before Contract...57

    Key Elements of Genuine Contact 58

    Story: Slowing Down to Speed Up 61

Holding the Coaching Relationship Together 62

    Administrative Level: Setting the Ground Rules 63

    Professional Level: What Are We Really Here to Do?......................63

    Psychological Contracting: The Unspoken Layer............................64

Pitfalls to Avoid 71

    Start Coaching Immediately Without Contracting..........................71

The Team and Sponsor Don't Understand the Difference Between Team Coaching and Skills Transfer 72

Omitted Sponsor 74

Objectives and Goals Are Vague 75

Negative Goals 76

Conclusion 76

Reflection Moment: Strengthening Contracting in Your Agile Team Coaching 78

Chapter 4: Rewriting the Team Imago 81

Self-organization in Teams: What Does It Mean? 82

The Group Imago: Our Inner Picture of "Team" 87

Boundaries, Roles, Authority, and Power: The Guardrails for Self-Organization 95

Common Traps and Ethical Considerations in Group Imago Coaching 103

Ethical Considerations 110

Conclusion 113

Reflection Moment 114

Chapter 5: Self-Organization Toolkit 117

Step 1: Contract & Context 119

Step 2: Elicit Individual Imagos 121

Step 3: Create a Shared Working Imago 128

Step 4: Calibrate Roles, Authority & Power 138

Step 5: Agree on the Operating System for Self-Organization 144

Step 6: Run Bounded Experiments 152

Step 7: Repair & Re-imprint 158

Step 8: Measure, Reflect, Sustain 165

Conclusion 172

Reflection Moment 174

TABLE OF CONTENTS

Part III: Navigating Challenging Situations 175

Chapter 6: Clearing the Roadblocks: Psychological Distance, Hidden Contracts 177

The Triangle of Psychological Distance 177

Diagnose Psychological Distance 185

Intervening Based on Psychological Distance 189

The Five Questions Tool 195

Conclusion 198

Reflection Moment 199

Chapter 7: Power Plays and Hidden Dynamics Revealed 201

Understanding the "Secret Life" and the Underlying Dynamics of Teams 202

Identifying and Addressing Specific Hidden Challenges 209

    Hidden Challenge 1: Power Imbalances and Authority Dynamics 210

    Hidden Challenge 2: Hidden Agendas and Unspoken Goals 212

    Hidden Challenge 3: Undiscussable Conflicts and Tensions........................214

    Hidden Challenge 4: Role Ambiguity and Boundary Issues 216

Psychological Games in Agile Team Coaching 219

    "Why Don't You/Yes, But" 220

    "I'm Only Trying to Help You" 223

    "If It Weren't For You . . ." 226

    "Ain't It Awful" 230

Conclusion 235

Reflection Moment: What Is Not Visible? 237

    Recognizing Hidden Dynamics 237

    Personal Role in Power Dynamics 238

    Spotting Psychological Games 238

    Surfacing the Undiscussable 238
    Reflecting on Systemic Roles 239

Chapter 8: Turning Resistance into Resilience 241

    The Roots of Resistance 242
        Fear of Change 242
        Lack of Trust and Psychological Safety 243
        Perceived Loss of Control 244
        Habitual Patterns and Group Dynamics (the "Immunity to Change") 245
        Conflicting Agendas 247
        Coach's Missteps and Contribution 248
    Strategies for Navigating and Overcoming Resistance 250
        Adopt an Empathic and Neutral Coaching Stance 250
        Work with the Present Moment (Here-and-Now Interventions) 251
        Facilitate Open Dialogue and Listening 253
        Address and Reframe Patterns or Stories 255
        Manage Difficult Behaviors Constructively 256
        Resolve (or Surface) Conflicting Agendas 258
        Leverage Clear Contracting and Re-contracting 260
    Assisting Teams in Building Resilience 263
        Define and Model Team Resilience 263
        Cultivate a Growth Mindset (Embrace Uncertainty) 265
        Foster Team Agency and Ownership 267
        Learn from History: Promote Reflection and Adaptation 269
        Strengthen Purpose and Leverage Strengths 272
    R➤R Flywheel + Resistance Radar: Practitioner Guide 274
        The R➤R Flywheel 275
    Conclusion 279
    Reflection Moment: How Do I Deal with Resistance in Teams? 281

TABLE OF CONTENTS

Chapter 9: Staying True 283
- The Team Is the Primary Client 284
- Confidentiality in Agile Team Coaching 285
  - Story 287
- Managing Conflicts of Interest and Multiple Agendas.........................288
  - Summary of Actions 291
- Shifting from Bystander to Contributor 291
  - The Boundary Between Bystanding and Contractual Engagement 295
- Developing Ethical Maturity 299
- Conclusion 303
- Reflection Moment: Ethical Check-up..304

Chapter 10: Going Virtual 305
- The Challenges of Coaching Virtual Teams 307
- Technological Demands and Digital Fatigue 308
- Building Trust from Afar 310
- Communication Gaps 313
- Blurred Boundaries 316
- Designing Engaging and Effective Virtual Sessions 318
- Key Practices and Interventions for Successful Virtual Coaching....................323
  - Virtual Contracting...323
  - Coach's Presence in the Virtual Space 327
  - Leveraging Digital Tools for Engagement and Collaboration 330
  - Fostering Team Dynamics and Accountability Remotely 332
- Conclusion 336
- Reflection Moment..338

Part IV: Enhancing the Coaching Craft 341

Chapter 11: What If We Don't Need Another Tool to Be Impactful? ..343

Understanding Vertical Development for the Coach: A Shift in Being 345

Why the Agile Team Coach's Vertical Development Matters 348

    Navigating Complexity and Ambiguity 348

    Working with Systemic Challenges 349

    Holding the Coaching Space Under Pressure 350

    Managing Multiple Stakeholders and Agendas 351

    Role-modeling Growth and Agility 352

    Supporting the Team Leader's Development 353

    Enhancing Ethical Maturity and Wisdom 354

Cultivating the Coach's Vertical Development 355

    Engaging in Coaching Supervision 356

    Receiving Individual Coaching (Being the Coachee) 358

    Engaging in Reflective Practice 359

    Continuous Learning (Horizontal Learning with Vertical Benefits) 361

    Seeking and Processing Feedback 363

    Confronting and Learning from Challenging Assignments 364

    Developing Systemic Awareness 366

Conclusion 368

Reflection Moment 369

Chapter 12: Pause, Reflect, Act 371

Core Concepts of Reflective Practice 374

    Deeper Learning: Adult Development and Double-Loop Learning 376

    Superficial vs. Transformational Reflection 378

Applying Reflective Practice: Agile Coaching Scenarios 380

    Scenario: Team Resistance 380

TABLE OF CONTENTS

    Scenario: Uncertainty in Facilitating a Difficult Conversation 382

    Scenario: Burnout, Ethical Dilemmas, or Identity Conflicts 384

Reflective Tools and Techniques 386

    Journaling Prompts and Exercises for Agile Coaches 386

    Transformational Journaling: Emotions, Assumptions, and Patterns 388

    Structured Reflection Frameworks for Coaches 390

Designing a Reflective Practice Routine 396

    Integrating Reflection into Daily, Weekly, and Sprint Rhythms 396

Common Pitfalls and How to Avoid Them 398

    When Reflection Turns into Rumination 398

    Beyond the Checklist: Authentic Engagement vs. Going Through the Motions 399

    Uncovering Blind Spots: Seeing What You Normally Miss 401

Conclusion 402

Reflection Moment: Reflect on Your Reflective Practice 403

Chapter 13: The Power of Supervision and Deliberate Practice 405

The Essence of Coaching Supervision 406

Models and Frameworks in Agile Team Coaching Supervision 413

    The 3 P's: Philosophy, Purpose, Process (PPP) 413

Hawkins' Seven-Eyed Model: A Systemic Lens for Agile Contexts 415

The CLEAR Model for Supervisory Sessions 422

Cultivating Deliberate Practice 427

    Integrating Deliberate Practice into Agile Coaching Development 428

Practical Application: Scenarios and Structures for Agile Coaches 433

    Navigating Complex Team Dynamics and Conflicting Agendas 433

    Addressing Ethical Dilemmas in Multi-Stakeholder Environments 434

    Managing the Coach's Emotional Responses and Biases 435

Setting Up Your Supervision and Reflective Practice Ecosystem 437
    Individual Supervision: Finding the Right Fit 437
    Group Supervision: Leveraging Collective Wisdom 438
    Peer Supervision Chains and Communities of Practice................................ 439
    Action Learning Sets for Collaborative Problem Solving 440
Overcoming Challenges in Supervision and Deliberate Practice 442
    Addressing the "Checklist" Mentality.. 442
    Bridging the Gap Between Theory and "Being".. 444
Conclusion 445
Reflection Moment... 448

Chapter 14: Mastering the Inner Game: Staying Grounded in Chaos 449

Recognizing Your Internal Signals—The Body, Mind, and Saboteurs 450
    Scenario Based on a Real Story 455
Instant Grounding—Pausing in the Moment of Challenge............................... 456
    Scenario Based on a Real Story (Continued) 459
Unhooking from Difficult Thoughts and Feelings—Defusion and Acceptance 460
    Scenario Based on a Real Story (Continued) 464
Reconnecting with Your Purpose and Values 465
    Scenario Based on a Real Story (Continued) 468
Shifting to Sage Mode—Leveraging Your Innate Powers 469
    Scenario Based on a Real Story (Conclusion)... 476
Integration and Continuous Practice—Your Coach's Toolbox 478
    Scenario Based on a Real Story (Final) 482
Conclusion 483
Reflection Moment... 484

TABLE OF CONTENTS

EPILOGUE: The Long Game: Beyond Frameworks to Living Systems 487

Appendix A: TA Cheatsheet for Agile Coaches 501

Appendix B: Techniques and Methods for Group Imago Coaching for Self-Organization 513

Appendix C: References 519

Index 525

About the Author

Roman Lobus is an Agile team coach and organizational change leader who helps teams and leaders turn complex work into steady, self-managed progress. He is a Professional Scrum Trainer with Scrum.org, coaching across Southeast Asia and beyond. Blending deep practice with rigorous training, Roman holds ICF-PCC accreditation, is a Certified Professional Co-Active Coach (CPCC), and is certified in Organization and Relationship Systems Coaching (ORSC). His approach draws on group dynamics, transactional analysis, and vertical development to make human systems visible and workable in everyday Agile contexts. With over 20 years in professional services and enterprise environments, Roman has supported transformations across sectors from finance and logistics to government and aviation. He regularly presents at international conferences, including XP, Scrum Day Europe, and Regional Scrum Gatherings, sharing practical playbooks for self-management and leadership.

Acknowledgments

This book exists because practice needed a companion. When I began coaching Agile teams, I could find methods and frameworks, but far less on the human work of helping a team become truly self-organizing. The gap showed up in real rooms—with sticky notes, awkward silences, competing agendas—and it was the people in those rooms who taught me the most. What follows is a thank-you to those who challenged me, steadied me, and opened doors so that this manuscript could meet the moment.

Early drafts of the "team imago" work were messy by design. I remember bringing an outline to a supervision circle and being asked, "Where's the evidence behind this leap?" That question sharpened Chapter 4 and, frankly, my coaching. I'm especially grateful to Sari van Poijle for her generous contribution to team coaching through transactional analysis (TA) — her writing and teaching helped me translate TA into pragmatic moves for Agile coaches. Her insistence on clean contracting and ethical clarity echoes throughout these pages.

In one engagement, a developer sketched their "ideal team" as a lighthouse and the "real team" as a tugboat stuck in fog. That drawing became a prompt I now use often. To all the leaders, Agile coaches, Scrum masters, and Agile practitioners I've worked with: You loaned me your challenges — conflicting agendas, hidden contracts, unspoken fears — and in doing so, you gave this book its spine. Your willingness to experiment, to test a consent decision here or a clearer boundary there, underpins the practical tone you'll find in the tools chapters.

Several employers created conditions where I could practice, fail safely, and try again. In particular, colleagues and leaders who supported coaching experiments and evidence-based decisions helped me refine the

ACKNOWLEDGMENTS

material on contracting, supervision, and measurement. I'm grateful for the space to do real work with real stakes. Any views or errors in this book are mine; gratitude is not endorsement.

To protect privacy, I've blended details and changed identifying features; examples illustrate patterns, not people. If you recognize a situation, it's likely because many teams face similar dynamics — and that is the point.

This manuscript was drafted across borders and time zones. With respect, I acknowledge the diverse communities and cultures in which these ideas were shaped and are now read. Wherever you are reading this, you bring your own context to the work; may this book meet you there.

Finally, to you, the readers. Perhaps you picked this up after a bruising sprint review, or because you sense your team can hold more authority than you currently allow. Thank you for trusting this book enough to try something. My hope is that these pages shorten your learning curve, steady your hand in the storm, and make your teams' work a little more human—and a lot more theirs.

Introduction

Why Self-Organizing Teams Matter More Than Ever

Agile ways of working have swept through industries, promising faster delivery, higher quality, and engaged teams. Yet behind every truly successful Agile initiative lies a key ingredient: a self-organizing team. In today's fast-paced, complex environment, no single manager or playbook can micromanage every decision. Teams need autonomy and trust to respond rapidly to change. In fact, the Agile Manifesto itself proclaims that "the best architectures, requirements, and designs emerge from self-organizing teams," and the Scrum Guide emphasizes that such teams *"choose how best to accomplish their work, rather than being directed by others outside the team."* In other words, Agile *works* when teams are empowered to work out the "how" themselves.

Why is this so urgent now? While generative artificial intelligence (GenAI) offers significant potential to enhance Agile teams, it also introduces a set of subtle but serious threats that teams must navigate with care. One of the most immediate risks is over-reliance. When teams begin to trust GenAI outputs without critical evaluation, they may unintentionally bypass the collaborative conversations that are core to Agile decision-making. AI-generated code, test cases, or user stories might seem efficient, but the team risks building the wrong thing faster without shared human understanding. The erosion of collective sense-making can lead to a fragile kind of self-organization—one where the surface looks productive, but the underlying cohesion and clarity are weak.

Another threat lies in the potential flattening of learning curves. Agile teams typically grow by navigating complexity together—resolving disagreements, experimenting, and refining their practices through feedback loops. If GenAI starts delivering ready-made answers, teams might skip over the discomfort that leads to deep learning. This could result in shallow agility, where teams appear adaptable but aren't truly developing the resilience or critical thinking needed for long-term improvement. There's also the risk that AI tools subtly reinforce biases, promote groupthink, or introduce opaque logic into decision-making. Without deliberate oversight, these risks can undermine psychological safety and trust within the team.

Research bears this out: lack of team empowerment is a top impediment to Agile success. The 17th State of Agile report[1] found that one-third of respondents saw teams *"not empowered to be self-organized"* as a significant barrier to Agile adoption. In short, enabling teams to self-organize is not a "nice to have"—it's critical for survival and success in the Agile age. Traditional management approaches and off-the-shelf resources often fall short here because they don't show how to *get* a team to that self-driven state. This book starts by recognizing that urgency and aims to fill that gap.

Envisioning Great Self-Organizing Teams

Imagine a small Agile team in action: Teammates huddle around a table with sticky notes and laptops, enthusiastically planning their next sprint. There's a buzz of energy and trust in the room. Everyone's voice is heard, ideas flow freely, and decisions are made collectively. Now extend that picture: When challenges arise, the team members instinctively rally

---

[1] https://2288549.fs1.hubspotusercontent-na1.net/hubfs/2288549/RE-SA-17th-Annual-State-Of-Agile-Report.pdf

together to solve them without waiting for a manager to tell them what to do. In Daily Scrum, they don't report status—they collaborate, adjusting to ensure the most important work gets done. If a blocker emerges, a developer and tester might pair up to tackle it, or the team might swarm on the issue until it's resolved. There's no finger-pointing or "that's not my job"—the team owns its outcomes together.

In a truly self-organizing team, you can feel a sense of ownership from every member. These teams aren't chaotic; they have clear goals and discipline, yet they also enjoy the freedom to decide *how* to reach those targets. The environment is safe enough for people to voice concerns and wild ideas, knowing their colleagues will consider them. Leadership is still present but takes a different form—more facilitative than directive. A Scrum master or Agile coach acts as a gardener, quietly creating conditions for growth, fostering trust, clarifying purpose, and then stepping back to let the team shine. You notice an engaged focus when you walk into such a team's workspace (or join their video call). Problems are met with curiosity and collective brainstorming rather than dread. The result? These teams consistently deliver value, innovate, and improve. They quickly adapt to change because they've learned to self-correct and self-manage. This is the vision of agility unleashed—a team of empowered individuals coordinating seamlessly, much like a jazz ensemble improvising a performance. And just as even the best ensemble benefits from a great conductor, so too does the best Agile team benefit from a coach who knows how to unlock their potential. With skilful coaching, an ordinary group can evolve into a high-performing, self-organizing powerhouse.

The Coaching Gap in Agile Practice

If self-organizing teams are so critical, why aren't they the norm? This issue lies at the heart of many Agile struggles. The truth is, it's one thing to *tell* a team to self-organize and quite another for them to actually do it. Agile

INTRODUCTION

frameworks assume teams will take on this responsibility, yet often fail to clearly outline *how* to achieve it. Many Scrum masters and Agile coaches find themselves trained in Scrum events, backlogs, and burndown charts, yet feel unprepared to tackle the human dynamics that can make or break self-organization. There's a gap in the literature and practice: While there are numerous guides on Agile mechanics, there are far fewer resources on the *art* of nurturing a self-organizing team. As a result, Agile practitioners are frequently left without a playbook for the most crucial aspect of their role—coaching the human side of agility.

Consider the common scenario: An organization "goes Agile," and teams are told they are now self-organizing. In theory, this means managers step back, and teams take ownership. In practice, old habits and hierarchies don't disappear overnight. Team members, long accustomed to being directed, may be unsure how to *behave* as a self-driven unit. As Scrum co-creator Ken Schwaber observed, being managed is deeply ingrained in our work lives; simply declaring a team self-managing often leaves them confused about what that really means. Without guidance, a team might slide back into waiting for orders or descend into chaos due to a lack of coordination. This frustrates everyone. Leadership laments, "Why aren't they self-organizing as expected?" while team members feel set up to fail. What's missing is coaching tailored to the team level. Traditional management training doesn't address this, and many Agile resources only scratch the surface, perhaps advising "trust the team" or "the Scrum master coaches the team in self-organization" (as the Scrum Guide mentions), but without concrete techniques. Agile coaches often learn through trial and error how to foster teamwork, resolve conflict, encourage participation, and build trust. It's a slow, uncertain learning curve. Clearly, we need more practical guidance on cultivating self-organization—guidance that draws not just on Agile theory but also on the rich discipline of professional coaching and group facilitation.

A Practical Solution: Agile Meets Professional Coaching

When I began my journey as an Agile coach two decades ago, the role felt fragmented, with scattered insights and no coherent guidance on effectively navigating the complexities of team dynamics within Agile contexts or how to organize the team-coaching process. Books either spoke theoretically about professional coaching, detached from the realities of Agile adoption, or offered dry methodologies with limited acknowledgment of the critical human factors. The literature lacked practical, actionable strategies specifically tailored for those of us coaching Agile teams.

This book originates from recognizing that gap and understanding that a solution exists. This solution (Figure I-1) merges Agile methods with established principles of professional coaching to help teams realize their potential. In the following chapters, you will be presented with a practical, experience-driven approach to developing self-organizing teams—an approach I have refined over 20+ years of coaching and leading teams in the field. It's not a theoretical formula but a collection of practices and insights tested in real-world Agile environments.

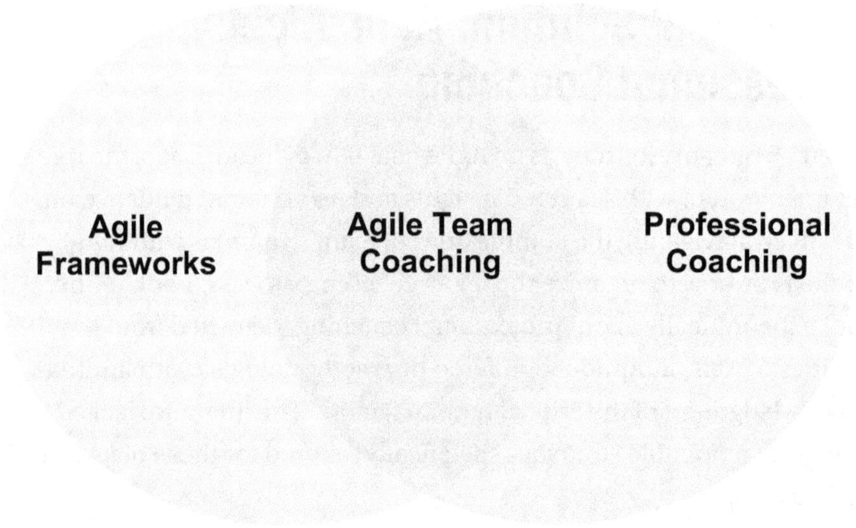

INTRODUCTION

Agile Frameworks   **Agile Team Coaching**   **Professional Coaching**

Figure I-1. *Agile team coaching = Agile frameworks + Professional coaching*

What does that mean in practice? It means that as an Agile coach or Scrum master you'll leverage techniques from the professional coaching world, such as deep listening, powerful questioning, and creating awareness, and apply them to your team's day-to-day collaboration. The International Coaching Federation (ICF) has defined a set of core coaching competencies that help coaches facilitate growth and change. By incorporating competencies like building trust, coaching presence, and evoking insight, you can go beyond simply managing tasks to truly transforming how the team collaborates. In fact, team coaching has become one of the fastest-growing disciplines in the coaching profession precisely because organizations recognize the need for this kind of guidance. ICF's own Team Coaching Competencies model defines team coaching as *"partnering in a co-creative and reflective process with a team on its dynamics and relationships in a way that inspires them to maximize their abilities and potential in order to reach their common purpose and shared goals."* That might sound abstract, but we make it very concrete

INTRODUCTION

for Agile contexts in this book. We will demonstrate how aligning Agile practices with these coaching principles leads to teams that don't just go through the motions of Scrum or any other framework or method but truly embrace continuous improvement and self-management.

What You Will Find in This Book

Mastering the Art of Creating Self-Organizing Teams is designed as a journey—one that will equip you with both the mindset and the toolset to coach teams toward self-organization. The chapters ahead are organized to gradually build your understanding and skills, with a combination of theory, practical frameworks, and real-life examples. Here's a preview of what's in store.

Part 1: Team Coaching for Agility
Chapter 1: Why Team Coaching?

We will look at why team coaching matters in Agile settings, how it differs from individual coaching, one-off team building, and pure facilitation, and how it aligns with Agile principles. You'll also see the common implementation challenges (role boundaries, resistance, "ROI" worries) and a pragmatic path to unlocking a team's self-organizing potential.

Chapter 2: Mastering the Fundamentals

This is a practical walk-through of the eight ICF Team Coaching Competencies translated into day-to-day Agile work (agreements, trust, listening, awareness, partnering, and growth). The chapter closes by clarifying team coaching versus Agile facilitation—when you're guiding the process versus coaching the team's mindset and relationships.

INTRODUCTION

Part 2: Coaching Techniques and Processes

Chapter 3: Sealing the Deal: Effective Contracting

This looks at how to create strong multi-party agreements that give coaching teeth and protection: sponsor alignment, team contracting, boundaries, confidentiality, feedback loops, and review cadence. You'll get a usable flow, questions, and artifacts that prevent the "nice conversations, no change" trap.

Chapter 4: Rewriting the Team Imago

Each person brings an inner picture of "how a team should be." This chapter shows how those "imagos" shape power, norms, and authority—and how to surface, compare, and reset them. You'll connect self-organization essentials with a three-level diagnostic to deliberately re-imprint a team image.

Chapter 5: The elf-Organization Toolkit

This presents a step-by-step toolkit you can run end-to-end: contract and context, elicit individual imagos, create a shared "working imago," calibrate roles and authority, define the team's operating system, run bounded experiments, repair and re-imprint, and sustain with measures. It includes ready-to-use exercises, prompts, and canvases.

Part 3: Navigating Challenging Situations

Chapter 6: Clearing the Roadblocks: Overcoming Issues with Contracting

This examines what to do when the coach–team–sponsor triangle drifts into hidden or split contracts. You'll learn to recognize psychological-distance patterns, re-balance the contracting triad, and re-contract without blame—plus a five-question lens to keep purpose, roles, and boundaries crisp.

Chapter 7: Power Plays and Hidden Agendas Revealed

This looks at how to work with a team's "secret life": unspoken norms, alliances, status games, and shadow leadership. You'll get humane ways to surface and rebalance power, as well as practical anti-patterns/interrupts for common psychological games so the team can act as one.

Chapter 8: Turning Resistance into Resilience

Read resistance as information—fear, safety deficits, lost control, competing agendas—and convert it into experiments that build agency and grit. You'll use the R→R flywheel and a "resistance radar" to move from pushback to progress the team owns.

Chapter 9: Staying True

This chapter examines ethics and boundaries when pressure mounts: keeping the team as the primary client, operating clear confidentiality levels, and avoiding the bystander stance. You'll anchor integrity in explicit contracts and role clarity so trust compounds over time.

INTRODUCTION

Chapter 10: Going Virtual

This looks at coaching distributed teams without losing safety, focus, or energy. Expect guidance on virtual contracting, session design to avoid fatigue, building trust at a distance, and keeping experimentation alive when you're all tiny squares on a screen.

Part 4: Enhancing the Coaching Craft

Chapter 11: What If We Don't Need Another Tool to Be Impactful?

Impact often comes from vertical development—expanding your capacity to hold complexity—rather than from adding techniques. You'll contrast horizontal versus vertical growth and adopt practices (supervision, reflective routines, being coached, feedback) that raise your signal-to-noise in the room.

Chapter 12: Pause, Reflect, Act

This shares a lightweight reflection loop you can run with any team (and yourself). You'll use reflection-in/on/for-action, journaling prompts, and sprint-sized reviews to turn experience into learning and learning into better choices next sprint.

Chapter 13: The Power of Supervision and Deliberate Practice

This looks at why no coach grows alone. You'll see how supervision safeguards ethics and accelerates insight, explore simple models, and adopt deliberate-practice drills that sharpen micro-skills—so improvement becomes systematic, not accidental.

Chapter 14: Mastering the Inner Game—Staying Grounded in Chaos

The nervous system is your primary tool. You'll learn to notice somatic cues, defuse sticky thoughts, act from values, and shift from saboteur to sage—so you can be the calm container teams need when it's stormy.

Whether you are new to Agile coaching or a seasoned practitioner looking to refine your craft, this book offers something for everyone. If you're just starting out, you'll gain a structured approach and avoid many common mistakes that new Scrum masters make. If you're experienced, you'll discover fresh perspectives, integrate professional coaching techniques into your practice, and perhaps validate lessons you've learned the hard way. The writing balances professional rigour with a conversational style—as if we're having a friendly chat about real challenges in the workplace (because we are!).

By the end of this journey, you will have a deeper understanding of cultivating a self-organizing team culture and the confidence to implement it. More important, you'll have experienced through examples and exercises how transformative it is when a team begins to organize itself—the increase in innovation, the rise in ownership, and the relief it brings to organizations, as problems can be addressed at the team level without constant escalation. This introduction lays the groundwork by establishing why this topic is urgent, painting a vision of what's possible, identifying the gaps, and presenting the solution this book offers. Now, with anticipation, turn the page, and let's begin mastering the art of creating self-organizing teams together. The journey to unlocking your team's potential starts here.

PART I

Team Coaching for Agility

CHAPTER 1

Why Use Team Coaching in the Agile Context

Agile practices and frameworks give teams a powerful engine, but team coaching is the oil that keeps that engine running smoothly and efficiently. Without attention to team dynamics, even the best Agile processes can stall. This chapter highlights why team coaching is not just a buzzword but rather a vital component in Agile. It empowers self-organization, nurtures collaboration, drives relentless improvement, helps teams weather change, and builds a sustaining coaching culture. By investing in team coaching, organizations enable their teams to truly embody Agile values rather than just go through the motions.

The Agile Landscape and the Growing Need for Team Coaching

I've worked with plenty of teams who say they're doing all the "right Agile things"—daily stand-ups, sprint reviews, visual boards, retrospectives. On paper, it looks like everything should be working. But underneath,

CHAPTER 1   WHY USE TEAM COACHING IN THE AGILE CONTEXT

something feels off. Collaboration is surface level. Decisions are slow. Energy is flat. When I ask what's going on, someone usually shrugs and says, "We don't really work as a team. Not yet."

That's where team coaching enters the picture.

Agile frameworks like Scrum and Kanban have changed the way we structure work. They encourage shorter feedback loops, shared ownership, and adaptability. The Agile Manifesto even points to self-organizing teams as the source of the best designs and solutions. But frameworks don't build trust. They don't teach teams how to navigate conflict, communicate openly, or hold each other accountable without fear. That's the invisible layer—the team dynamics—and it matters just as much as the processes.

In practice, an Agile team's success often hinges less on whether they're using Scrum or Kanban and more on how they show up for each other: how they make decisions, respond to failure, and learn and grow together. And these are exactly the kinds of things team coaching helps unlock.

Unlike individual coaching or one-off team-building activities, team coaching is an ongoing developmental partnership with the team *as a whole*. It focuses on how the team functions as a living system—how it communicates, learns, makes meaning, and aligns around purpose. Think of it less like giving a team a motivational pep talk and more like helping them see their own playbook more clearly so they can rewrite it together.

Many Agile coaches and Scrum masters are pulled into this space intuitively, recognizing that sticky team dynamics can't be solved by better backlogs or more Jira automation. But it's not always obvious how to navigate it. Coaching a team is fundamentally different from mentoring individuals or facilitating a workshop. It requires a shift in stance and skillset. That's why in 2020 the International Coaching Federation (ICF) formally introduced Team Coaching Competencies—recognizing it as a distinct and increasingly essential discipline.

Team coaching is no longer a luxury in today's complex, high-change environments. It's becoming a vital part of how Agile teams mature—not by fixing what's broken, but by helping teams become more aware, intentional, and, ultimately, self-directed.

How Team Coaching Differs from Other Practices

To clarify the concept, it's important to differentiate team coaching from other team-development practices like individual coaching, team building, and facilitation, as described here and summarized in Table 1-1.

Individual Coaching: Individual (one-on-one) coaching targets a person's personal development, goals, or career. For example, a Scrum master might coach a team member to improve their technical skills or confidence. *Team coaching*, however, focuses on the team as a whole—the "system" of people and their interactions. Instead of concentrating on one person's growth, the goal is to enhance collective performance and alignment. The coach collaborates with team members, helping them improve communication, resolve conflicts, and align on goals as a unit, rather than in isolation.

Team Building: Team building typically consists of one-off events or activities (workshops, retreats, trust falls, escape rooms, etc.) designed to boost camaraderie and morale. While these activities can foster momentary trust or friendship, their impact is often short-lived if deeper working habits do not change. *Team coaching is an ongoing process*, not a one-time event. A team coach collaborates with the team over time, through real work situations, to instill lasting improvements in their collaboration. Consider team building as a spark—it can ignite positive feelings—while team coaching is the steady fuel that keeps the fire burning and growing.

CHAPTER 1   WHY USE TEAM COACHING IN THE AGILE CONTEXT

Facilitation: Facilitation involves guiding a group through a meeting or process, focusing on achieving a specific outcome (such as making a decision or solving a problem) during that session. A facilitator remains neutral regarding content, managing the process so the team can think and work effectively in the moment. Team coaches often *use facilitation skills*, but they go further.

Facilitation versus Coaching: Facilitation typically centers on *what the team is doing* (the task at hand), whereas team coaching also addresses *how the team is doing it*—the underlying relationships, mindsets, and interactions. For instance, a sprint planning meeting facilitator might ensure that everyone's ideas are heard for the plan; while facilitating, a team coach will also observe how team members communicate or avoid topics, later helping the team reflect on those interaction patterns. One description puts it well: A facilitator manages the team's process and keeps them on task, while a team coach "is listening to what is not being said," noticing unspoken tensions, gaps in understanding, or hesitations that reveal growth opportunities for the team. Coaching has its distinctive focus, format, and impact, which is different from other modalities (see Table 1-1).

Table 1-1. *Team Coaching Versus Other Team-Development Practices*

Practice	Focus	Format	Lasting Impact?
Individual Coaching	Personal growth, mindset	1:1 conversations	High for individual
Team Building	Camaraderie, morale	One-off event	Often short-lived
Facilitation	Structured process, decisions	Meeting-based	Focused on outcome
Team Coaching	Team dynamics, system growth	Ongoing engagement	Deep and developmental

In summary, team coaching is a distinct approach that supports Agile adoption by focusing on the team's behavioral excellence and cohesion, rather than just their ability to follow a framework. It's about *coaching the team to develop itself*, rather than solely coaching individuals or facilitating events. This distinction matters because Agile teams, to truly reach high performance, often require guided help to navigate their group dynamics and become self-sustaining, continuously improving units.

How Team Coaching Aligns with Agile Principles

One of the strongest arguments for team coaching in Agile is its natural alignment with core Agile values and principles. Agile is more than a process or framework; it's a mindset and a culture. Team coaching provides the support and feedback loop needed to embody Agile principles in practice. Let's examine several key Agile tenets and how team coaching supports each.

Empowering Self-Organizing Teams

A fundamental Agile principle is to build projects around motivated individuals and give them the environment and support they need, trusting them to get the job done. Self-organization means the team figures out the best way to accomplish its goals rather than being micromanaged. Team coaching directly empowers this. An Agile coach acts not as a boss, but as a servant leader who encourages the team to take ownership of decisions. Through coaching techniques (like asking powerful questions, reflecting observations to the team, and encouraging the team to design their own solutions), the coach helps the team build confidence in self-management. For example, if a team relies too much on a manager or Scrum master to make decisions, a coach might step in to facilitate a conversation where the team defines roles and decision-making rules for itself. Over time, the team coach gradually steps back as the team learns to self-organize effectively. This guidance accelerates the team's journey to autonomy. It aligns with the Scrum master's duties as well—the Scrum master is described as coaching the team in self-organization, and team coaching skills enhance this ability. When done well, team coaching creates an environment of safety and trust where team members feel empowered to fill gaps, make decisions, and experiment on their own, which is exactly what Agile aims for.

Fostering Collaboration and Communication

Agile teams rely on intense collaboration—"individuals and interactions over processes and tools" is the very first value of the Agile Manifesto. Open communication and close collaboration are critical for success in fast-moving Agile projects. Team coaching works to strengthen the relational "glue" of the team. A coach observes communication patterns and facilitates improvements, perhaps encouraging quieter team members to voice their thoughts, helping the team establish norms for active listening, or mediating misunderstandings before they escalate. By doing so, the coach helps unlock honest dialogue and better collaboration. Psychological safety is a huge part of this equation; it's known from Google's Project Aristotle research that *teams with high psychological safety are more innovative and effective.* Team coaches explicitly focus on building that safety. For instance, in a sprint retrospective, if only a few voices dominate, the coach might introduce a check-in round so everyone shares, or use a retrospective exercise that surfaces difficult topics in a safe way. Over time, the team learns how to communicate more openly, even when the coach isn't present.

Driving Continuous Improvement

Continuous improvement (Kaizen) is another pillar of Agile. Agile teams are expected to regularly reflect and adapt—for example, through sprint retrospectives at the end of each iteration. Team coaching reinforces this principle by ensuring that improvement discussions lead to real change in team behavior. A team coach often plays a key role in retrospectives, not by solving problems for the team, but by *facilitating the team's own reflection* and pushing them to dig a bit deeper. For example, if a team's retrospectives have become superficial ("everything is fine"), a coach might notice stagnation and introduce a different retrospective format to uncover growth areas. Or if the team identifies an action item to improve (say, "reduce interruptions during focus time"), the coach might hold them accountable by revisiting that item in the next session and asking what progress was made. This gentle pressure and guidance help the team build a habit of continuous improvement rather than treating retros as a checkbox exercise. It aligns perfectly with the Agile principle of regularly adjusting behaviors for effectiveness.

Furthermore, team coaching introduces *reflective practices* into the team's workflow. Beyond the formal retrospective, a coach might encourage small practices like daily check-ins ("What's one thing we could do better today?") or periodic team health checks. They might use tools like a "team radar" to help the team assess itself on various dimensions (quality, collaboration, product value, etc.) and spot areas to improve. The coach is essentially building the team's "muscle" for self-examination and adaptation. Over time, the team internalizes this and continuously improves on its own, which is the ultimate goal. In essence, team coaching turbocharges continuous improvement: It not only supports the formal Agile events meant for reflection, but also weaves a mindset of learning and adjusting into the team's everyday work.

CHAPTER 1   WHY USE TEAM COACHING IN THE AGILE CONTEXT

Navigating Change and Complexity

Agile teams frequently operate in complex environments, where traditional cause-and-effect thinking breaks down. In the complex domain (as defined by Dave Snowden's Cynefin framework), cause and effect can only be understood in hindsight, and patterns of success emerge rather than being predefined. In other words, outcomes develop over time; they cannot be engineered upfront with certainty. Team coaching plays a strategic role in helping Agile teams thrive under these conditions by encouraging an experimental mindset and adaptive practices. Coaches guide teams to embrace probe–sense–respond approaches, running small, parallel, safe-to-fail experiments to determine what works and what doesn't. This approach is essential for complex work, where "one can only ascertain cause and effect after the fact." By treating each iteration or sprint as a safe-to-fail learning opportunity, Agile teams can reveal valuable insights and emergent practices that would remain hidden in a purely analytical or predictive approach. Team coaches reinforce this by framing experiments not as projects to be right or wrong, but as probes that make emergent possibilities more visible. When an experiment yields a promising result, the team can amplify it; if it fails, the team contains the impact and learns from it. In short, coaching helps teams navigate complexity by shifting the culture from avoiding failure to learning from safe failures.

The Evolving Role of the Agile Coach: From Directive to Facilitative

An Agile coach's role can be tricky to navigate. Many Agile coaches start as experts in Agile practices or experienced Scrum masters—they're used to advising teams on *what to do*. However, team coaching calls for a shift from a primarily directive stance to a more facilitative and, well, coaching stance (see Figure 1-1). In practical terms, this means less "telling" and more "asking." Instead of being the hero with all the answers, the coach becomes a guide on the side, helping the team discover answers. This doesn't happen overnight; it's an evolution in the coach's mindset and skills.

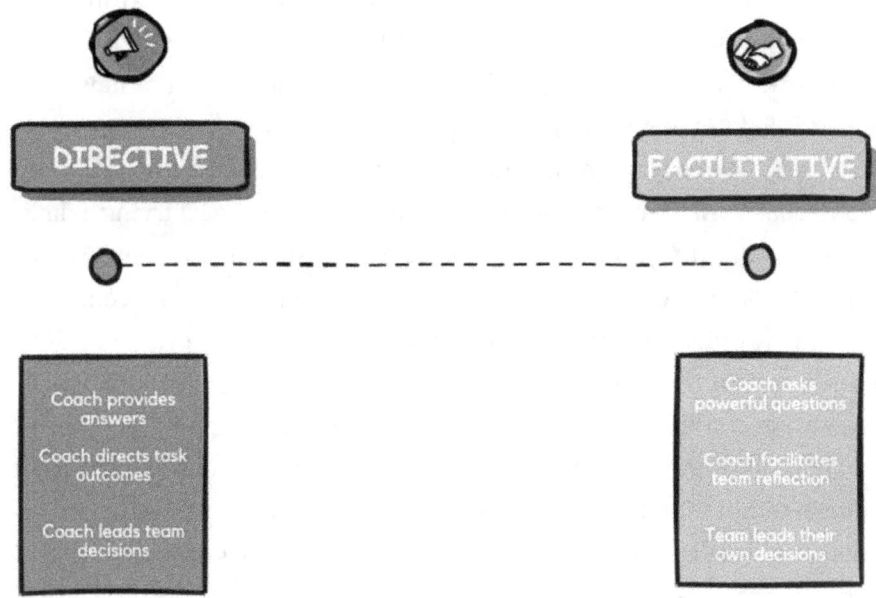

Figure 1-1. *From telling to asking*

In the early stages with a team, an Agile coach might need to be somewhat directive—for example, teaching the basics of Scrum or setting up initial Kanban boards. But the coach should hand responsibility to the team as quickly as possible. They start asking questions like, "How do *you* think we should handle this impediment?" or "What options do we have to meet the sprint goal?" This encourages the team to think for themselves. A coach will use techniques from professional coaching, such as active listening, powerful questions, and maybe reframing what team members say to help them gain insight. If a team member asks the coach, "What should we do to improve our code quality?" a directive answer would be,

CHAPTER 1 WHY USE TEAM COACHING IN THE AGILE CONTEXT

"You should start doing X practice." A facilitative coaching response might be, "What have you noticed about when quality slips? What could we change in our process to catch issues earlier?" The latter prompts the team to analyze and own the solution. It's the classic give-a-man-a-fish versus teach-to-fish scenario.

This doesn't mean an Agile coach never gives advice. Mentoring and teaching are part of the Agile coach "stances" too (as described in frameworks like Lyssa Adkins' Agile Coaching Competency Framework). The art is in knowing *when to mentor versus when to coach*. For example, with a very novice team, more guidance is initially needed. But even then, a good coach will pair any advice with questions: "I suggest trying a daily 15-minute planning huddle. How does that idea sit with the team? How might we adapt it to fit your context?" As the team matures, the coach deliberately pulls back from providing answers. They may even play dumb at times to spur the team's problem-solving—"Hmm, I'm not sure how to resolve that conflict between you two. What ideas do you have to address it?" This can feel uncomfortable to coaches who have a lot of expertise; there's a temptation to jump in and fix things. Balancing this is indeed a challenge (we'll revisit it under "Challenges"). But making that shift is crucial to grow the team's self-reliance.

A practical tip Agile coaches use is to discuss the coaching approach with the team explicitly. For instance, the coach might say: "There will be times I act as a mentor (share Agile best practices) and times I act as a coach (ask questions and not answer). If you feel you really need expert advice, let me know; otherwise, I'll likely respond with questions to help you find *your* answer." This manages expectations and enlists the team in the process. Over time, the team starts to internalize this approach. Team members begin coaching each other in a similar way—asking questions instead of always handing out solutions. That's when you know the coach's facilitative style is rubbing off and the team is developing a coaching culture internally.

Finally, an Agile coach's role also involves supporting team dynamics (not just tasks and workflow). This means the coach often observes how the team interacts and occasionally steps in to hold a mirror up for the team. For example, "I noticed in the last discussion, every time John started to speak, he got interrupted. Is that something we want to address as a team?" This kind of intervention is facilitative—it's not scolding, it's helping the team see a dynamic they might be blind to. Handling such moments with care and neutrality is part of the coach's craft. In essence, the Agile coach moves fluidly between *mentor, teacher, facilitator, mediator,* and *true coach.* However, the overall trend is toward enabling the team's thinking and decision making, not substituting for it. As one industry commentary noted, in a coaching culture, even leaders move "from instructing to mentoring" and "from controlling to empowering." The Agile coach epitomizes that shift, acting as a catalyst for the team's growth.

Addressing Team Dynamics and Relationships

Agile team coaching isn't only about processes and tasks—a lot of it is about people: how they relate, communicate, trust, and handle conflict. Team dynamics can make or break an Agile team's performance. Unspoken tensions, personality clashes, or lack of trust will silently undermine velocity and quality far more than any technical impediment. Thus, a significant part of team coaching is devoted to observing and improving the "people dynamics" within the team.

One key practice here is helping surface *unspoken issues.* Many teams avoid difficult conversations—perhaps two team members have a lingering disagreement that's never been resolved, or the team has concerns about a stakeholder but won't voice them. An Agile coach uses their outsider perspective to spot these undercurrents. Maybe during meetings they notice a lot of side-eye or that certain topics always get quickly dropped. The coach can gently bring these up in a safe setting. For example, in a retrospective, the coach might say, "I sense there might be some hesitation in discussing X. What are our thoughts on that?" or even speak to individuals one-on-one to encourage them to bring issues to the team. Coaches sometimes facilitate crucial conversations—high-stakes discussions the team needs to have. They might use techniques from conflict coaching or nonviolent communication to help team members express themselves constructively. The goal is to clear the air because unaddressed issues will fester and damage collaboration.

Psychological safety again plays a big role here. The coach continually works to maintain an environment where team members feel it's okay to be honest. A practical example: If a team member criticizes an idea and someone else goes silent, the coach might later check in with the silent member, assuring them that their perspective is valuable. Or if someone makes a blaming remark ("The testers always slow us down"), the coach may intervene to reframe it ("It sounds like there's frustration about our process. What is actually causing the delays?"), steering away from personal attacks to the underlying issue. By modeling respectful communication, the coach helps the team build trust and openness. Over time, team members learn to have these tough conversations more directly and maturely themselves, without the coach mediating.

Another aspect is team norms and behavior patterns. A coach might help the team establish or refine their working agreements; e.g., "We agree to start meetings on time, one conversation at a time, assume positive intent," etc. If the team has set norms but isn't following them, the coach will call attention to that gap in a supportive way. For instance, "We all agreed to give each other a head's-up about changes, but in the last sprint, a major change was made without notice. How can we honor our agreements better?" This reinforces accountability to shared norms, which is key for a self-organizing team.

CHAPTER 1 WHY USE TEAM COACHING IN THE AGILE CONTEXT

Handling conflicts is certainly a part of addressing dynamics. The coach may play the role of a neutral mediator in a conflict between team members or between the team and an outside party. They ensure each side feels heard and help find common ground, or at the very least, mutual respect. The coach might introduce techniques such as rotating someone to play "devil's advocate" in discussions, or use retrospectives specifically focused on team relationships (sometimes called "team health retrospectives").

A powerful tool coaches use is here-and-now intervention. This means addressing something in the moment it happens. For example, if two people start arguing in a planning meeting, a facilitator might postpone that discussion. A coach, however, might pause the meeting and help the team reflect: "We seem to have a conflict emerging. What's really at stake for us here? Let's take a few minutes to unpack this because it's important for our teamwork." This can feel risky, but it's often where breakthroughs happen—the team starts discussing how they interact, not just the task, which can lead to deeper understanding and improved relationships.

Coaches are trained to notice subtle cues: body language, who talks after whom, who never disagrees openly, etc. These cues can indicate trust levels or unresolved issues. Bringing them into the team's awareness is part of the value a coach provides. For example, "I notice in our meetings the developers rarely speak up after the product owner shares her view. Is there perhaps an assumption that her view can't be challenged? How do we feel about that?" Such a question can open up a dialogue about power dynamics or assumptions, which, once addressed, can free the team from unhelpful habits. *It's often said the coach works in the "spaces between" team members—listening for what's not being said.* By illuminating those spaces, the coach helps the team strengthen their relationships and work together more joyfully and effectively.

Importantly, an Agile coach maintains confidentiality and impartiality when dealing with team interpersonal matters. Team members must trust that the coach isn't taking sides or gossiping about their issues to higher-ups. This trust allows them to be honest about interpersonal challenges. The reward is huge: A team that has worked through conflict with the help of a coach often emerges much stronger, with higher mutual respect and confidence to handle future bumps on their own. Given that Agile relies on close teamwork, investing time in team relationships is investing in the heart of Agile success.

Challenges in Implementing Agile Team Coaching

While the benefits are compelling, implementing team coaching in an Agile context isn't without its challenges. Both organizations and coaches face hurdles in making this a smooth and effective journey. Being aware of these challenges can help in proactively addressing them.

Balancing Coaching with Directing (When to Coach Versus When to Lead)

One of the biggest challenges for Scrum masters or Agile coaches is knowing how to balance a coaching stance with a directive stance. In practice, there are times when the team might genuinely need direction—say, a critical deadline looms, or the team is totally stuck and inexperienced—and other times when stepping back and coaching is more beneficial for long-term growth. Finding this balance is tricky. Coaches can err on the side of doing *too much*, effectively disempowering the team by providing all the answers, or doing *too little*, leaving a very immature team floundering with no guidance. The key is situational awareness. Early on, a coach might need to be more hands-on (teaching, mentoring, making some decisions to get momentum), but should always look for opportunities to hand over responsibility to the team. This often involves a mindset shift for coaches coming from traditional management; they must resist the urge to control. As mentioned earlier, in a coaching culture, leaders move "from directing to facilitating . . . from controlling to empowering," and that's easier said than done when pressure is high. It helps to explicitly discuss this balance with stakeholders; for example, agreeing with management that the coach will prioritize team growth even if, in the short term, the team's output might dip as they learn. Another helpful tactic is getting supervision or mentorship for the coach (if available)—someone who can observe or debrief with the coach and point out if they're falling into the trap of being too directive or too hands-off. Self-awareness is crucial: Coaches need to constantly ask themselves, "Am I doing something the team could be doing for themselves?" and if yes, step back. Conversely, "Is the team floundering in an area where they lack the skill, and I haven't given them any guidance?"—then step in appropriately. It's a dance that gets better with experience and reflection.

Distinguishing the Team Coach Role from the Scrum Master (and Other Roles)

There can be confusion in organizations about who does what, especially if there are multiple roles like Scrum masters, Agile coaches, line managers, etc., all interacting with the team. In some setups, the Scrum master *is* effectively the team coach (Scrum itself positions the Scrum master as a coach for the team in Scrum principles). In other cases, organizations have separate Agile coaches who may work across several teams (sometimes focusing on higher-level organizational coaching too). It's important to clarify these roles to avoid stepping on toes or leaving gaps. For example, if an Agile coach and a Scrum master both attend a retrospective, who leads it? They should coordinate so it's clear—maybe the Scrum master facilitates, and the Agile coach observes and gives meta-feedback later, or vice versa. A lack of clarity can also lead to the team "shopping around" for answers; e.g., if the coach is urging them to self-solve a problem while a manager or other role is still in directive mode, telling them what to do, it sends mixed messages. Organizations should define how team coaching relates to existing roles. One approach is to treat *team coaching as a function, not necessarily a full-time position*; the Scrum master can fulfill much of it, and an Agile coach (if present) might focus on advanced team dynamics or multi-team issues. Some companies are even renaming Scrum masters to "team coaches" to emphasize the coaching aspect. The challenge is also for the individuals in these roles: A Scrum master might need to upskill in coaching to truly fulfill the team coach role, or an Agile coach might need to establish trust and rapport with Scrum masters so it's a partnership, not a competition. Clear communication, role agreements, and sometimes formal RACI matrices (Responsible, Accountable, Consulted, Informed) can help outline who does what. Ultimately, all parties should align on a common goal: helping the team thrive. If that stays front and center, role turf wars can be minimized.

Measuring Impact and ROI of Team Coaching

Organizations rightly ask, "How do we know if this team coaching is working? What's the return on investment (ROI)?" Unlike more straightforward process changes, the impact of coaching can be diffuse and qualitative. Team coaching deals with human behavior changes that are not as easily quantifiable as, say, cycle time or defect count (though those may improve as a result). It's a challenge to attribute improvements directly to coaching because many factors influence team performance. However, it's not impossible to measure. One approach is to use surveys or assessments before and after coaching engagements; for example, team health checks, psychological safety surveys, or 360-degree stakeholder feedback. These can show shifts in communication, clarity, trust, and

CHAPTER 1 WHY USE TEAM COACHING IN THE AGILE CONTEXT

collaboration. Another approach is to set concrete goals during contracting (e.g., reduce deployment lead time from ten days to five days) and track those metrics, acknowledging that coaching is one contributor among others. The International Coaching Federation suggests measuring *return on expectations (ROE)*—essentially checking if the agreed outcomes (better communication, higher engagement, etc.) are observed. Agile gives us empirical data each iteration (velocity, customer feedback, etc.), which can serve as indirect indicators. A coached team might show a steadier velocity or more frequent releases, for instance. It's also valuable to gather qualitative evidence: testimonials from team members ("We feel much more confident now"), stories of how they handled a crisis better than before, etc. Presenting a mix of quantitative and qualitative data to sponsors can justify the coaching investment. Still, this remains a challenge—sometimes improvements are obvious to those involved but hard to prove to outsiders. Being proactive in defining success criteria during contracting (e.g., team self-assessment scores, specific business outcomes) and then collecting data is the best strategy. And sometimes a little faith is needed—as the saying goes, not everything that counts can be counted. Leadership should look at team coaching as building long-term capability, akin to leadership development, which may not yield a tidy ROI number immediately but pays off through more adaptable and high-performing teams.

Overcoming Resistance to Coaching

Not everyone greets the idea of team coaching with open arms. Teams or individual team members might be skeptical ("Is this going to be touchy-feely stuff? I just want to code."). Managers might resist ("Why do we need a coach? Isn't that what I pay the team lead for?"). There can be fear that coaching will mean airing dirty laundry or that it implies the team is underperforming (a stigma, like "we need coaching because we're bad"). Overcoming these perceptions is a real challenge. The coach often needs to do some selling and education. One effective method is to frame coaching positively and *not as remediation*. For instance, positioning it as "This team is doing well, and we want to invest in you to go from good to great," rather than "We have problems to fix." Also, emphasizing confidentiality and psychological safety from the start helps alleviate fears that coaching is a means to judge or report on people. Some team members who've never experienced coaching may simply not know what it is and thus be wary. The coach can address this by explaining what a typical coaching session looks like, perhaps sharing examples of outcomes from other teams (without naming companies if confidential). It's also helpful to get a quick win or two early on. If, early in the engagement, the coach facilitates a session that helps the team resolve a nagging issue or conflict, people will see the value firsthand. That can turn skeptics into advocates. Involving the team in designing the coaching process (as mentioned, co-creating the agenda) also reduces resistance because they have agency. At times, resistance can come from outside the team; e.g., a manager might feel threatened that the team listens to the coach more. In such cases, the coach should actively keep that manager in the loop, even involve them appropriately (maybe invite them to a part of a session or provide them non-attributable feedback about improvements the team is making). Showing how coaching aligns with the manager's goals (e.g., "This will help your team deliver more reliably, which helps you") can win them over. Persistence and patience are key—some folks might only buy in after they start *feeling* the benefits, which could take a few sprints.

Investing in Coach Development

For Scrum masters or Agile coaches to be effective team coaches, they need continuous development. This is a meta-challenge—organizations must recognize that coaching requires training and practice. It's not automatically gained by being a good project manager or developer. Professional coaching skills (like deep listening, powerful questioning, facilitation of group processes, conflict mediation, etc.) often need to be learned. Agile coaches benefit from training in these areas (for example, attending ICF-accredited coaching courses or Scrum Alliance's Certified Team Coach program). However, not all organizations provide support or budget for this development. Thus, coaches may struggle, applying trial and error. Another aspect is supervision or mentoring for coaches, which is common in professional coaching circles but still new in Agile coaching. Having a veteran coach with whom to debrief tough situations can massively improve a less-experienced coach's effectiveness. If an organization is serious about team coaching, it should invest in building the coaching competency of its Agile leaders. This challenge is also personal: As a coach, committing to your own growth is vital. It can be uncomfortable; coaches might have to confront their own blind spots, biases, or habits (like the tendency to step in too much). Engaging in reflective practice (journaling about coaching sessions, seeking feedback from the team about the coaching, etc.) is important for improvement. The good news is that the Agile community is increasingly aware of this—there are coaching meetups, communities of practice, and resources to learn from. Agile team coaching is being connected with professional standards like the ICF competencies, signaling a maturation of the discipline. So, the challenge is being addressed gradually, but any Agile coach should personally acknowledge: *To better coach others, I must continuously better myself.*

Despite these challenges, none are insurmountable. They require mindfulness, support, and sometimes creativity to address. In many cases, simply being aware of the pitfalls (such as the temptation to direct or the need to clarify roles) will help you navigate around them. Agile coaches who succeed in tackling these challenges often become the linchpins of their organization's Agile success—they pave the way for a healthier, higher-performing Agile ecosystem.

CHAPTER 1   WHY USE TEAM COACHING IN THE AGILE CONTEXT

Conclusion: Unlocking Agile's Full Potential Through Team Coaching

For Agile coaches and Scrum masters reading this, consider this a call to action. Reflect on how you can incorporate or enhance team coaching in your work. Perhaps start with something as simple as dedicating part of your next retrospective to discuss *how* the team is working together (beyond the technical issues), or practicing "asking instead of telling" in the next team huddle. Small coaching interventions, done consistently, will accumulate into significant changes in team behavior and results.

Leaders should also note that supporting team coaching (through training, allocating coaching time, and being open to its findings) will pay dividends in the form of high-performing, self-sufficient teams. Recall that Agile is about individuals and interactions and responding to change; team coaching directly amplifies those aspects by focusing on the people and how they interact in the face of change.

In conclusion, embedding team coaching into the fabric of Agile practice helps unlock its full potential. It transforms Agile from a mechanical process into a living, learning way of working. Teams not only perform Agile, they also embody Agile—adaptable, collaborative, and continuously improving entities. If you are on the journey of mastering the art of coaching self-organizing teams, know that you are contributing to something profoundly powerful: You're helping create workplaces where people communicate openly, trust one another, innovate freely, and take ownership of their success. That is the promise of Agile, and team coaching is key to fulfilling it.

CHAPTER 2

Mastering the Fundamentals: Essential Competencies for Agile Team Coaches

In Agile environments, effective team coaching competencies are essential for cultivating self-organizing, high-performing teams. Agile frameworks like Scrum emphasize that teams must be self-managed and adaptive, which means an Agile team coach (often a Scrum master or Agile coach) must possess more than technical know-how; they must excel in guiding human dynamics. The International Coaching Federation (ICF) has defined a set of Team Coaching Competencies that serve as a professional standard for coaching teams, providing a clear framework for the skills and behaviors coaches need. These eight competencies form the backbone of masterful team coaching and closely align with Agile values and principles. In fact, Agile's demand for empowered, self-directed teams has created a strong need for coaches who can foster collaboration, trust, and continuous improvement.

CHAPTER 2 MASTERING THE FUNDAMENTALS: ESSENTIAL COMPETENCIES FOR
            AGILE TEAM COACHES

This chapter introduces each of the ICF Team Coaching Competencies (1 through 8) and examines their application within Agile team settings. We will explore how each competency supports the four core values of the Agile Manifesto—Individuals and Interactions, Working Product (Working Software), Customer Collaboration, and Responding to Change—along with relevant Agile principles. We also delve deeper into how team coaching differs from (and complements) Agile facilitation, ensuring that, as a coach, you know when to facilitate and when to coach more deeply. By the end of the chapter, you will understand how mastering these fundamental competencies enhances your coaching practice and fosters sustainable agility and improved team performance.

Competency 1: Demonstrates Ethical Practice

Demonstrating ethical practice is the foundation of all coaching work. This competency means the coach upholds ethics and standards and acts with integrity and honesty in all interactions. In an Agile team context, ethical practice entails treating the team as the client and safeguarding their trust. ICF emphasizes that a team coach *"coaches the client team as a single entity,"* meaning the coach's primary loyalty is to the team as a whole rather than to any individual or external stakeholder. For example, if a team member confides a personal concern or admits a mistake, the coach honors confidentiality and addresses the issue at the team level only as appropriate, rather than using that information in a way that could betray trust. The coach also *"maintains the distinction between team coaching, team building, training, consulting, mentoring, facilitation and other modalities,"* ensuring clarity about their role. This distinction is critical in Agile environments—the team coach must be transparent about when they are coaching versus when they are offering advice or facilitating an event so the team isn't misled. Ethical Agile coaches are careful not

CHAPTER 2   MASTERING THE FUNDAMENTALS: ESSENTIAL COMPETENCIES FOR AGILE TEAM COACHES

to abuse authority; for instance, they avoid "fixing" the team by secretly taking control of decisions and instead guide the team to arrive at its own solutions within agreed boundaries.

Ethical practice in Agile coaching directly supports the Agile value of "Individuals and Interactions" over processes and tools. By maintaining confidentiality and fairness, the coach creates a safe space for individuals to interact openly without fear of exploitation. This builds mutual respect—a cornerstone of any self-organizing team. It also aligns with the Agile principle that we must "build projects around motivated individuals" and "trust them to get the job done." Trust can only flourish when the coach consistently behaves ethically and models integrity. For example, during a sprint retrospective, team members might share sensitive feedback about team dynamics or leadership. An ethical coach ensures this conversation remains respectful and does not leave the room inappropriately. They might remind everyone of the working agreement that retrospective data stays internal, thus reinforcing trust. Should the coach also serve as a facilitator or have a managerial role, they take extra care to "maintain trust, transparency, and clarity when fulfilling multiple roles"—perhaps by explicitly stating, "Now I'm offering an observation as a Scrum master, not as your coach," if they need to momentarily give advice. In summary, Competency 1 underpins all others: It professionalizes Agile coaching by grounding it in ethics, which in turn engenders the trust needed for Agile teams to thrive.

Competency 2: Embodies a Coaching Mindset

Embodying a coaching mindset means to approach coaching with a stance of openness, curiosity, and continuous learning. ICF defines this competency as developing and maintaining a receptive and client-centered mindset. In practice, Agile team coaches with a coaching

CHAPTER 2   MASTERING THE FUNDAMENTALS: ESSENTIAL COMPETENCIES FOR AGILE TEAM COACHES

mindset demonstrate self-awareness, ongoing reflective practice, and a commitment to personal growth, much like the Agile principle of continuous improvement. In fact, the ICF Team Coaching Competencies encourage coaches to engage in supervision or mentoring *"for support, development, and accountability when needed,"* highlighting that even coaches should continuously improve their craft. In an Agile setting, this might involve the coach seeking feedback from the team on their facilitation of a retrospective, or working with a mentor coach to refine their approach to a team that is "stuck." For example, after a challenging iteration where team morale dipped, an Agile coach might reflect on their own biases or triggers during that period. They could keep a learning journal or discuss in a supervision session how to better remain objective and supportive. This behavior models the growth mindset for the team: Just as the team is expected to inspect and adapt, the coach does so for their own performance.

Agility is about adaptability and learning, so a coaching mindset perfectly aligns with the Agile value of *"Responding to change over following a plan."* The coach remains flexible in the face of team changes, treating setbacks as learning opportunities rather than failures. For instance, if the team decides to change a process mid-sprint during a daily Scrum, a coach with a proper coaching mindset will encourage the experiment and remain curious about the outcome, rather than insisting on sticking to the original plan. They stay objective and aware of team dynamics and patterns as they unfold, checking their ego at the door. This mindset also supports Individuals and Interactions, as the coach stays present with the individuals on the team, paying close attention to their evolving needs rather than being overly wedded to coaching "by the book."

In real-world terms, embodying a coaching mindset might mean the coach practices active listening and empathy even when tension is high, or takes a moment to center themselves before facilitating a conflict resolution discussion. By being mindful and non-judgmental, the coach creates an atmosphere where team members feel seen and understood.

Ultimately, this competency ensures the Agile coach is agile themselves—embracing change, learning continuously, and viewing challenges through a lens of possibilities rather than problems. It lays the groundwork for a resilient team culture where adaptability and improvement are the norm.

Competency 3: Establishes and Maintains Agreements

Establishing and maintaining agreements is about creating a clear, shared understanding of the coaching engagement and the goals, roles, and ground rules involved. For ICF, this competency means the coach partners with clients and stakeholders to co-create explicit agreements about the coaching relationship, process, and outcomes. In an Agile team context, this begins with aligning expectations: The team coach works with the team (and often the team's leader or sponsor) to agree on how coaching will support the team's Agile journey. This often includes explaining *"what team coaching is and is not, including how it differs from other team development modalities."* For example, at a team's kick-off or during a reset with a struggling team, the coach might clarify, "I'm here to help the team improve how you work together. I won't be solving problems for you like a consultant, nor teaching technical skills like a trainer, but I will facilitate conversations and ask questions to help you find your own solutions." Such clarity prevents misunderstandings—the team knows the coach isn't there to micromanage or play project manager, and managers understand that team coaching isn't a one-time team-building workshop but an ongoing process.

Establishing agreements in Agile teams can involve creating a team coaching contract or alliance (see more on contracting in the next chapter). This could cover logistical agreements (e.g., the team will dedicate an hour every two weeks for a coaching retrospective focused on team dynamics) as well as behavioral agreements (e.g., confidentiality rules or a norm that team members will give the coach permission to challenge them). The coach "partners with all relevant parties, including the team leader, team members, stakeholders, and any co-coaches, to collaboratively create clear agreements about the coaching relationship, processes, plans, and goals." In an Agile context, one such agreement might be with the product owner and Scrum master on how they will share responsibilities for improving the team; for instance, agreeing that the coach focuses on team dynamics and collaboration, while the product owner clarifies product goals. Another example is establishing a working agreement among team members (often done in early sprint retrospectives or team formation workshops). While the working agreement is created by the team (with the coach facilitating), it aligns with this competency because the coach is ensuring the team explicitly agrees on how they will work together, from meeting norms to how they handle conflict. This fosters a sense of ownership and clarity that is vital for self-organization.

This competency supports the Agile value of "customer collaboration over contract negotiation" in spirit because it emphasizes collaboration in defining the "contract" of coaching. Instead of a top-down mandate, the team coach and team collaboratively define how they will work, mirroring how Agile prefers collaboration to rigid contracts. It is also tied to "Individuals and Interactions," since crafting agreements requires open dialogue and consensus among people. By maintaining these agreements, the coach holds the team (and themselves) accountable for the commitments made. For instance, if it was agreed that "everyone has an equal voice in retrospectives," the coach would remind the team of this agreement if they noticed only a few people talking during the session. Keeping agreements visible and reviewing them periodically is part of maintaining them. This consistency builds trust (reinforcing Competency 4) and ensures that the coaching process stays on track toward the agreed goals. In summary, Competency 3 sets the stage and guardrails for the coaching engagement so that all parties move forward with a common understanding, much like an Agile team aligns on a "definition of done" or a team charter to guide their work together.

Competency 4: Cultivates Trust and Safety

No team can perform optimally without trust and psychological safety. Cultivating trust and safety is, therefore, a crucial competency, requiring the coach to create an environment where all team members feel safe to be honest, to take risks, and to be vulnerable in the service of learning and growth. ICF highlights that a team coach should *"create and maintain a safe space for open and honest team member interaction," "promote the team viewing itself as a single entity,"* and *"encourage participation and contribution by all team members."* In practice, this means the Agile coach actively works to include every voice on the team and to foster mutual respect. For example, in a daily Scrum, an Agile coach might notice that one team member hasn't spoken for days; exercising this competency, the coach could gently invite that person's input or follow up privately to ensure they feel safe raising issues. During sprint retrospectives, trust and safety are paramount—team members need confidence to discuss failures or conflicts without blame. A coach cultivating safety might start a retrospective with a safety-check exercise (asking team members to indicate how safe they feel to speak up anonymously) or explicitly remind the team of the prime directive (that the retrospective is a blameless space). They also intervene if they observe behavior that threatens safety. For instance, if one member starts to attack another's idea, the coach may pause the discussion and establish respectful communication guidelines.

Cultivating trust and safety directly supports the Agile Manifesto's focus on "Individuals and Interactions," since individuals only interact openly when trust exists. It also underpins the principle that *"the best architectures . . . emerge from self-organizing teams"*—self-organization flourishes in a high-trust environment where team members feel safe to take initiative. Moreover, Google's landmark "Project Aristotle" research into team effectiveness found that psychological safety was the number one predictor of high-performing teams. Teams *"with a strong sense of psychological safety fostered an environment where members felt comfortable expressing their thoughts and ideas openly, leading to more productive discussions and innovative solutions."* An Agile coach keeps this in mind and actively nurtures that atmosphere. This can involve small behaviors, like ensuring meetings are free of judgmental language, and larger interventions, like coaching the team through resolving interpersonal conflicts.

One practical example is handling conflict in an Agile team. Instead of avoiding it (which can erode trust), a coach skilled in Competency 4 will facilitate a healthy dialogue, setting ground rules like "attack the problem, not the person." They might use techniques such as round-robin sharing (so each person's perspective is heard) or employ a retrospective activity where team members write down what they appreciate about each other before tackling improvement areas, thus reinforcing respect. By *"partnering with the team to identify and resolve internal conflict"* in a constructive way, the coach helps the team build confidence that issues can be raised and resolved safely. Over time, this competency leads to a culture of transparency and safety, where team members freely share impediments (improving efficiency) and admit mistakes (accelerating learning). Agile teams with high trust move faster; for example, a team that trusts each other is more likely to speak up early about risks or to ask for help, preventing small problems from turning into big ones. In summary, Competency 4, "Cultivates Trust and Safety," is a linchpin of Agile team coaching because it enables all other Agile practices (from pair programming to retrospectives) to be executed honestly and effectively. When a coach masters this, they pave the way for a truly collaborative and resilient team.

CHAPTER 2   MASTERING THE FUNDAMENTALS: ESSENTIAL COMPETENCIES FOR AGILE TEAM COACHES

Competency 5: Maintains Presence

Maintaining presence is the art of fully engaging and being aware of the moment, with both the team and the unfolding process. For a team coach, presence means bringing one's complete attention, using all senses and intuition to tune into what is happening here and now. The ICF competency description notes that a coach uses their *"full range of sensory and perceptual abilities to focus on what is important to the coaching process."* This can be challenging in a live Agile team setting—conversations are fast-paced, multiple people may speak, or emotions may run high. A coach demonstrating presence stays mentally and emotionally available to the team, rather than getting distracted or overwhelmed. They show up with a centered, calm demeanor, even amid chaos or uncertainty. For example, imagine a sprint planning meeting where the team is anxious about an unmet deadline; team members might be speaking over one another. An Agile coach with a strong presence will pay close attention to both the words being said and the mood of the room. They might notice a particular comment that signals a more profound concern and gently bring the team's focus to it ("I sense a lot of concern around quality—shall we explore that?"). Or if tensions rise, the coach might call for a short break or a moment of reflection, effectively encouraging the team to pause and reflect on their interactions. This helps the group regain composure and thoughtfulness.

Presence also involves agility in the coach's responses. The ICF framework mentions the coach *"moves in and out of the team dialogue as appropriate."* In other words, the coach knows when to step in and when to step back. In Agile facilitation, this is akin to the idea of *holding the space*: sometimes the team needs the coach to actively guide (for instance, intervening to ask a powerful question when the discussion stalls), and other times the coach should allow the team to struggle a bit and find its own path (e.g., remaining silent a little longer so that a shy team member musters the courage to speak). A real-world scenario could be a daily Scrum where the conversation veers off-topic into problem-solving an issue. A present coach gauges whether this tangent is valuable team collaboration or a derailment. If it's the latter, they calmly refocus the team ("Let's take that discussion offline and keep our stand-up to the agenda")—but if it's the former (the team organically addressing an impediment), a present coach might consciously decide *not* to interrupt the flow. This split-second judgment comes from being fully attuned to the team's dynamics in that moment.

This competency supports Agile values by ensuring "Individuals and Interactions" get the coach's primary attention, not rigid agendas or tools. It also aligns with the Agile principle of face-to-face conversation, which is the most efficient and effective communication method. A coach's presence, especially in face-to-face (or real-time virtual) interactions, sets the tone for mindful communication. When the coach is fully present, it encourages the team members also to be present with each other, listening and responding more genuinely. Additionally, maintaining presence ties to "Responding to Change" because a present coach can detect subtle changes in team morale or understanding and address them immediately, rather than following a scripted plan that might no longer fit. For instance, during a team launch event, the coach might sense that the team is fatigued after a long day and decide to postpone a complex team-building exercise (adapting the plan to the reality of the moment). In sum, maintaining presence is about *being there* for the team in a way that is attentive and adaptable. It's a skill that allows the coach to catch the "little moments"—a hesitant tone, a confused look, a sudden silence—that, when noticed, can lead to important insights or timely interventions. Coaches who master presence become anchors for their Agile teams, providing steady guidance and a clear mirror through which the team can see itself more honestly.

CHAPTER 2   MASTERING THE FUNDAMENTALS: ESSENTIAL COMPETENCIES FOR AGILE TEAM COACHES

Competency 6: Listens Actively

Active listening is a hallmark of any good coach, and when coaching a team, it becomes even more nuanced. Listening actively in the context of a team means not only hearing the content of what each team member says but also observing *how* things are said, noticing what is *not* being said, and understanding the interplay of different perspectives within the group. According to the ICF Team Coaching Competencies, a coach "*notices how the perspectives shared by each team member relate to other team members' views and the team dialogue.*" The coach also pays attention to the team's collective communication patterns and energy. For example, in a product backlog refinement meeting, one developer might quietly raise a concern about a user story's complexity, but the topic might quickly shift as others move on. An active-listening coach will notice that the concern didn't get addressed and that the developer's body language shows frustration. They might interject, "I want to loop back—John raised a concern about complexity. John, could you say more about that?" By doing so, the coach validates that person's voice and ensures the issue isn't lost. This benefits the team by preventing small concerns from festering or being ignored.

This competency also involves listening for underlying meanings and team dynamics. An Agile coach should be attuned to things like tone of voice, patterns of who speaks after whom, or recurring themes in team conversations. For instance, the coach might pick up that two team members frequently disagree in planning sessions but never in retrospectives—a cue to explore whether there's a hidden conflict or a healthy debate. ICF notes that an active-listening team coach "*notices verbal and non-verbal communication patterns among team members to identify potential alliances, conflicts, and growth opportunities.*" This might manifest as the coach observing that whenever the QA engineer speaks, the developers exchange glances (possible alliance or shared viewpoint), or that certain ideas proposed by junior members get overlooked until a senior member repeats them. These insights allow the coach to bring awareness to the team. They might say in a retrospective, "I've noticed something: when we discuss design changes, our testers often don't get a chance to weigh in. How can we improve on that?"—thereby prompting the team to adjust and become more inclusive in discussions.

Active listening by the coach also serves as a *model* for the team. Agile teams benefit when members listen to each other (it improves collaboration and reduces misunderstandings). The coach implicitly teaches these behaviors by demonstrating deep listening—summarizing discussions, asking clarifying questions, and showing empathy. For example, during a heated sprint review, the coach might paraphrase a stakeholder's feedback for the team: "So, what I'm hearing is the customer loves the new feature but is worried about its performance on mobile, is that right?" This not only confirms understanding but also shows the team how to clarify feedback instead of reacting defensively.

This competency reinforces the Agile value of "Individuals and Interactions" by elevating the quality of communication. Good listening ensures interactions are meaningful and that individuals feel heard. It's also linked to "Customer Collaboration"—an Agile team coach who listens actively can help bridge communication between the team and its customers or product owner. For instance, if a customer is present in a review or a planning session, the coach might pick up on customer concerns that the team misses, and later ensures the team addresses them. Additionally, active listening supports "Responding to Change." By listening carefully, a coach can detect early signals of change (e.g., a slight hesitation when the team discusses a requirement could indicate emerging uncertainty) and encourage the team to respond.

In Agile events, active listening is vital. In retrospectives, it helps the coach hear not just the explicit retrospective data (like "we didn't meet our commitment") but also the emotions or subtext (maybe disappointment or blame). The coach might reflect back to the team, "I sense some frustration around our sprint commitment. What's behind that?" This invites a deeper conversation about root causes (perhaps unrealistic planning or external pressure) that might otherwise remain hidden. In daily stand-ups, active listening enables the coach to catch if someone glosses over an impediment ("everything's fine" said hesitantly) and later gently probe if help is needed. All these actions flow from the coach's attentive ear and eye on the team. In sum, Competency 6, "Listens Actively," is the coach's radar. By using it well, the coach gathers the real information necessary to guide the team, ensures everyone's voice is acknowledged, and helps the team learn to communicate more effectively and empathetically.

Competency 7: Evokes Awareness

Evoking awareness is the competency where coaching truly shines as being distinct from mere facilitation. It's about sparking new insights, challenging the team to think in new ways, and helping them *see* what they might not see on their own. The ICF definition involves the coach using techniques like powerful questioning and observations to broaden the team's perspective, and specifically for team coaching it means the coach "*challenges the team's assumptions, behaviors, and meaning-making processes to enhance their collective awareness or insight.*" In an Agile team setting, evoking awareness often happens by asking thought-provoking questions during moments of reflection. For example, in a sprint retrospective, beyond capturing what went well or not, an Agile coach might ask, "What patterns have we noticed across the last few sprints in how we collaborate with our stakeholders?" Such a question invites the team to step back from the day-to-day and consider a broader view of their interactions and processes. It may prompt realizations like, "We tend to rush demo preparation at the last minute each time," or "We've stopped doing mid-sprint check-ins with our UX designer, and that's causing late surprises." These *a-ha* moments are the seeds of improvement.

CHAPTER 2   MASTERING THE FUNDAMENTALS: ESSENTIAL COMPETENCIES FOR AGILE TEAM COACHES

Evoking awareness can also mean holding up a mirror to the team. The coach might use data or observations to help the team gain insight. For instance, the coach might bring up an observation: "In the past month, I've noticed we've reopened five bugs on average per sprint, whereas three months ago it was only one. What do you think this is telling us?" This kind of prompt helps the team analyze their own behavior and outcomes, leading them to pinpoint causes (maybe rushed testing or unclear requirements) and thereby become aware of areas to address. Another real-world example: During a team conflict, the coach might ask each person involved, "What outcome do you truly want in this situation?" Often, this question makes people aware of their shared goals (e.g., both parties want the project to succeed, not to win an argument), shifting them from adversarial positions to a problem-solving mindset.

This competency is strongly tied to the Agile principle that *"at regular intervals, the team reflects on how to become more effective, then tunes and adjusts its behavior accordingly."* The coach's role in those regular intervals (retrospectives or other reflection workshops) is largely to evoke the insights that lead to tuning and adjusting. By challenging assumptions—for example, "What might be the impact if we continue doing X this way?"—the coach helps the team consider changing a habit or process that isn't serving them well. It also aligns with "Responding to Change" as a core value, since awareness is often the precursor to adaptive change. A team doing something out of habit may not change until someone helps them become aware of the need or opportunity to change. The coach fulfills that role.

It's worth noting that evoking awareness isn't always comfortable for the team. A skilled Agile coach uses this competency with care and respect, pushing just enough to expand the team's thinking without lecturing or creating defensiveness. For example, if a team is very quiet and avoids conflict, the coach might surface this pattern gently: "I notice in our meetings we rarely have debate. How might we be avoiding tough conversations?" Such a question can raise awareness of a teamwork issue (perhaps an overemphasis on harmony stifles candid feedback) and start a discussion on improving it. Similarly, the coach might use creative techniques, such as retrospective exercises, metaphors, or even role-playing, to help the team see issues from different angles. An exercise in a remote Agile team retrospective might be "Draw our team as a ship weathering a storm." The emerging drawings and metaphors can make the team aware of feelings or dynamics they hadn't articulated in words (maybe someone draws a hole in the hull, indicating they feel there's a hidden problem, etc.).

The evoking awareness competency differentiates *coaching* from simply coordinating Agile processes. It's what helps teams break out of autopilot and continuously learn. By mastering this as a key competency, an Agile team coach serves as a catalyst for the team's growth in understanding. Each new insight the team gains—whether it's a realization about improving their workflow or a deeper understanding of each other's motivations—enhances the team's ability to self-organize and innovate. Ultimately, evoking awareness involves enabling the team to see the bigger picture and the systemic forces at play, allowing them to make conscious, informed decisions on improving.

Competency 8: Facilitates Client Growth

The final competency, "Facilitates Client Growth," focuses on turning insights into action and fostering sustainable development for the team. In ICF terms, this means the coach collaborates with the team to translate learning into forward movement—setting goals, experimenting with new behaviors, and tracking progress. Within Agile, this competency aligns with the philosophy of continuous improvement (Kaizen) and the emphasis on delivering incremental value. After all, having a retrospective insight (awareness) is useful, but the real power comes from acting on it in the next sprint. The ICF Team Coaching Competencies specifically note that a coach *"encourages dialogue and reflection to help the team identify their goals and the steps to achieve those goals."* In practice, an Agile coach does this routinely: helping the team pinpoint improvement goals (like "improve our code review process" or "increase test automation coverage") and facilitating the creation of concrete action items or experiments to pursue that goal.

Consider a typical scenario at the end of a retrospective. The team has discussed several issues and possible improvements. A coach applying Competency 8 will guide the team to *choose* one or two actionable improvements to implement in the next sprint. For instance, if the team became aware that their Definition of Done is unclear (evoked awareness), the coach might help them set a growth goal: "By next sprint review, we will draft and agree on a refined Definition of Done and apply it." The coach doesn't dictate the goal but facilitates the team in formulating it. They might ask, "Which of these ideas do we want to commit to trying in the next sprint?" and then, "How exactly will we do that? Who will take ownership to get us started?" This ensures the team leaves the room not just with insights, but also with a plan, however small, to grow and improve.

Facilitating growth also entails accountability and support. In subsequent sessions, the coach will check in on those action items: "Last sprint we decided to hold a mid-sprint demo with stakeholders to get early feedback. How did that go?" If the team struggled to follow through, the coach could explore why, without judgment, perhaps adjusting the plan or helping remove obstacles. In Agile events, this might manifest as quick follow-ups at the start of retrospectives: "We tried pair programming two days a week—what did we learn from that experiment?". It's similar to the "adapt" part of the Inspect & Adapt cycle—the coach helps the team *adapt* by implementing changes and learning from them, thus fostering growth. Over time, these incremental changes compound, and the team's capabilities and performance develop in a sustainable way.

This competency is strongly aligned with "Working software (product) over comprehensive documentation" in a metaphorical sense; it's about tangible outcomes (team improvements) over just theoretical discussions. The coach focuses the team on taking action that will yield real improvements in their work (their "working" team process), rather than just talking about problems or writing down issues in a document no one addresses. It also ties to "Customer Collaboration" because many growth actions involve improving collaboration either within the team or with stakeholders (for example, "let's involve the customer earlier in our demo process" is a growth step that enhances collaboration). And of course, it reinforces "Responding to Change," since a continuously growing team is better equipped to handle new challenges and evolving project needs.

Another aspect of facilitating growth is helping the team set and achieve longer-term developmental goals. An Agile coach might work with the team to create a vision of what "high performance" looks like for them in, say, six months. This could involve a facilitated session where the team imagines their future state ("If we were a rock-star Agile team, what would be different?"). From this vision, the coach helps them derive concrete steps or milestones. For instance, if the vision includes "we release to production with zero downtime," the team might set a goal to adopt continuous delivery practices, and break that into steps like training on CI/CD tools, pilot releasing a small service, etc. The coach then supports them through these steps, celebrating progress and learning from setbacks.

In essence, Competency 8, "Facilitates Client Growth," is where coaching delivers results. It ensures that all the trust built and all the awareness evoked lead to real change and improvement. For Agile teams, this means better adherence to Agile principles, higher performance, and more value delivered to customers over time. A coach who is adept in this competency helps the team solve today's problems and build the muscle to improve on their own continuously. This creates a sustainable agility—the team continues to grow and adapt even long after the coach is gone. In other words, the coach's legacy is a self-propelled engine of improvement within the team, which is the ultimate goal of Agile coaching.

CHAPTER 2   MASTERING THE FUNDAMENTALS: ESSENTIAL COMPETENCIES FOR AGILE TEAM COACHES

Team Coaching vs. Agile Facilitation

It's important to clearly distinguish team coaching from Agile facilitation, as the two terms are related but not interchangeable. Many Agile practitioners, especially Scrum masters, spend considerable time facilitating: guiding teams through Scrum events (daily Scrum, sprint planning, etc.) and ensuring discussions are productive. Agile facilitation, on one hand, is about making process interactions effective; for instance, keeping meetings on schedule, ensuring everyone has an opportunity to speak, and helping the team reach decisions. Team coaching, on the other hand, delves deeper into the team's development, focusing on the relationships, mindset, and systemic dynamics at play within the team. According to ICF, *"Facilitation is about enhancing communication and achieving clarity; the work remains on the surface and does not delve into an analysis of the team dynamics. Team coaching goes deeper than facilitation—exploring the subsurface dynamics of individual team member personalities, sub-groups, and how they might affect team performance."* In simpler terms, a facilitator might help plan the agenda and maintain the flow of conversation, but a coach is attentive to *how* people relate, what tensions or unspoken assumptions underlie the discussion, and how the team can learn from what's happening. There is often a continuum between facilitation and coaching, and a skilled Agile coach moves seamlessly along this continuum as needed.

Let's illustrate the difference. Imagine that during a sprint retrospective a debate arises about whether to adopt a new testing framework. An Agile facilitator would ensure the conversation stays respectful and on-topic, perhaps using a decision-making technique (like dot voting) to help the team choose, and then moving the meeting toward its conclusion on time. An Agile team coach, while capable of those facilitation tasks, also pays attention to deeper aspects: Why is this debate arising? Is there trust in the team around technical decisions? Are all voices being heard equally?

Are there fears or identity issues at play (e.g., a tester feeling their role is threatened)? The coach might intervene not just to manage time but also to pose a question that surfaces underlying concerns ("I notice our QA engineer hasn't spoken about this yet—I'd like to hear your perspective, especially regarding how this might affect our workflow."). Or the coach might sense that the debate is actually a proxy for a bigger issue (perhaps frustration with code quality) and gently bring that to light. After the meeting, a facilitator's job is done once the decision is made, but a coach might follow up by coaching the team on how they can handle technical disagreements in the future, turning it into a growth opportunity.

Another way to distinguish them: Agile facilitation is often about *the here-and-now task* (getting through the meeting, solving the problem on the table), whereas team coaching is about *the ongoing evolution of the team*. Agile facilitation focuses on immediate outcomes (e.g., a decision, an estimate, an action-item list). In contrast, team coaching focuses on building the team's capabilities (e.g., improving communication, increasing psychological safety, helping them become more self-aware and self-managing). Both are crucial—in fact, effective Agile coaches must have strong facilitation skills as part of their toolkit—but team coaching adds an extra dimension of depth. The ICF competency model acknowledges that team coaches may "wander into facilitation mode" frequently, yet they also maintain a broader coaching stance. A good Agile coach will explicitly switch hats: sometimes acting as a facilitator (neutral, process-focused), and other times as a coach (reflective, asking questions, highlighting learning). They might even inform the team: "I'm going to put on my facilitator hat now to help structure this discussion," versus "Now, as a coach, I'm hearing a pattern we might need to examine."

It's also worth noting the relationship between team coaching and other team development modalities, like mentoring, training, or consulting. The ICF competency for ethical practice reminds coaches to maintain distinctions between these modalities. For example, if an Agile team is brand new to Scrum, they might genuinely need training (teaching the Scrum principles) or mentoring (specific advice based on experience). An Agile coach might provide that instruction (or find someone who can), but when coaching, they step back from providing answers and instead help the team discover their own. Agile coaching, as defined by thought leaders (e.g., the Agile Coaching Institute's framework), includes a blend of teaching, mentoring, facilitating, and professional coaching. The art is knowing which stance to take when. Team coaching is a professional coaching stance where the growth of the team is the focus, whereas Agile facilitation is a stance ensuring that the team's processes and interactions in the moment are smooth.

In summary, team coaching versus Agile facilitation can be viewed as *depth versus surface.* Agile facilitation is the surface-level enabling of teamwork (important for day-to-day functioning), while team coaching involves the deeper work on team dynamics and development (important for long-term excellence). An Agile team coach wears both hats, but this chapter and this book emphasize that to create truly self-organizing teams, one must go beyond facilitation into the rich domain of coaching. By understanding this distinction, you, as a coach, can be more deliberate about when you are merely facilitating an Agile practice and when you are leveraging a coaching move to help the team grow. Both are valuable, but it's the coaching that ultimately helps the team improve not just the *what* of their work, but also the *how* of working together.

Conclusion

Mastering these eight ICF Team Coaching Competencies is akin to mastering the art of nurturing an Agile team's journey from formation to high performance. Throughout this chapter, we have seen that each competency—from Ethical Practice to Facilitating Growth—provides essential support for Agile values and principles. They are not abstract coaching ideals but rather practical guideposts for daily behavior and interventions that significantly impact team outcomes. By maintaining a professional, ethical stance, an Agile coach builds the trust without which Agile cannot function. By embodying a coaching mindset, the coach remains adaptable and resilient, modeling the very agility we seek to instill in teams. The coach lays a foundation of alignment through clear agreements, mirroring Agile's emphasis on collaboration and shared understanding. In cultivating trust and safety, the coach unlocks a team's potential to innovate and handle conflict constructively, fulfilling the promise of "Individuals and Interactions" seen in the Agile Manifesto. Presence and active listening make the coach a keen instrument tuned to the team's frequency, catching the nuances that can make or break a sprint. And by evoking awareness and facilitating growth, the coach turns each iteration, each ceremony, into an opportunity for the team to learn and improve, thus embedding continuous improvement into the team's DNA.

The impact of mastering these competencies on team performance is profound. A coach operating with these skills can transform a group of individuals participating in Agile ceremonies into a cohesive Agile team that embodies the principles of agility. Over time, the need for heavy coach involvement diminishes as the team internalizes these ways of working. In other words, great coaches work to *make themselves eventually unnecessary* by empowering the team. This is the essence of sustainable agility: the ability of the team to continue adapting, improving, and performing even as conditions change or when the coach's engagement concludes. Organizations that have teams coached in this way often see lasting benefits—improved product quality, faster delivery, higher employee engagement, and innovation—because the team has become self-organizing and resilient.

CHAPTER 2 MASTERING THE FUNDAMENTALS: ESSENTIAL COMPETENCIES FOR AGILE TEAM COACHES

It's also worth noting that aligning Agile team coaching with the ICF competencies, as we have done, serves to professionalize the role of the Agile coach. It means that Agile coaching isn't just ad-hoc advice and facilitation; it's grounded in proven coaching standards and ethics, lending credibility and consistency to the practice.. The competencies provide a roadmap for Agile coaches to develop themselves continuously. For instance, you might reflect: "How can I listen more actively in the next meeting?" or "Am I truly keeping our coaching agreements, and have they changed as the team has evolved?" Using the competencies as a lens for self-inspection is a powerful way to improve coaching effectiveness.

PART II

Coaching Techniques and Processes

CHAPTER 3

Sealing the Deal: Effective Contracting

Contracting is where team coaching really begins—not with the team session itself, but with how we come together to define *why* we're doing this work and *what* we're trying to achieve. It's not just a formal agreement; it's a conversation that sets the tone for the entire coaching journey.

At its core, contracting is about clarity. It brings all parties—the sponsor, the team, and the coach—into alignment around purpose, goals, and outcomes. I see it as the moment we move from good intentions to shared commitment.

Done well, contracting serves two big purposes. First, it creates the conditions for effective outcomes by giving us a clear North Star to aim for. Second, it dramatically reduces the risk of misunderstandings, scope creep, or fuzzy expectations down the road—things that can quietly erode trust or derail progress if left unchecked.

But this process isn't just about signing off on deliverables or agreeing on timelines. It's about surfacing what success looks like for *everyone* involved. That includes organizational goals—like improving cross-team collaboration or accelerating delivery—as well as personal hopes and fears, especially from team members who may be unsure about what coaching actually means for them.

CHAPTER 3   SEALING THE DEAL: EFFECTIVE CONTRACTING

A strong contract doesn't just define responsibilities; it creates safety. It clarifies what role I'll play as the coach, what's expected from the team and sponsor, and how we'll handle bumps in the road. I always make space to talk about what happens if something's not working—because in complex human systems, that's not an "if," it's a "when."

In my experience, teams can tell when this step has been rushed. And when it hasn't—when we've taken the time to co-create the agreement with honesty and transparency—they step into the process with more confidence and ownership.

So while it might be tempting to breeze through contracting as a procedural step, I treat it as foundational. It's where trust begins, expectations take shape, and the real work of coaching becomes possible.

Why Contract

Current research[1] indicates that coaching supervisors believe 51% of the challenges executive coaches face are related to the initial contracting process. This underscores how a lack of clarity and thoroughness in the initial agreement (see more in Table 3-1) often underlies later difficulties in the coaching engagement.

---

[1] Systemic Coaching Delivering Value Beyond the Individual (Peter Hawkins, Eve Turner, 2020)

CHAPTER 3　SEALING THE DEAL: EFFECTIVE CONTRACTING

Table 3-1. Pitfalls of Weak or Absent Contracting

Misunderstandings and Unmet Expectations	Without clear agreements, misunderstandings between the coach, team, and sponsor can lead to frustration and unmet expectations. *Example:* A sponsor hires an Agile coach expecting them to "fix" the team's productivity issues. Meanwhile, the coach assumes their role is to facilitate team growth and self-organization. As a result, after a few months, the sponsor is frustrated because they see no immediate increase in velocity, while the coach is focused on improving team dynamics—leading to unmet expectations and friction.
Unclear Goals and Scope	Vague objectives due to poor contracting make it difficult to measure coaching success, leading to a lack of focus and direction. *Example:* A Scrum master requests team coaching, saying they want "better collaboration." However, there is no clear definition of what success looks like. Should the team have more frequent discussions? Should they resolve conflicts more openly? Should they improve their ability to challenge ideas? Without specific goals, the coaching efforts lack direction, and after several sessions the team still doesn't see tangible improvements.
Ethical Dilemmas	Ambiguous roles and confidentiality gaps can create ethical dilemmas, such as conflicts of loyalty or mishandling sensitive information. *Example:* A team leader asks the Agile coach to provide private feedback on individual team members' performance. The coach is caught in an ethical dilemma—should they maintain confidentiality or report their observations? If confidentiality wasn't explicitly agreed upon in contracting, the coach risks damaging trust with the team or losing credibility with leadership.

(*continued*)

Table 3-1. (*continued*)

Role Confusion	Unclear boundaries can lead to role overlap between the coach, team leader, and members, causing confusion and conflict. *Example:* A product owner expects the Agile coach to facilitate every sprint planning session, believing it's the coach's responsibility. Meanwhile, the Scrum master assumes the coach will step in to resolve conflicts within the team. The coach, however, sees their role as enabling the team to take ownership. Without role clarity, coaching creates dependency instead of fostering self-sufficiency.
Unspoken Expectations and Dynamics	Ignoring hidden expectations can leave key issues unaddressed, leading to dissatisfaction and disengagement. *Example:* A manager brings in an Agile coach, hoping they will help the team "work harder." However, this expectation is never stated explicitly. The coach, focusing on team well-being and sustainable pace, encourages the team to push back against overcommitment. This leads to dissatisfaction on all sides, as the sponsor feels the coach is undermining business goals, while the team believes coaching is meant to protect them from pressure.
Lack of Accountability	Unclear agreements make it hard to hold the coach, team, or sponsor accountable, weakening commitment and follow through. *Example:* A team goes through Agile coaching sessions but fails to apply what they've learned. Since contracting didn't establish accountability measures—such as action items, progress tracking, or regular sponsor check-ins—no one follows up on implementation. Coaching sessions become interesting discussions rather than drivers of real change.

CHAPTER 3   SEALING THE DEAL: EFFECTIVE CONTRACTING

Erosion of Trust and Safety	Strong contracting behaviors—such as defining objectives, roles, and commitments—build mutual trust and a shared sense of purpose. *Example:* A sponsor asks the Agile coach to "secretly observe" the team's behaviors and report back. The coach initially agrees but later realizes this undermines psychological safety. When the team finds out, they lose trust in the coach, seeing them as a management informant rather than a neutral facilitator. This damages the coaching relationship, making it impossible to foster open discussions.
Challenges with Data and Feedback	Clear contracting on confidentiality and disclosure helps prevent ethical pitfalls and ensures transparency with both sponsors and clients. *Example:* During a retrospective, the coach collects anonymous feedback on team challenges. However, leadership later demands access to the raw, unfiltered data. Since no confidentiality agreements were made upfront, the coach is now caught between maintaining team trust and meeting sponsor expectations. This situation could have been avoided if contracting had established clear rules for data handling.

51

CHAPTER 3   SEALING THE DEAL: EFFECTIVE CONTRACTING

Contracting = Alliance Building

In team coaching, contracting isn't a one-off formality—it's an ongoing act of building a strong, shared alliance. It creates the foundation for trust, clarity, and commitment between the coach, the sponsor, and the team. When done well, contracting answers a vital question: *What are we committing to, together?*

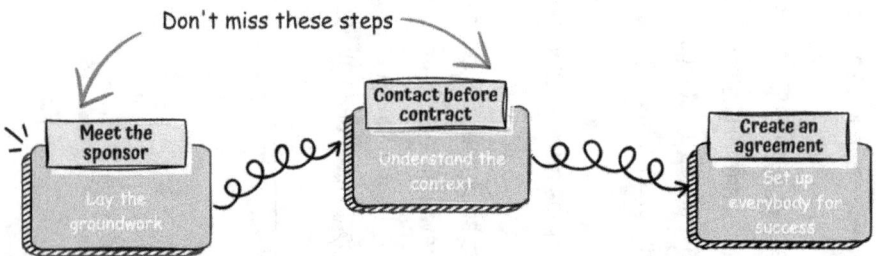

Figure 3-1. Contracting flow

To build this kind of alliance, contracting unfolds in three interconnected steps (see Figure 3-1).

1. **Sponsor alignment: setting the intentional frame**

    The process begins with the sponsor—the leader or stakeholder commissioning the coaching. This conversation is where the coach gains clarity on the organizational context, the sponsor's goals, and any known team dynamics. It's also an opportunity to explore the unspoken: Are there hidden agendas? Misaligned expectations? Unrealistic timelines?

    Effective sponsor contracting includes the following:

    - Clarifying the *purpose* of the coaching engagement
    - Surfacing desired outcomes (and checking if they are team-owned or leader-imposed)

- Agreeing on boundaries, confidentiality, and feedback loops
- Discussing how progress will be measured and communicated

This first step sets the tone. If a sponsor expects the coach to "fix the team," the expectation must be reframed: the coach's role is to *enable*, not rescue.

2. **Team member interviews: listening before leading**

Before engaging with the entire team, the coach frequently holds individual or small group discussions with team members. While there isn't formal contracting yet, these discussions are vital for establishing psychological rapport and setting the stage for team-level agreements.

These interviews serve several purposes, as follows:

- Understanding each person's view of the team's strengths, challenges, and goals
- Gauging the team's readiness and appetite for change
- Uncovering differing perspectives and interpersonal dynamics
- Building early trust and demonstrating a coaching stance of curiosity, not judgement

While these conversations are exploratory, they are not yet the full *contract*. They help shape what needs to be addressed when the team comes together for a shared agreement.

3. **Team contracting: building the coaching alliance together**

The final step is a facilitated team conversation where the actual coaching agreement is co-created. This is the moment when the coach and team align on what the coaching is for, how they will work together, and what success looks like. It also includes surfacing fears, assumptions, and practical considerations that may remain hidden.

This contracting conversation includes the following:

- The team's desired outcomes for the coaching journey
- Roles and responsibilities (coach, team members, leadership)
- Norms around feedback, confidentiality, and psychological safety
- Agreement on how to handle resistance, setbacks, and celebrations
- Time commitment, cadence, and scope of the coaching work

This is not just about logistics—it's about *ownership*. When a team helps shape the agreement, they are far more likely to stay engaged, take risks, and grow together.

Too often, contracting is rushed or limited to a quick kick-off meeting. But effective coaching relationships don't just happen; they are designed. Without these three steps, coaching risks becoming a service provided *to* the team rather than a partnership *formed with* them.

Whether you call it a "contract," "alliance," or "working agreement," what matters most is that the commitment is mutual, conscious, and co-created. The alliance is not static—it evolves as the coaching journey unfolds. As new insights and challenges emerge, the agreement can be revisited and refined.

Ultimately, contracting is what transforms coaching from a transactional service into a transformational partnership.

Meet the Sponsor

Meeting with the team coaching sponsor before contracting is crucial in establishing a strong foundation for the engagement. These early discussions clarify the coaching context and expectations, ensuring initial alignment.

No two sponsor meetings are ever quite the same. Sometimes, I'm greeted with a neatly structured plan and a list of "team issues." Other times, it starts with something vague like, *"There's just something off with the team."* Regardless of how the conversation begins, this is the moment I start sensing the lay of the land—what's happening on the surface and what might be brewing underneath.

Team coaches are usually brought in by someone in a leadership role—a sponsor, team lead, or key stakeholder—who's seeking support with team development. This first meeting is where we explore whether coaching is the right intervention and what the sponsor is really hoping to shift. It often involves peeling back layers of assumptions, expectations, and sometimes urgency.

One of my go-to questions is: *"What prompted you to reach out now?"* It's a simple opener but often uncovers unspoken tensions, sudden performance concerns, or long-standing dynamics that have finally reached a tipping point. These early conversations help me understand the sponsor's perspective, their hopes for the team, and how this coaching effort fits within the broader organizational picture.

CHAPTER 3 SEALING THE DEAL: EFFECTIVE CONTRACTING

I want to know what's important to the sponsor—but also what might be *too* important. Is there pressure to "fix" something fast? Are there conflicting expectations between leaders? Has the team even been told coaching is coming? These are subtle cues that shape how I approach the engagement.

Understanding the company's strategy, vision, and goals matters too. Coaching isn't just about helping teams feel good—it has to serve the business. So, we talk about outcomes, alignment, and the kind of change the organization is ready (or not ready) to support.

And then there's the invisible stuff: hidden agendas, interpersonal politics, or unvoiced frustrations that could quietly derail the coaching work. I've learned to listen for what's not being said as much as what is. Sometimes, what the sponsor *really* wants is transformation. Other times, they just want the noise to go away.

It's also crucial to establish boundaries and confidentiality upfront. I clarify what information stays within the team and what I might loop the sponsor in on. Setting these agreements early builds trust and reinforces a psychologically safe environment for everyone involved.

This meeting isn't just about assessing fit—it's where rapport is built, clarity is created, and expectations start to align. It also sets the stage for broader multi-stakeholder contracting, which later brings the team into the conversation.

In short, spending quality time in these early sponsor meetings is an investment. It reduces misunderstandings, reveals organizational dynamics, and sets a solid foundation for everything that comes next. And when done well, it marks the real beginning of the coaching journey—not just for the team but for the entire system around them.

Tip The following are some questions that might be helpful during a conversation with a sponsor:

1. Tell me about the team. What development objectives have you identified for their coaching?
2. Has the team received any feedback? If so, how did they respond?
3. What type of development support has the team received so far?
4. What business goals and performance expectations does the organization have for this team in the next 6–12 months?
5. How has coaching been introduced to the team? What was their reaction?
6. What organizational (division, department) norms should I be aware of to maximize my effectiveness as a coach?

Contact Before Contract

Agile coaching often fails when frameworks and ceremonies are introduced before teams are psychologically ready. This results in mechanical compliance rather than genuine agility or self-organization. The principle of *contact before contract* prevents this by prioritizing human connection before formal agreements.

CHAPTER 3 SEALING THE DEAL: EFFECTIVE CONTRACTING

When teams begin working with a coach, they may feel uncertain, wary, or unclear about what to expect. Yet beneath that uncertainty lies a common human need—the desire to be seen, understood, and accepted. If we move too quickly into defining structures and goals without addressing this, we risk shallow compliance instead of meaningful commitment.

Drawing from transactional analysis (TA), *contact* refers to the psychological proximity that enables authentic interaction. It means truly recognizing the other as a person—not just a role or a task performer. Without this genuine connection, any contract—explicit or implied—can become fragile, performative, or even counterproductive.

Establishing real contact helps prevent unconscious psychological "games"—manipulative or defensive behaviors that can derail collaboration. When people feel genuinely acknowledged and respected, they are more likely to show up fully and engage honestly in shaping how they work together. This is true in therapy, business, leadership—and especially in coaching Agile teams.

Key Elements of Genuine Contact

1. **Authenticity.** Be real, not performative. People quickly pick up on inauthenticity, which undermines trust. As a coach, it's more powerful to be grounded and human than to hide behind expertise.

2. **"I'm OK—You're OK" mindset.** Approach the relationship with mutual respect. This healthy stance from TA ensures you neither elevate yourself nor diminish the team.

3. **Awareness of psychological games.** Stay alert to unconscious communication patterns that sabotage trust. Recognize and gently surface these to enable more open and productive dialogue.

4. **Cultural attunement.** Be sensitive to how different cultures express connection. What builds trust in one team may feel invasive or distant in another.

5. **Stay curious and adaptable.**

Tip Use their language, not Agile jargon. Agile is a tool for achieving goals. What do their problems appear to be?

In Agile, we emphasize *individuals and interactions* over *processes and tools*. That begins with making real contact before formalizing any agreements. In team coaching, this means resisting the urge to "get things going" too quickly with charters, working agreements, or improvement plans.

Instead, invest in the conditions that make such agreements meaningful. Here's how this might look in practice:

1. **Build psychological safety first**

   Before jumping into sprint ceremonies or improvement work, create a space where team members feel safe to speak up, take risks, and be vulnerable. This lays the foundation for adult-to-adult transactions in TA.

2. **Recognize the team as a system**

   Acknowledge the team's efforts, tensions, and achievements—both collectively and individually. Positive strokes help strengthen the team's sense of identity and cohesion.

3. **Facilitate with authenticity**

   Don't show up as the expert with answers. Instead, bring your full self—sharing relevant experiences, owning your uncertainties, and modelling the kind of openness you wish to invite.

4. **Create space for emergence**

   Give the team permission to experiment, and protect them from premature evaluation. Agility thrives in an environment where people are free to learn in public.

5. **Tune in to cross-cultural dynamics**

   In diverse or global teams, adjust your coaching approach to respect cultural differences in hierarchy, directness, and emotional expression. What fosters connection in one context might feel inappropriate in another.

Arrange a series of conversations with the team members to understand their perspective and sense what the situation looks like for them.

Only after this foundation of contact is in place should an Agile coach move toward contracting—defining how the team will collaborate, what "done" means, how they'll measure progress, and where they want to improve.

As Agile practitioners, our first contract isn't written—it's felt. When we make real contact, we unlock the team's capacity for self-organization, ownership, and agility.

CHAPTER 3   SEALING THE DEAL: EFFECTIVE CONTRACTING

Story: Slowing Down to Speed Up

When I first started coaching a newly established product team in a global financial services company, the client was keen for results. "They require a definition of done, working agreements, and a retrospective process—can you get them there within two weeks?" the delivery manager asked.

But in the initial session with the team, I sensed hesitation. Cameras stayed off, voices were guarded, and there was a quiet undercurrent of resistance. I could've pushed ahead with the formal contracting—what their goals were, what success looked like—but something told me to pause.

Instead, I took a different approach. I invited them into a short "team mapping" exercise where each person shared a little about their background, what brought them to this team, and what energizes or drains them at work. I also shared my own journey—not as a credentialed coach, but as someone who's made plenty of mistakes in Agile adoption and still believes deeply in teams.

That small act of vulnerability changed something. The next session felt lighter and more open. People began addressing each other directly. One developer remarked, "I've never been asked what matters to me before. This feels different."

Over the following few sessions, we built psychological safety through listening circles, appreciative interviews, and strengths spotting. Only then did we co-create working agreements and a team backlog of improvement experiments. The team owned these decisions because they were rooted in real connection—not imposed structure.

Looking back, I'm convinced that had I rushed into formal contracting, the team would've complied—but only on the surface. By making contact first, we unlocked their ability to shape their own ways of working with ownership and pride.

CHAPTER 3   SEALING THE DEAL: EFFECTIVE CONTRACTING

Tip The following are some questions to use when interviewing the team members:

1. What feedback has the team received from the manager or anyone else in the organization? How did you feel about that feedback?
2. What does the organization (division, department) need from the team regarding goal achievement and performance in the next 6–12 months?
3. Are you pursuing coaching on your own initiative, or has it been suggested?
4. What is your experience with or perception of team and Agile coaching?
5. What cultural norms should I be aware of to be as effective as possible?

Holding the Coaching Relationship Together

Over the years, I've learned that great team coaching doesn't start with tools, techniques, or even the team—it starts with the contract. And not just the signed piece of paper, but the deeper, layered agreements that shape how we work together.

In practice, contracting happens on three distinct levels: administrative, professional, and psychological (Figure 3-2). I didn't always have names for these levels early in my career—I just knew that when something felt "off" in a coaching relationship, it usually traced back to something that wasn't clearly agreed upon. Over time, I came to realize

CHAPTER 3   SEALING THE DEAL: EFFECTIVE CONTRACTING

that these three levels are essential anchors, especially in the messiness of team coaching where multiple voices, expectations, and pressures collide.

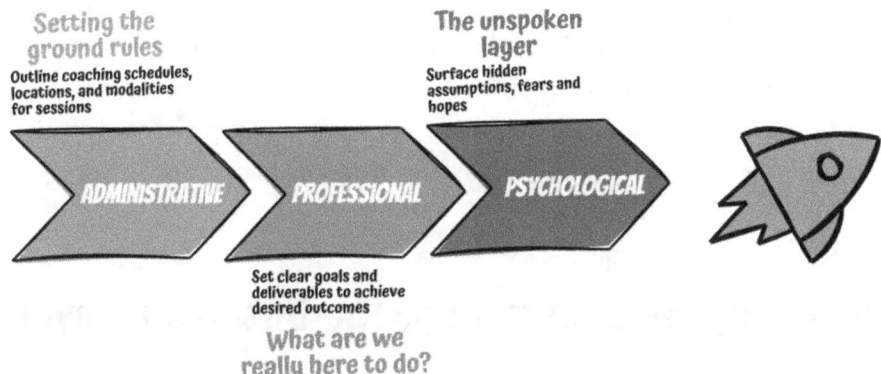

Figure 3-2. *Three levels of contracting*

Administrative Level: Setting the Ground Rules

This is the nuts and bolts stuff. How often are we meeting? Who's in the room? What happens if someone cancels? Are we charging a flat rate or per session? Who's paying—and what are they expecting in return?

It may sound transactional, but getting this clear upfront makes everything smoother later. I've been in engagements where vague admin terms led to misaligned expectations, awkward conversations, or even loss of trust. So now I treat these logistics as the scaffolding that holds the coaching container steady.

Professional Level: What Are We Really Here to Do?

This level is where we define the purpose and scope of the coaching. Are we focused on helping a team navigate change? Strengthening collaboration? Addressing persistent conflict? I work with the sponsor, team leader, and sometimes the team themselves to co-create a shared purpose.

63

This is also where roles and boundaries come into play. What's expected of me as a coach? What's the team's responsibility? What can the sponsor expect to hear—or *not* hear? We discuss confidentiality, ethics, what coaching is (and isn't), and how we'll measure progress.

Professional contracting ensures we're all pulling in the same direction—and it becomes even more important in complex setups with multiple stakeholders. Clarity here keeps things from derailing when inevitable tensions arise.

Psychological Contracting: The Unspoken Layer

Here's where it gets interesting. This level is about the assumptions, fears, hopes, and unconscious dynamics that shape how we relate to each other in the coaching process. It's not something you always define explicitly on day one, but I've learned to surface and attend to it early.

For example, is the team secretly worried this coaching is just a disguised performance review? Is the sponsor expecting me to "fix" the team? Is there a team member quietly resisting the whole thing because they've had a bad experience before?

Sometimes, it's about deeper group dynamics—power struggles, unspoken hierarchies, cultural tensions, or emotional residue from past leadership changes. If we ignore this layer, it almost always shows up later as resistance, silence, or misalignment.

The psychological contract is about building safety. It's about showing up with presence, curiosity, and empathy. And it's about creating a working alliance that can hold discomfort, challenge, and growth.

Team coaching is a multi-stakeholder game. You're not just contracting with one person; you're contracting with a whole system. That means expectations will clash, dynamics will shift, and things will get messy. That's why I've found it essential to revisit and refine the contract *throughout* the engagement, not just at the beginning.

Let's Professionalize It!

These three levels of contracting are directly linked to several ICF Team Coaching Competencies:

Demonstrates Ethical Practice: All three levels of contracting are foundational to ethical practice:

- Clearly communicating the parameters of the coaching relationship (administrative and professional levels) aligns with understanding and applying coaching standards.

- Maintaining confidentiality (professional level) is a key ethical standard.

- Being sensitive to the team's dynamics and potential power imbalances (psychological level) relates to demonstrating integrity and honesty.

- Maintaining trust, transparency, and clarity when fulfilling multiple roles in team development (professional level) is crucial for ethical conduct.

Establishes and Maintains Agreements: This competency directly addresses contracting:

- The administrative and professional contracting levels are essential for partnering with the client and relevant stakeholders to create clear agreements about the coaching relationship, process, plans, and goals. This includes logistics, fees, scheduling, and the scope of work (administrative level), as well as the objectives, roles, responsibilities, and ethical guidelines (professional level).

- Partnering with all relevant parties, including the team leader, members, stakeholders, and co-coaches, to collaboratively create clear agreements covers all three levels, including understanding expectations and potential unspoken dynamics (psychological level).

Cultivates Trust and Safety: The psychological level of contracting is fundamental to building trust and safety:

- Creating a safe space for open and honest team member interaction requires awareness of the psychological dynamics and implicit expectations within the team.
- Establishing clear boundaries (professional level) contributes to a safe and trusting environment.

Evokes Awareness: While not directly about contracting, a well-contracted relationship (especially at the psychological level) allows the coach to challenge assumptions and meaning-making processes more effectively. Understanding the team's psychological landscape helps the coach to facilitate deeper insights.

Facilitates Client Growth: Clear agreements (across all levels) help the team identify their goals and the steps to achieve them. Understanding the psychological contract can inform the goal-setting process and ensure alignment with the team's underlying needs and motivations.

Here is a contracting framework I use in my practice. This level handles the practicalities (see Table 3-2)—what needs to be in place for the coaching actually to happen. While it may seem procedural, clarity here prevents the kinds of small misunderstandings that can undermine trust or cause friction later on.

CHAPTER 3   SEALING THE DEAL: EFFECTIVE CONTRACTING

Table 3-2. Administrative Considerations in Coaching Agreements

Administrative	
Scheduling	Who arranges the meetings? How often, how long, and where?
Location	Onsite, remote, or hybrid?
Documentation	What records are needed? Who creates and stores them? Is there a need for logs?
Rescheduling and Cancellation	What happens if a session needs to be moved?
Reporting Logistics	Who reports to whom, and how often?

This level (see Table 3-3) focuses on the *coaching content* and the *boundaries* of the relationship. It's about establishing a shared understanding of the work ahead and the roles we all play in it.

Table 3-3. Foundation Contracting Themes

Professional	
Initial Exploration and Purpose	• What is the purpose that requires them to be a team? This question helps to define the core reason for the team's existence and aligns the coaching with that purpose. • What are the perspectives of the different stakeholders on the work that needs doing? Exploring stakeholder perspectives early ensures alignment with the coaching objectives.

(continued)

Table 3-3. (*continued*)

Professional	
Defining Success and Outcomes	• How would you know if this team coaching had been successful for you? Clarifying goals at the start allows revisiting them throughout the coaching engagement. • What would "effective outcome(s)" mean for these stakeholders? Defines how success will be measured from different perspectives. • How will we judge whether the coaching is effective? What are the expected outcomes from working together? Establishes clear metrics for evaluating the impact of the coaching. Ensures mutual understanding of what the coaching aims to achieve. Helps define the specific focus of the coaching.
Understanding the Coaching Approach and Needs	• How do you describe your approach to coaching? Aims to understand the coach's underlying principles and typical coaching process. • How will we distinguish between coaching, mentoring, consulting? Assists in diagnosing and defining the developmental needs of the team and organization.
Ethical Considerations	• What is our confidentiality agreement? What gets shared outside the coaching space—and under what conditions? What does the company require of you, according to its own rules and procedures? Is that acceptable? Addresses confidentiality and compliance with organizational policies.

CHAPTER 3 SEALING THE DEAL: EFFECTIVE CONTRACTING

This is the most nuanced level—and often the most important. The psychological contract (possible themes are shown in Table 3-4) addresses the *underlying expectations, assumptions, and emotional dynamics* between the coach, team, and sponsor. These are rarely articulated upfront, but they profoundly shape the coaching experience.

Table 3-4. Relational Coaching Agreements

Psychological	
Feelings and Expectations	• How do we really feel about this coaching relationship? • What assumptions or hopes might we be holding—about each other or the process?
Trust and Safety	• How will we be honest and respectful with each other? • What needs to be in place for psychological safety to emerge?
Differences and Diversity	• What "secret" fears do we have—especially related to differences in role, culture, or background? • How will we deal with misunderstandings, including those rooted in diversity or identity?
Relational Dynamics	• What might go wrong? How will we handle it if it does? • How will we end the relationship, either by completion or through a no-fault exit?
Perceptions and Power	• How do we perceive each other? • How might others view our relationship? • What role do power dynamics play here—and how will we name and work with them?

Creating a psychological contract is the most difficult part, in my opinion. It might even require a separate session—a workshop to explore it properly.

CHAPTER 3   SEALING THE DEAL: EFFECTIVE CONTRACTING

Set the Context

"Today, we're going to explore the *unwritten contract* we all carry into this work—what we secretly hope will happen, what we might be anxious about, and what outcomes we expect beyond the stated goals. This helps us get honest about what's in the room, even if it's never been said out loud."

Pose the questions (individually or in pairs):

- What are your hopes for this coaching engagement?
- What do you think are others' hopes, as far as you can sense?
- What are your fears about this engagement?
- What fears might others be carrying, from your perspective?
- Is there anything you personally expect to gain from this, even if it's not the official goal?
- What might others expect to gain that hasn't been explicitly named?
- Now that you're more aware of these undercurrents, are there any actions you want to take?

Debrief in the group:

- Invite sharing selectively—no one has to disclose everything, only what feels safe and useful.
- Look for patterns, unspoken tensions, and mismatched expectations.
- Use this insight to revisit or co-create the formal coaching agreement or team working agreement.

CHAPTER 3   SEALING THE DEAL: EFFECTIVE CONTRACTING

Tip   Consider the following:

- **Create safety first**. Start with individual reflection or small groups to warm up trust.

- **Be transparent**. Model your own responses with vulnerability: share a hope and a fear.

- **Normalize the exercise**. Explain that hopes and fears are normal—even healthy—as long as they are named and not left to drive behavior unconsciously.

- **Link to contracting**. Use what surfaces to adjust expectations, clarify roles, or renegotiate agreements if needed.

This exercise strengthens the *contact before contract* principle by surfacing what's usually left unsaid. It also enables more authentic contracting, where both spoken and unspoken dynamics can be acknowledged.

Pitfalls to Avoid

Omitting elements of the contracting framework can lead to all sorts of problems, and even seasoned Agile coaches can fall into pitfalls that undermine the coaching process right from the start.

Start Coaching Immediately Without Contracting

Many coaches, eager to make an impact, jump straight into coaching without first clarifying expectations or just having an initial conversation with the sponsor. While the desire to help the team feels rewarding, coaching can quickly become directionless without discussing roles, responsibilities, and outcomes. The urge to prove your value is natural, but without clearly defining success, both the team and stakeholders may struggle to see tangible results.

Some internal coaches believe contracting is only necessary for external consultants. In reality, clear agreements are essential for all Agile coaches, regardless of their role within the organization.

The Team and Sponsor Don't Understand the Difference Between Team Coaching and Skills Transfer

While organizations primarily focus on achieving results, they may not always be concerned with how an Agile coach facilitates that process. However, this distinction is crucial for both the coach and the team. Sponsors often expect Agile coaches to take a directive approach—identifying problems, prescribing solutions, like the ability to facilitate Scrum events or apply certain techniques (e.g., Impact Mapping, Lean UX canvas), and ensuring the team follows them. This expectation aligns with a traditional sports coaching model, where skill transfer is the priority.

In contrast, an Agile coach's role is not to dictate solutions but rather to help teams develop self-awareness and take ownership of their ways of working. Rather than prescribing methods, the coach fosters reflection and supports teams in shaping their own norms and practices.

When there is misalignment, the sponsor may expect the coach to take charge and drive performance improvements while waiting for the team to take ownership. This gap leads to frustration—sponsors see little visible change, and teams remain unaware that they must take responsibility for their growth.

CHAPTER 3 SEALING THE DEAL: EFFECTIVE CONTRACTING

Clear contracting around roles and responsibilities helps align expectations. It defines when the coach will step in to provide training on specific competencies and when the focus will shift to exploration—allowing the team to determine what works best for them.

Tip These questions can help to surface misalignment around team coaching and training:

What specific outcomes are you expecting from this engagement—do you need the team to acquire new knowledge and techniques, or do you want them to enhance their collaboration, ownership, and adaptability?

This clarifies whether the focus is on knowledge acquisition (training) or deeper behavioral and mindset shifts (coaching).

Do you expect me to provide solutions and best practices upfront, or are we working toward enabling the team to discover their ways of working through guided reflection and experimentation?

Training often involves delivering predefined solutions, whereas coaching fosters self-discovery and team-led problem-solving.

How will we measure success—by the team's ability to recall and apply specific Agile practices or by their ability to self-organize, navigate challenges, and continuously improve without external direction?

This helps distinguish between competency-based success (training) and behavioral and systemic transformation.

CHAPTER 3   SEALING THE DEAL: EFFECTIVE CONTRACTING

Omitted Sponsor

For team coaching to be effective, the contracting process must involve the sponsor—whether it's a manager or another key stakeholder invested in the coaching engagement.

Sponsors and teams often view coaching engagement through different lenses. While sponsors may focus on business outcomes, teams may prioritize internal dynamics. Contracting bridges this gap, ensuring alignment on both perspectives and clarifying what success looks like from an organizational standpoint. Without the sponsor's involvement, success criteria may remain vague or disconnected from business needs.

Contracting also sets clear expectations for the level of commitment required, ensuring all parties understand the effort and engagement needed for coaching to be successful. Without early involvement, the sponsor may remain disengaged or have unrealistic expectations, leading to limited support for the coaching process.

Furthermore, without a sponsor's visible support, the team may view coaching as an external intervention instead of a leadership-backed initiative. This might result in disengagement, skepticism, or outright resistance.

Without proper contracting, sponsors may unintentionally undermine coaching by prioritizing urgent business goals over genuine learning. This pressure compels teams to focus on delivery at the cost of reflection and experimentation—ultimately rendering coaching ineffective.

Excluding the sponsor from contracting can also create false expectations. They may assume the coach's role is to "fix" the team rather than enable it to develop its own capabilities. This misunderstanding can lead to unrealistic demands, misaligned success metrics, and potential conflict.

Ultimately, contracting without the sponsor creates misalignment, weakens organizational support, and increases the likelihood of coaching's being perceived as ineffective.

CHAPTER 3 SEALING THE DEAL: EFFECTIVE CONTRACTING

Objectives and Goals Are Vague

When discussing desired outcomes, teams often express them in vague terms, such as *"We want more psychological safety"* or *"We'd like team members to be more respectful."* While these are valuable aspirations, they lack specificity. Without a clear behavioral manifestation, they leave too much room for interpretation.

Terms like *respect* or *psychological safety* are subjective—one person might define *respect* as speaking politely, while another sees it as being constructively challenged. Without clear definitions, expectations remain ambiguous, making it difficult to measure progress.

It's crucial to probe deeper. Instead of accepting the first response, ask clarifying questions to uncover what these aspirations look like in practice. Helping teams articulate concrete behaviors ensures the desired change is clear, actionable, and measurable.

Tip Ask questions that help define the desired outcome in observable behaviors. This ensures clarity and alignment on what success looks like. For example: *"Can you describe a specific situation where you felt respected? What was happening?"*; *"If the team had strong psychological safety, what behaviors would be visible? What kinds of conversations would take place?"*

Encourage the team to describe real-life examples or situations in which they have experienced (or would like to experience) these behaviors. This will make abstract concepts tangible and measurable.

CHAPTER 3   SEALING THE DEAL: EFFECTIVE CONTRACTING

Negative Goals

A request for team coaching may arise when management or a team recognizes certain issues. This could lead to an initial conversation centered on what they dislike or wish to avoid, such as, *"The team doesn't take responsibility for product quality"* or *"I want to prevent disruptions in operations."* People often articulate their concerns in terms of what they wish to avoid. While this offers valuable context, it does not clarify what success looks like. It's challenging to envision absence; there should be something in its place.

When this type of sharing becomes a pattern, I usually say, *"You've talked about what you don't want or wouldn't like to have, but it's like walking into a supermarket with a list of things you don't want to buy—you'll still leave empty-handed unless you know what you do want. What would you like to achieve from coaching?"*

Framing coaching around what to avoid can be a trap. Without a positive goal, it's difficult to assess whether meaningful progress has been made. We create a clearer path for meaningful change by shifting the conversation toward desired outcomes.

Conclusion

- **Contracting is foundational**, not transactional. It sets clarity around purpose, outcomes, roles, responsibilities, confidentiality, and expectations, significantly reducing potential misunderstandings and conflicts.
- **Three-step contracting process**: (1) Aligning expectations clearly with sponsors; (2) Conducting individual team interviews to build rapport and psychological safety; (3) Co-creating explicit team agreements that drive ownership and commitment.

- **Watch out for common pitfalls**, such as unclear goals, sponsor omission, role confusion, negative goal framing (what teams don't want), ethical dilemmas, and confidentiality gaps—all of which can derail coaching effectiveness.

- Contracting operates on three distinct levels:
  - **Administrative**: practical logistics (scheduling, fees, cancellations).
  - **Professional**: defining clear coaching objectives, roles, and measurable outcomes.
  - **Psychological**: uncovering hidden expectations, fears, power dynamics, and emotional undercurrents.

- **Prioritize human connection ("Contact before Contract")**: Investing time in establishing genuine, authentic relationships and psychological safety is crucial before formalizing agreements.

- **Explicitly include sponsors** in early contracting conversations to align organizational objectives with team coaching expectations, preventing misalignment or unrealistic expectations.

- **Clearly define measurable behavioral success indicators** (e.g., observable changes in team behaviors, interactions, or performance outcomes), ensuring clarity and alignment throughout the coaching process.

CHAPTER 3   SEALING THE DEAL: EFFECTIVE CONTRACTING

Reflection Moment: Strengthening Contracting in Your Agile Team Coaching

- Have you clearly documented what success will look like for this coaching engagement?

- How will you regularly revisit these outcomes with the team and stakeholders to ensure continuous alignment?

- Have you identified and validated explicit measures (qualitative and quantitative) to track the coaching progress regularly?

- Which stakeholders have you not yet adequately engaged in contracting? What might their concerns or hidden expectations be, and how will you clarify these?

- Identify any assumptions you're currently making. How will you test them explicitly in your next interaction?

- Identify one unspoken expectation or "hidden agenda" within your current team. How will you surface and address it openly during the next team session?

- What cultural or behavioral norms have you noticed in the team that might influence their openness to contracting? Outline steps you'll take in your next session to respect and work with these dynamics.

- Write down your explicit understanding of the confidentiality expectations with your team. How will you validate and confirm this with the team and sponsors?

CHAPTER 3   SEALING THE DEAL: EFFECTIVE CONTRACTING

- Define clearly what falls inside and outside your coaching scope. How will you communicate these boundaries transparently?
- List three ways you'll validate that all team members and stakeholders genuinely share the same understanding of the coaching agreement.

CHAPTER 4

Rewriting the Team Imago

Agile frameworks like Scrum rest on self-organizing teams—groups that manage their own work and process. Yet many teams struggle to truly self-organize. Why? One oft-overlooked factor is the mental image each person carries of "how a team should be." This internal picture is known as the group *imago*, a concept from psychology meaning the unconscious template of what a group is or ought to be. Every team member brings their own group imago shaped by past experiences—families, schools, former jobs. These ingrained images quietly drive our norms, how we use power, and what we expect of leaders. In short, self-organization is either hindered or helped by the imago in each team member's mind.

If team members' imagos clash with each other or with the realities of Agile, the team can spin its wheels. For example, if some carry an imago that "a real team has a strong manager who must approve everything," they will hesitate to take initiative, undermining self-management. Others might have an imago of an idealized "flat" team and bristle at any directive, seeing it as oppressive. These hidden expectations can cause conflict or passivity that looks like resistance but is really an imago mismatch. The result: self-organization stalls.

As an Agile coach or Scrum master, you may have introduced Scrum events and taught collaboration techniques, yet your team still isn't self-organizing as hoped. Perhaps decision making is awkward, authority is unclear, or old hierarchies haunt the team dynamic. By explicitly working with the group imago, you can surface and reset those hidden "team pictures" that each person holds. Doing so accelerates genuine self-management: When everyone updates their internal picture to align with the team's purpose and context, they can then choose norms and behaviors deliberately rather than unconsciously reenacting old patterns. In other words, using the imago concept helps a team move from defaulting to outdated norms toward designing their own way of working.

In the pages ahead, I'll lay the foundations of self-organization and the group imago.

Self-organization in Teams: What Does It Mean?

In plain terms, a self-organizing team manages its own work and processes without needing heavy direction from above. The team members decide who does what, when, and how, rather than a boss assigning tasks or micromanaging. In Scrum, this is emphasized strongly: *"They are also self-managing, meaning they internally decide who does what, when, and how."* The Scrum Guide (2020) even upgraded the terminology from "self-organizing" to "self-managing" to stress that the entire Scrum team (developers, product owner, Scrum master) shares responsibility for planning and adapting their work. In practice, that means a Scrum team should, for example, pick which backlog items to tackle in a sprint, figure out the best approach to build them, adjust workload among themselves, and resolve day-to-day problems—all without a manager directing these decisions.

CHAPTER 4 REWRITING THE TEAM IMAGO

Why is self-organization so highly valued? Research by experts like the late J. Richard Hackman has shown that when teams are given autonomy and clear goals, they often perform better than those under strict control. Hackman, who coined the term *self-managing teams*, identified that such teams handle not only the execution of tasks but also monitor and manage their own processes and progress. He described a progression (see Table 4-1) of team autonomy—from manager-led to self-governing—where responsibility shifts from management to the team across execution, process monitoring, and design, culminating in teams that also set their own direction.

In other words, the team doesn't just do the work; it also keeps itself on track and continually improves its processes. This has profound implications: Managers must step back from daily supervision, and teams must step up to address impediments, adjust plans, and hold themselves accountable. Done right, self-organization can lead to more motivation, faster decision making, and solutions that those closest to the work devise (often yielding better results than top-down orders).

One useful way to distinguish between different kinds of teams is by looking at where responsibility sits for core aspects of work—execution, monitoring, design, and direction. Table 4-1 contrasts how these responsibilities shift across four types of teams: manager-led, self-managing, self-designing, and self-governing. It highlights the increasing degree of autonomy and ownership as teams move from being directed by management toward governing themselves.

CHAPTER 4   REWRITING THE TEAM IMAGO

Table 4-1. Team vs. Management Responsibilities

Responsibility ↓ / Team Type →	Manager-led Teams	Self-Managing Teams	Self-Designing Teams	Self-Governing Teams
Executing the Team Task	Team	Team	Team	Team
Monitoring & Managing Work Process/Progress	Management	Team	Team	Team
Designing the Team & Its Organizational Context	Management	Management	Team	Team
Setting Overall Direction	Management	Management	Management	Team

However, self-organization is not anarchy or the absence of leadership. It operates within constraints and clear objectives. Hackman noted that effective self-managing teams still need certain enabling conditions. These include a clear boundary (knowing who is on the team and what roles they play), a compelling direction (a clear, motivating goal for the team's work), an enabling structure (appropriate team size, skill mix, norms of conduct), a supportive context (resources and information the team needs), and expert coaching when needed. In other words, management's job shifts to setting the stage—defining the team's purpose, composition, and context—and then letting the team figure out the best way to achieve its mission within that framework.

CHAPTER 4   REWRITING THE TEAM IMAGO

Another perspective on cultivating self-organization comes from complexity science. Glenda Eoyang's CDE model describes three conditions that influence how self-organization emerges in any complex adaptive system: containers, differences, and exchanges. In a team context, the container is what holds the team together; e.g., the project scope, the team's membership, or physical workspace. Differences are the significant distinctions within the team—skills, personalities, priorities, or any diversity that could generate creative tension. Exchanges are the interactions or flows between team members—communication patterns, feedback loops, and sharing of resources. By tweaking these conditions (see Figure 4-1), we can affect the team's self-organizing behavior. For instance, a very large or loose "container" (like an undefined team boundary or too broad a mission) leads to slow or ambiguous self-organization. In contrast, a tighter container (clear team membership and scope) tends to help the team gel faster around a clear order. Similarly, if there are no differences among team members (everyone has the same skills and viewpoint), the team may stagnate. Still, if differences are too great or too many, the system can become chaotic. And the exchanges matter: A team with rich, frequent communication and feedback will self-organize more quickly than one with weak, infrequent exchanges. As a coach, you can adjust constraints (see Figure 4-1)—for example, clarifying team boundaries (container), introducing new perspectives or information (differences), or improving communication channels (exchanges)—to influence the team's self-organization. In complexity terms, you're neither imposing a top-down order nor leaving it totally random; you're guiding the conditions that allow an effective order to emerge.

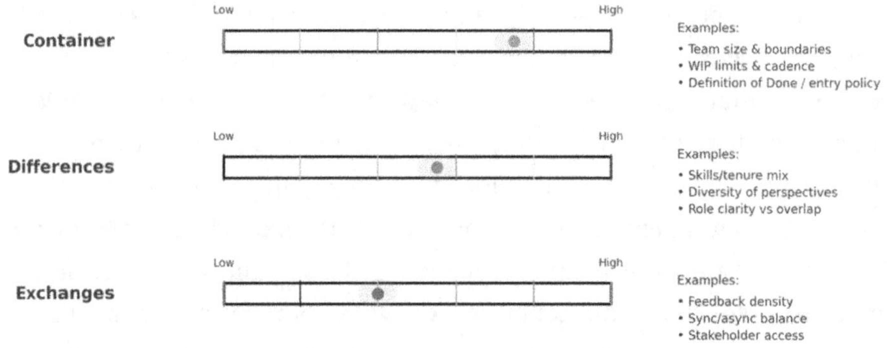

CHAPTER 4 REWRITING THE TEAM IMAGO

Container
Low — High
Examples:
- Team size & boundaries
- WIP limits & cadence
- Definition of Done / entry policy

Differences
Low — High
Examples:
- Skills/tenure mix
- Diversity of perspectives
- Role clarity vs overlap

Exchanges
Low — High
Examples:
- Feedback density
- Sync/async balance
- Stakeholder access

Figure 4-1. CDE "tuning" panel—adjust the knobs to shape conditions for self-organization

The role of the Scrum master or Agile coach is crucial here. In Scrum, one of the Scrum master's services is "coaching the team members in self-management and cross-functionality." This involves teaching and mentoring the team to take on responsibilities that a traditional manager might have handled. It means encouraging the team to solve their own problems, facilitating team decision making, and removing impediments that block self-organization (like overly restrictive policies or a hovering boss). It's a delicate dance: You provide enough support and clarity that the team feels safe to self-organize, but you resist the temptation to micromanage or step in whenever there's uncertainty. When managers or coaches panic and override the team's autonomy (what some Agile practitioners call *agile micromanagement*), it undercuts the very principle of self-organization. Teams need space to learn and even to stumble a bit as they find their groove.

In summary, self-organization is about teams' owning their work and process within clear boundaries and goals. It's enabled by thoughtful constraints (clear roles, goals, norms) rather than by free-for-all chaos. In the next section, we'll explore how each individual's internal model of a team (their group imago) can either accelerate or impede a group's journey toward true self-management. As you'll see, one of the most significant barriers to self-organization can be the mental baggage people carry from their past group experiences. By becoming aware of and actively shaping the team's shared imago, you create the conditions for autonomy to really take root.

The Group Imago: Our Inner Picture of "Team"

Have you ever joined a new team and felt like it reminded you of a past experience—maybe a family dynamic or a prior company's culture? That feeling comes from your group imago. The group imago is *"the mental image of what a group is, or should be like, that you carry with you from other experiences—probably starting with your family of origin."* It's an unconscious template in your mind that tells you *"how a team should operate and how people in it should behave."* We all have one, and usually we aren't aware of it until it clashes with reality.

The term *imago* (Latin for "image") in this context was introduced by Dr. Eric Berne, the founder of Transactional Analysis (TA), who studied group behavior in the 1960s. Berne observed that people enter groups with pre-formed expectations and roles in mind, often modelled after the first group we ever experience—the family. For example, someone who grew up in a strict household might unconsciously expect any group to have a strong authority figure and clear rules. Another person from a very nurturing family might expect a team to feel like a supportive circle of friends. These internal pictures influence how we perceive others' actions and how we behave in a team. They're like invisible lenses. If something in the team doesn't match our imago, we feel dissonance or anxiety—"this isn't how it's supposed to be!"—and we might try (often subconsciously) to change the team to fit our imago, or change our role within the team to fit what we think is needed.

CHAPTER 4   REWRITING THE TEAM IMAGO

The five stages of imago development can be summarized as follows:

1. *Provisional Imago* – When someone first enters a new group (e.g., a newly formed Scrum team), their image of the group is full of fantasy and driven by the need to belong and feel safe. They project hopes and script-based expectations onto the team. At this stage, a person might think, *"This team will finally be the perfect supportive family I never had,"* or conversely, *"I bet this will be like my last job—full of politics."* We often say, *"You get the group you deserve,"* meaning people tend to seek out or interpret groups in line with their life script. In Agile terms, during the Forming stage, team members are polite and optimistic but largely guided by preconceived notions rather than by reality.

2. *Adapted Imago* – As reality begins to intrude (the team has its first conflicts or disappointments), people start adapting their mental image. Berne noted that initially, *"when you come into any group, you first look at the leader"* and relate to them based on your imago. Only after that do you start noticing other members. In this stage, you might witness storming behaviors: disagreements about how to do things, testing of the leader's authority, or frustration when the group doesn't meet idealized expectations. This friction between *"how I imagined it"* versus *"how it really is"* is actually a critical adjustment process. The team member is grappling with forming a *real* identity in the group. This often shows up as agitation or conflict around processes, which is a sign that imagos are colliding with reality.

For the coach, seeing open conflict here is actually positive—it means people are explicitly working through differences, rather than silently retreating.

3. *Operative Imago* – In this stage, a more active negotiation happens between the individual and the group. The person recognizes, "If I want to truly belong, some things about this group (or myself) might need to change," and likewise, the group tests how much it will accommodate the individual. Berne described this as a bilateral negotiation for belonging: The individual asks, *"Can we do X differently so I feel I fit in?"* and the group implicitly asks, *"Will you adapt to how we do things?"* In Agile teams, this corresponds to late Storming into Norming: Members are openly suggesting changes to team norms, roles, or workflow (*"Could we communicate differently?"*, *"Can I take on this responsibility?",* etc.), and the team is working out agreements. When handled well, this leads to a cooperative contract among team members—not just an individual's contract with the leader. The imago is shifting from a one-way ideal imposed on the group to a two-way understanding.

4. *Secondarily Adjusted Imago* – At this point, enough adaptation has occurred that internal adjustments no longer consume the person's energy; instead, it is freed up to focus on the task and goals. In Berne's terms, the imago is now *"secondary adjusted"* to the group-as-it-is, allowing real collaboration. True collaboration emerges not only from structural and relationship factors, but also from this cumulative

subtotal of adjustment—people being able to say, *"I brought my imago, we've negotiated our realities, and now I'm ready to cooperate with who you actually are."* In Tuckman's model, this aligns with the Performing stage: the team works smoothly toward goals, having resolved most internal tensions. The individual feels like a full member. They have "given up" the unrealistic parts of their fantasy and accepted the group's imperfections, and in doing so can contribute wholeheartedly.

5. *Clarified Imago* – Finally, the person's internal picture of the group is fully aligned with the reality of the group's identity, purpose, and membership. There's no significant gap between expectation and actuality, no lingering illusions. Berne observed that in therapy groups, once people clarified their imagos completely, they often lost interest and were ready to leave—because the group was no longer serving as a stage for working out old internal issues. In a work setting, however, a clarified imago typically means the team member is *"ready to work fully, and celebrate success."* All their energy can go into productive teamwork since none is siphoned off to manage psychological dissonance. A hallmark of a team operating with clarified imagos is that *"their goodbyes are as good as their hellos"*—meaning when the team adjourns or a member leaves, it's handled in a healthy, appreciative way with no unresolved baggage. (In teams where imagos never fully clarified, departures tend to be messy or filled with regret and "phantoms.")

CHAPTER 4   REWRITING THE TEAM IMAGO

Petruska Clarkson, a contemporary TA researcher, expanded on Berne's ideas and linked the group imago to stages of group development. Clarkson and colleagues, like Adrienne Lee, correlated Berne's imago development stages with Tuckman's famous *"forming, storming, norming, performing"* model. The gist is that as a real group evolves through stages, each individual's imago of the group is also evolving—updating (or failing to update) to match the group's reality better. Clarkson identified additional nuances like the "secondarily operative" imago and the "historical" imago. Without drowning in terminology, what's useful to know is that our internal image of the team can change over time. Initially, it's based on fantasy and past ghosts, but as we work together, ideally it becomes more aligned with the actual people and purpose of this team (what Berne called a "clarified imago"). Keith Tudor (2013) even suggested adding new phases like the secondarily operative imago (an interim adjustment before being fully clarified) and a historical imago stage when looking back at a team that has ended. The details are beyond our scope, but they underscore that the imago is dynamic—it can be updated with conscious effort.

It's important to note that individuals (and whole teams) can get stuck at early imago stages and fail to reach full effective collaboration. For example, a team might loop in chronic conflict (stuck in Adaptation/Storming) or develop surface harmony without real trust (stuck between Operative and Secondary Adjustment, never fully negotiating differences). As coaches, we aim to help teams progress through these stages—not by forcing it, but by creating conditions and interventions that support healthy adaptation. The sooner people adapt their "group fantasy" to the group's reality, the more they can operate from their adult ego state and from a position of power and potency. In other words, closing the gap between *should* and *is* liberates the team's potential.

One practical implication is that unconscious processes require creative techniques to surface. Because group imago lives partly below awareness, a coach can't just ask "What's your group imago?" and get a clear answer. Instead, non-verbal or projective exercises can tease it out. For instance, you might ask team members to draw a picture of the team (or of an ideal team versus the current team), which can reveal hidden hopes or fears. Another method is a "family constellation" exercise: treat the team as a family and have members physically arrange themselves or objects to represent positions; this can expose how someone perceives power distances or alliances. Even a simple reflective prompt like *"How was your family when you were growing up, and how do you (perhaps unconsciously) wish this 'work family' would be?"* can spur valuable insight. The key point here is that acknowledging and adjusting each member's group imago is foundational work for deeper self-organization. It moves the team from a collection of private assumptions to a shared understanding of "who we are together."

Why does this matter for coaching Agile teams? Because every team member starts with a different "group template" in their head. If unexamined, these templates can collide. Imagine one developer's imago says, "Questioning the leader is dangerous" (perhaps from a past toxic job). While another's imago says, "If you disagree and don't speak up, you're a coward" (maybe from an open, academic background). When a contentious topic comes up, the first person may fall silent and defer, while the second person debates passionately—and each thinks the other's behavior is "wrong" or puzzling. It's easy to misinterpret these clashes as personal conflicts or resistance to change, when in fact they are imago clashes. Each person is acting in accordance with an internal blueprint of how a group should function.

A powerful implication here is that when team members seem passive, resistant, or in repeated conflict, the root could be mismatched imagos rather than unwillingness or incompetence. As a coach, you can help surface these unconscious pictures and foster understanding. Often, just realizing *"Oh, we each had a different mental model of a 'team'!"* diffuses tension. It shifts the conversation from blaming individuals to examining assumptions. It also opens the door for the team to actively shape a shared imago that serves their goals, rather than being driven by private, outdated ones.

There are some related concepts worth mentioning. One is the idea of "phantoms" in the group imago. Berne noted that "a phantom is left whenever a well-differentiated member leaves a group, and it persists until the mourning process is completed, if it ever is." In other words, when someone significant exits (a long-time manager, a charismatic team member), the image of them can stick around in the team's collective imago. The team may still unconsciously act as if that person (or their influence) is "in the room." For example, months after a domineering tech lead has left, developers might catch themselves thinking "What would Tech Lead X say about this design?" or hesitate to make decisions they think X would have vetoed. This is a phantom at work—an "ectoplasm" of a past member haunting the present. Phantoms can hold a team back, keeping them tied to old authority patterns. Part of coaching for self-organization is helping the team acknowledge and release phantoms—essentially, update their group imago to match the current membership. We'll discuss techniques for this, like the "phantoms sweep."

Another concept is how the leader figures in our imago. When we join any new group, Berne suggested, the first thing we do (often subconsciously) is size up the leader and our relationship to them. Only after that do we really notice and integrate with our peers. This is why early in a team's life people might be overly focused on the team lead or manager (or Scrum master, or whoever they perceive as holding authority), sometimes to the exclusion of peer relationships. As the group imago develops through stages, members start differentiating and relating to each other more fully, not just through the leader. Clarkson emphasized that each stage of group development has a corresponding leadership task; for instance, in the Forming stage (when imagos are provisional and full of fantasy), the leader's job is to provide safety and clarity, basically to check those fantasies against reality. As the team storms, the leader must weather challenges and model respect so that imagos can adapt rather than shatter. As a coach, you often work closely with formal leaders (or designated team leads) to ensure they provide what the team needs at each stage, which in turn helps team members adjust their internal models from *"This is what I imagined the team to be"* to *"This is what the team really is, and I accept that."* Berne believed that the more an individual's imago matches the reality of the group, the more they can operate from an adult ego state—meaning rational, present, and effective. Conversely, the bigger the gap between one's fantasy image and the group's reality, the more energy is wasted in frustration or wishful thinking. Part of our coaching mission is to narrow that gap.

In practical terms, working with the group imago means helping team members articulate their assumptions about teams, examine those assumptions against what the team actually needs, and then co-create a new, shared "team image." This shared imago becomes a guiding vision for how they want to behave together. It's like agreeing on an "operating manual" for the group that everyone actually buys into, because they helped write it. Instead of hidden clashing blueprints, there's one transparent, evolving blueprint. When teams do this, they often find a new sense of ownership and empowerment. They move from language like "They won't let us . . ." or "I was waiting for permission . . ." (signs of an old imago where authority lay elsewhere) to language like "*We* decided . . ." and "Let's try this" (signs of a clarified imago with shared power). In fact, a shift in language from "they" to "we" is one marker of imago change we can watch for.

To summarize, the group imago is a core lens for understanding team behavior. It reminds us that people don't enter a team as blank slates; they bring expectations that can either help or hinder self-organization. The good news is, imagos are not fixed. Through conscious work (dialogue, reflection, experiments), a team can update their collective picture to better fit their context and goals. The upcoming framework in this chapter will leverage that. We'll make the implicit images explicit, then intentionally craft a shared image of the team's desired way of working, and then implement structures and practices to make that image a reality. In doing so, we essentially accelerate the "group maturity" process, helping the team reach a clarified imago and effective self-organization faster than they might through trial and error alone.

Boundaries, Roles, Authority, and Power: The Guardrails for Self-Organization

Before introducing the coaching framework, we need to highlight some structural fundamentals: boundaries, roles, authority, and power—sometimes abbreviated as BART in group dynamics. These are the scaffolding on which a self-organizing team stands. If that scaffolding is weak or wobbly, the team will be anxious and dysfunctional, no matter how many trust falls or Agile games we play. As one organizational consultant quipped, *"If the boundaries between different roles and tasks are not clear, it usually requires some form of authority to bring the required clarity."* In other words, confusion about who is responsible for what will inevitably demand someone to step in and *"*lay down the law." That "someone" might be a manager, or it might emerge informally as a power struggle between team members. Neither is healthy for true self-management.

Clear boundaries answer the question: Who is inside this team and what is inside our scope? Boundaries can be physical (e.g., co-located in one room) or virtual (a defined membership list, a sprint). They also include time boundaries (e.g., our team meets daily for 15 minutes, or we work in two-week iterations) and task boundaries (what work is ours versus what is someone else's responsibility). When boundaries are unclear or constantly violated (say, outsiders regularly assign tasks directly to team members, or team members aren't sure if they're also on another team), the team's autonomy is undercut. People don't feel "safe" to self-organize because they're unsure what territory is truly theirs. A stable container, to use the complexity term, is needed for order to emerge. Especially after a crisis or reorganization, re-establishing clear boundaries is reparative; it helps a fragile team recover trust. As TA consultant and author Sari van Poelje notes, *"It's a reparative experience to be in a group where the boundaries are clear, where the leadership holds their task, [and] where the members have their [roles defined]. . ."* Think of boundaries as the walls of a sandbox: If the walls are solid, the team can play creatively with the sand inside; if the walls collapse, the sand scatters everywhere.

Roles provide clarity on who does what in the team. In Agile teams, we often define roles like product owner, Scrum master, developer, etc. Still, even within a development team, there can be roles (e.g., someone owning DevOps, someone mentoring juniors, etc.). Roles aren't just job titles; they encompass the expected responsibilities and authority that a person has. When roles overlap or are ambiguous, it's a structural problem that cascades into personal conflict. For example, if two roles are unclear and overlap, the people in those roles will have conflict about who has the power, who has the influence, whose work it is. We've all seen this: Two team members both think the other was supposed to handle a task, so it falls through the cracks; or, conversely, two people both try to drive a decision, leading to turf wars. From a coaching perspective, a key intervention is to clarify roles explicitly. This may involve writing down responsibilities, negotiating handoffs between team members, or even redefining roles to better fit the team's current situation. In Scrum, for instance, the roles are defined by the framework (PO, SM, Developers), but in reality, many teams need to discuss what that means for them: *Does the Scrum master schedule the meetings, or do we rotate facilitation? Does the PO make the call on release dates, or is that collaborative?* Clear answers to such questions prevent a lot of friction. They also empower self-organization by eliminating the guessing game. Team members can take initiative within their role boundaries confidently, rather than constantly checking, "Is it okay if I do this?"

CHAPTER 4   REWRITING THE TEAM IMAGO

Authority is about who has the right to decide or to enforce. In a traditional hierarchy, authority is defined by position: e.g., the manager has hire/fire and sign-off authority, the team members don't. In self-organizing teams, we redistribute and clarify authority. For example, the team might collectively have authority to plan their sprint and choose how to build a feature, while the product owner has authority to set priorities of what needs to be built. Making these authority boundaries explicit is critical. When people aren't sure if they truly have authority, they may either seize too much (stepping on others' toes) or abdicate and revert to "waiting for the boss to decide." Both extremes impede agility. After a crisis or when trust is low, explicitly stating who has authority for what can actually be soothing. It's paradoxical: We think of "empowerment" as giving people more freedom (which it is), but empowerment thrives on clarity. As a coach, you might need to facilitate a discussion to map out decision rights—who can decide unilaterally on what, which decisions require consultation or consent, etc. When a team knows, for instance, that "Our rule is any spending above $5k goes to management, but below that we decide" or "The QA lead can reject a release if quality is at risk, otherwise devs can self-approve," they feel a sense of contained autonomy. They have a playground with fences they can trust.

This ties to the idea of containment in psychology—providing a holding environment. Clear authority and role definitions create spaces better able to contain anxiety and unleash creativity. Without containment, people either become anxious (and freeze or fight) or they roam outside bounds and get into trouble. Neither is creative or productive.

Finally, power in a team can be formal or informal. Formal power comes with roles and authority: e.g., a tech lead may have formal say on technical decisions. Informal power is about influence: Who do people listen to? Who sways opinions in team discussions? Often, a seasoned developer or a charismatic personality wields a lot of informal power regardless of their title. Self-organizing teams aren't power-free utopias; they just use power differently. The goal is to have power dynamics that are healthy and transparent. Healthy, meaning no single individual dominates to the team's detriment (no "tyrants" or unchecked *de facto* bosses), and transparent, meaning everyone recognizes who has influence or decision rights in what areas. An Agile coach may help by mapping the power structure. Prompts like *"Who has the power?"* in your team coaching can help surface the real dynamics. For instance, perhaps the manager nominally has power, but the team actually follows the architect's direction more—that's worth acknowledging. Once known, the team can decide if that dynamic works or needs adjusting. Sometimes it's about shifting power to align with Agile values: e.g., encouraging that quiet "hidden leader" to speak more, or coaching a dominant member to create space for others.

In sum, self-organization does not mean the absence of structure. It flourishes within an appropriate structure of well-defined boundaries, roles, authority lines, and understanding of power. Many teams that fail at "self-organization" are actually suffering from a lack of this explicit structure—what we might call "under-containing." They were told *"you're self-organizing; now, go forth!"* without clarity on goals, roles, or limits, and naturally chaos ensued. The remedy is to add just enough structure to provide safety. On the flip side, a coach must avoid "over-specifying" everything. If you rigidly prescribe every aspect of how the team should function, you kill emergence and ownership; the team becomes self-managing in name only, still following the coach's or manager's script. Finding the sweet spot—enough structure to contain anxiety, enough freedom to let the team's intelligence and creativity emerge—is an art.

As you coach, keep checking these fundamentals: Are our boundaries clear and respected? Does everyone know their role and how it connects to others? Do we know who has authority for various decisions, and is that working? Who holds power or influence, and is that helping the team? If you strengthen these guardrails, the team will have a solid platform to truly self-organize and not collapse at the first sign of stress.

CHAPTER 4   REWRITING THE TEAM IMAGO

When a team hits a snag—be it conflict, low performance, or change resistance—it's easy to zoom in on the immediate issue (say, two members arguing) and miss deeper causes. Effective coaching employs multi-level diagnosis: looking at the individual, interpersonal, team, and even organizational levels to understand what's really going on. This prevents what we call *"local fixes"* that don't stick because the real problem lies elsewhere.

Sari van Poelje developed a useful model of diagnosing on three levels (see Figure 4-2):

- **Structural level:** This is about the formal design of the team or organization—boundaries, roles, hierarchy, processes (especially decision-making processes). Questions here include: *Is the team's purpose clear? Are membership and boundaries defined? What are the formal roles, and how do they interrelate? How are decisions supposed to be made (and are those processes followed)?* A lot of issues start here. For example, if a product owner and a team lead both think they have final say on prioritizing work, that unclear role boundary (structural) will inevitably cause friction (relational) and frustration (psychodynamic). An Agile cue: clarify core roles (product owner, Scrum master, developers) and their decision domains. Also, consider external boundaries: Does the team know who its stakeholders are and how to interface with them? Structural gaps or overlaps often manifest as persistent decision gridlock or power games. *Tip*: When in doubt, firm up structure first—it's easier to fix a role-clarity issue than to mend hurt feelings after a long power struggle that a clear role could have prevented.

99

CHAPTER 4   REWRITING THE TEAM IMAGO

- **Relational (interpersonal) level:** This looks at the informal dynamics and relationships in the team—who likes whom, informal cliques, alliances, social "rank," communication patterns. Every team has unspoken norms about influence: perhaps the senior developers carry more weight in technical discussions, or one extrovert sets the meeting tone. We ask: *Who carries weight in discussions? Who is quiet or ignored? Is there a "hidden" leader?* Sometimes an official leader isn't the one truly motivating the team—maybe an unofficial guru is. At the relational level, we also watch for recurring conflict pairings (e.g., two teammates who always seem to butt heads) or unhealthy silence (e.g., disagreements that never surface). In Agile coaching, tools like personas or team radar charts can help visualize these dynamics. Noticing relational patterns informs where to intervene: Perhaps pair a quiet member with a more vocal one in a facilitation role to shift the dynamic, or bring awareness to an informal hierarchy that's excluding some voices.

- **Psychodynamic (intrapsychic) level:** This is the deepest level, dealing with subconscious patterns, transference (people projecting past experiences onto current relationships), and of course the group imago. Here we ask: *What does this situation remind team members of? Are people reacting not just to present events but also to something in their personal history?* For instance, if a team member reacts very strongly to any form of feedback, could it be tied to a past bad experience with criticism? Are there recurrent emotional patterns in the team—like a cycle of idealizing a plan and then crashing into disappointment—that might indicate an underlying shared script? The psychodynamic lens is also where we'd examine the team imago content; e.g., "It's interesting, whenever a conflict arises, the team behaves as if a parent figure must intervene—is this an imago of needing a parent-like leader?" Working at this level often involves surfacing those hidden feelings or references: *"What does this conflict feel like to each of you? Does it echo something familiar?"* It can be abstract, but even simple questions can help a team realize, *"We're not really mad about this task, we're reenacting an old pattern of designer versus developer from our last company."* Once that's conscious, they can break the pattern.

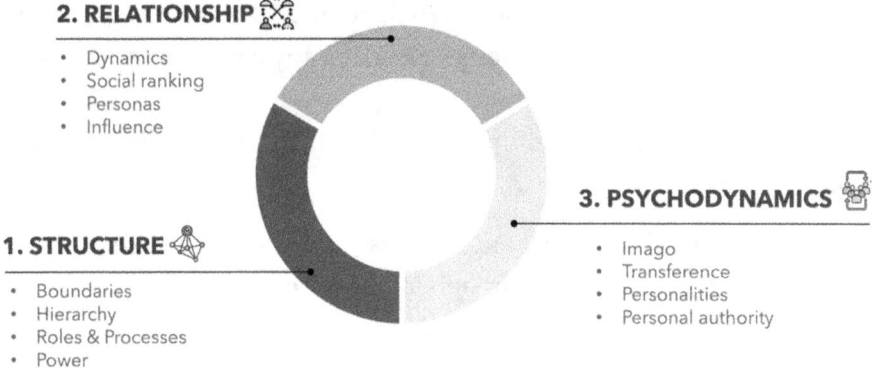

Figure 4-2. Three levels of diagnostics

The link between levels is critical: they aren't isolated; they influence each other. *"A problem at the structural level causes problems at the relational and psychodynamic levels,"* Sari van Poelje notes. The example given earlier fits perfectly: unclear roles (structural) ⇒ people conflict over power (relational) ⇒ that conflict triggers personal past issues (psychodynamic). Likewise, unresolved psychodynamic issues (say, a lingering phantom or trust wound) can sabotage relationships and even lead people to undermine structural changes. When diagnosing, it's like being a doctor checking multiple systems of the body—sometimes a knee pain comes from a hip misalignment. Sari uses the metaphor: *"If you have a pain in your neck, it might mean your hip is not aligned,"* and teams work similarly. So if a retrospective reveals interpersonal tension, don't just assume "team members need conflict training" (relational fix)—also check, for example, if their goals or roles are colliding (structural cause).

For Agile coaches, there's also the individual level and organizational level beyond the team to consider. Individuals have personal development needs or stressors outside the team. And the organization's culture or policies (HR rules, reward systems) might undercut team self-management (for instance, if managers are still rated on how much they control decisions, they'll never truly empower teams). Thus, a full diagnosis might span individual ↔ team ↔ organization. This framework scans three contracting levels as well—the individual member, the team as a whole, and the organization's expectations—ensuring any coaching intervention aligns across these.

In practice, before you "jump to a tool" to fix something, do a quick multi-level scan:

- Structural: Are there any obvious structural issues here (unclear goals, roles, membership, process)?

- Relational: What's the emotional climate and interaction pattern? Any subgroup dynamics at play?

- Psychodynamic: Does this scenario ring any bells in terms of past patterns (imago issues, phantoms, underlying anxieties)?

CHAPTER 4 REWRITING THE TEAM IMAGO

By identifying the right level at which to intervene, you maximize impact. For instance, if the real issue is structural (e.g., two product owners fighting over scope), you can facilitate a boundary clarification meeting (structural solution) rather than doing a team bonding workshop (which might scratch the surface but not resolve the turf war). Conversely, if the structure is sound but morale is low because of a recent trauma (say, layoffs), you might focus on psychodynamic interventions like a closure ritual or a session to voice fears, rather than tinkering with roles (which are fine).

In the upcoming framework, group imago coaching for self-organization, we will touch on all these levels. Eliciting individual imagos is psychodynamic work; creating a team charter and roles is structural; establishing norms and feedback loops touches relational patterns, and so on. Keep this diagnostic triad in mind; it will help you choose the appropriate tool from the toolkit. Structural fixes can prevent relational and psychodynamic turbulence. When you see symptoms at one level, consider causes at the others. The result is more-targeted coaching—a bull's eye instead of buckshot. And your team will feel it: interventions actually addressing their real pain points, not superficial team-building band-aids.

Common Traps and Ethical Considerations in Group Imago Coaching

While coaching teams toward self-organization can be deeply rewarding, it also comes with challenges and potential pitfalls. This section highlights some common traps Agile coaches or Scrum masters might encounter, as well as ethical guidelines to ensure your coaching remains professional, respectful, and effective. Being aware of these will help you navigate tricky situations with integrity.

103

CHAPTER 4 REWRITING THE TEAM IMAGO

Common traps to avoid are as follows:

1. *Skipping the Forming/Naming stage:* One trap is to dive straight into work tasks without properly forming the team identity and agreements (perhaps due to pressure to deliver fast). This often backfires. If you don't invest time in establishing purpose, roles, and norms, the team will likely flounder or experience conflict later because imagos remain unaligned. It's impossible to skip stages—the issues will surface eventually.

   Avoidance: Even under tight deadlines, allocate at least a short kickoff for introductions and basic agreements. Explain to stakeholders that this is necessary groundwork for long-term efficiency.

2. *Over-relying on authority (not letting the team self-organize):* Some coaches or Scrum masters, especially if new or coming from a management background, may fall into "command-and-control" habits—solving every problem for the team, dictating solutions, or always stepping in. This undermines self-organization and keeps the team in a dependent state.

   Avoidance: Resist the impulse to provide all the answers. Remember, your role is to guide the team to solve their own problems. Ask guiding questions instead of directives, and tolerate a bit of team struggle as long as it's safe—that's how they learn. Like a parent with a growing child, gradually give more autonomy. If you catch yourself being the first to speak in every meeting, step back and let silence draw out team members instead.

3. *Avoiding conflict (premature peacekeeping):* It's uncomfortable to see team members disagree sharply, and a trap is to smooth it over too quickly or discourage any arguing. This can lead to artificial harmony where issues go underground (and imagos stay unadapted). If members aren't even implicitly storming, that's a bad sign.

    Avoidance: Recognize that some conflict is necessary for growth. Don't rush in to "calm everyone" at the first sign of tension. Instead, facilitate it constructively: Set ground rules for a fair fight and encourage expression of concerns. A team with zero conflict may actually be stuck in Norming/Storming with suppressed feelings. Encourage them to voice dissenting opinions. When you do intervene, focus on how they're arguing (ensure respect), but let them hash out the what (the actual differences).

4. *Coach imposing personal imago or agenda:* As coaches, we have our own experiences and biases (our own group imago of the "ideal team"). A trap is imposing that model on the team rather than facilitating their unique path. For example, maybe you had a fantastic experience with a particular framework or tool in another team; you might force Team X to adopt it even if it doesn't fit their context. Or you might unconsciously favor the dynamic that matches your comfort zone (e.g., you prefer quiet, so you quell lively debate even if it's productive).

Avoidance: Practice self-awareness and humility. Continuously reflect: "*Am I pushing this because it truly serves them, or because I like it?*" Gather feedback from the team about your interventions. Supervision or peer coaching can help spot when your own script is interfering. A good mantra: *"Enable the team to be their best version, not my version of best."*

5. *Neglecting individual dynamics:* While focusing on the "team as a whole," a trap is overlooking that it's made of individuals with personal needs and growth areas. For instance, one team member might be struggling with confidence or feeling excluded, but if the coach only looks at group-level output, that issue festers.

   Avoidance: Balance group interventions with occasional check-ins one-on-one. Especially after intense conflicts or changes, see how each person is doing. As per TA, each individual's script can play out in group; notice if someone repeatedly takes a certain role (like the "rescuer" or the "rebel") and address it privately if needed. Just ensure any individual coaching doesn't undermine their trust in the team (keep confidentiality, and encourage them to share feelings with the team if appropriate).

6. *Overloading with too many changes at once:* Teams have limited capacity for change absorption. If a coach introduces too many frameworks, tools, or process changes in short order, the team can become overwhelmed and resistant. For example,

CHAPTER 4   REWRITING THE TEAM IMAGO

insisting they adopt five new canvases, three new meeting types, and a dozen new metrics in one month will likely cause burnout or cynicism.

Avoidance: Prioritize and iterate. Introduce improvements gradually, observe impact, and stabilize before the next. Remember Agile itself: inspect and adapt in small increments. Also, get team buy-in for changes; if they co-decide to try something, it sticks better than a coach decree.

7. *Ignoring organizational context:* Sometimes coaches work intensely with the team but ignore the larger company culture or structure that may hinder the team. This trap is focusing on micro (team) and ignoring macro (org). The team might self-organize well internally, but if organizational policies (hierarchy, reward systems, etc.) don't support it, the team could hit a wall.

    Avoidance: Engage with management and stakeholders. Educate them on what the team is doing and why. Try to align performance evaluations to team outcomes instead of individual heroics, for instance. If certain constraints are non-negotiable, at least make them explicit to the team so they can adapt. Be the team's advocate in the org, but realistic about what can change. Not doing so might inadvertently set the team up to be punished for self-organizing (e.g., if a manager expects the TL to command but the team is now democratic, conflict can arise).

8. *Misdiagnosing the root cause:* A trap is intervening at the wrong level because of a misdiagnosis. For example, if a team's poor performance is due to unclear strategy (structural level), a coach might wrongly assume it's a team dysfunction and start doing trust exercises (relational level), which won't solve the strategic void. Or labeling a member as "difficult" (psychodynamic) when actually the role definitions are unclear (structural).

    Avoidance: Use the multi-level diagnostic approach. When a problem arises, pause and think: Is this structural (e.g., unclear goals, roles, external pressures)? Relational (team interpersonal issue)? Psychodynamic (personal script or emotional issue)? Check facts: Have roles changed recently? Did something external disrupt them? Talk to people to glean different perspectives. Only then decide on intervention. If uncertain, experiment with addressing one level and see if the issue persists or shifts.

9. *Becoming indispensable (job security trap):* Some coaches fall into making the team overly reliant on them (perhaps subconsciously to feel needed or secure in their position). They intervene in every retrospective, solve every impediment themselves, and maybe even become the *de facto* team spokesperson always. This stunts the team's self-organization and growth—essentially, the coach becomes a crutch.

Avoidance: Your aim is to work yourself out of a job with that team. Continuously empower them to take on your functions (facilitating, impediment removal, coordination). Celebrate when they do things without you. If you notice they ask you for every minor decision, start redirecting: *"What do you all think we should do? You have the expertise."* Build them up so that if you stepped away, they'd still thrive. It's bittersweet but necessary—like a teacher watching graduates leave the class.

10. *Dealing with "problem" team members incorrectly:* Sometimes one individual might consistently disrupt self-organization—maybe a highly ego-driven senior, or someone who doesn't buy into Agile values and undercuts team decisions. A trap is either ignoring it (hoping it resolves itself) or coming down authoritarianly (which can violate trust or your role boundaries).

    Avoidance: Approach such cases with a mix of empathy and firmness. One strategy: one-on-one coaching with that person; explore their perspective (maybe their group imago leads them to not trust peers, etc.). Provide feedback on the impact of their behavior on the team's goals. Involve them in solutions: *"How can we meet your concern while still honoring team agreements?"* In some cases, it might require escalation: Involve their manager if it's harming deliverables or others. Ethically, you must also ensure that one person doesn't poison the team environment (the whole group's welfare is at stake). Use tact and try to help them integrate, but also set boundaries of acceptable behavior per the team's contract (e.g., disrespect or consistently sabotaging decisions cannot be ignored). Removing a team member is a last resort, but a possibility if all coaching fails and the team cannot function; do so only in consultation with HR/management, not unilaterally.

Ethical Considerations

- *Cultural sensitivity:* Be mindful of cultural differences in communication, authority perception, conflict style, etc. For instance, some cultures avoid open conflict or direct criticism so that the Storming stage may be subtle (people might withdraw rather than argue). Ethically, adapt your approach—maybe use anonymous feedback techniques or one-on-ones more in such contexts, and slowly build comfort for direct dialogue. Don't impose, say, a very Western confrontational retro format on a team that might find that deeply uncomfortable. Learn about your team members' backgrounds and adjust. Also, ensure team norms don't inadvertently marginalize someone (e.g., scheduling all team events around alcohol if someone doesn't drink for religious reasons; find inclusive ways to celebrate).

- *Avoid dual roles confusion:* If you are an external coach, this is simpler, but if you are, say, also their line manager or have administrative authority, be clear when you're coaching versus when you're managing. Ethical coaching requires a level of neutrality and non-

CHAPTER 4 REWRITING THE TEAM IMAGO

evaluation. Mixing roles can confuse team members ("If I reveal a weakness in retro, will my manager-coach dock my performance review?"). If you have both roles, be transparent: e.g., "In this retrospective, I'm wearing my facilitator hat, not judging anyone. I'm here to help us improve. Your candor won't negatively affect performance appraisals." Then stick to that promise. Some coaches recuse themselves from direct performance evaluation to maintain trust.

- *Respect autonomy and Adult ego state:* TA encourages relating at the Adult–Adult level (respectful, equal human beings). Ethically, treat team members as autonomous adults capable of growth and decision making. Avoid patronising or manipulating. For example, don't use TA insights as a trick ("I know their Parent ego can be guilted, so I'll do that to enforce a behavior."). Instead, share relevant insights, educate the team in simple TA concepts if it helps (many teams appreciate learning about dynamics like Parent-Adult-Child ego states, which gives them language to discuss interactions). Empower them with knowledge rather than using it behind the scenes to control them. Always obtain buy-in for interventions; e.g., if you want to introduce a novel exercise, explain its purpose and get agreement rather than springing surprises that can feel like psychological tricks.

- *Continuous consent:* Especially for deeper exercises or any team change, maintain an attitude of seeking consent. At the start of an exercise, I often ask, "Is everyone okay trying this out? If at any point you're uncomfortable, we can pause." This gives agency and respects boundaries. Similarly, if new team norms are being proposed and someone is silent, check in—don't steamroll quiet dissent. Ethical facilitation ensures all voices are heard or at least invited.

- *Cultural change ethics:* As a coach, you might also be pushing some cultural changes (like moving from a blame culture to a learning culture). This is positive, but, ethically, be mindful of pace and effects. People can feel destabilized if change is too fast. Ensure that in advocating for change you aren't disparaging current values that people hold dear. For instance, if the company historically valued individual heroics and you're moving to team collaboration, some veterans might feel their past contributions are devalued. Ethically, honor the past while guiding to the future: "That approach got us here and had merits, but to tackle current complexity, we believe a more collaborative approach will serve us better." It respects those who identified with the old model.

In sum, ethical coaching (check out more on ethics in Chapter 9, "Staying True") for self-organization centers on respect—respect for individuals' dignity, for the team's collective intelligence, for the truth, for confidentiality, and for your professional boundaries. It also means being a role model of the values you preach: trust, transparency, and integrity. Boundaries are important, and managing the emotional field of a group responsibly is an ethical charge too: to be aware of how your actions influence the team's emotions and to handle that influence with care, not for personal power or negligence.

By avoiding the traps and adhering to ethical principles, you not only help the team succeed, but you also build your reputation as a trusted coach with whom teams and organizations will want to work. Agile team coaching, done ethically, contributes to a healthier workplace where people can grow, and that ultimately is what enables self-organization to flourish in a sustainable way.

Conclusion

Self-organization does not happen by decree; it emerges when teams are given both the space and the support to redefine how they work together. At the heart of this lies the group imago—those often invisible inner pictures of what a team "should" be. Left unexamined, imagos can hold a team hostage to outdated habits or conflicting expectations. Brought into the open, however, they become a powerful lever for transformation.

By working consciously with imagos, an Agile coach helps the team replace inherited patterns with deliberate choices. This process begins by surfacing individual assumptions, then building a shared team image that reflects the current purpose and context. From there, the team can agree on concrete ways of working—decision-making protocols, roles, norms, and feedback loops—that anchor their new identity. In effect, they trade unconscious repetition for conscious design.

The journey is rarely linear. Teams will cycle through stages of hope, conflict, negotiation, and renewal as imagos shift. Coaches play a vital role in holding the container through these transitions, ensuring that moments of friction become opportunities for growth rather than setbacks. Over time, the shared imago becomes self-reinforcing: it provides a compass in times of uncertainty and a reference point when old patterns threaten to resurface.

CHAPTER 4   REWRITING THE TEAM IMAGO

Within the broader context of Agile coaching, rewriting the team's imago is not a one-off intervention but rather a continuous practice. Each new member, each organizational shift, and each significant challenge re-opens the question: *Who are we as a team, and how do we want to work together?* Teams that learn to revisit and reshape their imago with intention are the ones most likely to achieve lasting self-organization—not as a static state, but as a living capacity to adapt, co-create, and thrive.

With these foundations—self-organization, group imago, BART, and multi-level thinking—under our belt, let's move into the next chapter describing Group-Imago Coaching for Self-Organization Framework (sorry, all good names were taken). This framework ties everything together into a step-by-step approach to help teams become self-organizing by leveraging the group imago concept.

Reflection Moment

1. What "team imago" do you carry, where did it come from, and how did it show up in one recent interaction?

2. Which single Hackman condition (Boundaries, Direction, Structure, Context, Coaching) is your biggest constraint right now—and what would "one notch better" look like in two weeks?

3. Where are our BART guardrails fuzzy (Boundary, Authority, Role, Task), and what one rule or visual would remove that ambiguity?

4. If you could nudge one CDE knob (Container, Differences, Exchanges) this month, which would you choose and what micro-change would you try?

5. Name a persistent symptom; at which level is the likely cause (structural, relational, psychodynamic), and what's the cheapest diagnostic you can run?

6. What's the current "we/they" ratio in our language, and which phrase will you replace next week to shift it toward "we"?

7. Which recurring decision has the most latency, and what's the smallest step to clarify who decides, by when, and with what input?

CHAPTER 5

Self-Organization Toolkit

Group-Imago Coaching for Self-Organization (GICSO) is a practical, step-by-step approach that helps a team become truly self-organized by working directly with the "group imago"—the often unconscious picture each person holds of how a team should function. It reveals those private templates, then guides the team to co-create a shared image of "who we are together," turning it into clear boundaries, roles, authority, power, and daily decision protocols.

Here's an overview of the steps:

1. **Contract & Context** – Set up a clear coaching agreement (with the team and stakeholders) and understand the context and goals for self-organization.

2. **Elicit Individual Imagos** – Draw out each team member's mental model of a team (their group imago)—their expectations, fears, and ideals.

3. **Create a Shared Working Imago** – Facilitate the team to build a shared "Team Image"—a collective vision of how they want to operate (team purpose, norms, roles, etc.).

4. **Calibrate Roles, Authority & Power** – Make sure roles and decision authorities are explicitly agreed upon, and discuss any shifts needed in formal/informal power.

5. **Agree on the Operating System** – Establish the team's own "OS"—the concrete working agreements, decision-making protocols, meeting cadences, work process rules, feedback mechanisms, etc., aligned to the shared imago.

6. **Run Bounded Experiments** – Encourage the team to try small, safe-to-fail experiments to practice self-management and adjust their imago and behaviors, without committing to permanent changes all at once.

7. **Repair & Re-imprint** – When old patterns or conflicts resurface (and they will), use quick interventions to repair trust, reinforce boundaries, and update the team image ("re-imprint" new experiences over old habits).

8. **Measure, Reflect, Sustain** – Track indicators of self-organization and imago shift, reflect on progress, and build sustaining practices like peer coaching so the improvement continues beyond the coaching engagement.

Let's go now, step by step. For each step, I'll explain its purpose, what activities it involves, and tips to do it effectively. I'll also sprinkle in techniques and tools you can use. By the end of this section, you should have a mental playbook for coaching a team through this transformative journey.

Step 1: Contract & Context

Every successful coaching engagement starts with clarifying the contract and context. In essence, this step is about answering: *What are we doing, why, and under what conditions?* It sets the foundation of trust and safety for the work ahead. Skipping this would be like starting a road trip without agreeing on the destination or who's driving.

Contracting is covered extensively in Chapter 3, "Sealing the Deal: Effective Contracting", which is why I'd like to mention just a few things to add on top of the existing guidance.

One helpful tool here is the Three-Level Contract Map. Draw three concentric circles or a matrix, as follows:

- Outer circle: *Administrative* – fill in logistics (we'll meet every Friday for one hour, etc.), who's coach, who's client(s).

- Middle: *Professional* – fill in the goals and success criteria everyone agrees on.

- Inner: *Psychological* – fill in agreed-upon norms, any fears named (e.g., "fear of being judged for speaking up")—team agrees not to ridicule any idea; or coach's disclosure: "I tend to jump in to help, but I will try to step back and let you struggle a bit, and you can call me out if I overstep." Yes, coaches should be aware of their own imago and tendencies; more on that in the "Common Traps" section of the previous chapter.

In summary, Step 1 is about setting the stage: clarifying *who is involved, what we're aiming for, and how we'll work together*. It's also about ensuring support—the whole organization around the team knows about and agrees to this journey. I often say to sponsors: *"We're about to empower this team. That means they might make decisions you used to make. Are you ready for that?"* If not, it's better to resolve those concerns now than have the team hit a wall later.

Take the time to do this contracting thoroughly. It might "cost" a meeting or two up front, but it pays off in smooth sailing later. When things get sticky (and they will at some point), you can refer back: *"We agreed that candor was okay, remember? So let's speak openly now,"* or *"Our goal was to handle decisions without escalation; how can we hold ourselves to that?"* The contract becomes your anchor.

Techniques for Step 1: Contract & Context:

- *Three-Level Contracting Map*: Draft a simple document or visual mapping the Administrative, Professional, and Psychological agreements. Review it with sponsor and team; get explicit agreement (even an email sign-off or nod in meeting).

- *Sponsor Alignment Checklist*: A list of questions to review with the sponsor (e.g., "What outcomes do you expect? What are non-negotiables? How will you support the team's autonomy? Who else needs to be informed?").

- *Team Expectations Exercise*: In the kickoff, ask team members, "What do you expect from me as a coach? What do you expect from this process? What are you worried about?" Write these on a flip chart. This surfaces psychological contract elements. Address them openly (e.g., if someone expects you to *"tell us exactly what to do,"* clarify your actual approach, which likely involves them finding their solutions).

- *Ethical Guidelines Reminder*: If you have a professional code (like Scrum Alliance or ICF or similar), share relevant bits (e.g., "I am not a therapist; if deep personal issues arise we can suggest resources, but within our sessions we focus on team functioning" or "I'll be transparent and I invite you to do the same"). This builds trust that you operate ethically.

- *Context Inquiry:* Conduct short interviews with key people around the team (their manager, a senior stakeholder, perhaps a few team members individually) *before* the main work starts. Ask about the team's history, what's working/not, and their hopes for this coaching. This not only informs you, but also shows people their input is valued.

By the end of Step 1, everyone should understand why this is happening and why it is happening now, and have bought into the process. There should be a sense of relief—"okay, we know the rules of engagement"—and perhaps even eagerness to get started because the desired outcome is clearly articulated.

Step 2: Elicit Individual Imagos

With the groundwork laid, we move into the discovery phase: uncovering each team member's individual group imago. The goal here is to make the invisible visible—to draw out those mental models and assumptions about teams that usually remain hidden. This can be one of the most eye-opening parts of the whole journey, both for you and for the team members themselves. Often, people have *never* been asked to reflect on "what a team means to me" or "what I expect in a leader"—it all operates in the background. By surfacing this, you create a rich shared awareness that, *wow, we have some different pictures in our heads!*

CHAPTER 5   SELF-ORGANIZATION TOOLKIT

It's important to do this in a safe, non-judgmental way. Emphasize that there is no "right or wrong" imago—they are all understandable given our different backgrounds. We're not here to critique someone's internal image, just to understand it and ultimately to choose what aspects serve us or not.

A few techniques are very effective for eliciting imagos:

> *Imago Drawing Exercise:* This is a creative, somewhat playful method to bypass intellectualization and tap into gut-level images. Give each team member a large sheet of paper and markers (or use a virtual whiteboard if remote). Ask them to draw two pictures: one of "our team when it's working at its best" and another of "our team when it's breaking down or struggling." Importantly, these drawings are metaphorical—stick figures, symbols, whatever. Encourage them to use symbols or scenes that represent how they experience the team. For example, someone might draw the team at its best as a soccer team scoring a goal, and at its worst as players arguing with no one tending the goal. Another might draw a family dinner table versus a family fight. Give them time (10–15 minutes) to sketch both scenarios. Then, have each person share and explain their drawings to the group. It's crucial that everyone listens without interrupting. As a coach, you facilitate by gently probing, *"Tell us about this element. . . . I see the manager is drawn very large in the second picture—what does that represent to you?"* Patterns will emerge: perhaps multiple people draw a common theme (like images of hierarchy or images

CHAPTER 5   SELF-ORGANIZATION TOOLKIT

of chaos). These are clues to the collective imago. Also note differences: one's ideal might be another's nightmare. Debrief by highlighting themes: "I notice a theme of authority—some see strong authority as positive (like the ship's captain in John's drawing), others see it as stifling (the puppet strings in Maria's drawing). Interesting! What do we make of that?" This can spark a rich conversation.

- *Relational Team Genogram:* A "genogram" in therapy is like a family tree mapping relationships. For a team, we adapt it to map each person's formative team experiences. Ask team members to individually reflect on significant teams/groups they've been part of in their life—family, school groups, sports teams, past work teams. Have them draw a timeline or diagram showing these groups (maybe 3-5 key ones). For each, note roles they played and one or two words describing the group climate (e.g., "My college project team—I ended up as the one doing all the work (role: solo hero); climate: disorganized/fun"). Then have them share highlights: *"What patterns do you notice in your journey? Were you often in a leader role, or a mediator, or a rebel? What was your best team ever and why? Worst team and why?"* This exercise connects their past to present. They might realize, *"I'm projecting my last job's dysfunctional team onto this one."* Or *"I felt safe in teams where someone clearly facilitated, so I tend to wait for that."* As each shares, others can ask gentle questions. This builds empathy ("Ah, that's why Alex values structure—he came from a chaos startup").

123

- *Imago Interview (10 Prompts):* Sometimes it helps to have direct questions to tease out assumptions. You can do this as a written reflection or a group discussion. Some powerful prompts include (see Table 5-1) the following:
  - "In a real team, who gets to decide what the team works on?" (Some might answer "the manager" or "the team collectively" or "the loudest person"—revealing their assumptions about decision making.)
  - "What's unsafe to say in a team setting?" (This uncovers taboos or fears; e.g., "It's unsafe to question the boss's idea" or "It's unsafe to admit you need help." These are gold to know, because they show current unwritten rules likely stemming from imagos.)
  - "If the team were really healthy, how would conflict be handled?" (Imago of conflict: avoid it? thrash it out? etc.)
  - "What must leaders do in a team?" (People's core expectations of leaders; e.g., "protect us," "give clear direction," "stay out of the way unless needed," etc.)
  - "What is each person *responsible* for on a good team?" (e.g., "everyone carries their weight," "people take care of each other," etc.)
  - "What are signs of a failing team?" (This elicits what *triggers* people; e.g., "missed deadlines, arguing, quiet meetings.")

- "Complete the sentence: *Teams are like ___.*" (Metaphor prompt—sometimes surprising: *"Teams are like families," "Teams are like a ship crew,"* etc., which reveals the mental schema.)

- "What's your personal pet peeve in teamwork?" (Often something that violated their imago in the past; e.g., "when only a few speak up" or "when there's no plan.")

- "Think of an ideal team you'd love to be part of—what three words describe it?" (Tells their aspirational imago.)

- "Think of the worst team situation—what made it that way?" (Tells their aversive imago—what they're trying to avoid.)

Table 5-1. Imago Interviewing Prompts

Prompt	What It Reveals
In a real team, who gets to decide what the team works on?	Assumptions about decision making and authority (manager-led vs. collective vs. dominant voices)
What's unsafe to say in a team setting?	Taboos, fears, and psychological safety limits that constrain openness
If the team were really healthy, how would conflict be handled?	Conflict resolution expectations—avoidance, open debate, mediation
What must leaders do in a team?	Core leadership expectations (directive vs. facilitative vs. hands-off)

(*continued*)

Table 5-1. (*continued*)

Prompt	What It Reveals
What is each person responsible for on a good team?	Views on accountability, workload fairness, and mutual support
What are signs of a failing team?	Triggers and red flags (missed deadlines, silence, arguing, disengagement)
Complete the sentence: Teams are like ___ .	Underlying metaphors and mental schemas (family, ship crew, machine, etc.)
What's your personal pet peeve in teamwork?	Sources of irritation linked to past team experiences; reveals "hot buttons"
Think of an ideal team you'd love to be part of—what three words describe it?	Aspirational qualities (trust, energy, structure, creativity, etc.)
Think of the worst team situation—what made it that way?	Aversive experiences and fears driving current defensive behaviors

You can have team members jot down their answers individually, then discuss them. Or do it in round-robin style verbally. If trust is still warming up, written first is good (maybe even anonymously collected and then read out, aggregated). The key is to draw out differences and commonalities in answers.

During this eliciting step, you, as a coach, are in listening and inquiry mode. Resist any urge to "solve" things here. Some statements might alarm you (e.g., "It's unsafe to admit mistakes on this team"—big red flag!). Note them, perhaps ask the group, "Others feel that too?" but don't jump to fixing just yet. We want the full picture out first.

Expect some aha moments among the team. They might realize, "Oh, not everyone sees our team the way I do." One person might say, "I assumed everyone wanted more hierarchy, but it sounds like half of you actually want more autonomy." These conversations set the stage for the next step, where we negotiate a shared team image out of this mosaic.

Also, be prepared for emotions or surprises. Talking about one's family-of-origin or past-team pain can trigger feelings. If someone shares "My last team betrayed my trust," acknowledge it: *"Thank you for sharing; that sounds painful. It's understandable you'd be cautious now."* As a coach, validate feelings, normalize them (many carry scars from bad team experiences), and highlight positives too: *"I hear a lot of passion for teamwork as well—like in those ideal descriptions."* We want to create a space where all these imagos can be put on the table without judgment.

Remember to capture key insights. If in person, I often use a whiteboard or sticky notes: we might list "Team should . . ." statements that pop up, like a collective brainstorm of assumptions. Or draw a spectrum on the floor and have people place themselves (e.g., "On the spectrum from 'leader should decide' to 'team consensus on everything,' where do you lean?"). Visualizing these differences helps everyone literally see the diversity of thought.

Techniques for Step 2: Elicit Individual Imagos:

- *Imago Drawing:* Two drawings ("team at best" vs. "team at worst"). Share and debrief for themes (authority, safety, etc.).

- *Relational Genogram of Work:* Personal timeline of past group experiences with roles and feelings. Share patterns noticed.

- *Imago Interview Prompts:* A list of 8–10 guided questions (some examples provided earlier). This could be conducted as a survey or a live discussion. Consider making it into a one-page Imago Interview Guide handout.

- *Anonymous Assumption Poll:* Use sticky notes or an online tool; e.g., ask, "Who decides if someone in the team isn't pulling weight?" each writes an answer, then reveal. Variation in answers can provoke discussion.

- *Family Metaphor Game:* Ask, "Which family member were you in your first team? (the big brother, the baby, the mom, the rebel teen, etc.)" This often brings levity and insight into the default roles people take.

By the end of Step 2, you should have a rich tapestry of the team's internal perspectives. It's like you've opened up everyone's head and peeked at the "team movie" playing in there. The team now recognizes that these images exist and vary. That awareness alone starts to loosen the grip of the unconscious imago; people might already start re-evaluating (*"Maybe my view of needing a strong leader isn't shared—what does that mean for us?"*). We're now ready to shape a unified picture collaboratively, taking the best of these imagos and aligning them into one shared team imago.

Step 3: Create a Shared Working Imago

Having explored where everyone is coming from, the team can now move to co-create a shared vision of how they want to be, effectively designing a new group imago together. This is a pivotal step: It's where the team shifts from individual expectations to a collective agreement. You might call the output a "Team Image Canvas," but it is explicitly informed by the imago work we just did.

Think of the Team Image Canvas as a one-page representation of the team's identity and operating agreements. It typically covers the following key elements:

- *Purpose and Mission:* Why does this team exist? What's our core mission or the goal that unites us? (Agile teams might phrase this as their product goal or sprint goal context.) A clear purpose aligns everyone and often helps resolve debates (if it doesn't serve the purpose, why are we doing it?). It's the north star on the canvas.

- *Primary Customers/Stakeholders:* Who do we deliver value to? Naming the end customer or internal client reminds the team it's *"us together serving them,"* which fosters unity.

- *Boundaries (In/Out):* Who is in this team (list of members, roles) and who is out? Also, what work is in scope versus out of scope for us? (e.g., "We develop features; Ops maintains the servers, that's outside our boundary but we coordinate.") And boundaries of time/space: Do we have core hours? Are we collocated or distributed? This section fights the tendency for boundary confusion. It can include how the team interfaces with outsiders (e.g., "All external requests funnel through the PO"—a boundary rule).

- *Roles and Responsibilities:* A clear mapping of formal roles on the team (PO, SM, developers, or other specific roles like UX lead, etc.), including *who* is in those roles and what each is responsible for. If multiple people share a role (e.g., five developers), clarify any specializations or rotating duties (like rotating who leads stand-up). This part should incorporate what we learned from earlier; e.g., if the imago interviews surfaced confusion about leadership, explicitly state,

"The Scrum master is the team's coach and facilitator, not a boss. They don't assign work; they help us improve our process."

- *Decision Rights and Process:* Outline how decisions are made in various domains. This is crucial. For example: "Product priorities: Product owner decides after seeking team input (advice process). Technical decisions: Team decides by consent—we discuss options, and if no major objections, we go with it. Hiring a new member: Team members interview and give input, the manager formally hires. Conflict between functions: Escalate to X if needed," etc. It might include specific protocols like consent decision making ("We agree a proposal moves forward if no one has a reasoned objection; objections must be based on its being not "safe enough to try") or the advice process ("Anyone can make a decision but must seek advice from those affected or knowledgeable"). By writing these out, you align everyone's expectations. No more hidden "who's really in charge" questions—it's on paper.

- *Power and Influence Norms (Power Signals):* This is a bit unique—here, the team articulates how one gains credibility or influence on the team. It might be something like: "We respect expertise: The most knowledgeable on a topic leads that decision (regardless of title). We also value collaboration: Influence comes from helping the team, not just individual brilliance." Or "Seniority in the company does not automatically mean you have more say in our team—all voices are equal on process matters."

Essentially, this is making informal power discussions explicit. It can reference things like how decisions are communicated ("We won't have decisions happening offline at the watercooler—decisions involving the team are brought to the team forum"). If the earlier power mapping found a "hidden leader," discuss it here: Do we want that person to have an official role, or do we agree that influence should be shared differently?

- *Team Norms for Interaction (Challenge & Support):* How do we want to challenge each other and offer help? This covers psychological safety and performance ethos. For instance: "It's okay to disagree openly in discussions—we see conflict as ideas clashing, not personal attacks. We will challenge ideas, not people. And when someone is struggling, we all chip in; asking for help is encouraged, not seen as weakness." Norms might include how we communicate (e.g., "No interrupting in meetings, use a parking lot for tangents, listen fully"), how we handle disagreements ("speak up in the moment, or request a separate session—no back-channel griping"), and how we ensure everyone's voice is heard ("if quiet, facilitator will invite you, or you can use a card to signal you want to speak").

- *Conflict and Repair Rituals:* Even with norms, conflicts or missteps will happen. The canvas should list how we will recover. For example: "If someone feels hurt or upset, they will (or can) request a one-on-one conversation using our Reparative Pair dialogue format (we'll describe that in Step 7). We won't hold grudges; we address issues within 24 hours if possible. If trust is broken, we do a 'trust reset' exercise." Perhaps there's a ritual like ringing a bell to pause a heated debate and then each person states the positive intent of the other's position—anything that fits the team. The idea is to have pre-agreed ways to handle breaches of the ideal.

- *"Phantoms" and History Acknowledgment:* If the team identified any phantoms or legacy habits (like "We still act like the old manager is watching"), explicitly name it on the canvas; e.g., "We acknowledge that *Person X* (former tech lead) is no longer here; we will not use them as an excuse or shield. We commit to let go of the 'What would X do?' mindset as we form our own identity." You could even have a small section for "Letting Go Of" listing any old rules or roles the team agrees to put to rest (maybe ceremonially).

- *Team Rituals & Cadences:* List regular events (daily Scrum, retros, etc.) with any team-specific tweaks ("Retros every two weeks, with rotating facilitator from team"). Also, any fun or bonding rituals can be decided upon ("Team lunch after each sprint" or "meme-of-the-week contest to keep us light"). These reinforce the unique culture they want.

This canvas (see Figure 5-1) can sound like a lot, but essentially it's combining elements of a team charter with elements of a working agreement and the deeper psychodynamic stuff we've uncovered. Keep it to one page or poster if possible—use bullet points or short statements.

CHAPTER 5   SELF-ORGANIZATION TOOLKIT

Figure 5-1. *Team image canvas*

So, how should you facilitate creating it? There are a few approaches, as follows:

- *Synthesis by Coach:* After the imago elicitation (Step 2), you might attempt a first draft of the canvas based on what you heard, then bring it to the team for discussion and editing. For example, you noticed half the team wants more voice, so you draft a norm—"We make decisions by consent, not by boss directive"—and see if they agree. This can be efficient, but be cautious: You are injecting your interpretation. Always validate with them: *"I heard this, did I capture it right?"*

- *Collaborative Brainstorm*: Go section by section with the team. For instance, start with Purpose: Ask them to craft a purpose statement together (could use round-robin suggestion or pair and share, then converge). Then Boundaries: Perhaps draw a circle on a whiteboard, label inside "Team" and outside "Not Team," and collectively fill it in (names of members inside, maybe names of key stakeholders just outside the boundary, etc.). Roles: List roles, fill in names, then discuss responsibilities (maybe each person describes what they see as their role's key tasks, while others chime in to clarify expectations).

- *Team Image Canvas Template:* Provide a pre-formatted template with headings (like an empty canvas) so they know what categories to fill in. Break them into small groups to fill in parts, then combine. For example, two people tackle the "decision rights" section, two tackle the "norms" section, etc., then review all together. This engages everyone and divides the work.

- *Use earlier outputs:* If they did drawings or interview answers, refer back. "In our ideal drawings, a theme was quick decision-making without needing the boss. How do we enshrine that? What decision process can we agree on to allow that?" Or "Many of you said an ideal team feels 'like family'—what does that mean in behavior? Let's set a norm from that; e.g., 'We care personally, challenge directly' (to quote Kim Scott)."

Throughout this, ensure everyone's voice is heard and integrated. If a member's idea isn't included, acknowledge it: "Alex suggested we all pair program 100% because that's his ideal of teamwork. The group seems to lean toward pairing when needed rather than always. Alex, are you okay with trying that approach and revisiting later?" The goal is a workable agreement for now—not perfect or set in stone. In fact, explicitly label it "Our Team Image v1.0—safe-to-try for the next two months, will adapt as needed." That helps people not over-negotiate every detail.

Ensure the shared image is realistic. Sometimes in their enthusiasm, teams come up with an ideal far from current reality (e.g., "We will always resolve conflicts immediately and never speak negatively"—noble, but perhaps too idealistic). Coach them to include reality checks: *"Is this something we can commit to consistently? If not, let's adjust."* The canvas should stretch them toward better behavior, but not set them up to fail or be a facade.

It's also helpful to highlight how this shared image differs from past patterns (legacy imago). For instance, "In the past, decisions were made outside the team; now we're saying they'll be made within the team with advice from stakeholders. That's a significant shift—is everyone on board? What will help us stick to that when pressure mounts?" These discussions re-imprint new norms over old ones.

By the end of Step 3, you'll have a tangible Team Image Canvas—likely a document or poster—that captures the team's agreements on purpose, boundaries, roles, authority, norms, etc. This is essentially the "blueprint" for their self-organization. It is the shared group imago they will aim to live by, rather than the conflicting private imagos from before. Many teams like to make it visible: Pin it on the team wall or start each retro by revisiting one section. One team I coached turned it into a graphic poster with icons (a lighthouse for purpose, handshake for norms, etc.) to keep it salient.

Techniques for Step 3: Create Shared Imago:

- *Team Image Canvas Template:* Provide a framework with sections like Purpose, Boundaries, Roles, etc., to fill in. Possibly pre-filled with some suggestions gleaned from Step 2 for discussion.

- *Phantoms "Sweep":* As part of the role/authority discussion, directly ask, "Are there any ghosts in the room we need to acknowledge?" If the ex-manager's spectre looms, name it and maybe do a little "farewell" —e.g., write that person's name on a sticky and move it outside the team boundary on the canvas, to symbolize they're no longer part of the decision loop. It's simple but symbolically effective.

- *Authority Ladder Exercise (see Figure 5-2):* If they struggle on decision rights, draw a ladder with rungs: from Tell (leader decides, no input) at bottom, up to Consult (leader decides after consulting team), up to Advice Process (anyone decides after seeking advice), up to Consent (group decision unless objection), up to Delegate (team decides without leader at all). For each type of decision (e.g., tech design, conflict resolution, taking time off mid-sprint, accepting new work, etc.), have them place it on a rung. This visualizes their comfort with autonomy per area. They might agree "For technical choices, we operate at consent—anyone can propose, we only stop if someone objects with reason. For spending company money, maybe consult the PO consults team, then decide." That becomes part of the canvas.

CHAPTER 5   SELF-ORGANIZATION TOOLKIT

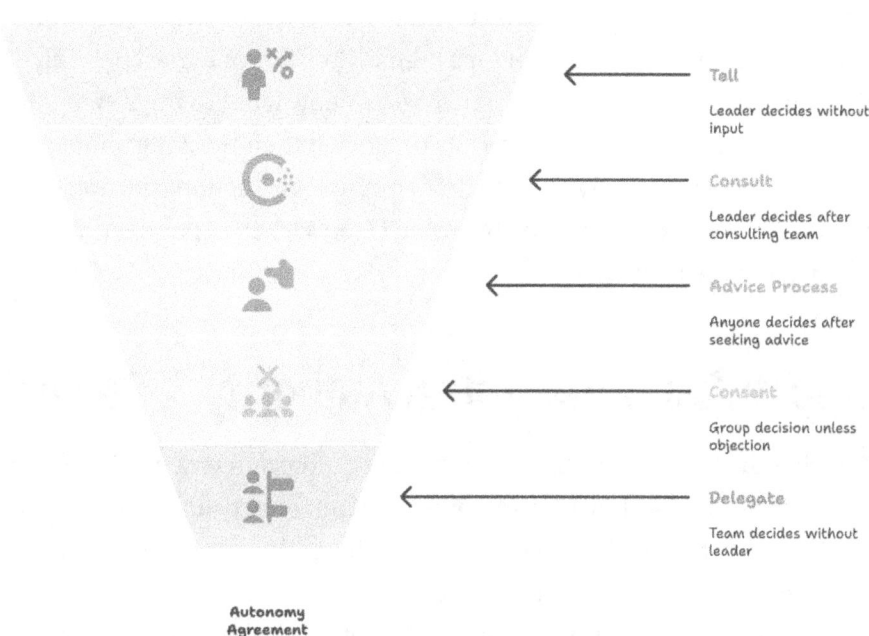

Figure 5-2. Authority ladder

- *Team Charter vs. Team Image:* If the company is used to "team charters," explain how this canvas is different and more. It integrates deeper assumptions. Emphasize common ground: *"We all wanted a more open, trust-based team—see how that shows up in our norms section."* This keeps them united in purpose.

- *Voting or Dot Voting:* If multiple options arise (say two different norms proposals), use dot voting to gauge majority, then see if minority can live with the majority choice (consent criteria: "good enough, safe enough"). Ensure no one has a serious objection left unaddressed.

At this point, the team should feel a sense of ownership and alignment. Often there's a noticeable energy uptick: *"This is our charter; we made this!"* It might not be perfect, but it's theirs. They've gone from possibly disparate expectations to a collective agreement. This is a huge step toward self-organization—they have literally organized their thinking about the team. In the next steps, we'll help them put this into action, starting with fine-tuning roles and power distribution (Step 4), which is a deeper dive into parts of the canvas.

Step 4: Calibrate Roles, Authority & Power

Now that the team has a shared picture and initial agreements, it's time to ensure that roles, authority, and power dynamics are calibrated correctly for self-organization. Essentially, we zoom in on the structural elements of the shared image to double-check they're clear and workable. Why dedicate a step to this? Because even a beautiful team charter can be undermined if, in practice, people are unclear about roles or if hidden power dynamics go unaddressed. This step is about solidifying the "who does what, who decides what, and how power flows."

First, clarify and assign any ambiguous roles. On some teams, beyond the standard Scrum roles, there might be grey areas like who leads architectural decisions? Who interfaces with another team on dependencies? Is there a project manager, or are we distributing those tasks among ourselves? The team should discuss and agree; maybe they decide to rotate a "Facilitator of the Week" role to run daily stand-ups and ensure equal voice. Or they designate a "DevOps Champion" among developers to coordinate infrastructure needs. List these roles and responsibilities explicitly. If someone has been unofficially doing something, either formalize it or consciously rotate it. For example, if Jane has been the one always taking notes, decide if that's her formal role or if it should rotate to share the load. Self-organizing doesn't mean no roles; it means *roles by conscious design* rather than by default or external imposition.

Next, map out authority in key workflows. I find it useful to take typical team activities (planning, coding, testing, releasing, reporting, conflict resolution, etc.) and ensure it's clear who has authority or final say at each point. This overlaps with what we did in the canvas, but here we might create a more detailed RACI-style matrix or R(A)R (Recommend-Agree-Request) model. The outline mentioned RCR (Recommend–Commit–Request), which sounds like a variant of decision rights allocation. Perhaps it means the following:

- Someone Recommends a course of action.
- Others Commit to implementing it.
- Or they Request changes if they disagree.

It's not a standard term, I know, but the idea might be to differentiate recommendations, decisions, and requests. Let's not overcomplicate—the bottom line is to ensure no decision falls through the cracks and no power struggle emerges because two people thought they had the same authority.

One practical tool: an authority ladder (which we already touched on). Use it to move one rung up where appropriate, consciously. For example, historically, maybe the product owner would *tell* the team the sprint goal (yes, not exactly how it should work in Scrum); now they'll *consult* the team or even get *consent* from the team to set it. Perhaps code standards used to be unwritten (people did their own thing); now, the team might delegate that to a pair to propose, and then everyone consents. Identifying even one area to "move the authority to the team" can be symbolic and empowering. It's like lowering the waterline on trust.

Power Mapping: We did a conceptual overview, but here you can engage in a tangible exercise. Draw a 2x2 matrix: formal power (high to low) versus informal influence (high to low). Have the team plot each member (and possibly significant outsiders, such as the manager) on it. For instance, a Scrum master might have medium formal authority (they don't boss people, but they have certain process authority), yet high influence if well respected. A junior dev might have low formal power, but maybe high influence if they're seen as the tech guru. A manager outside the team might have high formal authority (they could override something), but ideally low involvement day-to-day. This map can provoke conversation: *"We see Alice (tech lead) sits in high informal influence, though formally she's just one of the developers. Is everyone comfortable with that? Alice, are you comfortable? If Alice has a lot of say informally, how do we ensure others still speak up? Do we want to adjust anything?"* Perhaps the team is fine with it ("Alice has expertise, we trust her"), or perhaps someone says, "Actually, sometimes I have an idea but assume Alice's view will prevail, so I stay quiet." Aha. That could lead to a norm tweak: Maybe Alice can consciously hold back initially to allow others to voice ideas. Or the team might implement a practice like *round-robin speaking* during design discussions so the soft-spoken get in before the loud ones. The key is to not treat power as taboo, but as something to be openly discussed and shaped.

A real example: In one team, the unofficial architect held so much sway that everyone defaulted to him. When we mapped this, he was at the extreme of both formal and informal axes (not a manager, but essentially had become one in influence). We decided to create a "Design Board"—a small group including him and two others—to evaluate options together rather than him alone. That distributed his power a bit and he was relieved to share the burden, while others felt more included in big decisions.

Also ask: Who has veto power, if anyone? In truly self-managed style, no single member should have absolute veto (except maybe on something in their expertise domain where safety is concerned). Often, teams say only the product owner can veto on scope, only the QA can veto a release for severe bugs, etc., and those should be used rarely. Make these explicit.

Revisit the BART elements quickly (Boundary, Authority, Role, Task):

- Boundary: Already defined who's in/out. Check if any stakeholders cross the boundary inappropriately (e.g., a director who bypasses the PO to directly ask a developer for something—how will the team handle that? Possibly by a "boundary protocol"—the dev directs them to the PO).

- Authority: Write down any remaining ambiguous areas (e.g., "If we can't reach a decision by consent, do we escalate to someone or default to PO's call or what?" Better to decide that now than in the heat of the moment).

- Role: Ensure every key function is covered by someone. If you find "we don't have anyone playing X role," that's a gap to address (maybe train someone or ask for a new hire, etc.). Also ensure no unwanted duplication: two people both thinking they are the final voice on something.

- Task: Make sure tasks needed for team effectiveness (facilitation, meeting notes, backlog grooming, etc.) are assigned or rotated. Self-organizing doesn't mean these tasks vanish—it means the team takes ownership of them.

One more important piece: leadership tasks at every stage. Petrsuska Clarkson and other TA coaches talk about leadership not as a person, but as tasks that need doing (especially in group development phases). For instance, early on, someone has to do the boundary setting, and later someone has to challenge the team to address norms, etc. In a self-organizing team, these leadership tasks can be *shared* or *rotated*. Discuss explicitly: *"How will we ensure the leadership tasks are covered?"*

CHAPTER 5   SELF-ORGANIZATION TOOLKIT

For example, "At kickoff, our Scrum master took the lead in clarifying goals (forming stage leadership). In Storming, maybe any member can call out issues. In Norming, perhaps the product owner emphasizes process adherence if it drifts. In Performing, maybe we all hold each other accountable." Basically, encourage that everyone leads in some way. This prevents the old imago of "one leader, many followers" from sneaking back in.

In practical terms, the output of this step might be the following:

- A refined Responsibility Assignment chart (who owns what decisions)

- A visible Power/Influence Map (could even be left on the wall to remind them, "Let's hear from those with less automatic influence.")

- A set of role descriptions or a RACI table for main activities

- If needed, an update to the Team Image Canvas if they decided to adjust something (like adding "All voices are equal on process" or "We rotate meeting facilitation" based on this talk

Techniques for Step 4: Roles, Authority & Power

- *Role Clarification Worksheet:* List each team member (and common external roles). For each, bullet their responsibilities, decision authorities, and how they coordinate with others. Review and tweak in group. This can be turned into a one-page "Who Does What" reference.

- *Authority Ladder Chart:* As mentioned, write common decisions (e.g., "priority trade-offs," "approving overtime," "design choices," "resolving personal

CHAPTER 5   SELF-ORGANIZATION TOOLKIT

conflict") on cards. Have the team place them on a ladder from the manager to the team decides. Discuss moving at least one rung more toward the team for each if possible.

- *BART Quick Scan:* Use a BART checklist (Boundary, Authority, Role, Task), perhaps at the end of a sprint. Actually, as a micro-tool, some teams do a quick retrospective check: each member writes one sticky for each B, A, R, T, answering "Is this clear? Any issues?" For now, we can simulate that by asking: "Do we all feel boundaries are clear? Any role overlaps? Any authority confusion? Any tasks being dropped or duplicated?" This catches anything we missed.

- *Power Map & Influence Paths:* As described, draw axes for formal/informal power. Place people. Then discuss "influence paths": How does information or influence flow? For example, maybe all ideas flow through one person to get to management—do we want alternate paths? If a quiet person has a great idea, what's their route to getting it heard? Designing some direct paths (like a suggestion box, an agenda slot, or a buddy system) can ensure power doesn't bottleneck.

- *Signals of Power Shifts:* Agree on how to signal if someone feels disempowered or steamrolled. Maybe a safe word or simply, "I feel like I'm not being heard—can we pause?" norm. Encouraging this will help maintain a balance of power.

- *Leadership Task Chart (if team is interested):* Draw the Tuckman stages and ask, "What is needed from leadership at each?" (Forming: clarity; Storming:

listening and conflict management; Norming: encouragement of new norms; Performing: growth, etc.). Then note how the team will handle that. Possibly assign who ensures what. It reinforces that leadership is a set of functions, not just one person's job.

By solidifying roles and authority, the team's earlier agreements become actionable. People know who is doing what and who decides what day-to-day. This prevents regression to old habits (like waiting for the manager, or two leaders pulling in different directions). It also gives confidence—each member can say, "Yes, I *own* this part, I'll run with it," or "I know exactly who to involve for that decision." In essence, we are aligning formal structure with the desired self-organizing behavior. With this clarity, we can proceed to building the day-to-day operating system of the team.

Step 5: Agree on the Operating System for Self-Organization

Think of this step as installing the "software" on the structural "hardware" we've set up. The operating system (OS) for the team refers to the regular processes, routines, and protocols that the team will use to manage itself. It's how the team will make decisions, coordinate work, and continuously improve—all in line with the shared imago and roles we established.

Without an intentional OS, even a well-meaning team can flounder. They might agree in theory to be self-managing, but when Monday comes, they aren't sure how to run a meeting without a boss, or how to choose between two approaches without a top-down directive. By agreeing on some key practical methods ahead of time, we give the team scaffolding to lean on. Importantly, the OS should be tailored to the team's context (not blindly adopting generic practices) and should be lightweight enough to guide, but not so rigid as to stifle.

Key components of the team OS include decision-making protocols, work process rules (like WIP limits), meeting formats, and feedback loops. Let's go through each.

Decision Protocols: We already clarified who has authority for what, but now let's agree on *how* those group decisions will be made in practice. Four popular ones we discussed are as follows:

- Consent Decision Making: Use this for decisions that affect everyone or where buy-in is crucial (e.g., team norms change, major architectural choices). The protocol is: propose ➤ clarify questions ➤ discuss ➤ call for objections ➤ if no *paramount* objections, it's approved. If there are objections, integrate them by improving the proposal or clarifying until objections are resolved or minimized. Emphasize what consent is: *"good enough for now, safe enough to try,"* not perfection or unanimous love. This allows forward motion. We might practice this on a small matter first, so everyone understands not to hold out for perfect, only raise objections if they truly believe the proposal would cause harm or regression. By codifying consent, you avoid endless consensus-seeking (which can frustrate or lead to false agreements).

- Advice Process: For many decisions, particularly those that don't require everyone's direct input, *anyone* can decide something but must first seek advice from (a) those affected and (b) subject matter experts. We can formalize: "If you see a process improvement needed, you can implement it after asking the team's thoughts. If you want to try a new tool, ask the one who will use it most and maybe someone with experience, then go for it." The team OS could state: "Default decision method:

advice process by initiator; major team policy changes: consent by whole team; emergency decisions: maybe one designated person or quick two-person consult." An example for emergencies: if production is down at 2:00 a.m., we don't convene a consent meeting—maybe a tech lead just fixes it and informs later (that's advice process in a sense: get advice if possible, but if not, act in best faith).

- RCR (Recommend–Commit–Request) or RACI Adaptations: If this is a known method in their context, define it. Possibly RCR means one person recommends a decision, a second commits (agrees and executes), and others can request modifications. It could be a variant for multi-stage decisions. If the team or organization is familiar with something like RAPID (Recommend, Agree, Perform, Input, Decide) or RACI (Responsible, Accountable, Consulted, Informed), incorporate that for clarity. The simpler the better, though—fancy acronyms matter less than shared understanding. The OS might simply list, "For feature prioritization: PO recommends, team commits or requests change; for code changes: developer recommends via PR, another dev reviews and commits (pull request process)." Actually, come to think, the whole Git workflow is a decision process—maybe map those too if relevant (like if any code needs a review—that's a built-in check).

- Escalation Path: Self-managing doesn't mean never escalating; sometimes an external decision or arbitration is needed. But define when and how. For instance, "If the team cannot resolve a conflict after two attempts and it's blocking work, we will seek the Scrum master's mediation, and if still unresolved, involve our department head as a last resort." The idea is to avoid silent, festering issues or running to the boss at the first hiccup. They have a protocol to try internally first (like conflict resolution steps in Step 7), then clear when it's okay to pull in a higher authority. Having this in OS ironically makes them less likely to escalate, because they trust there's a safety valve if needed.

Work-in-Process (WIP) and Work Rules: Agile teams often benefit from explicit limits and definitions of how work flows. This aligns with their self-managing OS by preventing overload and chaos, as follows:

- WIP Limits: If they use Kanban or even within Scrum, they might set a limit like "No more than 2 tasks in progress per person at a time" or "Only 3 user stories in development at once for the whole team." This forces prioritization and collaboration (if the limit is reached, the team swarms to finish something before starting new). The team can decide what's reasonable. Maybe they don't formally adopt Kanban, but they say, "We won't each work on separate things in isolation; we'll often pair or at least not have eight things for eight people concurrently." That fosters communication and prevents thin spreading.

- Interrupts: Many teams struggle with interruptions and unplanned work. A good OS will define how to handle those. For example: "Urgent production issues override sprint scope but have a pipeline: We dedicate at least one person on rotation to handle them so others can focus. Non-urgent requests go to the product backlog for next planning." By agreeing on this, the team self-organizes how to respond to chaos rather than management swooping in.

- Minimal Viable Meetings: Decide what meetings to have and who must attend. Self-organizing teams can and should adjust their meeting cadences. For example, "We'll do backlog refinement every Thursday with PO + 3 devs rotating." The key is *they* decide what serves them, and they commit to making those meetings effective (or to change them if not).

Feedback Loops: These ensure the team is reflecting and adjusting—a hallmark of Agile:

- Retrospective Rhythm: Confirm they will do retrospectives and how; e.g., "We will have a retrospective at the end of each sprint (or every two weeks) focused not only on product, but also on our team process and dynamics (teamership)." Perhaps specifically allocate 15 minutes in each retro to check on how self-organization is going ("Are we sticking to our agreements? Any new tension in roles or processes?"). This catches drift early.

- Peer Feedback: Encourage something like a monthly or quarterly *"team 360"* or simple feedback rounds. For instance, a feedback dojo: one hour where one team member is in the "learner seat" and others share feedback/coaching with them, then rotate next time. Or simply "buddy feedback" pairs that meet biweekly. If everyone's comfortable, an OS might say, "We give each other real-time feedback; if something bothers you, tell the person within 24 hours." But many teams need a structured moment to do it. The OS could schedule that: e.g., first retro of the month includes a segment where each says one thing someone else did well and one suggestion (with psychological safety guidelines in place).

- Metrics/Indicators Review: Decide what signals of improvement or issues the team will monitor. Possibly tie to the Self-Organization Health Indicators mentioned later: e.g., "We will track how many decisions we escalated versus handled ourselves." If that number spikes, it's a sign to discuss why. Or track "cycle time from work ready to work done—is decision latency an issue or not?" Choose a few meaningful metrics that the team itself finds useful (not just what management wants). It could be qualitative pulses like a quick monthly survey "Do you feel the power distribution on the team is fair?" If someone says no, that triggers a chat.

In short, this OS step is about operationalizing the team's ideals into everyday practices. A concrete example outcome might be a one-page "Team Working Agreement" document (some overlap with the canvas, but more focused on process). It might be a bullet:

- Meetings/Events: Daily Scrum at 10 a.m., sprint planning Monday 2 p.m., Sprint Retrospective Friday 3 p.m., etc.

- Decision rules: Use consent for X, advice process for Y, escalate Z if needed. Try to use integrative discussions rather than majority voting if possible (they might explicitly say "we avoid simple majority vote because we value addressing concerns; only use vote as last resort if time-bound").

- Work process: All work visible on the Jira board, no adding items mid-iteration without team agreement, etc. Work-in-progress (WIP) limits: three in dev, two in the test column at once.

- Interrupt handling: e.g., "On-call person rotates weekly for production issues, who is freed from new sprint commitments accordingly."

- Knowledge sharing: e.g., pair programming at least on complex tasks, code reviews required for all PRs (these are development OS specifics).

- Continuous Improvement: e.g., retrospective frequency, any other improvement techniques like pair rotation or cross-training.

- Tool use norms: e.g., "We will use Slack channel X for urgent comms, email for external, decisions documented in Confluence," etc. This avoids confusion or siloed info.

By explicitly agreeing on these, the team reduces friction. When Monday comes, they're not wondering, "Should we meet or not? How do we decide on this bug fix?"—they have a playbook. Of course, they can and should evolve it as they learn. But it's easier to steer a moving car than to start from zero each time.

Techniques for Step 5: Operating System:

- *Decision Protocol Cheat Sheets:* Provide visual cheatsheets for consent (e.g., a flowchart: Proposal ➤ Questions ➤ Objections? No ➤ done; Yes ➤ resolve ➤ etc.), and for the advice process (steps listed). This helps members follow the method in real time. Some teams stick these on the wall or have them open during meetings.

- *Team Working Agreement Session:* Dedicate a meeting after roles (or part of the same workshop) to nail down the working practices. Could be facilitated by asking "What do we want to keep or change about how we currently do X?" for various X (meetings, comms, coding, etc.). If the team is already doing Scrum, start from Scrum ceremonies and ask if there are any changes. Document their decisions.

- *Safe-to-Try Commitments:* Emphasize that these OS elements can be experiments; e.g., "Let's try 3x/week stand-ups for one month and then evaluate if it's enough." Write that review date down. Agile is about inspect and adapt; their OS is not sacred, it's just what they think is best now.

- *Visualize Process Rules:* Sometimes, a simple diagram of their workflow with WIP limits and roles can be drawn and posted. Or a checklist for "Definition of Done" (if not in place), which is part of OS, ensuring quality without external policing.

- *Peer Coaching Dojo:* Introduce the idea of a periodic session where team members practice coaching each other. For example, one person presents a challenge (maybe about team functioning), another acts as coach (maybe the Scrum master), and they use the imago lens (prompt questions like "What does this situation remind you of?") to help. This not only solves issues but also builds internal coaching skills, making the team more self-sustaining.

- *Schedule Reflection:* Actually put a recurring calendar event a few weeks out—"OS Review"—to remind them to reflect on these processes. It's easy to slip into old habits or find something isn't working and forget to fix it. A 30-minute OS check every so often helps. The OS is not static.

By the end of Step 5, the team's machine is well oiled: roles clear, processes defined. They should feel a sense of agency: "We have our own way of working that we chose." It's a big confidence booster. They also have reduced reliance on the coach or manager to tell them how to run things, because they've set that up themselves. Now the next step is to put this OS into practice through experiments and gradually build the habits that make all these agreements a lived reality.

Step 6: Run Bounded Experiments

Even with a shiny new framework of roles and processes, behavior doesn't change overnight. Step 6 involves translating agreed-upon *intentions* into real *actions* and *habits*, utilizing the experimental approach. Why experiments? Because trying new ways of self-organizing is a learning process, so it may not work perfectly at first, and that's okay. Experiments give the team permission to try something short-term and evaluate rather than feeling they're making irreversible commitments. It creates a culture of *"safe-to-try"* changes rather than endless debate or fear of making a mistake.

We want to identify a few leverage-point changes that can shift the team's imago and behavior. Based on everything so far, certain patterns likely emerged where the team wants to improve. For example, maybe historically the Scrum master always facilitated every meeting, so one experiment could be rotating facilitation to reinforce shared leadership.

CHAPTER 5   SELF-ORGANIZATION TOOLKIT

Or if the product owner was a bottleneck, maybe experiment with an advice process decision in one sprint (like letting the team decide a minor priority after seeking PO's input).

Safe-to-Try Cards: One technique is creating "experiment cards" with a hypothesis format:

> If we do X (change/practice),
>
> then we expect Y (positive outcome)
>
> as evidenced by Z (measurable or observable indicator).

For example:

- *If we rotate the daily Scrum facilitator each week, then team members will develop facilitation skills and equalize participation, evidenced by quieter members leading some stand-ups confidently by the end of the month.*

- *If we implement the advice process for design decisions, then decisions will be faster and still well informed, evidenced by fewer meetings needed and no drop in quality in the next sprint.*

- *If the product owner only steps in to break ties after an advice round among developers, then developers will feel more ownership, evidenced by at least two instances of devs resolving a priority conflict themselves in sprint 5.*

These are essentially small self-management "experiments" that target the team's behavior and imago. The horizon is typically short: two to four weeks, maybe a sprint or two. The experiments should be bounded—clearly define the duration and scope so everyone knows it's not permanent if it flops. This lowers resistance to trying.

Some experiment ideas are presented here:

- Rotate Facilitation: Each team member (or at least each role) takes a turn facilitating a ceremony (daily Scrum, retro, etc.). This tests the norm that leadership is shared and that others can step up, challenging any imago that "only X can lead meetings."

- Peer Coaching on Backlog Refinement: Pair a developer with the product owner to co-lead a refinement session—the developer handles part of the discussion. Hypothesis: This cross-role experience will increase mutual understanding and reduce "us vs. them" feeling.

- PO Steps Back: For one sprint, the product owner deliberately does not intervene in intra-team decisions (unless asked) and lets the team resolve priority conflicts through the agreed protocol. Hypothesis: Team realizes they can handle it, shifting "We need PO's permission" imago to "We commit as a team." Evidence might be that the PO only had to step in once instead of five times during that sprint.

- Advice-process Decision Pilot: Pick a domain, e.g., tooling. "We need to choose a new testing framework." Instead of the manager deciding or a whole team meeting for consensus, one volunteer leads and uses an advice process (consults QA, devs, etc., then makes a call). Observe how the team responds and the quality of the outcome. Hypothesis: People accept the decision even if not everyone would've chosen it, because they were consulted, showing trust in the advice process.

- Sprint Goals by Team: Perhaps historically the PO gave sprint goals. Experiment: Have the team propose the sprint goal based on the backlog, PO gives advice and final okay (reverse of usual). See if this increases understanding of the goal and buy-in.

- WIP Limit Enforcement: If they set a WIP limit, treat it as an experiment: for two sprints, stick to it strictly. Hypothesis: Finishing rate and collaboration improve, evidenced by less idle or blocked work.

- Trust Repair Ritual Use: This is more Step 7, but you can test something like a "check-out" ritual at day's end or a "frustration forum" weekly to see if surfacing issues proactively helps. Hypothesis: Addressing minor gripes weekly prevents major blow-ups, evidenced by retro feedback that tensions feel lower.

To manage experiments do the following:

- Limit to a few at a time—maybe two to three concurrently, otherwise it's too many variables and overhead.

- Assign an owner to each experiment to champion it and gather data; e.g., "Jane will note how many times devs needed PO to intervene vs. previous." Or "We'll do a quick poll at the end: did rotating facilitation feel beneficial or chaotic?"

- Use a visible experiment board or chart. This could be a section on the team wall or digital board listing experiments, with columns like "Planned – Running – Concluded – Result." Each experiment card goes through this. At retros, review them: Which succeeded, which need tweaking, which to drop?

Encourage a mindset that experiments are not failures even if results aren't as hoped—they're information. If rotating the daily Scrum lead didn't improve participation, discuss why. Perhaps the quiet person still didn't feel comfortable leading—maybe they need training, or maybe stand-ups need reformatting. That learning is valuable. The team might decide to adjust the experiment and try again, or conclude "we tried, maybe that one isn't for us right now."

Also highlight positive deviations: Sometimes an experiment yields side benefits. For instance, rotating facilitation might reveal someone's hidden skill in running meetings, which could lead them to take on more Scrum mastery tasks, freeing the actual SM to focus elsewhere. Celebrate these discoveries—it reinforces experimentation.

Experiments also help to update the imago through experience. Remember Berne's idea: As your imago adapts to group reality, you operate more in the adult ego state. By living the new norms in experiments, team members gather new "evidence" about group functioning, which revises their unconscious expectations. For example, someone who thought "no one but the manager can handle conflict" sees a peer mediating a spat successfully, which directly challenges and updates their imago. Over time, these experiences accumulate into a new default view of "how our team is."

Make sure experiments are tracked to conclusion. It's easy to start them and forget. Put a reminder, e.g., "End of Sprint 5: evaluate Experiment X." In that retro or meeting, ask: *"Do we adopt this practice, tweak it, or drop it?"* If adopted, it might become part of the official OS (update your working agreement). If drop, note why (maybe revisit later under different conditions). If tweak, modify and run for another cycle.

Techniques for Step 6: Experiments:

- *Safe-to-Try Brainstorm:* In a session, ask the team, "What's one thing we could try for a few weeks that might improve our self-management?" Use sticky notes or a round-robin to gather ideas. Filter to pick a couple that seem promising and not too risky. The phrasing "safe-to-try" frees them to suggest bold things without fear (since if it's unsafe, the group will say so).

- *15–30 Day Bet Cards:* Use index cards or a template to write the hypothesis as described. Ensure each has a timeline and measures. Might literally write "Experiment: X. Duration: 2 weeks. Measure: Y." Pin these up.

- *Hypothesis Template:* Provide them a simple formula to fill (If..., then..., by/as measured by...). This makes them think of cause-and-effect and measurement, building analytical habits.

- *Buddy System for Experiments:* Pair up team members to co-own an experiment; e.g., quiet person + outspoken person co-own rotating facilitation experiment; they support each other. This also increases buy-in (someone is personally invested in showing it works).

- *Daily/Weekly Check-ins:* During an experiment, quickly check: "How's the experiment going? Any adjustments?" This could be two minutes in daily Scrum or Slack.

- *Celebrate Completions:* When an experiment concludes, especially if successful, celebrate! Even a little "We did a new thing!" acknowledgment. It builds a positive feedback loop for continuous improvement.

CHAPTER 5   SELF-ORGANIZATION TOOLKIT

Through experiments, the team essentially practices being self-organizing in increments, rather than just declaring it. It's the difference between reading about swimming and getting in the pool. As they rack up successful experiments, confidence grows, and their new self-image ("we are a self-managing team") solidifies. They also become more resilient; because they are used to trying stuff and adapting, they won't collapse the first time something doesn't work as planned.

Now, inevitably, there will be times when, despite all these efforts, the old patterns or problems resurface; maybe conflict flares or someone reverts to "I'll just ask the boss." That's where Step 7 comes in: having ways to repair breaches and re-imprint the new ways so the change sticks.

Step 7: Repair & Re-imprint

No transformation is perfectly smooth. Step 7 is about what to do when the team stumbles or backslides—when old imago-driven behaviors bite back or when conflicts and tensions arise. The two R's here are Repair (fixing damage in relationships or agreements) and Re-imprint (reinforcing the new patterns over the old ones).

Despite best efforts, there will be moments when someone unconsciously acts according to their old group imago. For example, under stress, a team member might exclaim, "We need our manager to decide this!" (slipping back to a dependency pattern), or a conflict might cause people to withdraw (if their imago equates conflict with danger). These moments are crucial—how the team handles them can either reinforce the old habits or further solidify the new, healthier norms. As a coach, you help the team navigate these with mindful interventions.

CHAPTER 5 SELF-ORGANIZATION TOOLKIT

Key scenarios and interventions:

- *Boundary Drift:* Over time, boundaries can erode. Perhaps a stakeholder started sneaking tasks directly to a dev again, or team members started doing work outside their agreed roles (like a dev making product scope promises to a client without PO). When you spot this boundary breach, it's time for a boundary reset ritual. What's that? It's a quick, intentional act where the team does the following:

    1. *Name the Drift:* Acknowledge openly what boundary was crossed (e.g., "We've noticed that our PO role boundary got blurred on Project X—multiple people directly committed to scope changes.").

    2. *Re-state the Boundary:* Remind everyone of the original agreement ("Recall, our agreement is that scope changes must go through the PO and team planning, not ad-hoc.").

    3. *Reinforce with a Small Ceremony:* This could be symbolic—maybe everyone literally signs the Team Canvas again under the boundary section, or the dev who overstepped says, "I hand this decision back to the PO—let's do it the right way." In a playful way, I've seen teams do things like drawing a "line in the sand" on the floor and each member stepping inside saying "I commit to staying within the team boundary for decisions"; it might sound silly, but physical acts can imprint memory.

4. *Adjust if Needed:* Maybe the drift happened for a reason—discuss if the boundary needs adjustment or more clarity to prevent future slips. Perhaps the stakeholder wasn't aware; the solution might be for the Scrum master to educate them or put up a visible "Team is in a sprint—do not disturb" sign metaphorically.

This ritual "containerizes" the incident as a learning moment and recommitment rather than letting it pass and slowly unravel trust.

- *Trust Breaks or Interpersonal Conflict:* Let's say two team members had a heated argument or someone felt disrespected. If not addressed, these can fester, leading imagos to devolve (e.g., one might start seeing the team as "unsafe" like a past bad team). Introduce reparative pairs. A reparative pair exercise is a structured dialogue between two people, typically facilitated by a coach or a neutral team member. The basic format is as follows:

  1. Each person in turn acknowledges what happened and their part in it ("I raised my voice and interrupted you in the meeting, which was not okay.").

  2. They express the impact on them ("When we fight like that, I feel anxious and start to shut down because it reminds me of my last job's toxic fights." The other might say, "I felt hurt and angry that my ideas weren't heard.").

CHAPTER 5   SELF-ORGANIZATION TOOLKIT

3. They each say what they value in the other or the relationship ("I value your expertise and I don't want us to be at odds—we both care about quality.").

4. They make a request of each other for the future ("I request that if I do something that upsets you, you tell me privately rather than in front of the whole team." And the other might say, "I request you let me finish speaking next time, even if you disagree.").

5. They each commit to something ("I commit to managing my tone and listening fully." "I commit to letting you know when I have an issue calmly.").

This structure ensures both sides feel heard and that the resolution is forward-looking. It's similar to techniques used in couples therapy (Imago Dialogue, ironically named, or Nonviolent Communication formats). As a coach, you guide them gently, ensure equal turns, and ensure that it stays respectful. Often, doing this in front of the team (if those two are comfortable) can actually strengthen overall trust. Everyone sees conflicts can be resolved openly and fairly, which imprints, "It's safe to address issues here."

- *"Stop-the-Phantom" Moments:* If you notice people referencing "the way X used to do things" (X = former boss or team member) or deferring to a non-present authority ("We should wait for the architect's opinion"—who's not even on the team), it's phantom

161

talk. Call it out kindly: *"I sense the phantom of X is in the room. Are we making this decision based on her imagined approval? How can we let that go?"* Sometimes I literally have an empty chair and say, *"Is X sitting here? No? Okay, then we can decide without her."* A more formal "stop-the-phantom" approach could be to do a farewell ritual: e.g., write that person's name or the old way ("old boss's approval") on a paper, then as a team throw it in a trash bin or erase it from the whiteboard. It sounds symbolic (it is), but those symbols matter to the psyche. Maybe at a retrospective, you allocate time to explicitly discuss any phantoms or outdated rules that crept back and ceremonially discard them. I recall a team that kept saying, *"We can't deploy on Fridays, the old VP forbade it,"* even though that VP was gone and maybe it wasn't relevant anymore. We examined why the rule existed (fear of issues over the weekend), updated it to a modern context (with current safe deployment practices, maybe it's fine). As a ritual, the team lead said, *"I hereby revoke the No Friday Deploy rule,"* and everyone clapped. It gave a sense of breaking free from a phantom hold.

- *Re-imprinting Positive Patterns:* When an old scenario recurs but the team handles it *differently* this time, highlight that—it's re-imprinting. For example, "Hey everyone, note this: Last month, a sudden scope change caused panic and a fight. This week, the same happened, but we saw you immediately go into problem-solving mode using the advice process, and no fight! This is a big change—kudos." Drawing attention to such instances reinforces the new imago:

"We are a team that can handle surprises calmly" replacing "We fall apart under surprises." You, as a coach, should be on the lookout for these milestone moments and celebrate them.

- *Micro-resets:* Sometimes a small mindful practice helps re-center. It could be something like at the start of each retro, doing a quick "How's everyone feeling?" check-in. If someone is harboring tension, they might mention it (*"I'm still annoyed about something from earlier"*), which can then be addressed. Or if a meeting gets heated, call a two-minute timeout: Have everyone take a breath or write down their viewpoint quietly, then resume with cooler heads. These micro-interventions prevent escalation and establish a norm of pausing and repairing in real-time.

The theme is making repair a normal, welcomed part of team life. Many teams avoid confronting issues because it feels awkward or they fear making it worse. But high-trust teams know that addressing and repairing is what keeps trust. As a coach, model this; e.g., if you accidentally overstep (maybe you gave advice when you should've let them find a solution), own it and reset: *"Folks, I realize I jumped in there—sorry about that. Let me step back, and you continue."* This shows it's okay to make mistakes and fix them.

Techniques for Step 7: Repair & Re-imprint:

- *Boundary Reset Checklist:* A short protocol script, like "When boundary X is violated: (1) identify it; (2) discuss why it happened; (3) restate the rule; (4) agree on adjustment or recommitment." Keep it handy.

- *Repair Ritual Plan:* Maybe write down the steps of the reparative pair dialogue on a card so the pair can follow it. Coach one or two team members in facilitating it if you're not around (maybe the Scrum master learns to do these).

- *Team Norm of Calling Out Phantoms:* Encourage team members to call each other out if they see phantom behavior, gently. A code phrase, e.g., "*Is that a phantom speaking?*" said with a smile, could cue someone to realize, oh, yeah, I invoked our ex-manager's name again. A little humor helps—some teams have a rubber duck named after the old boss that they pass around as a signal, "the phantom of the boss is here."

- *Visual: Old vs. New Table:* Consider a small poster listing "Legacy Imago vs. Emerging Imago" signs. For instance:

    - Legacy: "Saying 'Let's ask the boss'" vs. New: "Saying 'What do *we* recommend?'"

    - Legacy: "Meetings where one person talks 90%" vs. New: "Meetings where all voices are heard."

    - Legacy: "Conflicts avoided or explode" vs. New: "Conflicts addressed and resolved in a timely manner."

  This table (sometimes given in outline under Visuals & Tables) serves as a reminder. When they catch themselves on the left side, they can correct course to the right side.

- *Supervision for Coach:* As a side note, as a coach, especially when dealing with deeper dynamics, it's wise to have your own supervisor or mentor to debrief challenging situations (for ethical safety as per common traps: guard against your own imago leak—maybe you hate conflict, so you inadvertently hush it too soon, etc. Getting an external perspective helps keep you effective and neutral.

By implementing repairs as routine "maintenance," the team's new norms and image become more and more resilient. Over time, these repair interventions will be done by team members themselves without coach prompting—a great sign of maturity. They'll catch a boundary slip or interpersonal issue and handle it in the moment. That's ultimate self-management: not the absence of problems, but the ability to self-correct when problems occur.

Also, each successful repair or adaptation re-imprints the notion that *"we can handle it."* The new group imago gets firmer: earlier, perhaps someone's imago said "teams fall apart when there's conflict"; after three instances where conflict was fixed constructively, their inner belief shifts to "teams can come out stronger from conflict." This psychological shift is huge for sustaining the change.

The last step in the framework focuses on how to maintain and keep improving this self-organizing capability long-term.

Step 8: Measure, Reflect, Sustain

Step 8 focuses on ensuring the gains are sustained and the team continues to grow after the formal coaching engagement concludes. It involves setting up measurements to track their self-organization health, reflecting on progress regularly, and instituting practices that help sustain and further develop their capabilities (like peer coaching).

CHAPTER 5   SELF-ORGANIZATION TOOLKIT

Measure what matters: To sustain momentum, it's helpful for the team to see concrete evidence of improvement (or catch early warning signs of slipping). Together, define a few Self-Organization Health Indicators. These can be a mix of quantitative and qualitative metrics, as follows:

- *Decisions Made in Team vs. Escalated:* Track the percentage of decisions the team makes using their agreed protocols without external escalation. For instance, "In the last quarter, 90% of product decisions were made within the team; only 1 of 10 was escalated to management," versus maybe when you started, it was 50%. Seeing that number go up is validating.

- *Decision Lead Time:* Measure how long it takes from issue identification to decision. If self-management is working, this should shrink (no waiting for someone's approval in another department). For example, "Time to decide on a design approach: down from 3 days to 1 day on average." That indicates more autonomy and efficiency.

- *Role Clarity Score:* You could do a simple survey, like each member rates "I am clear on my role and others' roles" from 1 to 5, and track the trend. Or "I feel decisions are made at the appropriate level," from 1 to 5. If you did such a survey at the start (maybe many disagreed), and now they agree strongly, that's a measurable improvement in structure clarity and empowerment.

- *"Power feels fair" Pulse:* Ask periodically, "Do you feel influence and contributions on the team are balanced and fair?" with a yes/no or scale. If someone starts feeling disenfranchised, you catch it early. Ideally, over time, the majority feels "yes, it's fair."

- *Frequency of Boundary Breaches:* How often did an external person bypass the team process or an internal person break protocol? It might be an anecdotal count. Ideally reduces to near zero. If it spikes, that's a sign to revisit Step 7 interventions.

- *Team Stability & Ownership:* Perhaps track retention or willingness to take on challenges. It's harder to quantify, but maybe use something like "Number of initiatives the team proactively started on their own" as a count.

Imago Shift Markers: More subjectively, watch language and behaviors:

- Are team members saying "we" more than "they" now? For example, did those who used to say "management wants us to do X" start saying "we decided to do X because . . ."?

- Are references to phantoms or past ways almost gone? (E.g., no one says "but last year we did it this way" anymore; they're focusing on now.)

- Are goodbyes and hellos handled well? Berne noted that clarified imago leads to healthy departures. If a member leaves, do they do it gracefully with knowledge transferred and team stable (sign of maturity), or is it chaotic? If the team can onboard a new member smoothly into their culture (with Canvas, OS explained, etc.), that's a marker.

- Team confidence: Maybe ask them, *"Do you feel you're a self-managing team now?"* Their own self-assessment matters. Initially, maybe many said "not really"; hopefully later you get, "Yes, we are, and proud of it."

These measures should be transparent to the team and ideally owned by them. Maybe the Scrum master or a rotating "team health champion" plots a simple chart or includes a slide in a sprint retrospective about "team process improvement." This keeps them accountable in a positive way and also shows stakeholders that self-organization is yielding results (to keep their support).

Reflect regularly: Apart from retrospectives, which we've covered, consider periodic, deeper reflections, such as the following:

- A quarterly "Team Health Retrospective" solely focusing on these self-org indicators and team dynamics (not delivery). Ask what's improved, what's slipped, why, and set goals for next quarter. Perhaps involve an outside facilitator or coach for an objective view (if you, as a coach, have rolled off, maybe do a quarterly check-in).

- Use any company surveys (like engagement surveys) to gauge improvement (e.g., if there's a question about whether "I have autonomy to do my job," you'd hope to see higher scores).

- Storytelling: Encourage the team to reflect by telling their story. Maybe at a department meeting, team members present "Our journey to self-organization:

What changed in a year." Putting it in narrative form consolidates their own understanding and imprints pride. It also helps others learn.

Sustain through peer coaching: To avoid backsliding, the team can adopt the following habits to coach themselves:

- *Peer Coaching Dojo:* Perhaps once a month or quarter, one team member volunteers a challenge they're facing (maybe team-related, maybe technical or personal growth). Another member acts as a coach (listens, asks questions, doesn't just solve). Rotate who coaches and who is coached. Over time, everyone practices coaching skills and being coached by peers, which fosters a supportive, developmental atmosphere akin to having an internal coach at all times.

- *Mentoring new members:* Make it part of the OS that when someone new joins, a team member coaches them on "how we self-organize here," explaining the team image canvas and norms. This both indoctrinates newcomers into the culture (so the progress isn't lost with turnover) and reinforces it for the mentor because teaching it re-imprints it.

- *Community of Practice:* If multiple teams are adopting self-organization in the org, form a Scrum master or Agile coach community where they share experiences. Even within the team, maybe someone is more passionate about dynamics—they can attend workshops or training and bring back new insights (continuous learning).

- *Recognition and Rewards Alignment:* Work with management to ensure the formal reward system supports self-org. For instance, if managers were previously the only ones to receive bonuses for team success, perhaps the team should now be collectively recognized. Or incorporate "demonstrated self-management" into performance reviews in a positive way. This step is more org-level, but sustaining often requires the environment not to contradict the changes. If the team knows they won't be penalized but rather praised for acting autonomously, they'll keep doing it.

- *Further Reading & Learning:* Provide the team with resources to continue learning about group dynamics, facilitation, etc. (Our "Further Reading" section will list some!). Perhaps during each retro, someone shares a nugget from an article they read to keep ideas flowing.

Essentially, make continuous improvement a habit—the team should feel *"we're never 'done' improving how we work,"* which is the heart of Agile anyway. The coach's goal is to become redundant: The team can self-correct and improve on its own. Sustaining mechanisms ensure that when you step away, they don't slowly drift back to old habits due to neglect or new pressures.

One thing to watch for: Sometimes teams do great while the coach is there (a bit like training wheels or just the Hawthorne effect of observation), but months later slip. By establishing these measures and habits, you create an early warning system. For example, if decision time starts creeping up or conflict avoidance patterns return, the team's own retrospective or metrics should catch it and prompt action—maybe they'll even reach out to you or another coach for a refresher session, which is fine. But ideally, they spot and address it themselves because they've learned how.

CHAPTER 5   SELF-ORGANIZATION TOOLKIT

Techniques for Step 8: Measure & Sustain:

- *Team Health Dashboard:* Maybe a simple radar chart or bar chart updated periodically with key metrics (autonomy, clarity, etc.). Some tools exist for team health (some Agile consultants use them), or DIY in Excel. It could even be fun, like a self-drawn thermometer poster for "self-management temperature."

- *Imago Language Audit:* Once in a while, analyze team communication for language shifts. Perhaps during one retrospective, review a recording or chat logs for signs of "we vs. they" or other telling phrases. It's a reflective exercise that can reveal subtle shifts or slippage.

- *Periodic Survey:* If you like data, use a consistent survey every X months; e.g., the Scrum Team Survey or something customized. Keep it short so they'll do it. Show trend lines.

- *Rotation of Roles:* To sustain learning, consider rotating some internal roles occasionally; e.g., if you had a designated meeting facilitator role, change it each quarter. That prevents over-reliance on one person and keeps everyone on their toes.

- *Revisit and Renew Team Image Canvas:* Suggest that once or twice a year the team sit down and review that Canvas from Step 3. Maybe in a year some things become obsolete (new tech, team goal changed, etc.). They can modify their working image accordingly—this is re-contracting at a higher maturity level. It's like renewing vows, adapting to current reality. Teams grow, so their shared imago should grow too.

- *Injecting Fresh Perspectives:* Sustaining doesn't mean stagnating. Encourage occasionally inviting an outsider to observe a meeting or retrospective. A fresh set of eyes (could be a peer from another team) may spot a blind spot ("Hey, I noticed the UX person hardly spoke—is that normal?" could reveal something). It's voluntary and non-judgmental, more like mutual coaching between teams.

To sum up Step 8: It's about keeping the flame alive. The team now has the skills and structures to self-organize—this step makes sure that the flame doesn't die out due to entropy. By measuring and visibly seeing their progress, they stay motivated. By reflecting regularly, they remain conscious and don't slip into autopilot. By building in sustaining practices (peer coaching, periodic resets), they ensure new challenges or changes (like new team members, new projects) don't knock them off course.

Conclusion

Self-organization isn't a slogan; it's a sequence you can run and re-run. You begin by contracting clearly—who's involved, why this change matters now, the goals, and the psychological ground rules—so when friction appears, you can point back to explicit agreements rather than personalities. That upfront clarity becomes your anchor when the seas get choppy.

From there, you make the invisible visible. Surface each person's private "team movie," then negotiate a shared picture of how you want to work. The Team Image Canvas is that picture turned into a one-page blueprint—purpose, boundaries, roles, authority, norms—kept visible and treated as a living agreement rather than a poster that gathers dust.

With a shared image in hand, you calibrate roles, decision rights, and power. This is where self-organization succeeds or quietly fails. Spell out "who decides what," map formal and informal influence, and make leadership a set of tasks the team shares and rotates, not a crown one person wears by default.

Then you operationalize all of it in a lightweight team operating system. Default to the advice process for most decisions; use consent when a choice affects everyone—"good enough for now, safe enough to try." Package the day-to-day in a concise working agreement so Monday morning is no longer a mystery.

Change sticks through short, bounded experiments. Run two-to-four-week bets tied to clear hypotheses and observable signals, limit yourself to a small number at a time, assign owners, and review outcomes at retro: adopt, tweak, or drop. Over time, these micro-bets rewrite the team's default expectations of itself.

Because the old imago will resurface under stress, you also normalize repair. Use micro-resets in the moment, a simple boundary-reset ritual when lines blur, and a reparative-pair dialogue when trust takes a dent. Treat repair as routine maintenance; the real milestone is when the team initiates it without you.

Finally, you sustain the gains by measuring what matters and reflecting regularly. Track the percentage of decisions made within the team, decision lead time, role-clarity, and "power feels fair" pulses, plus tell-tale language shifts from "they" to "we." Make these indicators transparent and own them together.

Mature teams don't avoid problems—they self-correct. Contract clearly, make the image shared, give power shape, codify how you operate, learn in small bets, repair quickly, and keep score on what counts. Do that, and the team's new image stops being an aspiration and becomes its reflex.

CHAPTER 5   SELF-ORGANIZATION TOOLKIT

Reflection Moment

1. When you think of your current team, what "hidden imago" assumptions (yours or others') might be shaping how decisions get made or avoided?

2. If your team created a Team Image Canvas today, which section (purpose, roles, decision rights, norms, rituals) would spark the richest—or toughest—conversation?

3. Where could your team realistically move one step up the authority ladder (e.g., from "manager decides" to "advice process")? What small experiment could you try to test that shift?

4. Think of a time when your team slipped back into old patterns. How might you design a quick "repair ritual" to both restore trust and reinforce the new way of working?

5. If you plotted your team on the Self-Organization Health Radar, which dimension would you rate highest and which lowest? What would it take to raise the lowest one by even a single point?

PART III

Navigating Challenging Situations

CHAPTER 6

Clearing the Roadblocks: Psychological Distance, Hidden Contracts

The initial stage of team coaching—contracting—is absolutely paramount for the success of the coaching relationship. How well a coach executes it will largely determine whether the interested parties attain the desired outcomes. Chapter 3 covers substantial information on how to kick off a coaching relationship with a team. Here, we will dive deeper into the challenges that sit at the psychological level of contracting.

The Triangle of Psychological Distance

In the realm of team coaching, particularly when it involves multiple stakeholders, Nelly Micholt's concept of "psychological distance" offers valuable insights. Her work, "Psychological Distance and Group Interventions" (1992), examined the relational distances in a three-party

CHAPTER 6   CLEARING THE ROADBLOCKS: PSYCHOLOGICAL DISTANCE, HIDDEN CONTRACTS

coaching contract and how misalignments can lead to dysfunctional dynamics. While her research was grounded in Transactional Analysis (TA) and often described in the context of a triangle between coach, individual client, and the client's organization, the principles readily apply to Agile team coaching, where one frequently navigates relationships between the coach, the team (as the coachee), and the wider organization or sponsor (such as a manager or department head).

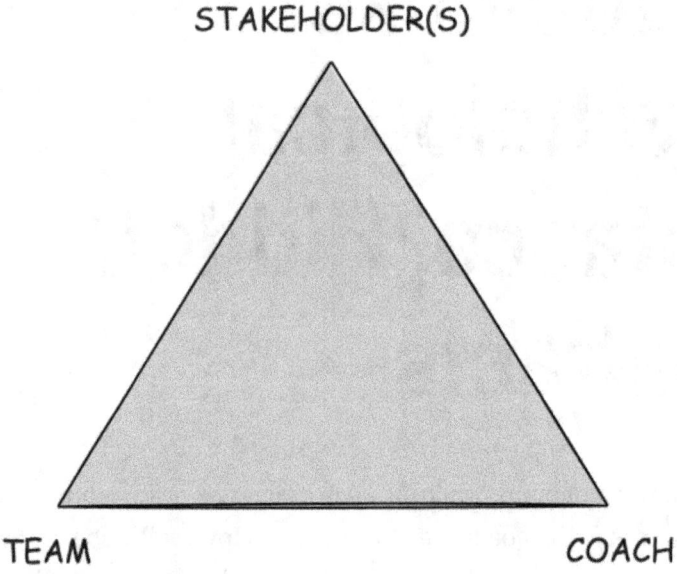

Figure 6-1. *Three-party coaching contract*

Micholt used the image of a triangle (Figure 6-1) to illustrate the coach–client–sponsor relationship and noted that problems arise when two of the three parties become too close (psychologically) and collude against the third. In an ideal scenario—what she calls a Type A contract—there is open discussion of expectations, clarity around confidentiality, and mutual respect among all three parties (coach, team, and sponsor). This means everyone is on the same page: The team understands the coach's role and trusts their intentions, the sponsor (e.g., a senior manager

CHAPTER 6   CLEARING THE ROADBLOCKS: PSYCHOLOGICAL DISTANCE, HIDDEN CONTRACTS

who brought the coach in) is clear on boundaries (like not using the coach as a spy on the team), and the coach maintains an equal commitment to supporting both the team and the organization's goals. In Type A, no one feels the coach is "siding" with someone else improperly—psychological distance is balanced.

However, if there's a lack of clarity or alignment, this scenario can slip into a "psychological game" where roles akin to the Drama Triangle (Persecutor, Victim, Rescuer) emerge. There can be three problematic configurations.

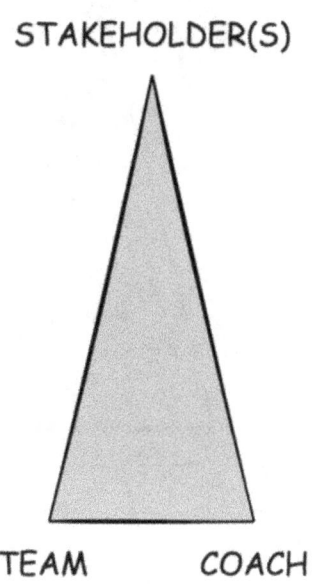

Figure 6-2. *Type B contract*

Type B contract (Figure 6-2): The coach and coachee (team) become too close, potentially colluding against the sponsor. For example, an Agile coach might over-identify with the team's grievances and begin to subtly join the team in blaming upper management for all problems. The coach might engage in "Isn't the management awful?" conversations with the team, thereby validating the team's victim stance and portraying the sponsor as the persecutor. In Micholt's terms, the coach and team share a Victim perspective against a common Persecutor (the sponsor), or sometimes the coach-team pair even assume a Persecutor role toward the sponsor (viewing them with derision). The danger here is that the coach loses objectivity and the trust of the sponsor; ultimately, this doesn't truly serve the team either – it indulges their sense of powerlessness instead of helping them constructively engage with the broader system.

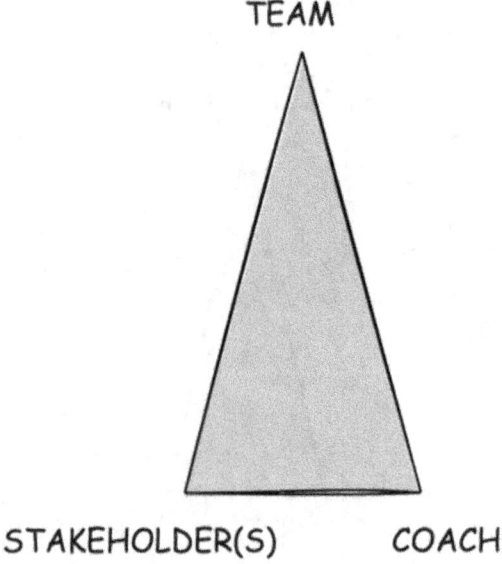

Figure 6-3. Type C contract

Type C contract (Figure 6-3): The sponsor and coach collude, leaving the coachee (team) as the odd one out. This may occur if a coach is hired by management with an explicit (or implicit) agenda of "fixing the team." The coach might then align more with management's perspective, perhaps sharing critiques of the team with the sponsor or focusing coaching goals on what the sponsor wants without involving the team's voice. In this case, the team feels done to; they might view the coach as an agent of the bosses (Persecutor) and themselves as victims of this alliance. Alternatively, the

CHAPTER 6   CLEARING THE ROADBLOCKS: PSYCHOLOGICAL DISTANCE, HIDDEN CONTRACTS

coach and sponsor might assume a well-intentioned Rescuer role—feeling sorry for the "struggling" team and colluding to help them at all costs—but this still puts the team in a one-down position (Victim) and can diminish the team's ownership of their improvement. Either way, trust between the team and coach erodes, and the coaching initiative can fail.

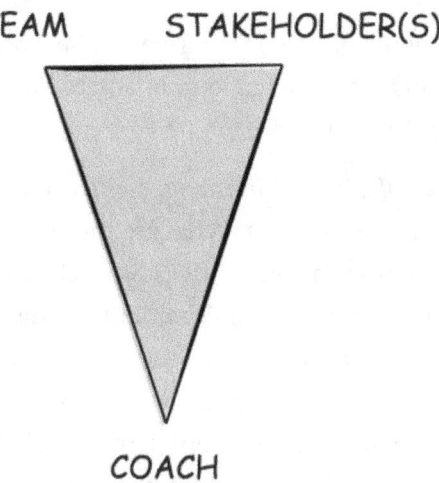

Figure 6-4. Type D contract

Type D contract (Figure 6-4): The sponsor and team align closely, effectively excluding or undermining the coach. In practice, this might look like a team and their manager both being skeptical of coaching—they privately agree that "this coaching thing is just a formality, we don't really need it"—so they may go through the motions, telling the coach what they want to hear but not truly engaging (sharing a sort of polite Persecutor stance toward the coach, who is kept at psychological distance as a Victim outsider). Alternatively, the team and sponsor might simply ignore the coach's input, colluding to maintain the status quo while appearing compliant on the surface. Another scenario Micholt describes is the coach stepping too far into a Rescuer role for both team and sponsor, effectively doing too much for them, which paradoxically invites them to adopt a

CHAPTER 6 CLEARING THE ROADBLOCKS: PSYCHOLOGICAL DISTANCE, HIDDEN CONTRACTS

passive or even resentful stance (Victim position) against the coach. A real-world example: a coach writes all the retrospective notes and action items themselves (Rescuer), the team and manager happily let them do it (Victims not taking responsibility), and later, if things don't improve, they collectively shrug, "well, the coach's plan didn't work" (making the coach the fall guy).

The lesson for team coaches is to strive for the conditions of a Type A contract from the outset of an engagement and to be vigilant for signs of sliding into B, C, or D patterns:

- *At the start of a coaching engagement, explicitly clarify the three-way agreement:* What are the coaching goals from the sponsor's perspective? From the team's perspective? How will confidentiality be handled— what stays in the team versus what gets reported out? (For instance, many coaches agree with teams that individual comments in a retro won't be shared with management verbatim, but perhaps general themes or progress might be.) How will success be defined and by whom? By ensuring these are discussed openly, you establish "a healthy understanding and respect between all three role players."

- *Maintain appropriate boundaries:* The coach should be friendly with everyone but not buddies to the point of losing professional objectivity. For example, if a coach finds the team venting about management frequently, the coach empathizes but also challenges or reframes toward solutions, rather than joining the dog-pile. Conversely, suppose a sponsor tries to use the coach as a confidant about team problems behind the team's back. In that case, the coach can encourage

CHAPTER 6   CLEARING THE ROADBLOCKS: PSYCHOLOGICAL DISTANCE, HIDDEN CONTRACTS

more transparency: *"These are important concerns— let's consider how we might address them with the team present."* The coach avoids being triangulated by not indulging secret talks or gossip from either side.

- *Keep both the team and sponsor appropriately informed and involved:* Maybe have periodic three-way check-ins (e.g., a monthly meeting where team representatives, coach, and sponsor discuss how things are going in a forward-looking, blame-free way). This prevents any party from feeling alienated. If, for instance, the organization's priorities change, the sponsor and team together update the coaching focus rather than the coach hearing only from the boss and arbitrarily shifting course on the team.

- *The coach must be aware of their own biases:* It's natural to sympathize with a team struggling under a harsh bureaucracy or to align with an engaging leader's perspective. However, we serve the system best by remaining an honest broker. One practical approach is to have separate access but equal regard. Perhaps you meet the sponsor periodically, one-on-one, to hear their concerns (so they feel heard and not in the dark), *and* you attend team meetings to listen to the team (so they feel supported and not spied on). Then you integrate perspectives. If either side begins to speak ill of the other in a way that feels like an alliance pull ("we're right, they're wrong"), the coach can gently introduce empathy for the absent party's point of view into the conversation, diffusing the collusion. For example, to a team griping about leadership, the coach might say, "It sounds like there's frustration with management decisions. Have we considered what pressures they might be facing? How can we communicate our needs to them?"—thus showing you're not just taking the team's side but also considering the sponsor's perspective, leading the team toward problem-solving rather than us/them thinking.

- *Emphasis on contracting aligns with the International Coach Federation (ICF) and other bodies' competencies around establishing agreements and upholding ethics:* Simply put, *no secrets, no surprises*. If the sponsor tells the coach something that affects the team, ideally, the coach encourages making that transparent (appropriately). If the team tells the coach something critical about the sponsor or organizational strategy, the coach either helps them address it or at least ensures it doesn't just fester as a secret complaint. When everyone knows where everyone stands, you approach the ideal of "healthy respect between all players."

In Agile coaching, this is particularly poignant because coaches often occupy an intermediary position—we champion the team's self-organization and well-being. Yet, we also serve as agents of the organization's desired change. If we lean too far in either direction, we lose effectiveness. For instance, a coach who merely becomes the team's mate and defends them against any outside feedback might unwittingly hinder the team's growth or prevent them from recognizing broader business needs (Type B trap). Conversely, a coach who solely advocates management's agenda and benchmarks to the team will be perceived as an enforcer, not a helper (Type C trap). And of course, if both the team and the organization dismiss the coach (Type D), nothing gets done. Thus, *balance and transparency* are the name of the game.

CHAPTER 6   CLEARING THE ROADBLOCKS: PSYCHOLOGICAL DISTANCE, HIDDEN CONTRACTS

Diagnose Psychological Distance

How do we know if one of these hidden distance problems is happening? In Agile coaching, we need to be part detective. Here are some ways to diagnose or sense psychological distance issues in your team coaching engagements:

> *Listen for "us vs. them" language:* Pay attention to how the team talks about the sponsor (and vice versa). If you hear things like *"They (management) don't understand us"* from the team, or *"This team just isn't getting it"* from the sponsor, alarm bells should ring. It suggests a divide. For instance, a Scrum master once confided, "Upper management just wants to micromanage us," and later that week the CIO told me, "These teams are so resistant to change." Clearly, each side saw the other as the problem—a sign that psychological distance was growing. When people start grouping themselves as "we" and others as "they," it indicates alliances are forming and possible hidden contracts.
>
> *Notice who talks to whom (and who doesn't):* In meetings that involve all three parties (team, sponsor, coach), observe the interactions. Is one party unusually quiet or detached? Maybe the manager avoids direct conversation with team members and only speaks to you as the coach. Or the team will address all remarks to you and not to their manager. That pattern can reveal who is closer to whom. For example, if the team only looks at the coach for answers in a meeting, they might see the coach as their safe ally and the manager as an

outsider. Or if the sponsor talks *about* the team to you instead of *to* the team, they might be distancing themselves. Silence, side-eye glances, and who people direct their comments to are clues about underlying distance.

Check alignment of expectations (explicitly): This serves as a proactive diagnostic tool. Periodically, ask each party, separately and together, *"What does success look like to you in this coaching engagement right now?"* or *"Are your expectations being met?"* If the answers diverge significantly, you've identified a hidden contract issue. For example, I did this check-in midway through a coaching engagement: The product director (sponsor) said, "Success means the team doubles their output next quarter." The team said, "Success means we finally get clarity from leadership and reduce churn." Wow—mismatch! Both thought the other was on the same page, but clearly they weren't. This kind of gap indicates psychological distance: They're not seeing things from a shared perspective. Misaligned expectations are a sure sign of an underlying distance or lack of true agreement.

Observe emotional cues and body language: As coaches, we're often highly attuned to team dynamics; extend that to the trio dynamic. Does the team get tense when the sponsor joins a meeting? Do people exchange knowing looks that exclude others? Perhaps the sponsor folds their arms whenever the team raises certain topics. These subtle cues can indicate discomfort or distrust. For instance, I noticed in one engagement that whenever we discussed Agile metrics, the engineering manager (sponsor) would sit back and smirk while the team lead's face fell—it turned out the manager and coach (me) had set some metrics targets offline, and the team lead felt blindsided and shut out. Those reactions signalled the issue *before* it was verbally acknowledged. If something feels "off" emotionally in the room, don't ignore it. It might be the hint of a hidden contract problem.

Gauge your own feelings and biases: This one is a bit introspective. Check in with yourself: *How do I feel toward the team and sponsor?* Coaches are human—we might click better with one side. If you find yourself sympathizing *a lot* with the team's complaints and dreading your update meeting with the sponsor, that's a sign you might be getting psychologically closer to the team and distanced from the sponsor. Or if you catch yourself thinking, "This team just doesn't get it, but at least I have the sponsor's backing," you might be overly aligned with the sponsor. Our internal bias can mirror the distance forming. Use yourself as an instrument: If you feel caught in the middle or pulled to one side, it's time to examine the dynamics more objectively.

Watch for information flow issues: Who tells whom what, and when? If you discover that the team made a decision but "didn't tell the boss yet" and they only confide it in you, that's a sign. Or if the sponsor has given new strategic direction but only told you and expects you to "handle the team," that's another sign. Ideally, important information should flow openly to all parties (remember transparency!). When info gets siloed, with the coach as a go-between, it indicates someone is out of the loop by design. That often points to an underlying trust issue or alliance (e.g., the team trusts the coach to tell the sponsor, or the sponsor trusts the coach to sell it to the team, but not direct trust between the team and the sponsor).

In essence, diagnosing psychological distance is about being alert to misalignments in words, attitudes, and overall vibe. Agile coaches often develop a sixth sense for team morale; extend that to the trio. Ask yourself: *Does everyone feel equally heard and valued right now?* If the answer is "hmm, maybe not," then you likely have a distance issue.

Micholt's framework also addresses psychological distance in a literal sense: how emotionally close each pair in the triangle is. If two are too close, the third becomes distant. The coach should therefore maintain the right distance, creating rapport and trust with both the team and the sponsor while also keeping enough professional distance to remain impartial. Think of it as balancing empathy and accountability. We empathize with the team's struggles and the sponsor's pressures alike, and we hold both accountable for their commitments (the team to growth, the sponsor to providing support and conditions for growth).

Coaches might practically leverage these ideas by conducting an initial contracting workshop. For instance, some team coaches hold a "kick-off" where the sponsoring leader, the team, and the coach discuss what coaching will look like. They might draw the triangle to discuss avoiding collusion and ensuring open three-way communication. The visual—a triangle with equal sides versus a skewed triangle—can be a powerful metaphor to show everyone: "We want *equilateral* here—equal, transparent relationships."

CHAPTER 6   CLEARING THE ROADBLOCKS: PSYCHOLOGICAL DISTANCE, HIDDEN CONTRACTS

Intervening Based on Psychological Distance

Once you've identified an imbalance—maybe the team and coach are tight and the sponsor's drifting, or another pattern. Table 6-1 outlines four common contract types, the red flags to watch for, and the interventions a coach can use to restore healthy dynamics.

Table 6-1. Rebalancing the Contracting Triangle

Contract Type	Description	Red Flags	Coach's Interventions
Type A	Balanced	Healthy dynamics	Nurture trust
Type B	Coach-Team too close	Blaming sponsor, gossip, "us vs. them" language	Re-establish three-way agreement, facilitate open dialogue
Type C	Coach-Sponsor too close	Coach seen as "spy," team feels victimized	Refocus on team's voice, transparency
Type D	Sponsor-Team too close	Coach excluded, token presence	Build credibility, clarify coach role

How do we bring things back into alignment? Intervening in these situations is a delicate but crucial part of our role. Here are some strategies to close the psychological distance gap:

> *Re-contract and reaffirm together:* When you sense a disconnect, it's time to get everyone back to the table (literally or figuratively). I often call for a *reset meeting* with the team and sponsor (and me as coach) to openly revisit our working agreement. This isn't a sign of failure; it's normal and healthy.

I might say, *"It feels like our initial goals might need updating. Can we all discuss what each of us needs and expects now?"* Then facilitate an honest conversation. Make sure each party voices their perspective. For example, the sponsor might say, "I realized I haven't been hearing much about progress and that worries me," and the team might say, "We were unclear on what you wanted to hear, so we assumed no news was good news." By addressing these concerns, you can adjust the explicit contract—maybe agree on a more frequent update cadence—or clarify how decisions will be made going forward. Think of it as a mini retrospective on the coaching relationship itself, embracing that principle of *inspect and adapt*. Remember, contracting is continuous, so revisiting it is not only okay, it's necessary.

Increase transparency across the board: This is huge. Shine light on everything (within reason) to ensure no one feels kept in the dark. If you've been having deep discussions with the team, find ways to summarize and share relevant insights with the sponsor with the team's consent. Likewise, if the sponsor gives you strategic input or pressures, encourage them to share it directly with the team, or do it on their behalf in an open forum. For example, instead of the sponsor quietly telling you "velocity must improve," have them join the next retrospective to express their concerns and hear the team's perspective. Transparency builds trust. It might be uncomfortable initially—people aren't used to exposing issues—but it prevents the poisonous triads of gossip and assumption. In practical terms, maybe start a shared "Coaching Kanban" board visible to all, showing what the coach is working on with the team, progress, impediments, etc. When everyone can *see* what's happening, there's less room for imagination to fill the gaps with worst-case scenarios.

Foster direct communication (coach as facilitator, not messenger): Often, when psychological distance grows, the coach ends up being a go-between messenger; don't get stuck permanently in that role. Instead, coach the parties to talk to each other more. For instance, if the team has an issue with how product priorities are being handed down, rather than carrying that complaint to the sponsor yourself, facilitate a session where the team can voice this to the sponsor constructively. You might prepare the team on framing their concerns objectively and prepare the sponsor to receive feedback openly. Then bring them together: maybe a focused workshop or a casual coffee chat, depending on the severity. The idea is to rebuild the bridge between the two sides. As a coach, I sometimes literally say in meetings, *"I notice we're discussing concerns about management decisions here—have we had this conversation with the manager yet? If not, let's do that. I can help set it up."* By prompting direct dialogue, you reduce the reliance on the coach as the only link. Over time, the team and sponsor start seeing each other as partners rather than adversaries. This closes the psychological gap because people tend to distrust *imagined* intentions less when they actually talk face-to-face.

Align on shared goals and values: One powerful way to break an us-vs.-them dynamic is to remind everyone of the common purpose. In Agile, we all ultimately want to deliver value, improve the product, satisfy customers, and create a sustainable pace; these are shared interests. I often bring the conversation back to *"What do we all want to achieve?"* For example, the sponsor might want faster delivery, but the team wants a sane workload—the shared goal there is *improving workflow efficiency without burning people out.* If I articulate that mutual goal, both sides nod. Now we're on the same team again, solving a problem together, rather than viewing each other as the problem. Collaboration is easier when we see we're aligned in purpose. You can even create a simple *joint vision statement* for the coaching engagement: "We (sponsor, team, coach) commit to working together so that this team becomes high-performing and happy, delivering great value." Corny as it sounds, having that visible and discussed can reframe the relationship positively.

Acknowledge and address feelings (the psychological level): When distance has formed, there are often lingering feelings of frustration, fear, or neglect in the air. Invite those feelings into the conversation respectfully. This can be as simple as the coach naming the elephant: *"It seems there might be*

CHAPTER 6   CLEARING THE ROADBLOCKS: PSYCHOLOGICAL DISTANCE, HIDDEN CONTRACTS

some frustration on the team's side about how decisions are made, and maybe some concern on the sponsor's side about hitting targets. Can we talk about those worries?" Encouraging each party to share *how they feel*—not just what they think—can be transformative. It humanizes the stakeholders to one another. A manager hearing "We felt unheard when the deadline changed without our input" from the team can be eye-opening. Likewise, the team hearing "I felt I was failing as a leader when our last project slipped" from the manager creates empathy. This leverages that Agile value of openness and respect. We create a safe space (psychological safety) for each party to voice concerns without blame. As those feelings emerge, misunderstandings often clear up. It's much harder to dislike or distrust someone when you've heard their genuine concerns and emotions.

Maintain an impartial stance (avoid taking sides): Throughout all of this, guard your neutrality as the coach. This doesn't mean being distant or cold; it means being equally supportive of both the team and the sponsor. You're an ally to *the relationship*, not to one side against the other. In practice, this might mean if the team starts venting to you about the sponsor, you listen empathically but also gently challenge any assumptions: *"I hear you're frustrated. Have we checked with [sponsor] why that decision was made? Maybe there's info we don't have."* And if a sponsor complains about the team, you might respond, *"I get that you're under pressure for results.*

Let's consider how we can share that context with the team and enlist their ideas to improve things." You become a model of a respectful, balanced perspective. This way, neither side sees you as the opponent or as completely "on the other side." Instead, you're the bridge or glue holding the triangle together. This role modelling also teaches them to approach each other with more empathy. Remember, as coaches, we often lead by example, demonstrating transparency, collaboration, and *courage* to address tough issues head-on.

Make it a continuous process: We fixed it once—great! End of story? Not quite. We should continue to monitor and adjust the relationships regularly. Build in checkpoints, perhaps as an agenda item in your regular sponsor check-in, like, "How are we all working together?" or in team retrospectives, "How is our engagement with leadership going?" In Agile teams, we don't assume that the initial plan will hold forever—we adapt. Similarly, don't assume the initial contracting (or a one-time fix) will last; keep updating the working agreements. Continuous improvement applies to the coaching relationship too. In fact, explicitly mention this: *"Let's periodically do a quick retro on our collaboration—what's going well among coach–team–sponsor, and what could be better?"* This normalizes the idea that our contract is dynamic. By doing this, if a new psychological distance starts creeping in (for instance, if there's a reorg and a new sponsor enters the picture), you catch it early and adjust.

CHAPTER 6   CLEARING THE ROADBLOCKS: PSYCHOLOGICAL DISTANCE, HIDDEN CONTRACTS

The Five Questions Tool

One of the practical tools I use to create balanced perspectives is a set of Five Questions from Christine Thornton that help structure thinking when contracting and preparing for team coaching work. These questions prompt a coach to consider critical aspects of the engagement systemically and relationally before diving in. The five core questions are as follows:

1. **Who wants the team to be worked with?** Identify the commissioning client or sponsor. Who is requesting or funding the coaching for this team, and what is their relationship with the team? Will that person (e.g., a manager or executive) be directly involved in the coaching or remain outside of it? Additionally, who is on the team and will attend the coaching sessions? Understanding who is in or out of the group and who genuinely wants the change helps clarify the power dynamics and expectations at play from the outset.

2. **What is the purpose of the work with the team?** Clarify the explicit goals and scope of the coaching engagement. What outcome does the sponsor expect, and what does the team itself hope to achieve? It's important to explore how this purpose was determined—was it imposed from the top down due to a problem, or co-created with the team? Moreover, inquire about what the team members do NOT want from the coaching. Often, teams have unspoken fears (e.g., "this isn't a therapy session" or "don't single anyone out"); bringing those to light

helps ensure the coaching contract addresses both hopes and anxieties. Having a clear, shared purpose (and boundaries regarding what coaching is or isn't) will align everyone involved.

3. **What is the organizational context of the team?**
Take a step back and consider the *bigger system around the team*. What is happening in the organization that forms the backdrop for this team's situation? For example, are there major changes (restructures, new strategies, market pressures) or cultural factors influencing the team? Paying attention to *context and multiple perspectives* is key to understanding a team system. A team is nested in a department, which is nested in an organization, within a broader society; *all these layers* can affect the team's dynamics. By mapping the context, the coach can better understand external influences on the team's behavior and tailor the coaching accordingly.

4. **Who or what am I invited to be to this team?**
Reflect on the role the team or sponsor might unconsciously push onto the coach. The coach is not a neutral actor; as soon as you enter the system, the team may relate to you in ways that reflect their internal dynamics. Ask: "What feelings do I have when I'm with this team, and what roles do I sense I'm being given?" Perhaps the team treats the coach as a rescuer, an authority figure, or an outsider to rebel against. These feelings are clues to underlying relationship dynamics. By noticing your own impulses (e.g., to "fix" things or to referee

arguments), you can gain insight into how the team might be projecting needs or fears onto the coach. This self-reflective question encourages coaches to use their own reactions as data about the group and respond thoughtfully rather than reactively.

5. **What are the structural considerations and boundaries?** Consider the practical setup and boundaries for the coaching work. This includes seemingly simple logistics that carry psychological weight: How often and for how long will the team meet with the coach? Will sessions be on-site or off-site? Who must attend, and is attendance voluntary or mandated? Are discussions confidential within the team, and what (if anything) will be reported back to the sponsor? These structural elements are part of what group analysis calls dynamic administration—they create a safe container for the team's work. Defining and agreeing on these boundaries up front prevents misunderstandings and builds a stable platform so the team feels secure to engage in coaching.

By exploring *who, why, what, context, roles,* and *how* upfront, an Agile coach can form a clearer contract with both the sponsor and the team. It ensures that the coaching intervention is anchored in the real purpose and context, that all stakeholders' roles are understood, and that the coach remains aware of relational dynamics from the outset. This preparation prevents common pitfalls, such as unseen agendas or mismatched expectations, that can derail team coaching.

Leveraging the concept of psychological distance involves guarding against hidden agendas within the coaching relationship. We've spent much of this chapter discussing hidden dynamics within the team, but it's equally important to consider the hidden dynamics *surrounding* the team, specifically among the team itself, those who have a stake in the team (managers, HR, etc.), and the coach. If those relationships go awry, even a skilled coach can find their efforts undermined. By following the guidance—clear expectations, no collusion, ethical contracting—a coach establishes a stable trust platform. From this foundation, the coach and the team can address the team's internal hidden challenges more effectively.

Conclusion

Psychological distance must be managed so that the coach acts as a bridge rather than a wedge in the system. A well-managed triangular contract ensures the coach's interventions gain credibility and that all parties feel supported, not threatened, by the coaching process. This alignment of coach, team, and sponsor becomes a powerful enabler for positive change, as it eliminates the meta-level dysfunctions that could otherwise sabotage the coaching efforts.

By naming these patterns—whether it is the coach over-identifying with the team, aligning too closely with a sponsor, or being left out altogether—we create the possibility of choice. A balanced "Type A" contract is not an accident but the result of deliberate effort: setting clear boundaries, honoring confidentiality, and continually revisiting agreements as the coaching journey evolves.

For Agile team coaches, the task is to walk the fine line of being close enough to build rapport yet distant enough to maintain objectivity. This requires vigilance, ethical grounding, and courage to challenge when the triangle begins to tilt. When we hold this balance, we help teams take ownership of their growth rather than slipping into dependency or blame.

Ultimately, clearing the roadblocks of psychological distance and hidden contracts frees the coaching relationship to focus on what matters most: enabling the team to step into self-organization with clarity, trust,

CHAPTER 6   CLEARING THE ROADBLOCKS: PSYCHOLOGICAL DISTANCE, HIDDEN CONTRACTS

and confidence. The next chapter will build on this by exploring the subtle forces of power and hidden dynamics that also shape how teams truly function beneath the surface.

Reflection Moment

Review each "stakeholder triangle" in turn, reflecting on the following:

1. How close do you feel to the client compared to the other stakeholders?
2. How might these levels of closeness show in your behavior?
3. How close do you think the team feels toward you compared to the other stakeholders?
4. What about the team's behavior might be leading you to this interpretation?
5. What's your speculation on how the third party perceives the relationship between you and the team?
6. What might the team members have said or done to spark your speculation?
7. What actions, if any, do you need to take to achieve balanced psychological distances?
8. What could you encourage the team to consider so as to prevent any imbalance?

CHAPTER 7

Power Plays and Hidden Dynamics Revealed

Experienced Agile team coaches understand that a team's behavior typically has two layers: the visible layer of planned tasks, meetings, and processes, and a hidden layer of unspoken dynamics. As a researcher of group dynamics, Christina Thornton says the latter is the "secret life" of the team. These hidden dynamics encompass the underlying relationships, anxieties, power plays, and unwritten rules that shape how the team operates daily. In a self-organizing Agile team, such covert factors can significantly affect performance and morale. For instance, a team might outwardly agree on decisions while secretly harboring unresolved conflicts or fears. These issues can undermine genuine collaboration and continuous improvement if they go unaddressed. This chapter delves into how to recognize and engage with these hidden dynamics in an Agile team coaching context. We will draw on established theories from systems psychodynamics and Gestalt coaching (see Appendices B and C) to illuminate how a coach can intervene effectively. By enhancing our understanding of the *unseen* forces at play—from unconscious team anxieties to unspoken expectations—Agile coaches, Scrum masters, and team leaders can better facilitate healthy, transparent team environments where self-organization thrives. In the following sections, we examine what constitutes a team's "secret life," identify specific hidden challenges (with techniques to address them), discuss psychological games, and conclude with practical guidance on managing these advanced aspects of team coaching.

Understanding the "Secret Life" and the Underlying Dynamics of Teams

Every team has an internal emotional landscape and set of unwritten norms—a "secret life"—that runs parallel to its official activities. While a team might be discussing sprint backlogs and release plans on the surface, unspoken tensions, alliances, fears, or resentments may be influencing those conversations. Research on group dynamics reveals that various hidden factors can influence team interactions, including unconscious biases, informal role and power dynamics, hidden agendas, covert alliances, emotional contagion, and even groupthink. These forces impact how team members communicate and make decisions, ultimately affecting performance and collaboration. In essence, with any team, there are really two teams present: the task-focused team that operates in reality and an implicit team engaged in a more "fantasy" agenda driven by unconscious motives. Renowned group theorist Wilfred Bion noted this phenomenon decades ago, observing that, besides the explicit work group, an unconscious group mentality exists, acting out hidden assumptions and emotions.

One common aspect of a team's secret life is the presence of undiscussables—topics or feelings everyone senses but nobody openly acknowledges. For instance, a team might have a "knowing" that a certain senior member's behavior is problematic or that the deadline set by management is unrealistic, yet these issues are never explicitly raised. When teams feel anxiety or threat (e.g., fear of conflict or reprisal), they often develop defensive routines to avoid confronting the underlying issues. Research in organizational behavior has found that teams instinctively develop defensive routines to cope with anxiety, such as feeling ignored or undervalued; these routines allow the team to avoid naming the real issues, but at the cost of blocking learning and adaptation. In other words, silence and avoidance become coping mechanisms; for example, team members might stay "professionally polite" in meetings, never challenging flawed decisions, because it feels unsafe to speak up. Over time, such patterns become part of "the way we do things," impeding honest dialogue and continuous improvement. Chris Argyris famously described how organizations and teams maintain organizational defensive routines that make certain conversations off-limits, creating a culture where people would rather avoid embarrassment or conflict than face the truth. In Agile contexts, which thrive on transparency and inspection/adaptation, these hidden routines are especially counterproductive since they directly undermine the inspect-and-adapt cycle.

Psychological safety is a critical prerequisite to bringing the team's secret life into view. Harvard professor Amy Edmondson defines psychological safety as *"a shared belief that the team is safe for interpersonal risk taking,"* meaning team members feel confident they won't be punished or humiliated for speaking up with ideas, questions, or concerns. People are comfortable being candid about problems or mistakes in a psychologically safe environment. By contrast, low psychological safety creates a culture of silence—a "Cassandra culture" where speaking up is belittled and warnings go unheeded. If team members fear retribution or ridicule, they hide real feelings and information, and the team's secret life will become more pronounced (and more toxic). Thus, psychological safety is the foundation that allows hidden dynamics to surface and be addressed. Many studies have shown that teams with higher psychological safety exhibit better decision-making, learning, and performance outcomes, largely because they can discuss the *undiscussables* and address issues before they escalate.

So what exactly might make up the "secret life" of an Agile team? It can take many forms (see Table 7-1):

- *Hidden agendas:* Personal motives or goals that individuals pursue without openly stating them. For example, a team member might quietly push for a particular technical design not because it's best for the product, but because it boosts their own status or workload comfort. Hidden agendas are essentially personal goals not explicitly shared with the group, yet they can influence behavior and decisions. These unspoken motives often lead to misalignment and mistrust if discovered.

- *Unspoken expectations and norms:* Team members may have assumptions about "how we should work together" that are never articulated. For instance, perhaps everyone expects the product owner to always make decisions, so they don't step up—but this was never agreed upon. Such unspoken expectations often result in frustration or "premeditated resentment" when others fail to meet them. A classic example is one team member expecting peers to work late hours because they do so, but never communicating this, eventually breeding quiet resentment. The cure is to make implicit expectations explicit through open conversation and working agreements.

- *Power dynamics and status differences:* Even in "flat" Agile teams, differences in experience, expertise, or personality can create power imbalances. Perhaps one senior developer's opinions carry disproportionate weight (the *hidden leader* dynamic), or team members defer to a loud, assertive colleague even when they disagree. Alternatively, if a manager or architect attends a Scrum event, the team might unconsciously relinquish its self-organizing stance and look to the authority for direction. These informal power plays can inhibit full participation; for example, quieter members might self-censor in the presence of a dominant figure. Unaddressed power dynamics often perpetuate inequality in contribution and prevent the best ideas from coming forward. Coaches need to be attuned to who speaks most, who speaks least, and whose opinions seem to carry unofficial authority.

- *Alliances and cliques:* Subgroups or coalitions can form within a team, sometimes along departmental lines (e.g., developers vs. testers), or personal friendships. These alliances might coordinate outside of official meetings or consistently back each other up in discussions. Hidden alliances can lead to "us vs. them" fractures within the team, even if everyone pretends unity. For example, developers and QA engineers might privately blame each other for defects rather than collaboratively solving problems, all the while keeping an appearance of politeness in meetings. Recognizing cliques and gently bringing the whole team into dialogue can help break down these silos.

- *Emotional undercurrents:* Teams, like individuals, have emotions. There may be fear, insecurity, anger, or cynicism beneath the professional facade. Perhaps the team is anxious about an upcoming re-org, or there's lingering anger because a past sprint failure was handled poorly by management. These emotions might manifest indirectly—sarcasm, unusually high stress over minor issues, or a general lack of enthusiasm. Emotional contagion is real: If one or two members are chronically frustrated, that mood can quietly spread through the team. Coaches often sense *"something in the air"*—a tension or malaise—even if no one states it. Surfacing and validating these feelings (for instance, in a retrospective, asking how people honestly felt during the sprint) can prevent them from poisoning morale.

- *Groupthink and conformity:* Sometimes the hidden dynamic is that too much agreement is happening. A team might present an illusion of consensus because dissent feels unsafe or socially unwelcome. If in meetings everyone quickly nods along to proposals—especially in the presence of a strong-willed member or a supervisor—the real opinions stay underground. Groupthink is dangerous because it masks real risks and suppresses innovation. The hidden life of a groupthink team may include private grumbling in the hallways after the meeting ("I actually thought that plan was terrible, but I didn't want to be the one to say it."). A coach needs to detect when consensus is possibly artificial and help the team establish norms that reward constructive debate and devil's advocacy.

Table 7-1. Diagnostics of Hidden Dynamics

Hidden Dynamic	What It Is	Typical Symptoms	Impact on Team
Hidden agendas	Personal goals not explicitly shared with the group	A push for certain decisions or designs that serve self-interest	Misalignment, reduced trust, covert resistance
Unspoken expectations & norms	Implicit assumptions about how team members should behave	Frustration over unmet assumptions, quiet resentment, uneven participation	Breakdown in collaboration, growing tension
Power dynamics & status differences	Informal influence based on seniority, personality, or role	Over-deference to certain members, self-censorship, "hidden leader" patterns	Unequal participation, loss of team self-management
Alliances & cliques	Informal subgroups that act in coordinated ways outside of full team visibility	Repeated agreement among some members, "us vs. them" mentality, side conversations	Fractured collaboration, loss of psychological safety, blame culture
Emotional undercurrents	Unspoken but felt emotions like fear, anger, or anxiety	Tension in the air, sarcasm, disengagement, overreaction to small issues	Morale degradation, burnout, miscommunication

(*continued*)

Table 7-1. (*continued*)

Hidden Dynamic	What It Is	Typical Symptoms	Impact on Team
Groupthink & conformity	Apparent consensus masking disagreement	Rapid agreement, lack of dissent, backchannel complaining after meetings	Suppressed innovation, risk blindness, passive resistance

These examples show how the visible life of the team (what's said and done openly) can differ from the hidden life (what people truly think or feel). Addressing this gap is crucial. Team coaches need to become skilled at spotting the underlying dynamics. This begins with sharp observation. As an external facilitator or Scrum master, you're well placed to notice patterns that insiders might overlook. For example, you might see that the same two people always speak first in stand-ups or retrospectives, or that when a certain topic comes up (like the involvement of a difficult stakeholder), the room falls silent and people avert their gaze. These are signs of deeper issues. In fact, a trained outsider can gather a great deal of data by observing who talks and how often, who interrupts whom, whom people look at when speaking, who or what gets blamed when things go awry, what topics are never brought up, who stays silent, and whose ideas are ignored. These observational clues, combined with expert questioning, can help link surface symptoms to the underlying causes within the team's psyche.

Identifying and Addressing Specific Hidden Challenges

It's important to remember that these challenges often overlap or interact; for example, a hidden power imbalance can lead to unspoken expectations and stifled voices, which in turn erode psychological safety. The coach must often deal with a cluster of issues together. The good news is that by tackling one, you often alleviate others.

Table 7-2 matches common hidden dynamics with coaching interventions you can bring into the room.

Table 7-2. How to Address Hidden Dynamics

Hidden Dynamic	Intervention Techniques
Power imbalances & authority dynamics	Use structured rounds, establish working agreements, mentor influential members privately
Hidden agendas & unspoken goals	Create space to surface personal goals, use one-on-one inquiry, align personal and team objectives
Undiscussable conflicts & tensions	Facilitate "Elephants in the Room," use humble inquiry, establish ground rules for feedback
Role ambiguity & boundary issues	Clarify roles using a matrix of responsibilities, revisit Scrum roles, run explicit contracting sessions
Groupthink & conformity	Introduce devil's advocate role, validate dissent, normalize differing opinions

None of these interventions are about "fixing" the team from the outside. Instead, they create conditions for the team to see its own dynamics more clearly and to take ownership of shifting them. By making the invisible visible, you enable the group to experiment with new ways of working that strengthen trust, balance power, and encourage fuller participation. Over time, this not only resolves immediate tensions but also deepens the team's capacity to self-organize—so they can face future challenges with greater resilience and autonomy.

Hidden Challenge 1: Power Imbalances and Authority Dynamics

What it is: An imbalance of power or authority in a supposedly self-organizing team. This could be formal (e.g., a manager or tech lead in the team holds positional power) or informal (e.g., a dominant personality or expert whom everyone defers to). Power dynamics are not always bad—expertise and leadership can be positive—but when unexamined, they create hidden hierarchies that contradict the team's intended autonomy. Team members might silently disagree with the "powerful" person but won't voice it, or they rely on the authority figure to make decisions, undermining self-organization.

Signs: Meetings are consistently steered by one or two voices; certain members rarely speak or seem hesitant when they do. The team may direct most comments to one specific person (watch who people look at when talking—if everyone's eyes flick to the lead developer whenever a technical question is raised, that's an indicator of deferred authority). Decisions outside of official team agreements; for instance, a decision gets made in a smaller meeting or by an individual offline and the team just rubber-stamps it. You might also notice subtle cues like body language of deference (nodding, little challenge) toward a particular person. In a retrospective, if suggestions always come from the same person and are accepted without question, groupthink under power pressure could be at play.

Why it's hidden: Often, people are uncomfortable openly acknowledging power differences, especially in Agile teams that philosophically value equality and collective ownership. So the dynamic goes underground. The influential person might not even realize others

CHAPTER 7   POWER PLAYS AND HIDDEN DYNAMICS REVEALED

are deferring to them (they might think silence equals agreement). The less powerful individuals might fear being labelled "not a team player" if they speak up, or they simply assume "that's just how it is here."

How to address: The coach can use facilitation techniques to redistribute power gradually. For example, use rounds or structured dialogue to ensure everyone contributes in discussions, not just the loudest person. Privately, a coach might gently mentor the influential person, making them aware of their impact ("I've noticed others rarely disagree with your ideas. How do you feel about that? Perhaps we can invite more debate to get the best outcomes."). In a team setting, introduce explicit working agreements about decision making; e.g., "We agree to hear at least two different options before we decide" or even rotate certain responsibilities to break habitual roles. Establishing open dialogue is crucial: talk *about* the team's decision-making process in a retro. The coach might ask, *"Do we feel everyone's voice is being heard equally? What might be influencing that?"*—an invitation for the team to acknowledge any imbalance. Often, just surfacing it ("I sometimes hold back because I assume Alice as tech lead has final say . . .") can prompt a corrective action, like Alice encouraging more input or the team clarifying that final decisions are group decisions unless otherwise decided. If a manager is part of the team (like a line manager sitting in a Scrum team), it may be necessary to have an explicit contracting, perhaps agreeing that in certain Scrum events or team meetings the manager participates as an equal team member or maybe steps back during sprint retrospectives to let open discussion flow. The coach can facilitate a candid conversation between the manager and team about how to handle differences in power; this builds trust that those differences won't be misused. In short, make the implicit power structure explicit. Once people can talk about it, they can consciously choose how to manage it (for instance, a senior member can agree to hold back initially to let others offer ideas first). Over time, these interventions should result in more balanced participation, where leadership is situational and not just defaulting to one person.

CHAPTER 7   POWER PLAYS AND HIDDEN DYNAMICS REVEALED

Hidden Challenge 2: Hidden Agendas and Unspoken Goals

What it is: When individuals or subgroups have personal objectives that diverge from the stated team goals, and they pursue these quietly. In an Agile setting, a classic example might be a team member who wants to learn a new technology (personal goal) so they keep pushing tasks or designs in that direction even if it's not agreed on by the team. Or a product owner who is secretly trying to make a case for hiring more people by demonstrating they can't get enough done, so their hidden agenda is to subtly resist process improvements that would increase velocity, to make the team look understaffed. Hidden agendas are by definition not openly shared, which makes them tricky.

Signs: Misalignment in execution that isn't explained by the official plan. One symptom could be a lot of side conversations or off-track work items that don't obviously tie into sprint goals. You might sense a person is "driving" a particular idea repeatedly without a clear rationale. If confronted gently, they may become defensive or evasive rather than straightforward. Another sign is repeated confusion or misunderstanding; for example, "I thought we agreed on X, but Bob seems to be doing Y." If Bob consistently does Y despite agreements, perhaps Y serves an agenda not fully articulated. Also watch for coalitions: two team members who always vote together or exchange glances; they might have a shared, hidden agenda (e.g., both lobbying for a tool they prefer). A more emotional sign is disproportionate reactions—if someone gets unusually upset when a certain topic is shelved or a decision goes a certain way, it could be because it conflicts with a personal wish they haven't voiced.

Why it's hidden: Individuals may fear that their personal goal will be viewed as selfish or not in alignment with the team or organization's interests, so they keep it under wraps. Sometimes the hidden agenda is subconscious—the person might not even fully realize their strong

CHAPTER 7 POWER PLAYS AND HIDDEN DYNAMICS REVEALED

attachment to an outcome is driven by a personal motive (like status, job security, etc.). In some cases, organizational culture discourages open disagreement with goals handed down, so people comply outwardly but subvert silently to meet their own needs.

How to address: The overarching solution is creating transparency and aligning individual goals with team goals. An Agile coach can help by fostering an environment where people feel safe bringing up personal aspirations or concerns. For instance, during sprint planning or retrospectives, explicitly ask, "Does anyone have any personal goals or constraints related to this work that we should know about?" This normalizes that individuals are allowed to have personal interests, and it's better to surface them. If hidden agendas are suspected, one-on-one coaching conversations can help. Talk to the person privately, expressing curiosity without judgment. "I notice you're very passionate about switching to Framework Z. What's important to you about that?" They might reveal, for example, that they feel it's crucial for their career to gain experience in Framework Z. Once that's known, you can work with them and the team: Maybe the team can accommodate some spike or experiment with Z that also benefits the product, rather than its being pushed in secretly. Clarify team goals and individual expectations in writing. When things are written down (like Definition of Done, success criteria for a project), it's easier to spot when behavior deviates. If misalignment persists, have a frank discussion with the whole team: "It seems we have different ideas of success. Let's revisit our team objectives and ensure we're all genuinely on board." Often, hidden agendas cannot survive in the light of open communication—either the person will voice it, or the group will call it out ("Why are we doing this again? Is there another reason?"). Fostering open communication and transparency is crucial to uncover and address hidden agendas. The coach might facilitate a session solely to air concerns or personal hopes for the project ("unmet needs" discussion). When people see that admitting a personal goal (like wanting to learn a new skill or needing something for their portfolio) won't get them shamed but rather supported or negotiated, they're more likely to put it on the table. From there, the team can find win-win ways to incorporate or at least acknowledge those needs, or the individual might realize they need to let go of some agenda for the greater goal. In cases where the hidden agenda conflicts with the team or organizational mission and cannot be reconciled, the coach might need to involve management; perhaps that individual is not in the right role or there's a deeper issue of trust with leadership that needs addressing. But generally, the earlier and more empathetically you surface differing agendas, the less damage they do.

Hidden Challenge 3: Undiscussable Conflicts and Tensions

What it is: Situations where conflict exists (or did in the past) between team members or between the team and an external entity, but it is swept under the rug. The tension thus continues to influence behavior, but no one is willing to talk about it openly to resolve it. Agile teams often value harmony, which can lead to a false peace where disagreements are suppressed rather than worked through. A typical scenario might be two teammates who clashed on a previous project; now they avoid each other or speak only curtly, and the rest of the team tiptoes around this rift. Or a team has an issue with their product owner's style but only jokes about it in private, never in the retro with the PO present.

Signs: Notice persistent avoidance patterns—certain people rarely interact directly or team up; some topics always get skipped. Meetings often omit genuine issues altogether (for example, every retro sidesteps the core problem everyone is upset about). You might notice nonverbal cues: eye rolls when someone speaks or visible discomfort (fidgeting, sighing) during discussions without voicing objections. Off-meeting gossip can also be a sign, as team members complain about each other or

CHAPTER 7   POWER PLAYS AND HIDDEN DYNAMICS REVEALED

someone else after the meeting, showing they didn't feel safe addressing it openly. Additionally, if minor issues provoke overblown reactions, it may indicate bottled-up unresolved tension. For example, a small scheduling disagreement suddenly escalates into a heated argument, likely reflecting a deeper, long-standing conflict that hasn't been openly addressed.

Why it's hidden: Conflict avoidance is a common team norm, either due to cultural expectations ("we're professionals, we don't argue") or fear of damaging relationships. There may also be a lack of skill in conflict resolution, so people simply prefer not to "go there." In some teams, a previous attempt to discuss a conflict might have gone badly, leaving a kind of scar, so an implicit rule forms like "don't bring that up again." Also, hierarchy can play a role: If a conflict is with someone of a higher status, others may not feel permitted to raise it.

How to address: Psychological safety is the essential ingredient to make conflicts discussable. So the coach should work on ground rules that encourage respectful debate and make it explicit that airing disagreements is healthy. One practical method is to introduce structured conflict discussion techniques. For example, use a retrospective activity like "Elephants in the Room," where you literally ask the team to write down things they feel are not being discussed (anonymously, if necessary) and then collectively discuss them. Or try a liberating structure like "Heard, Seen, Respected" for feuding parties to express what they want each other to know. The key is to create a container in which it feels safe to bring up the tough stuff. The coach often acts as a neutral facilitator or container of the group's tension, staying calm and empathetic even if emotions run high, which reassures the team that conflict won't destroy them. Edgar Schein's concept of humble inquiry can be useful: Ask genuine, open-ended questions to draw out concerns in a non-threatening way. For instance, "I sense there might be some lingering frustration around how the last release went. What's everyone's perspective on it? Let's get all views on the table." By normalizing that differences in perspective are expected, not embarrassing, you chip away at the taboo. If two individuals

215

have a personal rift, it can help to facilitate a focused dialogue between them (with ground rules). Each gets to speak while the other listens and then paraphrases, and vice versa; the coach ensures a fair process and keeps it civil. Sometimes, teams benefit from learning a conflict model (like Nonviolent Communication or Crucial Conversations framework) to give them tools to express themselves constructively. The coach might even do a mini-workshop on giving feedback or expressing concerns using "I" statements. The transformation often happens when one brave person tests the water by bringing up a mild concern and, instead of backlash, they experience acceptance. For example, a team member says in retro, "I was upset that my work got changed without asking me"—and the group simply discusses and addresses that. Everyone learns, "Oh, we can talk about these things!"—and bigger conflicts start to feel safer to tackle. Lastly, it's important to follow up: Once a hidden conflict is surfaced and hopefully resolved, ensure it stays resolved or at least that progress is maintained. A coach might check in during later sessions: "Earlier we talked about communication issues between dev and QA. How are we feeling about that now? Is there anything else we need to clear?" This shows that it's not one-and-done, but an ongoing openness. Over time, this builds a culture where conflict is seen as a pathway to improvement rather than a dreaded minefield. This is vital for Agile teams because if conflict is handled well, it results in better ideas and stronger trust; if handled poorly (or avoided), it undermines collaboration and quality.

Hidden Challenge 4: Role Ambiguity and Boundary Issues

What it is: Unclear roles, responsibilities, or boundaries that lead to confusion and unspoken tension. In Agile teams, we often expect cross-functionality and flexibility, but that can sometimes blur lines too much. For example, if it's not clear who is accountable for final decisions on backlog prioritization (product owner vs. team consensus) or if a Scrum master oscillates between facilitative coach and task manager, team members may have unspoken frustrations about people overstepping or neglecting duties. Hidden role dynamics can include things like someone acting as an unofficial "boss" or people assuming others will handle something when it's actually not assigned (leading to gaps).

Signs: Tasks falling through the cracks or being double-worked. Team members frequently complain about others not doing "their part" (perhaps in side conversations), indicating mismatched expectations of roles. You might see two people consistently clashing or stepping on each other's toes—e.g., a designer and a developer arguing over who has final say on UI decisions—but never formally resolving the ownership. If decisions take a long time or require "approval" outside the team, maybe the boundary of team autonomy isn't clear (e.g., do we need our manager's OK or not?; if unclear, folks will either assume yes or no and conflict). Another sign: a team member doing work outside their area of expertise but not communicating it, possibly out of a sense of duty or assumption, which can later lead to resentment ("I had to do testing *and* my dev work, because no one else took it"). That resentment may stay unspoken.

Why it's hidden: Discussing roles and boundaries can feel awkward, as if one is jostling for power or complaining. Many teams just "muddle through" ambiguities, and people adapt silently or harbour private gripes. In Agile, since we want to be collaborative, individuals might fear that raising a role issue (like "I think this is not my job") will make them seem not agile or territorial. Additionally, early-stage teams may not yet have the psychological safety to negotiate roles openly, so they often live with confusion instead.

How to address: Clarify, clarify, clarify. The coach can facilitate a roles and responsibilities discussion or workshop. One effective method is simply creating a chart of key activities and assigning who leads each. For Scrum teams, revisit the definitions: ensure everyone genuinely understands the intended accountabilities of the product owner, Scrum master, and developers, then discuss how to implement those in practice (since every team is a bit different). If a specific boundary issue causes friction (for instance, between two roles), bring it up neutrally: "I've noticed some confusion about who should approve UI changes. Can we as a team decide how to handle that going forward?" Encourage them to set a policy or principle. For example, "We trust the designer's call unless it impacts architecture, then dev and design decide together." Promote explicit contracting within the team, not just assuming "someone will do X." In sprint planning, if something remains an open question ("Who will speak to the customer about this?"), assign a name to it. If outside roles (like stakeholders or managers) interfere or are ambiguous, the coach might need to facilitate a meeting with those parties to clarify; e.g., "Dear manager, when should the team involve you, and when do they have full authority? Let's agree on that." Many hidden role tensions dissolve simply by making implicit assumptions explicit and negotiating them. The coach should also observe for unofficial roles that people play—like a team member always acting as the mediator in conflicts, or another as the ideas person—and reflect that to the team, which can help distribute those "hats" more evenly to avoid overload on one person. Another concept is "boundary spanning": sometimes teams aren't sure where their responsibility ends and another team's begins. This can cause either conflict or things falling through. An Agile coach might organize an alignment session between two teams or between the team and management to clearly delineate scopes. Overall, when everyone knows what their role is and is not, there's less room for resentment and assumption. And if circumstances require role flexibility (as Agile often does), that's fine, but explicitly agree on how to handle it (e.g., "When QA needs help, developers will pitch in on testing, but they will check in first rather than duplicate efforts."). With clarity, hidden frustrations become voiced expectations. A team that has clearly defined and agreed-upon roles and working arrangements is a team with less confusion and more trust, as people feel their contributions and boundaries are respected.

Those are some of the primary hidden challenges that Agile team coaches may encounter. Each requires slightly different tactics, but common themes emerge: increasing transparency, fostering open communication, building trust and safety, clarifying uncertainties, and addressing emotional undercurrents. By systematically identifying and addressing these issues, the coach helps the team remove impediments not only in their process (the obvious impediments) but also in their human interactions and environment. This paves the way for the team to self-organize and continuously improve, unencumbered by invisible weights.

Psychological Games in Agile Team Coaching

Team coaching engagements can sometimes be derailed by psychological games—repetitive, unconscious interaction patterns defined in Transactional Analysis (TA) theory. These games often involve hidden agendas and role-switching on the Drama Triangle with players unconsciously taking on Victim, Rescuer, or Persecutor roles (see Figure 7-1 below).

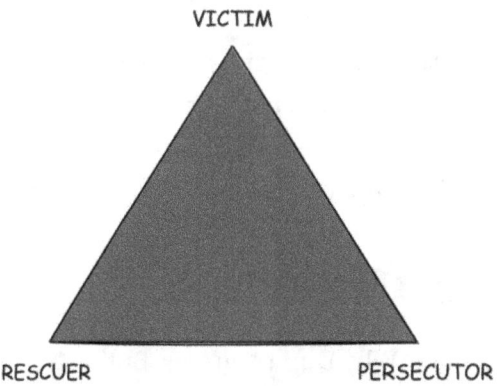

Figure 7-1. Drama Triangle

CHAPTER 7 POWER PLAYS AND HIDDEN DYNAMICS REVEALED

They typically end in frustration or a negative "payoff" (such as feeling vindicated, superior, or victimized) rather than a constructive resolution.

One of the clearest ways to understand how psychological "games" play out in teams is through the Game Formula, first described by Eric Berne. A game is not just casual banter—it's a predictable sequence of interactions that starts innocently but ends with someone feeling frustrated, blamed, or diminished. Figure 7-2 illustrates this pattern step by step, showing how a seemingly harmless exchange escalates into a negative emotional payoff.

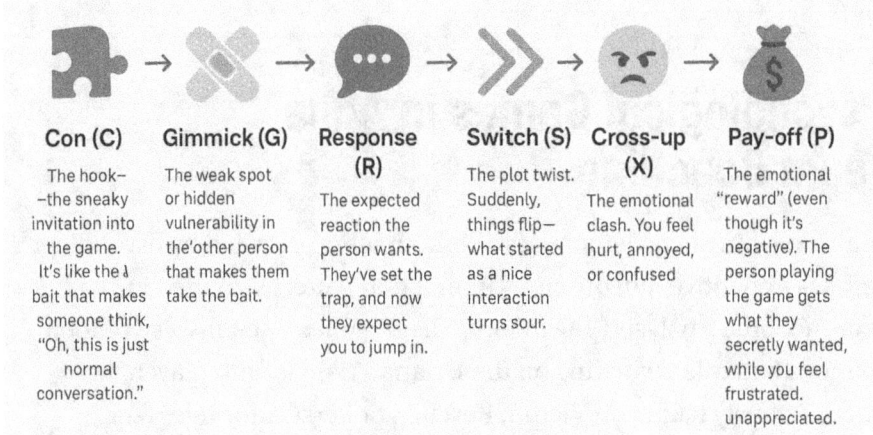

Figure 7-2. The formula of a psychological game

Here, we identify several common TA games in team coaching contexts—between the coach and the team, the team and external stakeholders, and the stakeholders and the coach—and discuss their structure, triggers, roles, impact, and strategies to interrupt them.

"Why Don't You/Yes, But"

Structure of the game: "Why Don't You/Yes, But" (often abbreviated *YDYB*) is a classic TA game in which one person (often in a Victim stance) asks for help with a problem, but reflexively rejects every proposed solution. On the surface, they appear to seek solutions, but in reality their goal is to reinforce the belief that their problem is unsolvable. Every suggestion from the helper is met with a "Yes, but..." followed by reasons why it won't work. The social level of the conversation appears as problem solving, while the psychological level is about maintaining control and validating the person's helplessness or the hopelessness of the situation. The game ends when the frustrated helper runs out of ideas or the seeker finally says, "See, nothing can help me," leaving the helper feeling inadequate and the seeker perversely satisfied that their dilemma is indeed unsolvable.

Common triggers and organizational manifestations: This game is frequently triggered when a team member or team voices ongoing problems (e.g., "We can't meet our targets due to X") and the coach or others jump in with advice. In a team–coach context, the coach (or a well-meaning colleague) suggests a solution, only to hear "Yes, but we already tried that," or "Yes, but that won't work here" each time. It can also occur between a team and external stakeholders; for example, management might propose solutions to a team's challenges, and the team counters every idea with "Yes, but..." excuses, effectively stonewalling change. The common trigger is a habitual complainer (Victim role) and a problem solver (Rescuer role) engaging under stress. Both may actually be avoiding the real underlying issue (such as fear of change or reluctance to take responsibility) by playing out this futile exchange.

Roles and Drama Triangle dynamics: In YDYB, the person saying "Yes, but" positions themselves as the Victim—feeling helpless with an unsolvable problem—and lures someone into the Rescuer role. The Rescuer (coach or stakeholder) spends energy trying to fix the Victim's issue. Eventually, a switch often occurs: the Victim may become a Persecutor, blaming the helper for "useless advice," while the would-be Rescuer feels unappreciated or inadequate, slipping into Victim feelings. For example, a team member complains about their workload; the coach suggests delegating tasks; the team member responds, "Yes, but no one else has the skills," cycling through ideas until finally they snap, "You're not really helping!" leaving the coach confused and the team member feeling validated in their belief that no one can help them.

Impact on team dynamics and coaching outcomes: This game damages trust and productivity. The helper (coach or stakeholder) becomes frustrated and might feel their expertise is being questioned, while the team or individual confirms a victim mentality, convinced their situation is hopeless. In a coaching session, repeated "Yes, but" exchanges hinder real progress; sessions get stuck in a cycle of problem admiration instead of solutions or learning. Team members may bond by collectively dismissing proposed changes ("yes, but that won't work in our industry"), which boosts resistance to new ideas and stalls the coaching process. It also risks placing the coach in a useless advisory role (Parent–Child dynamic) rather than a collaborative Adult–Adult relationship.

Strategies for spotting and disrupting the game: Coaches should be attentive to the classic pattern of serial "Yes, but . . ." responses—a strong sign that a game is happening. To break it, stop giving direct advice once you see the loop. Instead, adopt an Adult stance: Ask open-ended questions or gently challenge the pattern. For example, a powerful question to ask the stuck team member is, "How is what you're doing now working for you?" This encourages them to reflect on their resistance rather than continue the cycle. Another option is to hand the issue back; e.g., "What solutions have you thought of so far?" or "Out of these ideas we discussed, which one do you see worth trying?" This shifts the person from Victim to an accountable problem solver. Sometimes, using an unexpected response can break the cycle; for example, deliberately agreeing that the situation seems unsolvable (reverse psychology), which often prompts the other person to reconsider or defend a potential solution instead of dismissing it. Importantly, the coach should avoid the trap of endless rescuing and return to a non-directive coaching style, encouraging the client to find their own answers. By naming the dynamic (with tact and empathy), setting an agreement for a more constructive conversation, and refocusing on the client's ownership of the problem, the "Yes, but" game can be defused. The coach might say, "I notice that we tend to find a 'but' for every idea—perhaps we should pause and clarify what outcome you truly want, so we can find a realistic way forward." The key is shifting the interaction back to an Adult-Adult collaboration instead of a Parent-Child struggle.

"I'm Only Trying to Help You"

Structure of the game: "I'm Only Trying to Help You" (sometimes abbreviated IOTHY) is a game where a person takes on the Rescuer role—offering unsolicited or excessive help—and eventually feels hurt or frustrated when the help is not appreciated or effective. The classic structure: Person A jumps in to "save" Person B (who hasn't actually asked for rescue). When B doesn't cooperate with or value the help, A becomes resentful and might snap with something like, "Fine, I was only trying to help you!" At the surface level, A's stated intent is benevolent support, but the ulterior aspect is that A may be seeking validation or control, and B's resistance allows A to feel wronged. Eric Berne described this game as one where the helper's advice or assistance is ultimately shown to be flawed or unwanted, allowing the helper to upstage others or feel superior before feeling unappreciated. In coaching contexts, this can play out as a coach who keeps switching techniques to help an unengaged team, or a leader who micromanages a team "for their own good." The payoff for the helper is often a sense of martyrdom ("I did my best and they didn't care") or moral high ground, while the other party gets to prove no one can help them or that the helper is overstepping.

Common triggers and manifestations: This game often begins with the Rescuer's over-involvement. In a coach–team relationship, a trigger might be the coach's noticing the team struggling and immediately stepping in with solutions or extra support, even if the team hasn't asked. Similarly, an external stakeholder (like a manager) might impose help on the team ("reorganizing" their tasks or offering constant advice) under the guise of assisting. Initially, the "helper" is in Parent/Rescuer mode, perhaps deriving self-worth from being needed. The team or individual (in Child or Victim mode) may passively accept or actively resist the interference. For example, a coach might observe a conflict within the team and intervene to mediate without obtaining permission or establishing context—the team members didn't ask for this help. They might quietly resent it or push back against it. Over time, if the team doesn't show gratitude or fails to improve, the coach's offers of help become increasingly forceful or desperate. The tipping point (the "switch") comes when the helper's uninvited assistance backfires. The team might say, "We never wanted your help in the first place," or simply continue failing, prompting the coach to feel annoyed or blame the team. The helper then moves into a Persecutor or Victim role, expressing irritation: "After all I've done, you won't cooperate—I was only trying to help!" Meanwhile, the team may feel persecuted by the unwanted help or vindicated that the coach's methods didn't work.

Roles typically played: Initially, the helper (coach or stakeholder) adopts the Rescuer role, and the team or team member is cast (or casts themselves) as the Victim needing help. Notably, the Victim role here may be unspoken; the person receiving help might not truly see themselves as helpless, which is why they resist. When the switch occurs, roles realign: the erstwhile Rescuer feels unappreciated and can become the Victim ("My efforts are not valued") or lash out as a Persecutor ("You're impossible to help"). The former "victim" (team) might then become Persecutor by rebuking the helper ("Leave us alone!"), or remain in a passive-aggressive Victim stance that nothing changed despite the helper's actions. In a Drama Triangle sense, "I'm Only Trying to Help You" often involves the Rescuer and Victim cycling into mutual resentment. Coaches themselves can fall into this game if they tie their self-esteem to fixing the client's issues. The coach keeps trying new techniques to rescue the team, and the team's continued stagnation or resistance eventually "proves" to the coach that the team is difficult (coach feels victimized) while the team proves that the coach's help wasn't useful.

Impact on team dynamics and coaching outcomes: The effect of this game is a breakdown of trust and independence. When a coach or leader repeatedly assumes the Rescuer role, the team may become overly dependent or start to resent it. This diminishes the team's confidence in their ability to solve problems on their own (since the coach always intervenes), and it reduces the coach's effectiveness (as the team either tunes out or resists the help offered). The relationship can fade into quiet sabotage; team members may nod or say "thanks" but not act on the coach's advice ("praising the coach without actually trying what is suggested," as one version called the "Peasant" game depicts). Simultaneously, the coach may feel increasingly frustrated or "burned out" from giving too much help. Ultimately, playing IOTHY causes a stalemate and strained relationships: the coach and team might each blame the other for the lack of progress. For example, a team may accuse the coach of pushing irrelevant tools ("We never needed those workshops you insisted on"), while the coach internally blames the team for being uncoachable, creating a toxic cycle. The coaching process can become stuck in this covert conflict, with outcomes and goals delayed while both sides unconsciously reenact a helper-versus-victim struggle.

Strategies for coaches to interrupt/resolve: The key to breaking "I'm Only Trying to Help You" is self-awareness on the part of the helper and a shift to a more collaborative stance. Coaches should monitor their own motivations: Are you helping because the client explicitly asked or because you feel compelled to "save" them? If you catch yourself jumping in too quickly, pause and contract. For example, ask permission before offering help: "I have some ideas—would you like to hear them, or do you prefer I just facilitate while you generate solutions?" This ensures the team remains in the driver's seat. It's also vital to address resistance openly

CHAPTER 7   POWER PLAYS AND HIDDEN DYNAMICS REVEALED

rather than plowing past it. If a team member is pushing back or passively not implementing changes, a coach can bring that up: "I notice we try different techniques, but things aren't improving. Let's discuss what's really going on—is the coaching meeting your needs? What might you be hesitant about?" By doing so, the coach moves out of the Rescuer role and into Adult-to-Adult dialogue, exploring the client's perspective. In cases where a stakeholder or manager is the over-helper, the coach can mediate by helping that person see the pattern; for instance, share feedback that the team feels micromanaged by well-intentioned "help," and guide the stakeholder to empower rather than over-direct. Structurally, one antidote to IOTHY is enforcing clear roles and boundaries in the coaching contract; e.g., the coach is there to facilitate growth, but the team must do the work; the manager will support resources, but not solve the team's problems for them. If you're the coach and find yourself thinking, "Why won't they appreciate all I'm doing?" it's a red flag. Step back and realign with the team's own goals instead of your personal agenda. As TA expert Jeremy Lewis notes, when a client actively resists and the coach keeps switching techniques or trying harder, it's time to stop and discuss the meta-issue (the client's reluctance) rather than continue a "helping" game. In summary, stay in the Adult ego state: offer help when invited, listen to the team's actual needs, and if you sense yourself becoming a martyr or the team becoming disengaged, use supervision or reflection to recalibrate. A useful mantra is: "Don't work harder than the client." Allow the team to experience natural consequences and learning, and provide support without overstepping. This collaborative, permission-based approach defuses the IOTHY dynamic and fosters healthier team autonomy.

"If It Weren't For You . . ."

Structure of the game: "If It Weren't For You" (often abbreviated IWFY) is a blame-shifting game where one party attributes their own lack of success or action to the interference or existence of another person or factor. Essentially, the player claims "I could achieve X, if only it weren't for [Person/Condition Y] holding me back." The structure involves a Victim who uses a Persecutor as an excuse for inaction or failure. In Berne's examples, this often occurs in personal relationships (e.g., a spouse saying they'd pursue a career "if it weren't for you" needing me at home). In a team coaching or organizational context, it might look like a team saying they'd be high-performing "if it weren't for" those meddling executives, rigid policies, or some difficult colleague. The real payoff for the person playing IWFY is that they avoid facing their own fears or responsibilities by externalizing the cause of their difficulties. They get to save face: As long as they can point to an outside obstacle, they have a built-in alibi for why they aren't succeeding. Meanwhile, the blamed party is kept on the defensive and often feels guilty or uneasy, which can give the blaming player leverage in the relationship.

Common triggers & manifestations: This game frequently emerges under stress when there are visible external constraints or antagonists that a team can latch onto. In team-stakeholder dynamics, for example, a team might be underperforming and rather than admit internal issues, they collectively decide "we'd meet our targets if it weren't for senior management constantly changing the priorities." Similarly, a coach-team relationship can fall into IWFY if the team (or coach) starts seeing the other as the reason goals aren't met; e.g., a coach thinks "this team would improve if it weren't for their cynical leader undermining the process," or a team complains "we'd adopt these new practices if it weren't for our coach's methods that don't fit our culture." A trigger is often a difficult change or challenge accompanied by frustration. It's psychologically easier to blame an outside agent than to deal with one's own fear of failure or need to change habits. We also see IWFY when there's a power imbalance: The nominal "victim" chooses a "persecutor" who has some authority or control. For instance, an Agile team might secretly be reluctant to embrace a new workflow, but they blame the delay on an external compliance rule ("we can't change because of regulations")—regulation becomes the persecutor. Or a team leader privately fears stepping up, so they hire a coach and then say, "If it weren't for my team's resistance, I'd be a great leader." Here the team is cast as the obstacle. The key manifestation is frequent external blaming statements. Listen for phrases like "We'd be fine if not for X" or "Because of them, we can't do our part."

Roles in the Game: The primary role of the person saying "If it weren't for you . . ." is that of the Victim, with the "you" (or "them/it") being assigned the Persecutor role. Unlike some games, the Victim in IWFY isn't necessarily looking for a Rescuer—they seek absolution or justification. However, Rescuers can get drawn in; for example, a coach hearing "we could succeed if not for management" might be tempted to play Rescuer by intervening with management on the team's behalf. This triangulates the situation further—now management is the Persecutor, the team is the Victim, and the coach tries to be the Rescuer. Often, the Victim in IWFY can also assume a Persecutor stance by blaming and even guilt-tripping the supposed culprit. The complaining player gains an advantage by keeping the blamed party on the hook and making them feel uneasy. In a team setting, members might collectively persecute the absent scapegoat (e.g., upper management) in conversations while claiming the powerless Victim role concerning their agency. In the Drama Triangle, this game reinforces a dependent, no-responsibility stance for the blaming side. It portrays the other side as an oppressive force, even if the reality is more complex. It's not uncommon for the actual dynamic to be that the "persecutor" was not as limiting as claimed; the restriction is partly an unconscious convenience for the Victim. For instance, a team might say, "If it weren't for our client's constant changes, we'd have delivered on time," when in truth, some internal inefficiencies also played a part, but focusing on the client's role absolves the team of full accountability.

Impact on team dynamics and outcomes: IWFY is toxic to growth because it externalizes responsibility and prevents learning. Teams caught in this game develop a fixed mindset that their fate is controlled by others. This can create a culture of learned helplessness or chronic complaining ("nothing's our fault"). It also deteriorates relationships with the blamed stakeholders or the coach. For instance, if a team constantly blames upper management for their issues, trust between the team and leadership erodes, and constructive dialogue is replaced by mutual suspicion. Likewise, if stakeholders hear the coach blaming the team (or vice versa), the coaching engagement loses credibility. The game can stall progress on goals, since the team doesn't fully engage in problem solving—why bother if "they" are stopping us anyway? Additionally, the morale within the team can be oddly two-sided: on one hand, the team may bond over a shared enemy ("ain't it awful what they make us do"—often blending into the Ain't It Awful game, see below), but on the other hand, they feel disempowered and cynical, which reduces initiative and innovation. From a coaching outcome perspective, IWFY severely limits the effectiveness of interventions. Any suggestion can be dismissed because "we can't do that unless they change." It essentially creates a deadlock, where the team waits for the external persecutor to remove the obstacle, and real change is postponed indefinitely.

Strategies to identify and resolve the game: Spotting IWFY is usually straightforward through the language: Listen for constant external attributions for internal problems. When you hear statements like "We'd be agile if it weren't for our old-school CEO," flag that pattern. The strategy for coaches is to gently challenge the narrative of helplessness and refocus the team on its locus of control. One approach is reality-testing questions: "What part of this situation is within your control?" or "If that obstacle weren't there, what would you be doing differently right now?" Then, "Is there a version of that you can try anyway?" This helps the team distinguish between real constraints and assumed ones and encourages creative problem solving in the face of barriers. Another tactic is to work on empowerment and reframing. For example, if a team blames strict regulations (a common persecutor) for inaction, the coach might reframe: "The regulations are fixed for now, but what choices do we have in how we meet them? Let's list what's still possible." This shifts the mindset from

CHAPTER 7   POWER PLAYS AND HIDDEN DYNAMICS REVEALED

victimhood to agency. When the "persecutor" is a person or group (like senior management), facilitating dialogue can break the game. The coach can encourage the team and stakeholders to communicate needs and constraints openly, rather than assume malign intentions. For instance, organize a session where the team can express to leadership what they need (constructively), and leadership can clarify their reasons; this can transform an IWFY blame game into a problem-solving session. It's also important to address any underlying fears that make the IWFY game attractive. Often, the team uses an external excuse to avoid confronting an internal issue (fear of change, skill gaps, etc.). A coach might use immediacy: "I sense that focusing on X (external) might be a way not to have to deal with Y (internal challenge). Does that resonate at all?" By bringing such insight to light (tactfully), the coach invites the team out of the game. In doing so, maintain a blame-free atmosphere—emphasize that the goal is not to assign fault (which feeds the game) but to find solutions. For the stakeholder at fault, if they are truly contributing to the problem, the coach can work with them to adjust while also highlighting how the blame dynamic is counterproductive. Ultimately, the antidote to IWFY is fostering ownership, helping the team articulate "Even if X is true, here's what we will do." By shifting focus from you/they to we/I, the game's spell is broken, and the team can move forward with a greater sense of power and responsibility.

"Ain't It Awful"

Structure of the game: "Ain't It Awful" is a group complaint-and-bonding game. It involves two or more people swapping pessimistic, critical, or miserable observations about situations or third parties, trying to one-up each other in a misery contest. The apparent aim is to share grievances or seek sympathy, but the real reward is that participants find satisfaction in complaining itself, reveling in how "awful" things are. According to Eric Berne, this often acts as a way to structure time (a "party game" in social settings), but in its game form it has a subtle competitive edge: who can lament the loudest or share the worst war story. For example, one person says, "Work is crazy, we're drowning in bureaucracy," another responds, "Ain't it awful? And our budget got cut again—we're doomed," then another contributes an even more dire story, and so on. The gloom intensifies until it usually ends with a "winner" who out-awfuls everyone (e.g., "We're utterly screwed because of X, Y, Z"), followed by an awkward silence. Everyone gets a "stroke" (recognition) from taking part, but it's negative strokes; they feel bonded through shared hardship but also frustrated and drained because nothing gets solved. In brief, the group pretends to seek solutions or meaningful discussion, but in reality they indulge in collective victimhood and blame. The roles typically involve multiple Victims (sharing tales of being victimized by circumstances) with an absent Persecutor (the situation or people being blamed). Sometimes, a participant acts as a superficial Rescuer by offering sympathy or even "I hear you" suggestions, but any positive shift is quickly knocked back into negativity (otherwise, the game would end).

Common triggers and manifestations: "Ain't It Awful" tends to surface when a team or group faces stress and uncertainty, and there's a temptation to bond over negativity rather than seek solutions. It can happen among team members during a coaching engagement; for example, after a tough change initiative, the team gathers (with or without the coach) and the conversation slips into "Isn't this just impossible? . . . Yes, it's terrible, and on top of that, did you hear what else they want us to do? . . ." It can also occur between the team and coach if the coach is not careful. Sometimes, to build rapport, a coach might empathize with the team's complaints about the organization, which can quickly turn into a mutual gripe session. Similarly, in team–stakeholder interactions, if an external stakeholder (such as a senior leader) meets with the team and begins lamenting about company problems, the team might join in the chorus of how awful things are (instead of focusing on the meeting's purpose). The trigger often is a new piece of bad news or a shared frustration that someone introduces with an emotional charge. Humans naturally seek social bonding, and complaining is an easy way to do that—it invites others to join in. For example, a stakeholder might casually say, "This market downturn has really killed our morale—nothing's working," and a team lead responds, "Ain't it awful? We also lost two people in our department," and then the griping begins. This is especially common in cultures where open conflict is discouraged; instead of confronting problems directly (which might cause conflict), people bond over how unresolvable or terrible things are. In a coaching setting, this can occur during retrospectives or group reflections, where the discussion shifts from focusing on improvements to commiseration about factors outside the room's control ("the clients, the system, the economy, etc.").

Roles and emotional payoffs: In "Ain't It Awful," participants predominantly take on the Victim role—everyone is suffering and blameless (the blame goes to the abstract "awful" situation or others not present). There isn't a distinct Persecutor in the room—it's often an external entity (like "the higher-ups," "the market," "those other departments"). If the coach is in the room and joins in, they too become a Victim alongside the team, which is a problematic loss of objectivity. Occasionally, someone in the group might position subtly as a Rescuer by saying "You poor things, that's so unfair" to someone else's complaint, but since they then share their own complaint, it's more of a reciprocal victimhood than true rescuing. The competitive aspect—trying to top each other's complaints—can inject a Persecutor-like one-upmanship dynamic; e.g., one-upping someone's awful story implicitly "defeats" the previous story. The person who delivers the most dramatically awful scenario "wins" the game (and gets a kind of gloomy admiration from others). This odd payoff structure means that each participant is actually seeking strokes for how bad their situation is. The emotional payoff is twofold: social camaraderie ("we're all in the same sinking ship together") and personal vindication ("I feel right to be upset because look how awful it truly is").

However, as Berne noted and practitioners observe, everyone leaves such a session feeling worse—drained and somewhat dirty—because the hidden message internalized is "we are powerless and the world is terrible." Over time, frequent playing of "Ain't It Awful" reinforces a negative, defeatist culture, where complaining is rewarded with attention and any suggestion of optimism or responsibility is subtly discouraged (since it would stop the game).

Impact on team coaching and culture: When "Ain't It Awful" becomes a pattern, it stalls progress and saps morale. In team coaching, if sessions turn into complaint festivals, the team wastes energy reaffirming problems instead of finding solutions. This can seriously undermine coaching results—action items get lost under "what's the point, it's all bad anyway" attitudes. Additionally, it can foster a harmful coach–team collusion. If a coach sympathizes too much, they might enable the team's passivity. In organizations, a team known for "Ain't It Awful" chatter may develop a reputation for negativity, causing stakeholders to dismiss their legitimate concerns. Internally, too much focus on how bad things are can erode psychological safety. Ironically, team members might fear being the "positive one" or offering ideas and so avoid breaking the unspoken pact of pessimism. It can also be contagious—new members learn that to fit in, they should join the gripe sessions. Regarding team dynamics, this behavior creates a shared Victim identity that can bond the team ("us vs. the cruel world") but also keeps them stuck. It's closely linked to learned helplessness and can pair with "If It Weren't For You" (where the team constantly claims nothing can improve because of external factors). For the coaching process, this means the coach's efforts to foster an empowered, proactive mindset face a tough challenge against the allure of "Ain't it awful" camaraderie. If unaddressed, it can derail the entire engagement into a chronic "problem-talk" cycle where sessions become venting exercises with little strategic planning or accountability.

CHAPTER 7   POWER PLAYS AND HIDDEN DYNAMICS REVEALED

Strategies to interrupt and re-focus: The antidote to "Ain't It Awful" is to inject possibility and personal responsibility back into the conversation, without dismissing legitimate issues. First, a coach should recognize when normal venting is sliding into this game; signs include repetitive cycles of complaint with escalating dramatization and no movement toward solutions. Once spotted, one strategy is to validate the feelings briefly, then pivot to solutions or reframing. For example: "I hear that you're frustrated with the new system, and it does sound challenging. Let's acknowledge that. Now, what are some things within our control that we can do to improve the situation?" This helps break the cycle by not feeding more fuel into the fire of complaints. Another tactic is to set time boundaries on venting. In a team meeting, one might say, "Let's take 10 minutes to air all the 'awful' stuff on our minds, get it out, and then spend the rest of the time problem solving." Often, when people know the gripe session has a clear end, they'll wrap it up and be more open to transitioning. Coaches can also challenge the group (gently) to consider different perspectives: "What would it look like if this problem were solved? What's an example of something that is working despite these challenges?" By asking for exceptions or positives, you invite the team to step out of pure victim mode. In some cases, introducing a bit of humor or absurdity can jolt participants out of the downward spiral; for instance, exaggerating the exaggeration: "Wow, by the sounds of it, absolutely nothing good has ever happened here! Are we sure about that?" said with a smile, can make people self-aware that they're spiralling. A key is also to avoid collusion. As a coach or leader, show empathy but don't top the team's complaints with your own, and don't simply nod along without eventually steering the discussion. If the team says, "It's hopeless," respond with, "It is tough, and yet I have seen you tackle hard things before—let's figure out one small step." Essentially, convert "Ain't it awful?" into "It is tough, so what shall we do?" It might also help to explicitly name the pattern (if rapport allows): "Hey, team, I notice we spend a lot of time in our meetings highlighting how bad things are. While it's good to acknowledge reality, I worry we might be getting stuck. Can we try shifting into a mode of what we can do, even if the situation isn't ideal?" This transparency can help the team catch themselves when they fall back into the game. On an ongoing basis, coaching should encourage a culture of solution-focused dialogue: for every problem raised, ensure the conversation includes brainstorming options or at least next steps. If external factors truly are awful, strategies might include influencing those factors (through communication upward, etc.) or accepting and adapting to them if they can't be changed—both are more empowering than endless rumination. Finally, reinforce any movement out of the victim stance: Praise the team when they shift from complaint to action (e.g., "I admire that instead of just saying 'ain't it awful,' you reached out to that other department to collaborate—that's a great move."). Over time, this positive reinforcement can diminish the payoff of the game (sympathy, camaraderie) and replace it with a healthier payoff (a sense of accomplishment and agency). By combining empathetic listening with firm redirection, a coach helps the team retire the "Ain't It Awful" habit in favor of more constructive communication.

Conclusion

Hidden dynamics and unseen challenges exist in every team—even (and sometimes especially) in Agile teams aiming for high collaboration and self-organization. Far from being "touchy-feely" side issues, these dynamics often determine whether a group of individuals simply go through the motions or become a true team that excels and continuously improves.

For Agile practitioners, Scrum masters, and team coaches reading this, the key takeaway is twofold. First, grow your awareness and diagnostic skills—learn to see what isn't immediately obvious, sense emotional undercurrents, and observe systemic patterns. Use the theories and examples as lenses; with practice, you'll start recognizing signals like,

CHAPTER 7   POWER PLAYS AND HIDDEN DYNAMICS REVEALED

"Ah, we're scapegoating again" or "There's an undiscussable topic lurking here," and be able to name it or plan an intervention. Second, foster environments that encourage openness and learning; often just surfacing a hidden dynamic respectfully can strip it of much of its disruptive power. As the MIT Sloan researchers highlighted, "Destructive and unconscious dynamics lose their power when they become visible and a topic for discussion." Once a team collectively recognizes a dysfunctional pattern, it can course-correct, especially in a setting of psychological safety. Your role as a coach is to facilitate that collective awareness and learning, not by preaching, but by guiding the team to discover insights themselves through skillful questions, activities, and sometimes pointed yet caring confrontations.

By understanding common psychological games and the drama roles involved, team coaches and organizational leaders can better recognize when interactions veer into game territory, rather than genuine problem solving. By naming the patterns, re-contracting ground rules for healthier interactions, and encouraging personal responsibility and solutions, a coach can transform these unproductive games into opportunities for insight and growth. In doing so, the team moves from a cycle of hidden agendas and "rotten feelings" payoffs to a more transparent, collaborative, and effective way of working—the ultimate goal of any coaching engagement.

It's important to acknowledge that this is advanced coaching work. It can be messy and requires a lot of patience. There will be times when trying to address a hidden issue initially makes things feel worse (for example, bringing a conflict into the open can create a heated meeting). However, this is often the storm before the calm—once they have navigated it, teams often report feeling relieved, heard, and ready to move forward together. As a coach, your steady presence and belief in the team's capacity to grow are crucial in those moments. Moreover, don't go it alone: Utilize peer coaches, mentors, or supervisors to reflect on your own blind spots. As we help teams confront their hidden dynamics, we must also be aware of our own. Continuous development in areas like facilitation, psychology, and organizational development will serve you well.

The reward for doing this work is substantial. When hidden dynamics are addressed, teams not only improve their performance metrics but often also experience a cultural shift. Meetings become more honest and effective. Team members solve issues directly rather than letting frustrations build up. There is an increased trust and a greater willingness to rely on one another. Creativity improves because people aren't walking on eggshells. Essentially, the team becomes more resilient, able to handle internal and external challenges, because they have no internal rot weakening them. This captures the true essence of a self-organizing team: not just managing workflows, but managing themselves—their relationships and interactions—in a healthy way. In Agile, we say the team owns its process. By extension, a high-maturity team owns its dynamics and actively works to improve them. As a coach, you eventually make yourself redundant in this aspect too: You impart the ability to recognize and discuss the previously undiscussable.

Reflection Moment: What Is Not Visible?
Recognizing Hidden Dynamics

1. What subtle cues have you noticed in teams that might indicate hidden power struggles or unspoken tensions?

2. Have you ever sensed that something important was not being said? How did you respond—or choose not to respond?

CHAPTER 7   POWER PLAYS AND HIDDEN DYNAMICS REVEALED

Personal Role in Power Dynamics

1. When coaching, do you tend to align more with authority figures, underdogs, or bystanders? What impact does this have on the team system?

2. What are your personal triggers or blind spots when power dynamics emerge in a team setting?

Spotting Psychological Games

1. Which of the psychological games discussed (e.g., "If It Weren't for You," "Why Don't You/Yes But") have you observed in teams you coach?

2. How do you usually intervene (or not) when you notice these patterns? What would you like to do differently?

Surfacing the Undiscussable

1. What practices have you used (or might try) to bring "undiscussables" into the light safely and constructively?

2. How do you cultivate psychological safety so that power and conflict can be addressed rather than avoided?

CHAPTER 7 POWER PLAYS AND HIDDEN DYNAMICS REVEALED

Reflecting on Systemic Roles

1. When entering a new team system, how do you assess who holds formal and informal power?

2. How do you avoid becoming entangled in team roles (e.g., Rescuer, Hero, Mediator) that may reduce your effectiveness as a coach?

CHAPTER 8

Turning Resistance into Resilience

Change within an Agile team often faces resistance. In the context of Agile team coaching, resistance refers to pushback, hesitancy, or defensive reactions that individuals or teams show when confronted with new ways of working or uncomfortable changes. Resilience, however, is the team's ability to adapt, bounce back from setbacks, and grow stronger in the face of those challenges. A Scrum master or Agile coach frequently encounters both; for example, a team might publicly agree to adopt Scrum practices while privately harboring doubts and quiet pushback. As discussed in earlier chapters, every team has two layers of behavior—the visible layer of plans, tasks, and ceremonies, and a hidden layer of unspoken concerns, power plays, and anxieties. If left unaddressed, that hidden "secret life" can undermine genuine self-organization and continuous improvement. The coach's role is to shed light on those hidden dynamics (like fears or unspoken conflicts) and foster an environment where they can be safely explored. This is vital because an Agile team's true strength comes not from avoiding resistance, but from working through it. When managed skillfully, today's resistance can become the foundation of tomorrow's resilience—the very process of confronting resistance can build a team's confidence and capacity to handle whatever challenges lie ahead.

CHAPTER 8   TURNING RESISTANCE INTO RESILIENCE

In this chapter, we'll explore how to turn resistance into resilience. We'll start by understanding why resistance occurs in the first place, examining common root causes, from fear of change to conflicting agendas (and even coach missteps). We'll then look into strategies for navigating and overcoming resistance, including the coach's stance, facilitation techniques, and the importance of clear agreements.

The Roots of Resistance

To navigate resistance, an Agile coach first needs to understand why it's happening. Resistance is rarely just stubbornness; it often masks deeper concerns or dynamics. Here, we examine several common roots of resistance in Agile teams.

Fear of Change

Perhaps the most prevalent source of resistance is the simple human fear of the unknown. Agile transformations ask people to step out of their comfort zones—to adopt new roles, learn new practices, or give up familiar routines. Team members may fear losing their expertise or status (*"Will I still be valuable on the team if I'm not the sole expert?"*), while managers may fear losing control or authority. Such fears can manifest as overt pushback (like openly arguing against a new process) or covertly as foot-dragging and avoidance. Often, individuals aren't resisting the idea of improvement; they are resisting the potential loss they associate with the change (loss of control, competence, security, or identity). In Robert Kegan and Lisa Laskow Lahey terms, they may consciously agree to change but simultaneously hold hidden "competing commitments" that act as an immunity to change; for example, a developer genuinely wants to improve team collaboration, but unconsciously resists pair programming because it threatens his self-image as the "go-to" expert.

Understanding that fear—whether fear of failure, fear of losing power, or even fear of embarrassment—is at the heart of much resistance helps the coach respond with empathy rather than frustration. As one example, some leaders in an Agile adoption had an unspoken fear of losing status in a flatter, team-centric model; this fear of diminished power became a hidden agenda that led them to undermine the change effort subtly. By recognizing fear-driven resistance, a coach can address the underlying anxieties (through reassurance, education, small experiments, etc.) instead of simply pushing harder on the change.

Lack of Trust and Psychological Safety

Resistance often thrives in an environment of low trust. If team members don't trust their leaders, the Agile coach, or even each other, they will understandably be hesitant to embrace new ways of working. When safety is low, people fear being punished or humiliated for being honest. As a result, resistance goes underground—team members nod along in meetings but later vent privately or simply disengage. A "culture of silence" can take hold, where team members prefer to avoid raising concerns or new ideas (since doing so has backfired before). In such cases, what appears to be passive resistance (e.g., chronic lack of input in retrospectives, minimal interaction in meetings) is actually a protective mechanism in a low-trust environment. Additionally, if the team doesn't trust the intent behind the change (for example, suspecting that management's Agile initiative is just a ploy to work them harder or cut jobs), they will resist it outright. Lack of trust can also be personal: If the Scrum master or coach hasn't built rapport or is seen as an outsider "imposing" changes, team members may resist even good advice. Hidden dynamics play a role here; teams might have unspoken narratives like *"Management doesn't really care about us"* or *"This coach is just a spy for our boss."* Without addressing the trust deficit, these narratives fuel ongoing resistance. Therefore, diagnosing resistance must include asking:

Is there a trust or safety issue underlying this? Often, the coach's answer must be the first step in creating a safer, more trusting space, rather than pushing the change itself. When people feel psychologically safe, what looks like "resistance" can quickly turn into open dialogue and cooperation, because team members finally feel confident that they won't be punished for engaging with the change.

Perceived Loss of Control

Agile is all about empowering teams, but during the transition it can sometimes feel to individuals as though they are losing control. A developer used to individually controlling technical decisions might resist collaborative practices like pair programming or collective code ownership, perceiving them as a loss of autonomy or craftsmanship. A line manager who is asked to adopt a servant-leader stance might inwardly struggle (or outwardly push back) because they perceive they are losing their familiar authority over the team. In some cases, resistance is a reaction to feeling that one's influence or status is being reduced. People who built success in the old system can feel alienated by the new system. For example, a project manager in a traditional setup might resist Scrum because it essentially eliminates their role as the taskmaster—it's a direct hit to their sense of control. Similarly, team members might resist certain Agile practices if those seem to take away personal control (*"Now we have to commit as a team rather than individually—what if others mess up my success?"*). This "loss of control" can also be felt at a team level: A team used to operating in silos might initially push back on closer collaboration or transparent progress tracking because it feels like a loss of control over their individual work or a loss of privacy. Confusingly, Agile is intended to increase autonomy and control (shifting it to the team), but during the change, individuals may not experience it that way. They might only see what they have to give up. A coach should recognize signs of this kind of resistance, often expressed as *"This Agile stuff is chaos"* or *"We *can't guarantee outcomes with these new methods,"* and help the team regain a sense of control within the Agile framework. This can be done by involving them in designing the change (thus giving back ownership), explicitly clarifying decision rights (so they know where they still have autonomy), and highlighting how Agile will increase their influence over doing the work (even if some old controls like detailed Gantt charts are gone). In essence, the antidote to perceived loss of control is choice and transparency. Invite the team to co-create their working agreements and emphasize the aspects of Agile that expand their zone of control (such as self-management and deciding how to meet sprint goals). When team members see that they are not losing their voice, but rather gaining a more meaningful one, their initial resistance often subsides.

Habitual Patterns and Group Dynamics (the "Immunity to Change")

Teams, like individuals, can develop habitual ways of responding that inadvertently resist change. These include subconscious group norms, defensive routines, and "immune systems" that kick in when something challenges the status quo. Teams under anxiety often fall back on defensive behaviors; for example, avoiding hard conversations or clinging to "the way we've always done it." Chris Argyris famously observed that groups maintain defensive routines to protect themselves from embarrassment or threat; however, these routines block learning and change. In practice, a team may smile and nod at a new idea during a retrospective, but then silently agree afterward, *"Let's just keep doing what we do—rocking the boat is not worth it."* Such habitual avoidance can appear as passive resistance or simply inertia. Another powerful lens on this is Kegan and Lahey's Immunity to Change model. Even when a team says it wants to improve, it may have unspoken commitments and assumptions that act like an immune system, preventing real change. For example, a team might state a commitment to quality, yet resist investing time in automation or Test-Driven Development (TDD) because secretly they're also committed to never slowing down output (perhaps driven by a fear that management will punish a dip in velocity). These hidden, competing commitments (stay fast and improve quality) create a system of resistance that must be uncovered to be addressed. Additionally, Transactional Analysis and group coaching models show that teams can unconsciously enter into "psychological games" when under stress (see more on that in Chapters 6 and 7). Misaligned coaching contracts can lead to exactly these dynamics; for instance, a coach overidentifying with a beleaguered team and colluding in blaming leadership (the coach and team as victims against the big bad management). Such hidden group dynamics sustain resistance by reinforcing an "us vs. them" mentality. Similarly, unspoken expectations act as hidden contracts that breed resistance when violated. Or management expects the team to "act like adults" without ever clarifying what that means, and then perceives their confusion as defiance. These unspoken norms and assumptions create friction under the surface. In short, many roots of resistance are systemic and hidden, not obvious on the surface. An Agile coach must therefore play detective. Listen for the pattern of resistance. Is it fear of something? A historical habit? A conflicting hidden commitment? A Drama Triangle game? By bringing these patterns to light (in a respectful way), the coach can help the team understand *why* they are resisting. This understanding is the first step to shifting the pattern.

Real-world example. A team resisted adopting peer reviews for months. Through coaching, it emerged that an unspoken norm in their culture was *"We don't critique each other openly"* (a defensive routine stemming from a fear of conflict). Once this was named and traced back to a past negative experience, the team could intentionally establish a new norm for safe, constructive feedback, effectively dismantling that "immunity to change." The resistance then dissolved because its protective purpose (avoiding hurt feelings) was addressed through a new, healthier mechanism (team agreements on respectful feedback).

CHAPTER 8   TURNING RESISTANCE INTO RESILIENCE

Conflicting Agendas

Another root cause of resistance is when different stakeholders have different definitions of success or clashing goals that haven't been reconciled. A classic example is a conflict between a team's agenda and a sponsor's agenda. Imagine a scenario: The department head (sponsor) brings in an Agile coach to "increase delivery speed," but the team is more concerned with reducing burnout and improving quality. If not openly discussed, these differing agendas will breed resistance—the team will quietly resist any "improvements" that feel like speed-at-all-costs, and management will view the team (and perhaps the coach) as resistant to change. Chapter 6 emphasized the importance of aligning the "three corners" of the coaching engagement (sponsor, coach, team) upfront to avoid this trap. If that alignment doesn't happen, hidden conflicting agendas surface later as resistance. A mid-engagement check at one company revealed a stark misalignment: The sponsor stated that success meant the team doubling its output next quarter, while the team claimed success meant gaining clarity from leadership and reducing waste. "Wow—mismatch!" was the coach's reaction. Each side had assumed the other was on the same page when, in fact, they were not. The result? The team had been subtly pushing back against hastily imposed changes aimed at increasing output, as those changes conflicted with their understanding of what the coaching was intended to achieve (namely, addressing the ambiguity and churn emanating from above). Conflicting agendas aren't always as glaring; sometimes, they show up as a general lack of buy-in. For instance, if a personal agenda drives part of the team (say, a developer resisting pair programming because they want to maintain a "rockstar" image, which they feel is threatened by equal collaboration), their personal goal (to stay special) conflicts with the team goal (share knowledge and collaborate), causing resistance. In other cases, organizational-level conflicts cause team resistance; e.g., the metrics and incentives in place reward individual heroics or hours worked, which conflicts with the Agile behaviors the coach is encouraging (teamwork, sustainable pace). The team will naturally resist the coach's message if following it means they'll be penalized per the old metrics. In all these situations, the underlying issue is a lack of alignment: People are pulling in different directions. The coach needs to surface and address these conflicting agendas, either by finding a unifying purpose or at least getting the conflicts on the table for negotiation. Often, reframing the conversation around the shared higher goal can help. For example, a product team and their manager were at odds—the manager wanted more features faster, the team wanted to invest in automation; the coach helped them see that both agendas served the higher goal of customer satisfaction (features and quality mattered), and facilitated a compromise on balancing new features with technical debt payoff. Until that conversation, the team's "resistance" to management's requests was really a principled stand for quality, but it came across as stubbornness. Only by aligning on the broader objective (happy customers) could they drop the tug-of-war and move forward together.

Coach's Missteps and Contribution

Lastly, we must acknowledge that sometimes resistance is triggered or exacerbated by the coach's own actions or missteps. Coaches are humans, and how we show up can either build buy-in or create pushback. One common mistake is poor contracting (or skipping it entirely). If a coach rushes into working with a team without establishing clear agreements, roles, and boundaries, it's easy to stumble into misunderstandings that lead to resistance down the line. For example, if confidentiality expectations weren't set, team members might resist sharing openly; or if the coach's role wasn't clarified, the Scrum master might resist the coach's involvement, feeling their turf is being infringed upon. Similarly, if a coach fails to "contract" for psychological safety—meaning they don't create a safe, agreement-backed space for coaching—teams may be wary and resistant from the get-go. Another misstep can be the coach's appearing to take sides or collude with one party. For instance, if a coach frequently meets the sponsor privately and shares critical observations about the team (even with good intent), the team may start to see the coach as an arm of management and resist opening up to them. Conversely, if the coach is perceived as too chummy with the team and constantly validates the team's complaints about leadership, managers may resist cooperating with the coach. Chapter 8 described this balance as psychological distance—if it skews, trust erodes. The ideal is a transparent, "no secrets, no surprises" stance.

A real-world example: A coach once agreed to a sponsor's request to "secretly observe" the team and report back misbehavior. When the team discovered this back-channel reporting, trust was shattered—they understandably resisted any further coaching, seeing the coach as a spy. A misstep in ethics and contracting effectively derailed that engagement.

Coaches can also prompt resistance by misreading the culture; for example, using aggressive confrontation in a culture that values harmony, or pushing too hard for change when the team's stress level is already high. Even a coach's communication style can trigger resistance (imagine a coach who talks in abstract coaching jargon to a team of pragmatic engineers—eye-rolls and disengagement may ensue). Lastly, failing to practice what we preach will breed resistance. If we encourage the team to be open and adaptive but we appear inflexible or defensive to feedback, the team will push back or tune us out. In summary, coaches must reflect on how their behavior might be inviting resistance. Often, a quick reorientation—re-contracting expectations, apologizing for a misstep, and adjusting one's approach to fit the team better—can dissolve that resistance. Having the humility to course-correct as a coach not only reduces resistance, but also models the very adaptability and transparency we seek to foster in the team.

CHAPTER 8   TURNING RESISTANCE INTO RESILIENCE

Strategies for Navigating and Overcoming Resistance

When resistance shows up, Agile coaches should have a few strategies up their sleeves to handle it and turn it around. Here are some key approaches a coach can use when working with a team that's pushing back.

Adopt an Empathic and Neutral Coaching Stance

Everything begins with the coach's stance—their internal posture and attitude toward the team. When resistance surfaces (be it open defiance or quiet disengagement), the coach's job is to remain calm, curious, and non-judgmental. In practice, this means not taking the resistance personally and not reacting with frustration or authority. Instead, embody the coaching mindset: a stance of openness, compassion, and curiosity. If a team senses the coach is disappointed in them or is "against" them, their resistance will only harden. But if they sense the coach is genuinely on their side, seeking to understand their perspective and help, they are more likely to open up. Techniques to embody this stance include practicing active listening (really hearing their concerns without interrupting or immediately fixing), expressing empathy (*"I can understand why this feels frustrating"*), and showing humility (*"I don't have all the answers either, let's figure this out together"*). A neutral stance also means avoiding taking sides in team disagreements; instead, align with the whole team's growth. In a tense retrospective, for example, an empathic coach might say, *"It's clear everyone cares deeply about this issue. My role is to help us have a constructive conversation where all viewpoints are heard."* This kind of statement underscores neutrality and shared purpose. Maintaining this centered stance can be challenging, especially if the resistance is directed at you (say, a skeptical manager questioning your value, or a team member who constantly dismisses your suggestions). Here, emotional self-management is key: take a breath, remember not to ego-clash, and respond with professionalism and curiosity. Oftentimes, simply modeling a calm presence in the face of tension has a powerful effect. It "sets the tone" of stability. A coach who stays present and objective amid conflict helps the team to self-regulate as well. Your steadiness provides an anchor.

Additionally, holding a positive regard for the team—believing that they are capable and resourceful even if they're struggling now—tends to become a self-fulfilling prophecy. An example scenario: a Scrum master is facing a team that resists doing sprint retrospectives (they say it's a waste of time). An authoritative stance would be, *"We have to do retros because Scrum says so, and I'm the Scrum master."* An empathic coaching stance would be, *"I hear you that past retrospectives haven't felt valuable. I wonder what we can change to make them worth our time? Let's experiment."* The latter invites collaboration and shows respect for their perspective, which can turn cynics into participants. Remember, your mindset as a coach is contagious—if you approach resistance as an adversary to be battled, the team will likely battle you; if you approach it as a puzzle to be explored together, the team is more likely to drop their guard. By being patient, respectful, and curious, you defuse the emotional charge and create conditions for resistance to be discussed openly rather than acted out.

Work with the Present Moment (Here-and-Now Interventions)

In the thick of a resistant moment, one of the most effective tools is to name and work with what is happening right now. Rather than ignoring tension or plowing ahead with your agenda, use the resistance as data and bring it into the conversation (skillfully). This is a very present-oriented approach inspired by the Gestalt theory: the idea that what's happening in the moment is exactly what needs to be addressed. For example, imagine during a planning meeting, you notice people exchanging glances or

CHAPTER 8   TURNING RESISTANCE INTO RESILIENCE

two team members sighing every time a particular topic comes up. A present-moment intervention might be: *"I'm noticing some heavy sighs and side glances when we discuss integrating that legacy system. What's going on for the team right now?"* By doing this, you are gently surfacing the undercurrent in real time. It signals to the team that it's okay to pause the formal agenda and discuss the real concerns at hand. Often, such interventions reveal the real source of resistance—perhaps the sighs indicate a lack of confidence in the integration approach, or frustration with a prior decision. Another aspect of working with the present moment is addressing emotions as they arise. If you sense frustration building, you might say, *"I sense some frustration in the room (or on this call). What needs to be voiced?"* If someone is withdrawing, you might gently invite them in: *"John, I notice you've been quiet—I'd value your perspective if you're comfortable sharing."* These here-and-now observations must be delivered *without judgment.* You're not accusing, you're inquiring. In Chapter 2, we saw an example of this kind of presence: during a heated sprint planning, a coach noticed a comment indicating deeper concern and brought focus to it: *"I sense a lot of concern around quality—shall we explore that?"* That simple intervention can redirect the team from surface arguments to the core issue (e.g., *"We're worried rushing this feature will introduce serious bugs"*). Working with the present also means being adaptive in the moment. If an exercise you planned is meeting resistance (the team's body language is closed off, or they're openly challenging it), address that rather than forcing it. You might pause the workshop and say, *"It appears this activity isn't resonating. Can we talk about what you really need right now?"* Perhaps they feel it's too elementary, or they're tired from another fire drill earlier in the day. By pivoting based on what is happening, you both respect the team's reality and often discover a better way forward. Sometimes "working with the present" involves literally taking a break. If tempers are flaring in a meeting, a coach might suggest a short timeout: *"Let's pause for five minutes. When we return, perhaps we can try to hear what each person needs from this discussion."* This can prevent escalation and allow cooler heads to prevail. Overall, this strategy is about acknowledging and leveraging the current experience instead of fighting it. It's amazing how simply voicing the unspoken can dissipate tension. Many teams have sighed in relief when the coach says what everyone is feeling: *"This change is hard, and it's okay that we're struggling with it."* Such here-and-now honesty often unlocks a productive dialogue, turning resistance into a topic the team can openly grapple with (rather than a silent force thwarting progress).

Facilitate Open Dialogue and Listening

Resistance often persists because people feel unheard or misunderstood. One of the coach's most powerful interventions is facilitating a dialogue where underlying issues can be safely aired. This goes hand-in-hand with psychological safety—team members need to know that it's acceptable to voice dissent or skepticism without repercussion. A coach can establish this by explicitly inviting perspectives: *"Let's hear from those who are skeptical about this change—what are your concerns?"* and by modeling non-defensive listening when those concerns come out. Sometimes, just giving space for the team to express why they're resistant dramatically reduces the resistance (people feel, "Finally, we're being listened to"). Use coaching techniques like paraphrasing (*"So, you're worried that adopting pair programming might slow us down, did I get that right?"*) to show you're trying to understand their viewpoint. Then encourage team-to-team communication as well: Have them listen to each other's concerns and ideas. The coach essentially becomes a facilitator of a difficult conversation.

In cases where resistance stems from conflict or tension between individuals or factions, you may need to facilitate a dialogue for conflict resolution. Establish some ground rules for the discussion to maintain respect (e.g., one person speaks at a time, focus on the issue rather than the person, etc.). By diplomatically bringing the issue on the table, the coach allows the parties to address it directly rather than through passive-aggressive resistance. Similarly, if a subset of the team is resisting a decision (perhaps QA engineers versus developers over a testing approach), set up a dialogue where each side can clarify their needs and concerns. Often, the coach may facilitate techniques such as nonviolent communication (NVC) or a structured round-robin, where each person speaks uninterrupted for a few minutes. The key is creating an environment where everyone feels heard. When people feel heard, they tend to become more open to influence in return; their defensive stance softens.

Facilitation also means guiding the conversation toward common ground or solutions once the issues are aired. You might ask, *"What outcome would address these concerns for you?"* or *"How can we adjust our plan so that you feel more comfortable moving forward?"* Sometimes resistance is resolved through compromise (maybe adjusting a deadline, providing extra training, or agreeing to try something for a limited time as an experiment). The simple act of engaging in dialogue can transform an adversarial dynamic into a collaborative problem-solving session. For example, a team was very resistant to adopting a new project management tool mandated by the Project Management Office (PMO). Rather than pushing it, the coach facilitated a dialogue between the team and the PMO rep: The team expressed their frustration (the last tool was buggy and wasted their time), the PMO explained the reasons for the new tool (better integration, compliance, etc.), and together they identified a few training and support actions that would address the team's concerns. The team's resistance dropped significantly once they felt their voice mattered in the decision. As a coach, you may also need to coach the stakeholders or leaders to participate constructively in such dialogues, ensuring, for instance, that a sponsor doesn't shut down the conversation with *"just do it"* language. When done well, facilitating dialogue transforms resistance from a standoff into a mutual exploration of "how can we make this work?"

By guiding the team to talk to each other rather than about each other, and focusing on issues, not personalities, you create a pathway for genuine understanding and movement forward.

Address and Reframe Patterns or Stories

Often, resistance is sustained by a repeating pattern or a narrative within the team. A coach spots these patterns and helps the team bring them into the open. For instance, you might notice that in every retrospective, any suggestion involving changes to the coding standards is immediately shot down by the same two senior developers—a pattern that indicates a possibly rigid mindset or fear. As a coach, you could address this pattern by reframing or inquiring: *"I've observed that whenever we discuss coding standards, we quickly decide it's fine as-is. I'm curious—is there an underlying concern about changing those standards that we haven't talked about?"* This invites reflection on a pattern that was previously only in the developers' subconscious. Similarly, pay attention to the stories the team tells about itself or others: *"Ops never listens to us,"* or *"We're just bad at estimates,"* or *"Management will never allow that."* These narratives create a mental model that breeds resistance (Why try if "they'll never listen"?). The coach can challenge and reframe these stories. For example, if the team believes *"management doesn't care about quality, only speed,"* the coach might bring evidence to the contrary or facilitate a meeting where management can express their genuine concern for quality, thereby updating the team's story. Another common pattern is for certain voices to dominate while others withdraw. This can lead to passive resistance from the quieter members (they resist by disengaging). A coach should actively intervene in these patterns: *"We've heard from the same few people on this topic; I'd like to invite anyone who hasn't spoken yet—what do you think about this change?"* Or for a dominant member, in private, coach them on making space for others.

Another pattern coaches should address is avoidance (a form of resistance). Perhaps the team continually delays the "retrospective" or keeps postponing a tough discussion for the future. Pointing out this avoidance gently can be powerful: *"I've noticed we've moved the retrospective three times this quarter. What might be behind our reluctance to reflect together?"* This can surface fears or beliefs like *"We think it's just going to be a blame session"*—which, once named, can be solved (e.g., by establishing the Prime Directive or using a different retro format to ensure psychological safety). It's important when addressing patterns to do so without blame. You're effectively holding up a mirror, not scolding. Use neutral language ("I notice ...", "It seems like ...", "What I'm hearing is ...") and invite the team to explore it with you. Once a pattern is acknowledged, the coach can help the team reframe it or experiment with breaking it. For example, if the narrative is "we always fail at change," help them reframe to *"we have learned a lot from past attempts; this time we can apply those lessons."* If the pattern is that decisions get made outside the team (leading them to resist decisions imposed on them), help them establish a new decision-making policy so they feel more ownership (thus breaking the victim mentality pattern). Ultimately, by making the implicit explicit, the coach removes the power that subconscious patterns have over the team. The team can then choose a different response. Over time, as they practice noticing and adjusting their own patterns, they become more resilient and self-correcting, which is exactly the goal.

Manage Difficult Behaviors Constructively

In some cases, resistance shows up through one or two individuals' challenging behaviors; for example, a team member who constantly interrupts or criticizes any new idea (the "naysayer"), or someone who withdraws and refuses to participate, or perhaps uses sarcasm and side comments that undermine meetings. These behaviors can derail the team and infect others with negativity, so the coach needs strategies to manage

CHAPTER 8   TURNING RESISTANCE INTO RESILIENCE

them while still respecting the person behind them. First, set or reinforce teamwork agreements that focus on respectful communication. If the team has none, co-create them ("We speak one at a time," "Critique ideas, not people," etc.). Then, if someone violates these norms (e.g., attacking someone's idea or making it personal), the coach should intervene immediately in a firm but respectful manner. For instance, *"Let's remember our agreement: we critique the idea, not the person. It's okay to disagree, but let's keep it respectful. What is your specific concern about the idea?"* This kind of real-time boundary-setting can neutralize a potentially toxic moment and also signals to the team that psychological safety is being protected (which in turn reduces resistance rooted in fear of attack). For chronic behaviors (like the perpetual naysayer), a combination of empathy and redirection works well. Acknowledge the value in their viewpoint (they often raise valid risks), but set a structure: *"I appreciate that you're looking out for potential issues. Could I ask that for each concern you raise, you also suggest an alternative or a way to address it? That would help keep our discussion constructive."* This transforms the behavior from pure resistance into participation in problem solving. If someone is resisting by withdrawing (maybe arms folded, no comments), consider addressing it privately. One-on-one, share your observation and concern: *"I've noticed you've been quiet in the last few meetings when we discuss X. I value your input; what's going on for you?"* It could be that the person feels it's not safe to speak, or they've disengaged out of frustration. By coaching them individually, you might help them re-engage or surface an issue that needs addressing with the whole team.

Preventive action is also important. Sometimes, difficult behaviors escalate because the environment allows it. As a coach, you can structure meetings to diffuse potential issues; e.g., use a round-robin format to ensure everyone speaks (lessening the chance for one person to dominate), or use time boxes for discussions (limiting filibustering), or utilize anonymous brainstorming tools (to get input from shy or cautious members without fear). These facilitation techniques can pre-empt

257

resistance behaviors. Another tool is positive reinforcement: Catch people (including the difficult individuals) doing something constructive and acknowledge it. *"I noticed in this planning session you raised a concern and also offered a possible solution—thank you, that really moved us forward."* This encourages more of the desired behavior. In handling difficult behavior, it's crucial to separate the person from the behavior. Make it clear you value the person as a team member, and you're addressing the behavior because it's hindering the team. Often, resistant behaviors are a sign that a person has an unmet need or concern. The chronically critical person might actually be anxious about the project failing. The disengaged person might feel their ideas were ignored earlier. By addressing the behavior and also investigating the underlying need, you not only manage the immediate disruption but also potentially resolve a source of resistance. In more extreme cases (e.g., someone actively sabotaging changes or being openly hostile), you might need to involve leadership or take a stronger stance, but even then, approach it as *"We have a problem to solve together,"* not *"You are a problem."* Maintaining the individual's dignity and inviting them to be part of the solution is more effective than public scolding or punishment, which often only breeds deeper resentment from them or others. In summary, timely intervention, clear norms, empathy, and structure are your allies in managing difficult behaviors. When handled well, even the "troublemaker" can turn into a powerful advocate for the team. Many coaches have seen naysayers transform into the most vocal supporters once their core issues were heard and addressed.

Resolve (or Surface) Conflicting Agendas

Conflicting agendas—whether between a team and its sponsor or within subgroups of a team—can lead to persistent resistance. A key strategy is to surface and align agendas through contracting and facilitation. If you suspect a conflict in goals is at play, bring the parties together for

CHAPTER 8   TURNING RESISTANCE INTO RESILIENCE

an alignment conversation. This could be as formal as a re-contracting session with the sponsor and team, or as informal as pointing out the discrepancy and mediating a discussion. For example, suppose a product owner is pushing for a scope that the team thinks is unrealistic; the team is resisting by sandbagging estimates or dragging their feet. The coach might facilitate a session where the product owner and team openly discuss their goals and concerns: *"Let's get everything on the table—what does success look like for each of you? Where do we feel tension in these goals?"* The coach ensures each side listens to the other. Maybe the product owner's agenda is driven by a customer commitment, while the team's agenda is not to accrue massive technical debt; both are legitimate. The coach can then guide them to find a solution that meets both requirements to an acceptable degree (perhaps by reducing the scope to meet the most critical customer needs while allowing time for refactoring to improve quality). With Agile teams, normalize that some tension between speed, quality, customer demands, team sustainability, etc., is natural. The coach's aim is to shift the mindset from competing agendas to a shared problem-solving approach. Emphasize the shared goals where they exist. In Agile, there's almost always a common higher goal—delivering value to customers, thriving as a business, etc. Refocus the conversation there: *"Ultimately, both the sponsor and the team want the product to succeed in the market. How can we get on the same page about achieving that?"* This reframing can reduce the feeling of opposition. Encourage transparency: If the sponsor has a non-negotiable priority, it should be stated openly; if the team has serious reservations or constraints, they should voice them. As a coach, you might literally act as a translator or mediator, ensuring each party's perspective is heard in terms the other can accept.

For internal team conflicts with conflicting agendas (e.g., developers vs. QA or front-end vs. back-end priorities), use techniques such as establishing shared working agreements or defining success. For instance, if Dev and QA are at odds, help them craft a team definition of "done" that incorporates both quality and speed so they are aligned on what they're

CHAPTER 8   TURNING RESISTANCE INTO RESILIENCE

collectively aiming for. In one coaching scenario, there were quiet turf wars between component teams—each wanted to optimize their piece at the expense of the whole, causing them to resist cross-team collaboration. The coach guided the creation of a shared purpose statement for all teams, serving as a reminder that they're all building one product for the customer, not competing products. This helped shift perspective and ease the resistance to working together. When agendas conflict, you may sometimes find that a higher-level leadership decision is necessary (for example, clarifying business priorities or adjusting key performance indicators, or KPIs). Part of the coach's strategy is then to facilitate those escalations constructively; e.g., helping the team articulate a clear ask to leadership (*"We need clarity on whether customer satisfaction or new sales take priority this quarter, because it's affecting our focus"*), rather than just stewing in resistance. In all cases, surfacing the issue is the prerequisite to resolving it. Resistance loves ambiguity. It's easy to resist something when goals are muddy because no one can be proven "wrong." By contrast, clear, agreed-upon goals shine a light that makes misalignment obvious and addressable. Thus, a coach navigating resistance will often find themselves in the role of an aligner—aligning expectations, aligning understanding, aligning metrics with desired behavior, and so on. When everyone is truly on the same page about the why and what of the change, much of the resistance loses its fuel. And if they're not on the same page, at least now it's out in the open and can be consciously dealt with (rather than fought in the shadows).

Leverage Clear Contracting and Re-contracting

Finally, one of the most preventive and remedial strategies for resistance is effective contracting—essentially, making clear agreements up front and revisiting them as needed. Contracting is where we define the purpose of the coaching engagement, roles, expectations, and boundaries. A well-crafted coaching alliance creates a foundation of trust and clarity that preempts many forms of resistance. For example, when a coaching engagement begins, explicitly discussing *"What does each stakeholder expect from this?"* can unveil hidden fears or hopes (perhaps a manager secretly expects the coach to "fix the team's attitude"—a red flag that needs to be addressed). By getting those on the table, the coach can clarify what's realistic and ethical, and ensure all parties commit to the same vision of success. Such a strong contract creates safety: The team knows the coach's role and that there are no hidden agendas, the sponsor knows how they'll be involved, and everyone knows how to raise concerns if things go off track. This clarity itself can ward off resistance born of misunderstanding. That said, even with good initial contracting, things change—priorities shift, new stakeholders join, or initial approaches prove unworkable. Coaches should treat contracting as an ongoing process, or "alliance building." If resistance is mounting mid-way through a coaching engagement, it may be time to re-contract—literally pause and renegotiate how we're working together. For instance, a team started resisting the coach's presence in their daily Scrums; the coach paused and revisited the agreement: *"Originally, we said I'd attend to observe and help improve team communication. It seems that may not be serving you now. How would you like to adjust this agreement?"* The team might then say, *"We'd like to have you only on Mondays, and on other days we'll brief you if issues come up."* By adjusting the agreement, their resistance (stemming perhaps from feeling micromanaged) was resolved. Clear contracting also applies at the micro level: Every meeting or workshop can benefit from a mini-contract at the start (e.g., *"Today we're trying a brainstorming game. Let's agree that all ideas are valid, and we won't critique until the next stage"*). If resistance emerges ("this game is silly"), you can point back to the agreement or adjust it by mutual consent.

In multi-party scenarios (coach, team, management) strive for Type A (see Chapter 8 for more) alignment—meaning the coach, team, and sponsor all have an open, trustful three-way contract. If you notice slippage toward a dysfunctional pattern (like the team and coach colluding

CHAPTER 8   TURNING RESISTANCE INTO RESILIENCE

against the sponsor or vice versa), call a reset meeting. In that meeting, reinforce transparency: *"Let's ensure we're all on the same page; if there are any concerns or new expectations, let's discuss them now."* Emphasize the "no secrets, no surprises" rule. For example, if the sponsor has started asking the coach for private progress reports, the coach should encourage making that a joint conversation with the team, as per the original contract on confidentiality. By maintaining a clean alliance, you prevent a lot of mistrust that breeds resistance.

It's also worth explicitly contracting around how to handle resistance or missteps! Chapter 3 noted that a good contract includes talking about *"what if something's not working?"* If from the outset you agree, *"If at any point someone is uncomfortable or feels this coaching isn't helping, we'll voice it and discuss how to adjust,"* then when resistance arises, it's not an elephant in the room—it's expected to be voiced as part of the working agreement. This meta-contract can make teams feel safer because they know they have a say in the process.

In summary, clear agreements are the guardrails that keep the coaching on track. Many resistances can be traced back to fuzzy expectations or broken trust, which solid contracting could have prevented. And when resistance does occur, revisiting and refining the agreements often provides a straightforward path to resolution. It might be as simple as, *"Let's all remind ourselves what we agreed to, and see if that still makes sense. If not, how should we change it?"* This collaborative approach treats the team as an equal partner in designing the coaching journey, which increases their buy-in. They are no longer resisting your plan; it becomes our plan, co-created and clear. The effect is empowering and thus resilience-building, as we'll discuss next.

CHAPTER 8   TURNING RESISTANCE INTO RESILIENCE

Assisting Teams in Building Resilience

Overcoming resistance is not the end goal; it's a means to an even more important end: a resilient, self-organizing team. Resilience in an Agile team context means the ability to weather challenges, adapt to changing conditions, learn from adversity, and continuously improve without losing morale or effectiveness. It's the quality that allows a team to take a hit (a failed sprint, a sudden pivot in priorities, a conflict) and emerge not defeated, but stronger and wiser. In fact, a team that has constructively worked through its resistance points often becomes more resilient. They've faced some "internal storms" and developed confidence in their ability to handle both internal and external challenges. In this section, I will focus on how a coach can actively cultivate and reinforce resilience in a team, turning the hard-earned lessons from dealing with resistance into habits and mindsets that prepare the team for whatever the future brings. Many of these themes tie back to earlier chapters on team coaching fundamentals (Chapter 2) and the deeper dynamics of teams (Chapters 6 and 7). Key aspects include mindset, agency, learning practices, and relationships:

Define and Model Team Resilience

It's useful to start by explicitly defining what resilience looks like for the team. Often, teams haven't considered this beyond vague ideas of "don't fall apart under pressure." A coach can facilitate a conversation or exercise to identify resilient behaviors. For example, ask the team: *"Think of a past project or sprint where things went wrong—what helped you get through it? What behaviors do we want to see when we face tough times?"* Common answers may be: *"We come together to problem solve rather than blame," "We support each other," "We stay adaptable and positive,"* etc. From such discussions, you can derive a team resilience checklist or agreement.

CHAPTER 8   TURNING RESISTANCE INTO RESILIENCE

Having this shared vision is powerful—it sets a positive tone that *challenges will happen, and we have a plan to address them.* It reframes setbacks as a normal part of the journey rather than failures.

The coach should also model resilience in their own behavior as an example. As noted in Chapter 2, an Agile coach who embraces change and views challenges through a *"lens of possibilities rather than problems"* lays the cultural groundwork for the team to do the same. For instance, if a crucial release suddenly fails, the coach's reaction might be, *"Alright, this is tough—but it's also a chance for us to learn something important. Let's do a quick incident retro and see what we can improve."* This response models calm and a focus on learning, not panic or finger-pointing. Over time, the team internalizes this approach. Psychological safety, which I've mentioned often, is foundational to resilience: A team that feels safe will confront issues early, preventing small problems from turning into crises. Google's research (Project Aristotle) found that psychological safety was the number-one predictor of high-performing teams, enabling productive discussions and innovation. That's essentially resilience in action—a safe team deals with problems while they're still manageable. So continually reinforce safety and trust (Competency 4 from Chapter 2) as you build resilience. When a team has transparency and no "internal rot" (no festering hidden issues), it can absorb shocks much better. In a resilient team, you'll observe things like honest communication even under stress, quick adaptation to new priorities, mutual support when someone hits a snag, and a lack of blame when experiments fail. These are signs that not only has resistance been overcome, but the capacity to handle future resistance or disruption is ingrained. Coaches should celebrate these behaviors when they occur (*"I'm really impressed with how we pivoted this sprint after the change request—that was great resilience in action"*). This helps the team recognize their own strength, reinforcing their identity as a resilient team.

Cultivate a Growth Mindset (Embrace Uncertainty)

A core ingredient of resilience is the growth mindset—the belief (coined by psychologist Carol Dweck) that abilities and situations can improve through effort, feedback, and learning. In contrast to a fixed mindset (*"We're just not good at X"*), a growth mindset says, *"We're not good at X yet, but we can learn."* Agile philosophy is inherently growth-minded, valuing adaptation over sticking to a fixed plan. As a coach, you want to instill this attitude in the team. Encourage the team to view challenges and even failures as opportunities to learn, rather than disasters. This directly combats the fear of failure that underlies a lot of resistance. For example, if a sprint goal is missed, a fixed mindset reaction might be, *"This is terrible, we failed, maybe we're just a bad team."* A growth mindset reaction would be, *"Missing the goal is disappointing, but let's investigate why. What can we learn for next time? Maybe our estimation was off or we encountered unforeseen technical debt—how can we adapt?"* The coach's language and facilitation can steer the team toward the latter. Use retrospectives not as gripe sessions but as positive engines of improvement. Normalize making mistakes as long as we extract insight from them. It helps to introduce the concept of *"safe-to-fail experiments."* For instance, if the team is resistant to trying a new practice (say test-driven development [TDD]) because they fear it might lower velocity initially, frame it as an experiment: *"Let's try TDD for one sprint as an experiment to see what we learn. It's okay if it doesn't go perfectly; we'll inspect and adapt."* This reduces the fear of uncertainty by treating everything as a learning trial rather than a permanent, high-stakes commitment. Also, emphasize incremental progress; a growth mindset thrives on seeing improvement, however small. Help the team set mini-goals and celebrate incremental wins (*"We improved our automated test coverage from 50% to 60%—that's progress!"*). This fosters an environment where the team is always looking

CHAPTER 8   TURNING RESISTANCE INTO RESILIENCE

for how they can grow, rather than whether they're "good" or "bad" at something. Importantly, a growth mindset also means embracing uncertainty and ambiguity as things that can hold opportunity. In today's VUCA world (volatile, uncertain, complex, ambiguous), resilient teams don't demand perfect clarity to move forward. As Chapter 6 pointed out, leaders (and teams) need to view uncertainty as an opportunity and stress as a catalyst for innovation, rather than as a threat. A coach can cultivate this by reframing ambiguous situations: *"We don't have all the answers about the new market demo—that's true. What does this uncertainty make possible? Maybe it gives us freedom to experiment with a creative approach since nothing is set in stone."* It might sound a bit Pollyanna-ish, but this kind of optimistic reframe helps shift the team's focus from what they can't do to what they can do. One technique is practicing scenario planning: rather than dreading unknowns, the team plays them out; *"If X happens, how could we respond? If Y happens, what would we do?"* This builds confidence that they can handle a range of outcomes. It's essentially inoculating them with *imagined adversity,* so real adversity is less shocking. Over time, a growth mindset culture means team members start challenging themselves. They volunteer for stretch goals, they say things like, *"Who would have thought we'd actually enjoy pair programming? We hated it at first, but look at us now."* They become more psychologically flexible, which is at the heart of resilience. And crucially, when individuals in the team demonstrate growth mindset behaviors (like openly admitting a mistake and showing what they learned), recognize and praise that. It reinforces to everyone that this is how we succeed here. In sum, by cultivating a growth mindset, the coach helps the team view resistance or setbacks not as indictments of their ability, but as natural steps in their learning journey. The team becomes less afraid of challenges (and thus less likely to resist changes) because they're confident they can navigate any challenge.

CHAPTER 8   TURNING RESISTANCE INTO RESILIENCE

Foster Team Agency and Ownership

A resilient team has a strong sense of agency. They believe, *"We can influence our circumstances and outcomes; we are not helpless pawns."* This belief in collective efficacy is a potent antidote to the victim mentality that sometimes underlies resistance. When a team feels they have ownership of their process and decisions, they're more likely to tackle problems head-on (since they see it as their responsibility) rather than passively resist or wait for someone else to fix things. As a coach, you want to continuously push appropriate decision-making power and responsibility into the team's hands. This is aligned with the principle of teams being self-organized. For example, if the team is resistant to a top-down change, instead of forcing it, involve them in shaping it: *"How would you design a solution for this issue? What do you think would work?"* By co-creating changes, the team's agency is honored. They go from feeling "done to" (which breeds resistance) to "doing with" (which breeds commitment). Be mindful not to inadvertently steal agency. Coaches can sometimes become overactive, solving problems for the team, especially under pressure. Chapter 7 warned about the coach falling into a Rescuer role, which paradoxically can feed a team's victim stance. For instance, a coach who routinely steps in to handle conflicts or writes up all the retrospective actions themselves might actually disempower the team. If the team learns "the coach will sort out our issues," they won't flex their own problem-solving muscles and might even become passively resistant (doing nothing and blaming the coach if things don't improve— *"Well, your coaching didn't work"*). Instead, encourage the team to take the lead. If a conflict arises, perhaps facilitate the first conversation, but then challenge the team to create their own conflict resolution pact moving forward. If retrospectives yield improvement ideas, have the team members volunteer to own the actions (rotate the ownership if needed)—don't let it always fall to the coach or Scrum master. When teams implement their own ideas, their confidence grows, which is resilience. They start seeing themselves as

CHAPTER 8 TURNING RESISTANCE INTO RESILIENCE

agents of change rather than targets of change. Another aspect of agency is giving the team permission to adapt processes to fit them (within the guardrails of Agile values). A textbook approach might not work perfectly for a specific team, and if they feel obligated to follow it despite pain, they'll either resist openly or comply superficially (which is another form of resistance—compliance without engagement). A coach can empower them by saying, *"It's your process—how would you improve it? What if this stand-up is too long; how can we make it better for you?"* This signals that the team has ownership of how they work. As they exercise this ownership, they become more proactive. Proactivity is a sign of resilience; rather than being knocked around by problems, a proactive team anticipates and addresses them. On a practical note, techniques like delegation poker or Responsible, Accountable, Consulted, Informed (RACI) matrices can be used to clarify and expand team decision rights. Also, encouraging the team to set their own stretch goals or improvement targets (instead of all goals coming top-down) boosts their sense of control. You may witness the transformation: A team that initially said, *"We were told to do Agile, whatever,"* shifts to saying, *"We decided to experiment with our sprint demo format to engage stakeholders better."* That linguistic shift from passive to active voice, from *"We were told"* to *"We decided,"* is huge. It means they see themselves as owners of their destiny in the project. Such teams handle setbacks better because they think in terms of solutions (*"What can we do about it?"*) rather than blame or surrender. In coaching terms, you are moving them along the spectrum from dependence to self-managing independence, which is a hallmark of high team maturity (and a coach's ultimate aim—to become redundant!). Note that building agency doesn't mean abandoning the team to sink or swim. It's a balance: You're still there as a safety net and guide, but you're consciously giving them the space to lead and solve. A practical example: If a critical production issue occurs, instead of the coach jumping to coordinate the firefight, let the team assemble and handle it (they'll likely do so faster, too, being domain experts). Afterward, in the retro, highlight how effectively they self-organized to resolve it, reinforcing their confidence. Each such experience of *"We handled it ourselves"* is like tempering steel; the team becomes stronger and less likely to shatter under stress. They trust their own capabilities, which means future changes or challenges are less intimidating. Resilience grows from the mindset *"We've got this."* The coach's role is to nurture that mindset through granting autonomy and celebrating responsible ownership.

Learn from History: Promote Reflection and Adaptation

Resilient teams are learning teams. They don't make the same mistake twice if they can help it; instead, they treat mistakes and past experiences as valuable data for improvement. One of the coach's key jobs is to instill a habit of *reflection* in the team—essentially, to bake the inspect-and-adapt cycle (together with "transparency" pillars of empiricism from the Scrum framework) into the team's DNA beyond just the formal events. We often think of the sprint retrospective as the main avenue for this, and indeed, retrospectives are powerful if done well. The coach should ensure that retrospectives are regular, safe, and action-oriented. The coach's facilitation must break barriers; e.g., introducing retrospective techniques that surface hidden issues (like anonymous surveys, the "elephants in the room" exercise, etc.) or using structured methods (like Agile's "Five Whys" for root-cause analysis) to dig into problems rather than glossing over them. The idea is to transform any failure or conflict into explicit lessons. When a team sees that every stumble leads to tangible improvements, they start to fear stumbling less. It's no longer *"Oh no, something went wrong"* but *"Something went wrong—let's figure out why and make sure we handle it better next time."* That's resilience: continuously bouncing back and *improving* from adversity. Encourage the team to document their learnings—not in a heavy, bureaucratic way, but perhaps in a living "team playbook" or improvement backlog. Some teams create a simple wiki or mural with two columns: *"What we've learned"* and *"Our agreed adjustments."* This visual reminder shows progress over time and can be especially heartening when things get tough ("Look how far we've come and how much we've overcome"). Apart from retrospectives, promote a general reflective practice. For instance, after a big release or project phase, facilitate a longer retrospective or "post-mortem" that involves all stakeholders, extracting system-level learnings. For personal reflection, consider introducing techniques like a daily reflection or journaling for team members, or even a buddy system where teammates discuss each week what they learned. Leaders in Chapter 6 were coached to regularly reflect on their transformation efforts (doing retrospectives on the change itself). Agile teams can do the same at their level. The coach might occasionally pose meta-questions to the team, like, *"How are we improving our improvement process? Are we getting better at learning?"* This invites reflection on their learning mechanism itself, leading to even more effective adaptation. Another angle is learning from others' history. A coach can bring in experiences from other teams or industries as learning material: *"When Company X adopted Agile, they struggled with QA integration at first—what can we learn from their story?"* or *"I've seen another team try a similar change; here's what went wrong for them, does that prompt any ideas for us?"* This can accelerate learning and resilience by *preparing* the team for potential pitfalls (so when they encounter them, it's *"Oh, we expected this, we know what to try"* rather than *"This is a catastrophe"*). However, always contextualize—no two teams are identical. Resilient teams also practice double-loop learning—not just solving the immediate problem, but examining and updating the underlying norms or assumptions that led to it. Let's say, in a retrospective, the team finds that slipping quality was due to skipping writing unit tests under deadline pressure. Single-loop learning would be "write tests next time"; double-loop might lead them to ask, *"Why did we feel we had to skip tests? Is there an assumption about deadlines versus quality we need to change? How can we work differently so we don't get in that squeeze again?"* This might result in a deeper change, like negotiating more realistic deadlines or improving continuous integration to give fast feedback. Coaches should gently push the team toward this deeper reflection when appropriate, as it yields more systemic resilience. Over time, the goal is for the team to adopt reflection as second nature—not just in retros, but on the fly. A term often used is becoming a "learning team" or a "deliberately developmental" team. You might hear team members say, *"Hold on, before we rush into the next sprint, what did we learn from the last one's failures so we don't repeat them?"* or *"We keep having testing crunches at the end—what does that tell us about our process?"* When the team itself is raising those questions without waiting for the coach, that's a huge marker of resilience. They are actively seeking to adapt. As a coach, at that point you can step back and applaud—they're doing what you aimed for.

One more practice to mention is celebrating growth from adversity. After a crisis is resolved or a conflict is worked through, bring the team together to *appreciate* what they managed to overcome. It's the concept of "post-traumatic growth" in psychology: People (and teams) often grow in confidence and skill after handling a tough situation. Make that growth explicit: *"Two months ago, we might have imploded when we lost our product owner and got a sudden scope change. But look, we adapted our plan, communicated openly, and delivered something we can be proud of. That's real resilience. Great job—what did we learn about ourselves from this?"* This not only reinforces positive identity but also locks in the learning. In summary, resilience = learning applied. A team that consistently turns experiences into improvements is continuously renewing its ability to handle future challenges. The coach's emphasis on reflection and adaptation ensures that resistance and setbacks feed the virtuous cycle of growth instead of the vicious cycle of defeat.

CHAPTER 8   TURNING RESISTANCE INTO RESILIENCE

Strengthen Purpose and Leverage Strengths

A team that knows why it exists and what it's inherently good at will weather storms with greater determination and confidence. Clarifying the team's purpose—their fundamental mission or the value they aspire to deliver—provides a stable beacon during change. When people are connected to a purpose, they can tolerate a lot more uncertainty and change because there's meaning behind it. As a coach, you can help the team articulate and frequently revisit their "North Star." For example, an Agile team's purpose might be *"to delight our customers with easy-to-use, reliable software that solves their daily problems."* If a big change comes down (say, adopting a new platform), frame it in terms of this purpose: *"How might this change help us fulfill our mission to delight customers? Let's find that line of sight."* This connection can transform resistance (which often stems from feeling "this change is pointless" or "this is just for somebody's bonus") into at least a grudging acknowledgment of necessity, if not enthusiasm. Conversely, if the team determines a change actually threatens their purpose (for instance, a policy that they fear will hurt product quality), that's useful data to escalate and discuss with stakeholders. Either way, purpose becomes a guiding filter and a motivator. Purpose also bonds the team; it's a shared "why." A team becomes more resilient when everyone is on board with why they do what they do. A practical step: Have the team co-create a purpose statement or elevator pitch for their work. Write it down and put it on the wall (or virtual workspace). Refer to it in meetings: *"Is this action aligned with our purpose?"* When inevitable conflicts arise or when morale dips, reconnecting to purpose can re-energize and focus the team on what truly matters.

Along with purpose, leveraging strengths is vital. Every team has strengths—technical skills, domain knowledge, interpersonal synergy, creativity, diversity of thought, etc. In times of stress, it's easy to get fixated on problems and weaknesses. A coach can help the team identify and use their strengths deliberately as a resilience strategy. Consider doing a *"strengths inventory"* session (some coaches use StrengthsFinder or similar tools, or something simple like asking each team member what they think the team's top three strengths are). Suppose a team recognizes that one of their strengths is a high level of trust and openness among themselves—that's a huge asset in tough times (they can speak candidly, support each other). Another team's strength might be deep expertise in their tech stack—so even if requirements churn, they can rapidly design solid solutions. When facing a challenge, remind them of these strengths: *"We've never tackled a client this big before, but remember, rapid prototyping is one of our fortes—we can create a small proof of concept to build confidence."* This instills a sense of *"We've got what we need to handle this."* It can also be useful to assign roles or tasks in crises that play to individuals' strengths; e.g., let the naturally calm, methodical person run point on an urgent bug fix (because they won't get flustered), or have the socially adept team member communicate the bad news to stakeholders (because they'll do it diplomatically and preserve trust). By deploying strengths optimally, not only does the team perform better under pressure, but also each member feels valued, which boosts morale when it might otherwise sink. A focus on strengths can be woven into regular ceremonies: In retrospectives, don't just ask, *"What should we improve?"* but also, *"What went well and how can we do more of it?"* (This is a common retrospective prompt: *"Keep doing, Start doing, Stop doing,"* where "Keep doing" is all about strengths and successes to continue.) This positivity balances out the negative and builds an identity of success. Agile coaches might introduce techniques from positive psychology or solution-focused coaching here; for example, asking the Miracle Question (*"If overnight a miracle happened and this problem were solved, what would we notice that's different—and which of those things are already happening even a little bit now?"*) to help the team see seeds of the solution in their current state. Identifying existing resources and positive practices gives hope and direction.

Another facet is aligning changes with core values or strengths of the team/company. If a team or organization prides itself on, say, innovation, then frame Agile changes as supporting greater innovation (which they do, by encouraging experimentation). If they value excellence, show how the changes lead to higher quality. Aligning with identity ("This is who we are") reduces resistance and boosts resilience because it feels like building on what's already strong. Finally, coaches should encourage recognition of individual strengths within the team. In a resilient team, members appreciate each other's contributions. A quick practice is to end meetings or retros with a round of appreciations (shout-outs for something a teammate did). It might sound touchy-feely to some, but it directly combats the demoralization that can occur in hard times. It reminds people of their competence and the value they bring. For example, *"I want to thank Ana for jumping on that production issue; her deep knowledge saved us,"* or *"Kudos to Devansh for keeping the mood light with humor when we were under pressure—it really helped."* These acknowledgments reinforce strengths and encourage teammates to lean on each other. A team that knows not only *"We can do this"* but also *"We have each other's back"* will be far more resilient in the face of any storm.

R➤R Flywheel + Resistance Radar: Practitioner Guide

I'd like to introduce you to a simple tool that helps manage team resistance. It is based on two elements: R➤R Flywheel (Recognize ➤ Reframe ➤ Re-contract ➤ Reinforce) with the Resistance Radar diagnostic. Use it as a sprint-sized improvement loop: small, frequent, measurable.

CHAPTER 8   TURNING RESISTANCE INTO RESILIENCE

The Resistance Radar turns messy behaviors into observable signals. The R➤R Flywheel turns those signals into a repeatable improvement cycle. You *Recognize* patterns with the Radar, *Reframe* mandates into choices, *Re-contract* clear roles and boundaries, and *Reinforce* with habits and evidence. Then you repeat.

Quickstart (run this each sprint):

- Review notes and events; mark signals on the Resistance Radar (Safety, Control, Incentives, Clarity).
- Draft a one-sentence hypothesis ("We think loss of control + fuzzy decision rights drive pushback.").
- Generate ≥2 viable options and pick a small, time-boxed experiment (2 sprints).
- Fill or update your contract (roles/decision rights, confidentiality, success measures, triggers).
- Track a tiny scorecard; hold a 15-minute weekly Resilience check-in (Win, Learn, Next Bet).

The R➤R Flywheel

The R➤R Flywheel is a lightweight improvement loop that transforms resistance energy into momentum for change (see Figure 8-1). Each cycle follows the same rhythm: Observe what's truly happening, alter the story and options, make the new agreement clear, then cement it with habits and evidence.

CHAPTER 8   TURNING RESISTANCE INTO RESILIENCE

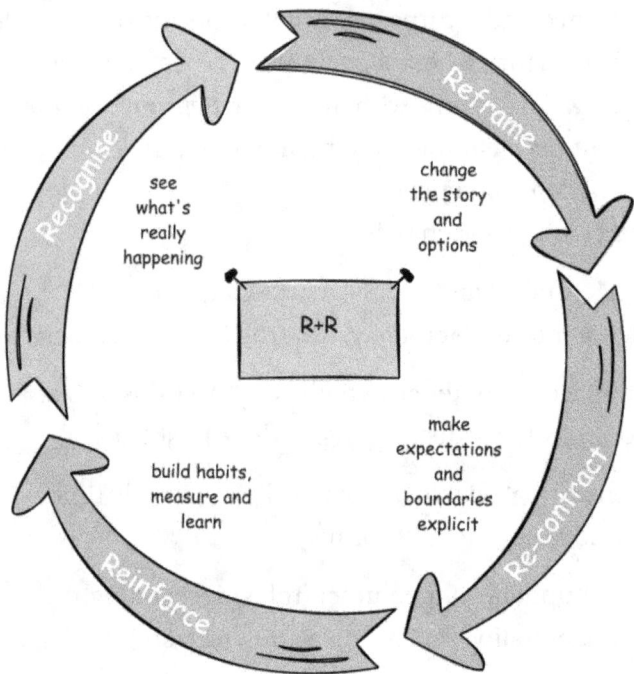

Figure 8-1. *R▶R flywheel*

Recognize — signals before stories

- Make resistance visible as data. Name here-and-now patterns; cluster signals into safety, control, incentives, clarity; draft a falsifiable hypothesis.

Reframe — from threat to choice

- Turn mandates into experiments and widen the option space. Make decision rights explicit; surface hidden commitments; propose a smaller, safer bet.

Re-contract — make the new deal explicit

- Convert the new frame into clear, living agreements. Use contracting; adopt "no secrets/no surprises"; set kill/scale criteria.

Reinforce — rhythm, measures, learning

- Run a 15-minute weekly ritual; track a tiny scorecard; use supervision or peer consults to catch drift and maintain momentum.

Recognize with the Resistance Radar

Use the Radar (Table 8-1) to transform behaviors into patterns. Mark observed signals, form a brief hypothesis, and select the first move.

Table 8-1. Resistance Radar

Safety	Control
☐ Silence in retros; few risks taken	☐ Micromanaging; demands for guarantees
☐ High defensiveness/blame language	
☐ Escalations avoid actual owners	☐ Tool/process mandate triggers pushback
☐ Psychological safety pulse low or falling	
	☐ Decision rights unclear or contested
☐ Bystander stance (see it, don't act)	☐ Refusal to abandon legacy practices
	☐ Requests for exceptions/side doors
Incentives	**Clarity**
☐ Heroics praised over stable flow	☐ Scope debates every sprint
☐ Shadow work bypasses the backlog	☐ Surprise escalations/late changes
☐ KPI conflicts (e.g., speed vs. stability)	☐ In/out ambiguous; weak entry criteria
☐ Rewards discourage learning time	☐ "No ticket, no work" not enforced
☐ Firefighting crowds improvement work	☐ Contract/re-contract cadence missing

Hypothesis (what must be true for this behavior to make sense):
_____

First Move (smallest safe experiment or contracting action):
_____

Tip If decision rights are unclear, run a 10-minute RACI/RAPID and update your contract.

Reframe

- Translate mandates into experiments (e.g., A/B two workflows over two sprints).
- Make decision rights explicit (who recommends, who decides, who's consulted/informed).
- Elicit hidden commitments (e.g., "no embarrassment") and propose a new pairing (learning > image).
- Ensure ≥2 viable options with visible trade-offs; record them in a decision log.

Re-contract

- Fill or update the contract together: purpose, scope, roles and decision rights, confidentiality and safety, working agreements, success criteria, metrics, escalation paths, and re-contracting triggers.
- Adopt the "no secrets/no surprises" rule with a visible decision log and a set update cadence.

Reinforce

- Run a 15-minute weekly "Resilience" ritual: Win, Learn, Next Bet.
- Track on a small, stable scorecard; prefer trends over single points.
- Pair metrics with qualitative learning notes; review monthly/quarterly.
- Use supervision/peer consults to catch drift and blind spots.

Conclusion

Resistance and resilience are two sides of the same coin in the journey of Agile team coaching. In this chapter, we explored how understanding and addressing resistance is actually part and parcel of developing a resilient, high-performing team. By digging into the roots of resistance—from fear of change and trust deficits to hidden dynamics and conflicting agendas—we see that resistance is rarely just obstinance. It is information; it's the team's way of signaling that something important lies beneath the surface. As Agile coaches and Scrum masters, our task is to listen to that signal, not fight it blindly. We apply the tools of our trade (presence, powerful questions, dialogue facilitation, contracting, etc.) to transform resistance into an opportunity for growth. In doing so, we create the conditions for learning, trust, and adaptability that define resilience.

What does a resilient team look like on the other side of resistance? It's a team that has learned how to learn. They surface issues and tackle them collaboratively instead of avoiding them. They have seen for themselves that working through conflict or uncertainty together makes them stronger and faster, not weaker. They trust each other and have each

CHAPTER 8   TURNING RESISTANCE INTO RESILIENCE

other's backs (the spirit of Ubuntu— *"I am because we are"*—is alive in their daily interactions). They own their process and outcomes, demonstrating agency; they don't wait to be told what to do, and they don't shy away from accountability. They've built confidence by weathering some storms: As we cited from Chapter 9, they have removed the "internal rot," so nothing inside is sabotaging them anymore; they can face external challenges with unity and integrity. Such a team is truly self-organizing and adaptive. They don't just do Agile practices; they embody an Agile mindset.

Importantly, resilience is not a static end-state—it's an ongoing capacity. That's why we stressed continuous learning and reflective practice. The most resilient teams keep growing; they have the humility to know they can improve and the optimism to believe every challenge is a chance to do so. For the coach, this means our role evolves into more of a guardian of that learning culture. Over time, you might find the team needs you less in day-to-day problem solving because they can handle it. In fact, a proud moment for a coach is when the team pre-empts a situation of resistance and navigates it themselves—maybe they hold a spontaneous mini-retrospective to clear the air after a heated meeting, or a team member steps up to mediate a conflict using techniques they've seen you use. That's a signal that resilience is taking root. In many ways, the ultimate goal of coaching is to make ourselves redundant by enabling the team to coach itself.

In wrapping up, let's reframe resilience as a core outcome of Agile coaching. Yes, we often talk about delivering value, improving velocity, increasing quality, but beneath those measurable outcomes, resilience is the enabling factor that makes them sustainable. A team that has resilience will continue to deliver value even when conditions are unfavorable. They'll maintain velocity (or recover it quickly) after a setback. They'll uphold quality not because someone tells them to, but because they take pride in mastering their craft through continuous learning. In a sense, resilience is what makes an Agile team self-correcting and self-sustaining. As coaches, if we leave behind a resilient team, we have done our job at the most fundamental level. We haven't given them fish or even just taught them to fish—we've taught them how to keep improving their fishing in ever-changing waters.

Reflection Moment: How Do I Deal with Resistance in Teams?

1. When resistance shows up, what observable signals do I notice first—and what do I habitually miss (safety, control, incentives, clarity)?

2. Where are decision rights still implicit? When did I last re-contract (and what were the triggers)?

3. Which metrics tell me resilience is improving? What does the trend say over the last four to six sprints?

4. How did I raise psychological safety without colluding with avoidance (here-and-now observations, admitting fallibility, normalizing micro-risk)?

5. Which KPI or incentive conflicts did I surface and renegotiate so teams aren't rewarded for anti-resilient behavior (e.g., heroics over flow)?

CHAPTER 9

Staying True

Agile team coaching rarely follows a straight path. One day, you're helping a team address tension surrounding delivery commitments; the next, you're in a quiet one-on-one where someone shares frustrations they'd rather not voice in a group. With shifting organizational goals, multiple stakeholders, and a dose of politics thrown into the mix, it's clear that coaching in this space demands more than mere good intentions. It requires a strong ethical backbone.

But here's the thing: Most Agile coaches don't work in regulated professions. There isn't a single licensing body or formal code that we all adhere to. That's why we need to *choose* to hold ourselves to a high standard. The ICF, for example, makes ethics the very first of its coaching competencies. Agile Alliance also drafted a code of ethical conduct to guide coaches toward integrity, transparency, and protecting others from harm. These frameworks don't provide all the answers, but they're strong compasses when things get murky.

Agile coaches must therefore be vigilant: practicing confidentiality, objectivity, and honesty even under pressure. They should adopt a mindset of continuous ethical awareness, asking at each step, "Am I respecting the team's trust? Am I acting with integrity?" This chapter explores how those principles play out in practice for Agile team coaches.

CHAPTER 9   STAYING TRUE

The Team Is the Primary Client

In Agile team coaching, the entire team, not just individual members, is treated as the client. The coach's job is to help the team achieve shared goals while acknowledging individual contributions.

A defining principle of team coaching is that the team is the primary "client." All individual coaching conversations and group sessions are understood to serve the team's collective purpose. This means contracting and setting goals at the team level: the coaching agreement is made with the team (often represented by a leader) and any sponsor, focusing on team objectives. For example, a Scrum master acting as a coach might co-create a coaching plan with the Scrum team, asking, "What do we, as a team, need to grow?"

Treating the team as a client requires balancing individual and team needs. Coaches must listen to every member while prioritizing the agreed-upon goals of the team. In practice, this may involve discussing personal issues only insofar as they impact team dynamics. For example, if a developer is facing a personal conflict, the coach can assist the team in establishing norms (such as a confidentiality agreement for one-on-ones) but should keep retrospective and planning meetings focused on the team's work. The coach must clarify that every session and insight is shared for the team's benefit, not for personal gain. (One useful model positions the team at the center of concentric client layers, reminding coaches that individual and organizational concerns ultimately contribute to team objectives.)

The ICF's Team Coaching Competency 1 explicitly instructs coaches to "coach the team as a single entity" and to maintain transparency when juggling multiple roles. By treating the team as a cohesive client, coaches help ensure equitable participation and avoid giving undue weight to one person's agenda.

Confidentiality in Agile Team Coaching

Agile team coaches operate across various levels of confidentiality: what is discussed in private one-on-ones, what is agreed upon to remain within the team, and what may be disclosed to sponsors or the broader organization. Establishing clear confidentiality boundaries in the contract is crucial. The ICF Code of Ethics makes this explicit: Coaches must ensure that *"prior to or at the initial meeting, my coaching Clients(s) and Sponsor(s) understand . . . the nature and limits of confidentiality."* In practice, this involves clarifying what the team can expect; for instance, agreeing that discussions in a private coaching session will not be disclosed to the manager without consent. In contrast, summarized lessons from team sessions may be shared.

All information obtained during the coaching engagement should be handled with care. The ICF code requires coaches to *"maintain the strictest levels of confidentiality with all parties as agreed upon."* In an Agile context, this often means honoring the "Las Vegas rule": by default, "what happens in retro, stays in retro." Agile coaching experts advise that all conflict-resolution or personal coaching sessions should likewise remain confidential. (If it's ever unclear, ask team members: "Would it be okay to share this insight more broadly, or keep it private?")

At the same time, coaches must inform clients and sponsors of exceptions. The ICF code calls explicitly for "a clear understanding with both Clients and Sponsors . . . about the conditions under which information will not be kept confidential (e.g., illegal activity . . . risk of danger to self or others)." For example, if a team member reveals intent to self-harm, the coach may need to break confidentiality to protect safety. Likewise, coaches should comply with any legal subpoenas. Documenting these boundaries in the coaching agreement protects everyone: The team knows what is confidential, and the coach is not put in a position of implicit spying for management.

CHAPTER 9   STAYING TRUE

When coaching internally (e.g., a Scrum master coaching their own team), it becomes even more important to spell out confidentiality. The ICF advises internal coaches to *"address . . . confidentiality and other reporting requirements"* in the contract. For instance, an internal Agile coach might agree that no details of a private discussion will be shared with HR or a sponsor unless legally required, but that they will give high-level feedback to the sponsor about team progress. Clear contracting—naming what is private to the team versus what will be summarized to others—is the best safeguard.

Tip

- **Contract early:** At the team's first coaching sprint or kick-off, co-create a confidentiality agreement. For example, agree that the coach will not report individual criticisms to management, and establish who will see session summaries.

- **Respect team space:** Honor team events (e.g., retros, backlog refinement) as "safe spaces." Encourage the team's "ground rules"—such as treating each other respectfully and not attributing comments outside the room.

- **Handle requests thoughtfully:** If a manager or a sponsor asks for details ("How are the retros going?"), offer aggregate insights ("We're identifying blockers and improving process.") rather than personal stories. When necessary, remind stakeholders of the confidentiality agreement.

By treating confidentiality as a core value, Agile coaches build trust. The team learns they can speak openly, and individuals feel safe. At the same time, coaches avoid being seen as secretive or inattentive by explicitly agreeing on limits (for instance, including legal obligations). In all cases, coaches should remember the ICF standard: rigorously maintain confidentiality and be transparent about exceptions.

Story

I was coaching a product development team in a large enterprise going through a bumpy Agile transformation. Things were polite on the surface, but flat. No real disagreement, no real energy either. It didn't take long to sense that important things were being left unsaid.

In a one-on-one, a senior engineer—let's call her Aisha—finally opened up. "I'm tired of pretending everything's fine," she said. "The leadership says they want empowerment, but they're still micromanaging. I feel like speaking up would just make things worse."

This was a breakthrough moment. Not because she was venting, but because her fear was shared. I'd heard quieter versions of the same concern from others, but this was the clearest, most heartfelt version yet.

A few days later, the sponsor (a well-meaning vice president) casually asked, "So, what are you hearing in your one-on-ones? Is there anything we should know about?"

The Dilemma:

This is the moment where many internal coaches feel stuck. Say too much, and you violate trust. Say too little, and you risk looking evasive—or even irrelevant.

What I did:

I paused and said, "There are some important signals emerging around voice and decision making. I won't share individual comments, but I can tell you there's a theme worth exploring. If you're open to it, I'd be happy to facilitate a team session to surface this safely."

The sponsor agreed. In that session, the team co-created a working agreement around decision rights, feedback loops, and leadership behavior they needed more of. Aisha didn't have to speak first—but when others echoed her concerns, she did. And it mattered.

Honoring confidentiality doesn't mean withholding value. It means translating insights into systems-level conversations without putting individuals at risk. And it means having the courage to hold the boundary when someone powerful wants "just a little peek."

Managing Conflicts of Interest and Multiple Agendas

In Agile environments, coaches often find themselves at the intersection of different stakeholders: the team's interests, the product owner's or manager's goals, and organizational demands. We covered the complexities of contracting with multiple parties in Chapter 8; here, we'll explore how these multiple agendas can create conflicts of interest if not managed ethically. The ICF defines a conflict of interest as any situation in which serving one interest could work against another. For example, an Agile coach who reports to engineering management but coaches the development team may struggle if the manager's targets conflict with the team's self-set improvements.

To navigate these tensions, clarity and transparency are key. *First*, coaches should disclose any dual roles or relationships at the outset. If the coach is both Scrum master and team mentor, they should state this role duality in the agreement. By openly acknowledging multiple hats, the coach avoids hidden agendas. If a genuine conflict arises later, the coach can renegotiate the agreement or even withdraw if necessary: ICF guidance suggests withdrawing from relationships *"if a conflict cannot be adequately managed."*

CHAPTER 9 STAYING TRUE

Second, use the coaching contract to align expectations. In multi-party engagements, it's wise to create a clear agreement with all stakeholders. For example, involve both the team and the sponsor in setting goals, and document how information flows between them. ICF Code II.10 cautions coaches to be "sensitive to the implications of having multiple contracts and relationships with the same Client(s) and Sponsor(s) at the same time." In practice, this might mean holding a kick-off workshop with the team and manager together so everyone hears the same purpose of coaching, and all agree on boundaries. Real-world case: A coach agreed with a team to focus on collaboration, but a sponsor later demanded metrics on productivity. Because the sponsor had been involved in the original scope setting, the coach could mediate the tension by revisiting and amending the agreement (perhaps adding a metric review meeting) rather than choosing sides unilaterally.

Third, maintain objectivity in the face of power dynamics. Team coaches often sense pressure (e.g., the product owner is persistent, or one team member dominates). Ethical practice requires the coach to *"actively manage any power or status difference"* and uphold fairness. For instance, if the product owner asks for a report on a reluctant developer, the coach should diplomatically explain confidentiality commitments and suggest alternative ways (maybe bringing the developer's concerns to a joint meeting). Coaches should refuse any request that would compromise their impartial role or the team's trust. If needed, ICF Code I.6 advises that internal coaches *"manage conflicts of interest ... through coaching agreement(s) and ongoing dialogue,"* including roles, responsibilities, and reporting.

Finally, build in checks. Some strategies include having co-coaches or rotating facilitators to avoid single-person bias, seeking feedback from a sponsor on the coach's neutrality, or simply pausing to reflect ("Is my advice favoring one side?"). Remember the ICF's insistence on professional integrity: Coaches should not use their position for personal gain. If a coach finds it hard to remain objective (for example, if friendships develop or performance reviews are tied to the coach's work), it may be time to involve a third party or advisor to preserve fairness.

CHAPTER 9   STAYING TRUE

Tip

- **Identify all stakeholders:** Map out everyone with a vested interest (team members, leaders, HR, etc.). Ensure all are included in the coaching contract.

- **Establish explicit multi-party contracting:** Co-create the agreement with the team and sponsor together. Clarify who sets the agenda and how updates occur. For example, say, "The team and I meet weekly; once a month I will summarize progress to the sponsor unless an issue of danger or ethics arises."

- **Maintain transparency:** Keep both the team and the sponsors informed about the coaching process without breaching confidentiality. If the sponsor is involved, agree on what summaries or metrics can be shared.

- **Check for conflicts:** Periodically ask: Does this decision benefit the team fairly, or is there an unaddressed agenda? Use ethical filters or discuss with a mentor.

- **Refer or withdraw if needed:** If a conflict becomes irresolvable (say, the coach must deliver results while also critiquing the boss), ethically, the coach may need to end the engagement rather than betray one party.

Summary of Actions

By proactively managing these tensions, coaches help to prevent misunderstandings. The ICF notes that ethical team coaching requires "maintaining trust, transparency and clarity" even when the coach plays multiple roles. In practice, this often means regular check-ins with sponsors to reaffirm agreements and a willingness to confront uncomfortable issues with integrity.

Shifting from Bystander to Contributor

In Agile teams, a bystander stance occurs when team members (or even coaches) notice problems or harmful dynamics but fail to act, assuming someone else will intervene. Psychologists describe this as the bystander effect, where individuals are less likely to help a victim when others are present. Agile teams can fall prey to this phenomenon; diffuse responsibility can lead to tasks or issues' being ignored, resulting in moral and practical problems. Ethically, each team member (especially the coach) has a duty to notice and act. In an Agile context, this means it is ethically incumbent on coaches and team members to remain vigilant. If nobody addresses an issue—whether it's a stalled user story, interpersonal conflict, or even harassment—the team fails its commitment to collaboration and respect. Ignoring warning signs violates core Agile values (like openness and respect) and coaching ethics (e.g., "treat people with dignity"). Thus, a bystander stance is not neutral; it carries an ethical cost. Coaches must model responsiveness: When they see a team member struggle or hear a quiet voice stifled, the coach has a moral responsibility to intervene, ask questions, and ensure all members are heard, rather than silently observing problems.

CHAPTER 9 STAYING TRUE

In every team, there's usually someone who hangs back. They speak less, offer fewer ideas, or quickly defer to others—even when they have something valuable to contribute. This behavior might look like shyness, but often it's something deeper.

Transactional Analysis (TA), a psychological framework, explains that many of our adult behaviors are shaped by the early messages we received growing up—what TA calls *injunctions*. One of the most common is an implicit message like "Don't be important." It's not usually said out loud, but it's *felt*: perhaps in a family where speaking up was discouraged or attention was reserved for others. As adults, people who carry this message may believe—consciously or not—that their ideas don't matter, that they shouldn't take up space, or that playing small is safer.

In Agile teams, this can show up in subtle but impactful ways. A team member may hesitate to raise concerns, avoid volunteering for challenging work, or deflect praise with comments like, "It was nothing." TA refers to this pattern as *discounting*—unconsciously ignoring your own value or relevance to a situation. The ethical issue here is clear: When certain voices routinely go unheard, the team doesn't just lose input—it risks reinforcing silent hierarchies where some dominate and others disappear. For example, a junior developer who's been carrying "Don't be important" may spot a serious problem but say nothing, leaving the team vulnerable.

And "Don't be important" is just one of many internalized messages. Others include "Don't be close," "Don't succeed," and "Don't belong." Someone who believes they don't belong might always linger at the edges of the team, never quite stepping in, even when they want to. These internal scripts distort team dynamics, often leading individuals to self-limit while others take up more space by default.

As coaches, it's our responsibility to notice this. That quiet team member might not be disengaged—they might be running a script they don't even realize is there. TA helps us understand these behaviors not as flaws, but as learned survival strategies. And it gives us a gentle imperative: creating space for those old messages to be questioned. Sometimes, all it takes is a well-timed question, a moment of genuine affirmation, or consistently inviting that person in. When the whole team feels safe to contribute, the team becomes not just more inclusive but also more intelligent and resilient.

Clear contracts and role definitions are not just process tools—they are also ethical instruments that protect team integrity and psychological safety. A working agreement or team charter explicitly co-creates the team's norms: how decisions are made, how conflicts are resolved, and how members treat each other. Research from Atlassian's Team Playbook finds that creating working agreements greatly improves team voice and commitment: 74% of teams felt *empowered to speak up* when such norms were established. In other words, defining how we work together reduces the bystander problem by assigning responsibilities rather than letting them fall through the cracks.

Similarly, team charters (inclusive of roles, goals, and values) foster psychological safety by making expectations explicit. A charter clarifies *who does what*, reducing ambiguity that breeds apathy. For example, if the role of "release manager" is clear, then no one can credibly dodge responsibility by assuming "someone else will do it." From an ethical standpoint, creating these contracts is a form of mutual respect: everyone agrees to be bound by the same rules, and everyone's autonomy is honored through consent. It also prevents hidden agendas or power plays. As a team charter newsletter notes, clarifying values and goals "improves predictability when interacting within the team, further fostering psychological safety." In short, establishing clear, shared agreements is an ethical act—it helps ensure no one is left feeling marginalized, and it compels each person to engage.

The coach's role in contracting is to facilitate and uphold these agreements. During iteration planning or team formation, the coach should prompt the team to discuss responsibilities (e.g., "What is each person's role in code review, documentation, testing?"). Returning to and revising the contract is also an ethical practice: It shows that the team takes commitments seriously and evolves norms when problems arise. Clear contracting and role definition give less "space" for bystander behavior; team members know what is expected of them and to whom they are accountable. In doing this, the coach upholds the ethical value of integrity—consistency between spoken values and actions—and protects the safety net that every team member deserves.

One of the most harmful manifestations of the bystander stance is when a coach starts exhibiting it. It might be a sign of burnout, but it is also a choice. Bystanding is fundamentally predicated upon the denial of obligation and responsibility for others.

Key ethical considerations of bystander behavior include the following:

- **Inherent involvement and influence**: Even when appearing silent or uninvolved, a bystander is *always* part of the system and influences the situation, either positively or negatively. By doing nothing, bystanders silently and unintentionally agree with prevailing dysfunctional dynamics.

- **Discounting of capacity**: Bystander coaches often discount their own ability to influence or take responsibility for change, using justifications like "It's not my problem," "I don't have the whole picture," or "Neutrality is the best option."

- **Maintaining dysfunctional patterns**: In organizations, the inaction of bystanding coaches can maintain and contribute to issues like team underperformance or persistent problems, consuming energy through anxiety rather than action.

A coach is not a neutral observer but an active participant, inherently influencing the group or team dynamic. Their role is multifaceted and goes beyond a simple "no help, no meddle" approach.

The Boundary Between Bystanding and Contractual Engagement

A perceived contradiction arises when a coach might fear "meddling" by addressing an individual's behavior in a team, especially if there's no explicit "individual help" clause in the contract. However, in Agile coaching, the coach operates under an overarching ethical framework that calls for active, responsible engagement within the system, as follows:

- **Systemic responsibility**: The coach is contracted to the *system* (the team, the organization), not just a static task. If an individual's behavior (or the collective's bystanding) is hindering the team's agreed-upon goals, psychological safety, or overall effectiveness, addressing it falls within the systemic responsibility of the coach.

- **Influence, not control**: The coach's influence is about creating awareness, forming options, and facilitating processes for change, not about controlling individuals or imposing solutions. This is distinct from "meddling," which implies intrusive, uncontracted interference outside the scope of improving the team/organizational system.

- **Ethical vigilance**: The professional constantly evaluates their stance, ensuring they maintain an "OK" position, are aware of their own feelings and countertransference, and are supported by supervision. This ongoing self-reflection is what allows them to navigate the "edges of disturbance" and prevent their interventions from becoming unethical.

- **Unconscious dynamics**: The coach's expertise lies in understanding unconscious processes and how they manifest in group dynamics. To ignore these, even if they appear as individual "problems," would be a professional failing and a form of bystanding, as these dynamics impact the contracted team goal.

The boundary between being a bystander and adhering to the coaching contract is crossed when the coach passively observes dysfunction that undermines the contracted goals of the system, under the misleading guise of non-interference. The coach's ethical responsibility extends to actively engaging with the evolving dynamics, including individual behaviors that affect the collective, within the framework of their multi-layered contracts, always aiming to promote autonomy, awareness, and the overall health of the system.

Agile coaches can draw on Transactional Analysis principles to design interventions that *ethically* break the bystander pattern. Strategies include the following:

- **Highlight and challenge discounting**: The coach can gently point out when team members discount themselves or others. For example, if someone says "Oh, I didn't really do much" about a contribution, the coach can affirm its value: "Actually, telling us that risk was important—it helped the team decide on a safer approach." This explicit recognition counters unconscious discounting (defined as "ignoring information relevant to the solution"). Team exercises (like round-robin retrospectives) ensure quieter members' insights are heard, pulling the "ignored" back into adult awareness. By surfacing these patterns, the coach raises awareness of the scripts at play. Calling attention to these helps team members reclaim their adult agency rather than slipping into a helpless stance.

CHAPTER 9   STAYING TRUE

- **Boundary work via contracting**: In TA, *symbiosis* occurs when people unconsciously depend on each other in child–parent ways. A coach can counteract this by reinforcing external boundaries: explicitly stating agreements (a form of adult-to-adult contract) and separating identities. For instance, having a "speaker's list" during discussions ensures one person speaks at a time, preventing dominant voices from smothering quieter ones. If someone habitually oversteps another's task, the coach might remind the team of the agreed-upon roles, thus reasserting clear boundaries. This adult–adult contract approach interrupts any covert symbiotic scripts (like "I do everything, you do nothing"). In practice, the coach may say, "Our agreement is that Alex handles deployment and Priya handles testing. Let's stick to those roles so we don't duplicate efforts or drop the task." Such boundary clarification is ethical: It ensures fairness and prevents exploitation of gaps.

- **Fostering +/+ relationships**: Transactional Analysis teaches that healthy interactions arise from an "I'm OK, You're OK" life position. The coach can encourage and model this stance. In team interactions, a +/+ (positive-positive) transaction means both parties feel recognized and valued. The coach might not just praise the speaker but also acknowledge the listener: "I appreciate how Jen listened and built on Sam's idea— that's great collaboration." Structuring communication norms (like active listening, yes-and brainstorming) builds mutual respect. Coaches can train teams in giving positive strokes: e.g., kicking off standups

297

by sharing "shout-outs" for help received, which counteracts any underlying "don't succeed" script. These practices affirm each person's worth, dissolving power imbalances.

- **Empathy and assertiveness training**: Coaches can bring structured exercises around empathy and "speaking up" (assertiveness). For instance, role-playing or discussing common scenarios (like witnessing a missed deadline) helps normalize the discomfort of intervening. A coach might hold a retrospective focused on "What stopped you from voicing that concern?" to surface feelings of fear or inertia. Then the coach could ask the team to brainstorm how anyone *can* speak up; this simultaneously increases awareness and generates solutions.

- **Third-entity facilitation**: In TA coaching it is sometimes helpful to refer problems to an external "task" or purpose (a "third entity"). The coach can frame a difficult issue not as a personal conflict but as a shared problem to solve. For example, instead of asking "Alice, why didn't you report this bug?", the coach might say to the whole team, "We all care about quality. What system can we create so that bugs get caught early, regardless of who notices them?" This adult-oriented framing removes blame and encourages collective responsibility. It's an ethical technique because it respects everyone's agency while redirecting focus to a mutually agreed-upon goal.

CHAPTER 9   STAYING TRUE

Throughout these interventions, the coach maintains an adult ego state—calm, curious, and respectful. The objective is not to shame bystanders, but to empower them. All steps are presented as part of a team's continuous improvement, aligned with Agile values. By drawing on TA concepts (like recognizing discounting, enforcing healthy boundaries, and promoting an "OK-OK" culture), the coach can shift the team out of passive roles. This upholds the coach's ethical role: enabling a +/+ environment where everyone can contribute, and ensuring that inaction is recognized and addressed.

In sum, tackling the bystander stance through an ethical lens means acknowledging the psychological and moral forces at play, affirming the dignity of each individual, clarifying mutual agreements, and using TA-informed methods to bring hidden scripts to light. By doing so, the Agile coach not only solves immediate teamwork problems but also honors a fundamental ethical commitment: protecting and empowering people within the Agile system. Left unchecked, bystander apathy harms individuals and the organization. But with vigilance and appropriate interventions, a coach can transform passive observers into engaged collaborators, strengthening the whole team.

Developing Ethical Maturity

Ethical agility is a skill honed over time, not a checkbox. Agile coaches should cultivate ethical maturity through reflection, supervision, and continuous learning. Professional bodies increasingly emphasize the coach's ongoing development. The ICF Code itself frames ethics as a living skill: It commits professionals to "continued personal, professional and ethical development" and to "cultivate our ethical growth . . . through continuous self-reflection."

CHAPTER 9   STAYING TRUE

A key practice is supervision and peer support. Coaching supervision (not to be confused with line management) is a reflective partnership where coaches bring dilemmas for discussion. Research notes that supervision explicitly "pays close attention to ethical practices . . . promoting adherence to standards . . . [and] helping coaches to identify subtle yet challenging ethical dilemmas." In Agile contexts, many coaches engage with mentors or "coaches for coaches" to debrief complex situations. For example, an Agile coach unsure how to handle a team member's mental health disclosure might seek a supervisor's perspective on balancing empathy and safety. ICF Team Coaching Competency 2 even recommends that team coaches leverage supervision "for support, development and accountability." By reflecting on our own choices with a safe peer group, we can detect blind spots (e.g., biases or burnout) before they lead to ethical slips.

It also helps to use structured ethical decision-making frameworks when dilemmas arise. The ICF has endorsed models (such as the one developed by Liora Rosen and colleagues) that prompt questions like "Who is affected?", "What are the coach's obligations?", and "What are the potential consequences?" Engaging in a step-by-step analysis can prevent snap judgments. In practice, a coach facing a conflict of interest might list the pros and cons of different actions, consult the ICF Code standards, and even role-play scenarios with a mentor. Even something as simple as a written decision tree ("If X happens, then notify; if Y, then refer out") can clarify the path forward.

A final aspect of maturity is knowing one's limits. Coaches should self-assess competence honestly: If the engagement drifts into areas outside coaching (e.g., psychological counseling, financial advising), the ethical move is to refer to another professional. The Agile Coaching Code stresses this: *"I will be honest with the client if I believe they need another form of professional help,"* and *"I won't claim abilities I do not have."* Similarly, the ICF Code urges professionals to "recognize personal limitations . . . seek support . . . [and] if necessary, promptly seek relevant professional guidance." An agile coach might thus say, "I'm not qualified to advise on organizational restructuring, but I can bring in a consultant," or bring the team's issue to HR if it's beyond the coaching scope.

Tip

- **Regular supervision/mentoring:** Schedule periodic sessions (e.g., monthly) with an experienced coach or peer group to review cases. Supervision builds a coach's competence and ethical awareness.

- **Reflective routines:** Keep a coaching journal or checklist: Note any ethical tensions and how you handled them after each coaching session. Over time, patterns emerge and lessons accumulate.

- **Use ethical tools:** When in doubt, apply a model (such as ICF's Ethical Decision-Making Model) or even simple frameworks (e.g., stakeholders chart, values alignment). These tools help structure decision making rather than relying on gut feeling.

- **Continual learning:** Attend workshops on coaching ethics, read case studies, and stay updated on codes (ICF revises its Code periodically). The profession expects coaches to be "open to other points of view" and "willing to acknowledge mistakes."

- **Cultivating humility:** Admitting "I'm not sure" and seeking counsel is itself an ethical stance.

CHAPTER 9   STAYING TRUE

By building these habits, Agile coaches develop what some call "ethical maturity": an intuitive sense of right action supported by reflective practice. For example, a coach might notice rising team tension and recall from supervision a technique to surface unspoken conflicts. Or a coach might identify their own fatigue before it harms the team and proactively rearrange priorities. In all cases, the goal is to integrate ethics into everyday practice. As the ICF Code underscores, ethical growth is ongoing: It's not just about knowing the rules, but about embodying values like honesty, fairness, and respect in every interaction.

Ethical practice is not optional for Agile team coaches; it is central to the role. Every decision—including how to handle confidentiality, which agendas to prioritize, and how to respond to dilemmas—should be guided by a clear moral compass along with an attitude of reflection. A coach who remains aware of their responsibilities to the team, to individuals, and to the profession will foster trust and drive lasting improvement. As the ICF affirms, maintaining ethical standards is a fundamental coaching competency. In practice, this means continuously asking oneself questions: Am I being transparent? Am I respecting all voices? Am I working in the best interest of the team? It also entails seeking help, learning, and holding oneself accountable.

Table 9-1 translates ethical competencies into Agile coaching scenarios, with examples of how to respond. It's not an exhaustive list, but it illustrates how abstract values like *confidentiality*, *integrity*, and *clarity* come alive in the messy realities of Agile environments.

Table 9-1. Agile Coaching Scenarios and Ethical Guidance

ICF Ethical Principle	Agile Coaching Scenario	Coaching Response / Application
Maintain Confidentiality	Sponsor asks what happened in 1:1s	Share only patterns/themes, not individual disclosures
Avoid Conflicts of Interest	Coach reports to sponsor but also works closely with team	Disclose dual role in contract; renegotiate or withdraw if conflict can't be managed
Act with Integrity and Transparency	Manager wants you to coach a team that hasn't asked for it	Ask for consent, hold a discovery session before proceeding
Define Clear Agreements	Coaching goals shift mid-engagement	Re-contract with all stakeholders, reset scope and expectations
Do Not Exploit Role or Influence	You're asked to give HR input that could affect promotions	Decline, or share a process-level reflection, not evaluative input
Commit to Professional Development	Facing burnout or bias but unsure how to proceed	Seek supervision, acknowledge limits, pause if needed

Conclusion

Ethical practice is not an abstract concept or an optional extra in Agile team coaching—it's what holds everything together when complexity, pressure, and human dynamics collide. From setting clear agreements to navigating confidentiality and conflicts of interest, the ethical coach chooses to act with transparency, humility, and responsibility, even when it's uncomfortable.

CHAPTER 9   STAYING TRUE

In this chapter, we explored what it truly means to *stay true*—to our values, the trust placed in us by teams and sponsors, and the professional standards we uphold. We examined everyday ethical tensions in Agile contexts, from blurred boundaries to bystander behavior, and offered ways to respond with clarity and compassion. Drawing on the ICF Code of Ethics and Transactional Analysis, we examined how internal messages and team dynamics can reinforce silence, hierarchy, or withdrawal—and how the coach can gently disrupt these patterns to foster equity and psychological safety.

Ethical maturity is not always having the right answer. It's about pausing to ask the right questions. It's about noticing the moment your neutrality wavers, your role gets blurry, or your integrity is at risk and having the courage to course correct. It's also about building habits of reflection, supervision, and continual learning so that ethics become not just what we *do* but who we *are* in our coaching practice.

In the end, ethical coaching builds more than trust—it builds the conditions for transformation. And that, more than any tool or framework, is what helps teams thrive.

Reflection Moment: Ethical Check-up

Take a moment to check in on yourself with the following questions:

- What ethical tensions showed up this week (if any)?
- Where did I honor confidentiality, and where was it tested?
- Did I experience any pressure to take sides or act outside my role?
- Did I hold space for all voices? Who went unheard?
- What am I learning about my ethical decision making?
- What will I do differently next time?

CHAPTER 10

Going Virtual

The way we work has undergone a seismic shift in recent years. Agile teams that were once co-located in the same office are now frequently dispersed across cities, countries, and time zones. Virtual teams—groups of people who primarily collaborate through technology rather than face-to-face—have become a norm rather than an exception. This trend has been driven by global forces, including digitalization, the push for talent without borders, and accelerators such as the COVID-19 pandemic, which rapidly normalized remote work. Agile coaching, traditionally done in person, must adapt to this evolving landscape. In this chapter, we explore what it means to "go virtual" with Agile team coaching, examining the challenges and opportunities of technologically mediated interactions.

Agile methods themselves originally assumed close collaboration and co-location; the Agile Manifesto famously stated that "the most efficient and effective method of conveying information . . . is face-to-face conversation." Yet today's reality is that many Agile teams are partially or fully distributed. This new context does not invalidate Agile principles, but it does require coaches and teams to apply them in a different way. As an Agile coach, you may find yourself supporting a Scrum team spread across three continents or facilitating a retrospective via video conference. The fundamentals of coaching still apply—the basics of listening, presence, and powerful questioning (see Chapter 2 on coaching fundamentals) are more critical than ever; however, the medium and environment introduce new nuances.

CHAPTER 10 GOING VIRTUAL

Why focus on virtual coaching? Because coaching an Agile team remotely is not simply "business as usual." It presents distinct challenges (see Table 10-1) in building trust, communicating effectively, and maintaining engagement, particularly without the benefit of a shared physical space. At the same time, it presents fresh opportunities: the ability to draw on a global talent pool, to coach across cultural boundaries, and to leverage digital tools for creative collaboration. This chapter will delve into both sides—the hurdles to overcome and the advantages to leverage—when coaching Agile teams virtually. We will cover the following:

- **Unique challenges and nuances of coaching virtual teams:** From technology hiccups and "Zoom fatigue" to the delicate work of building trust across a screen

- **Key practices and interventions that set virtual Agile coaching up for success:** Including explicit virtual contracting, maintaining coach presence online, leveraging digital tools, fostering team dynamics and accountability, and even coach self-care.

Table 10-1. Differences Between In-person and Virtual Coaching

Aspect	In-person Coaching	Virtual Coaching
Sensory input	Full body cues, energy shifts, spatial cues	Limited to visual/audio in constrained frames
Connection quality	Rich, embodied presence	Flatter, disembodied interaction
Informal interaction	Easy (hallway chats, coffee breaks)	Requires intention and scheduling
Group energy awareness	Immediate and intuitive	Muted or ambiguous
Intervention timing	Can rely on felt sense of the room	Requires structured observation and questions

CHAPTER 10   GOING VIRTUAL

The Challenges of Coaching Virtual Teams

Coaching a team remotely introduces new challenges (Figure 10-1) that even experienced coaches may not have encountered in traditional settings.

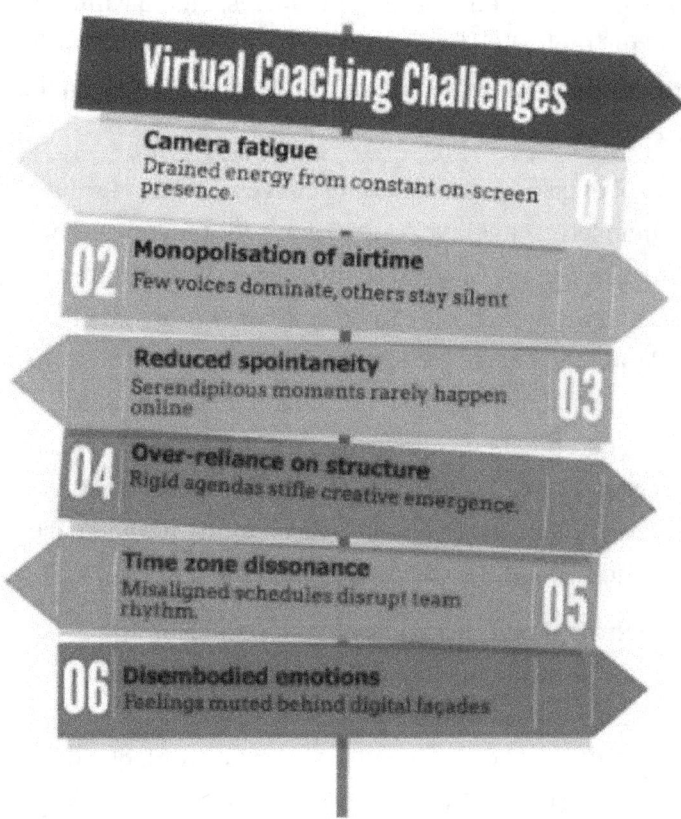

Figure 10-1. Virtual coaching challenges

307

CHAPTER 10   GOING VIRTUAL

Technological Demands and Digital Fatigue

Technology is the lifeline of any virtual team—without it, collaboration wouldn't be possible. Coaches must contend with a basic prerequisite: ensuring that the team has the right tools and that everyone can use them effectively. Video conferencing, chat platforms, digital whiteboards, and project tracking tools (like Jira or Trello) all become critical infrastructure for Agile teams. This reliance on tech brings its own set of challenges and stressors, as follows:

- **Tool overload and learning curves:** Teams may find themselves juggling Zoom/Teams for meetings, Slack for messaging, Miro for whiteboarding, and more. Using multiple tools can be overwhelming initially. Part of the coach's role is helping the team choose the simplest, most effective toolset and build confidence through practice. Sometimes, a quick tutorial or a low-stakes trial run (like a fun practice retrospective on the new whiteboard app) can boost confidence and ease anxiety about new technology.

- **Technical glitches and access issues:** Nothing disrupts a coaching session more than dropped connections, audio echoes, or "Can you see my screen now?" moments. These are unavoidable in virtual settings. As a coach, be prepared with backup plans (for example, if video fails, have a dial-in line or chat to keep communication going). Normalize these hiccups so they cause minimal frustration—a calm acknowledgment and a quick switch to plan B can maintain momentum. It's also wise to set clear expectations upfront about what to do if someone disconnects ("If anyone drops off the call, we'll pause for two minutes and then continue, and they can catch up via the recording or notes"). Such agreements help prevent confusion during tech failures.

- **"Zoom fatigue" and cognitive load:** Spending hours in virtual meetings can be draining in ways that in-person work is not. Research from Stanford has identified several reasons for "Zoom fatigue," including the intense eye contact, seeing your own face constantly, reduced mobility, and the extra effort required to read non-verbal cues over video. Both coaches and team members may experience mental exhaustion more quickly during online sessions. This can manifest as people losing focus, feeling unusually tired, or becoming irritable after extended screen time. Awareness of digital fatigue is vital. Coaches should consider scheduling breaks, using audio-only during parts of a session, or encouraging participants to occasionally turn off self-view (so they aren't distracted by their own image).

In essence, technology acts as both an enabler and a potential barrier in virtual coaching. A savvy coach focuses not just on which tech tools are used but also on *how* they are used. Do team members know the features (mute, chat, hand-raise) that can make meetings smoother? Are there ground rules about muting when not speaking to reduce noise, while also balancing expectations to stay present (not multitasking on mute)? When technology is well-managed, reliable, user-friendly, and as unobtrusive as possible, it becomes second nature, allowing genuine human collaboration to flourish. However, if mismanaged, tech glitches and fatigue can seriously undermine trust and productivity within a team.

CHAPTER 10   GOING VIRTUAL

Building Trust from Afar

Trust is the foundation of any effective coaching relationship and high-performing team. In a co-located setting, trust can build organically through casual hallway conversations, shared lunches, and the daily rhythm of working side by side. In virtual teams, however, trust and psychological safety (the feeling that one can speak up or take risks without fear of ridicule) require *deliberate cultivation*. The distance can breed misunderstanding or a sense of disconnection (see Table 10-2 for signals) if not actively managed.

Table 10-2. What Disconnection Looks Like in Virtual Coaching

Signal	Possible Meaning	Coaching Response
Frequent video off	Disengagement, fatigue, privacy needs	Check-in individually, renegotiate norms
Fast agreement with little debate	Groupthink or fear of dissent	Introduce devil's advocate or dissent rounds
Repetitive complaints post-meeting	Lack of safety in open forum	Use async reflection tools or anonymous prompts
Silent participants	Power dynamics or disengagement	Invite explicitly, rotate facilitation roles

One key challenge is the lack of face-to-face warmth and informal bonding. When all interactions are task-focused video calls or text chats, team members miss out on getting to know each other as people. Coaches often need to create opportunities for the "small moments" that build rapport. This might include starting meetings with brief personal check-ins ("One non-work win this week . . .") or encouraging virtual coffee chats or team-building activities. Research and experience confirm that personal connection builds trust and eases self-organization. Something as simple as each team member sharing their working-from-home setup or introducing their pet on a call can humanize remote colleagues.

Real-world example: A colleague of mine, an Agile coach at a tech startup, noticed her distributed team felt like "strangers." She instituted a Friday virtual lunch where everyone joined a video call to chat about non-work topics. After a few weeks, team members began reporting they felt more connected and were more comfortable raising concerns in regular Scrum events—a direct boost to psychological safety.

Managing power dynamics and psychological distance is another facet of trust-building in virtual contexts. In Chapter 9, we explored how power differences and group dynamics impact coaching. Virtually, some of those dynamics shift. On the one hand, being just another square on the screen can level the playing field. There is evidence that "power distance" (the tendency to defer to authority) is reduced with the use of remote communication tools. For example, a junior developer might find it easier to voice an opinion in a typed chat than in a physical meeting where senior managers loom large. On the other hand, virtual setups can also exacerbate power imbalances in subtle ways. If part of the team is co-located (say, at headquarters) and others dial in remotely, the remote folks may feel like second-class participants, perceiving that the in-room people have more say or are "in the loop" more. Additionally, those who are more assertive verbally or have more reliable tech connections might dominate online conversations. As a coach, you must be keenly attuned to these dynamics. Is one voice consistently absent on calls? Does a particular subgroup always drive decisions? Proactively facilitate to ensure everyone is heard: use round-robin sharing, explicitly invite input from quieter members, or use anonymous survey tools to surface dissenting views. By naming and normalizing the challenges ("It's harder to sense when someone has something to add on a call—let's be intentional to pause and ask"), you create an environment where trust can grow even across distance.

Another trust-related nuance is the need for greater transparency and follow-through. In a remote team, doubts can easily grow ("What is John doing? I never see him online, can I trust he's working?"). Agile practices, such as daily stand-ups, visible digital backlogs, and regular demos or reviews, become more than just process rituals—they serve as trust-builders by providing reassurance that everyone is contributing. As an Agile coach, encourage the team to make work visible and to communicate progress or blockers often. Simple habits such as updating task boards daily or sharing end-of-day summaries in the chat can help build reliability. Trust also increases when team members feel "in the know," so over-communicate context and decisions in virtual settings. For example, if a meeting is held with only part of the team, share notes with everyone so nobody feels left out. This level of inclusion requires a conscious effort in distributed teams to combat the "out of sight, out of mind" phenomenon, where remote colleagues might unintentionally be excluded from information loops.

Finally, cultural sensitivity is essential for building trust remotely. Virtual Agile teams are often international, consisting of members from diverse national and regional backgrounds. Cultural differences can influence how trust develops. Some cultures depend more on personal relationships and informal chats to build trust, which can be more challenging in a virtual setting. Others may be highly task-focused and find relationship-building efforts uncomfortable. As a coach, be aware of these differences and seek a balance that respects various needs. Promote empathy by encouraging team members to learn about each other's backgrounds and working styles. Even simple things like understanding time zone differences ("Maria is eight hours behind most of us, so she has a different routine") and showing consideration can help foster trust. Psychological safety in a multicultural virtual team may also require clarifying norms; for example, explicitly stating that *all* ideas are welcome and that polite disagreement is healthy. In some cultures, people might hesitate to contradict openly, especially in virtual forums; you may need to establish alternative feedback methods, such as an anonymous suggestion box or private messages to you as a coach.

Communication Gaps

Effective communication is at the heart of Agile teamwork, yet communicating well is decidedly harder when your team is not in the same room. Virtual communication gaps can take many forms: missed nonverbal cues, written messages that convey an unintended tone, people talking over each other on conference calls, or simply the silence of team members who don't feel comfortable speaking up in a remote forum. These gaps are often compounded by cultural and language differences on distributed teams, making communication a nuanced challenge that Agile coaches must continuously address.

One major issue is the loss of rich non-verbal communication. In face-to-face settings, coaches and team members rely on body language, facial expressions, and tone shifts to gauge how messages are received. On a video call, you get a limited view—perhaps just your head and shoulders—and in pure audio or text, you lose all visual cues entirely. This can lead to misunderstandings. For example, a suggestion met with silence in a virtual meeting might be interpreted as agreement, whereas in person, you might notice furrowed brows signaling confusion or dissent. To bridge this gap, virtual coaches encourage more explicit communication. That could mean asking for verbal confirmation ("Let me pause—is everyone comfortable with this decision?") or using the available tools, such as the reaction icons or the chat window, to quickly poll sentiments. As a coach, you might say, "Drop a thumbs-up emoji if you're on board, or a question mark if you have concerns," giving an easy way for unspoken reactions to surface.

CHAPTER 10   GOING VIRTUAL

Another approach is to vocalize the non-verbal cues. As a coach, you might model saying things like, "I'm noticing some quiet right now—often that can mean people are processing or perhaps hesitant. Is there an unspoken concern we should address?" This encourages people to share what might otherwise go unsaid. It also connects back to the psychological safety point: You are explicitly telling the team it's okay to voice uncertainty or disagreement, which is essential for Agile teams to operate honestly.

Cultural nuances significantly influence communication styles, and these differences can become particularly apparent in virtual teams. Variations in language skills can impact participation—someone working in a second language may be less inclined to jump into a quick discussion on Zoom. Norms around interrupting, directness, and politeness can also clash. For example, team members from cultures that value indirect communication might avoid openly disagreeing during a call but could privately express concerns later. Conversely, a culturally direct teammate might give blunt feedback in chat that others see as rude. Misunderstandings are common when you lack the context that physical co-location provides. As the coach, you act as a bridge and interpreter at times, helping the team establish shared norms that respect differences. This could involve explicitly rotating meeting facilitation or speaking order to ensure all voices (including those who culturally wait for an invitation to speak) are heard. It might also involve setting guidelines like "Assume positive intent" to prevent negative interpretations of terse emails or messages.

Real-world example: I was working in a multi-national team spread across several locations in Europe and Asia. A Dutch member (more senior in rank) gave harsh feedback to another member, who was in Malaysia. The Malaysian colleague visibly looked embarrassed, and his face turned red. Eventually, he stopped talking to the Dutch colleague. When I had a debrief with the Dutch counterpart, it transpired that she didn't mean ill; it's just the straightforward way in which the Dutch communicate.

One practical approach is co-creating a team communication charter. This could be a short set of agreements about how the team will communicate. For example, *We agree to use our Slack channel for daily informal updates, and email only for formal decisions. We will not assume tone from text—when in doubt, we'll ask. We will adapt to each other's time zones by not expecting instant replies after hours.* Bringing Chapter 3's contracting principles here, these are essentially communication contracts. The coach can facilitate this discussion, ensuring that cultural perspectives are represented. Perhaps one team member shares that in their culture, saying "no" directly is hard, so the team agrees on a phrase like "I have a different perspective . . ." as a safe way to disagree. These little agreements go a long way in smoothing cross-cultural collaboration.

Time zones are another communication hurdle. If your Agile team spans from California to Singapore, real-time communication windows may be slim. This forces some communication to be asynchronous, via recorded videos, detailed written updates, or shared documents. Agile coaches should guide teams on mastering asynchronous communication, such as writing clearer user stories or ticket updates, since you can't instantly turn to a colleague for clarification.

Lastly, active listening becomes even more vital for coaches in a virtual environment. In remote coaching, you often have to "listen" beyond just words: pay attention to pauses, voice tone, and the quality of text responses. If someone's contributions in chat suddenly shorten from sentences to one-word answers, that might signal disengagement or frustration. It's harder to notice these things remotely, so we must train ourselves to recognize subtle cues. Repeat back or summarize more often to confirm understanding ("So, Alex, if I heard you right, you're concerned about the deadline, correct?"). This not only ensures clarity but also demonstrates to the speaker that they were heard, building trust in communication.

CHAPTER 10   GOING VIRTUAL

Blurred Boundaries

When work occurs in the same place where one lives, and colleagues span different time zones, boundaries can become blurred in virtual teams. Both coaches and team members frequently struggle with maintaining a healthy work-life balance, effectively managing their availability, and preventing burnout. In an office, there were physical cues for boundaries—people leaving for the day, or a meeting room door closed for a private discussion. In virtual work, those cues vanish. Agile coaches need to help teams establish and respect boundaries and create new norms that fit the virtual context.

One major boundary issue is the feeling of being "always on" and available. Team members might feel pressured to respond to messages at all hours, especially if their colleagues are in different time zones and working while they're off. Without clear guidelines, a 9 p.m. ping from a coworker can pull someone back into work mode. From the outset, discuss and agree on expectations around responsiveness and working hours. For example, a team might agree on a norm like: "Unless it's marked urgent, no one is expected to answer messages outside their local work hours. We will delay sending non-urgent communications or use scheduling features to respect off-hours." As a coach, you can model this behavior—avoid sending late-night emails yourself, or, if you must, add a note, "No rush—for tomorrow." This demonstrates respect for personal boundaries.

Linked to this is the challenge of time zones. If an Agile team is globally distributed, scheduling meetings becomes a puzzle of fairness. Without care, the same people could end up consistently taking meetings at inconvenient times (e.g., 10 p.m. or 5 a.m. local). This breeds resentment and fatigue. A good practice is to rotate meeting times to share the inconvenience or find overlapping hours that reasonably balance the pain. Coaches should facilitate an open conversation about scheduling. Perhaps the daily stand-up is done in two groups to accommodate different zones, with a hand-off message bridging them. Or the team decides that, on alternate sprint reviews, the time will be reversed so that the other half of the world gets a break. The key is to demonstrate empathy for each other's personal time. When team members see that their well-being is valued, it strengthens trust and commitment.

Another boundary-related nuance is the intrusion of work into personal life (and vice versa). On a video call, you might catch glimpses of someone's home—kids in the background or a personal bookshelf—which can be humanizing, but also underscores that work and home have collided. Team members might struggle to "log off" when the office is just a laptop on the kitchen table. Coaches can encourage healthy practices; for example, they can suggest that the team define a norm, such as "No meetings during lunchtime," or implement "Focus hours" when messaging is kept to a minimum, allowing people to engage in deep work. Some teams establish a collective quiet hour each day or week, during which no meetings are scheduled, giving everyone permission to step away or catch up. Additionally, invite the team to share strategies that work for them – one person might signal day's end by literally shutting their computer and going for a walk. At the same time, another might use separate browsers or accounts for work versus personal use to create a mental separation. By talking about these practices, the team normalizes the idea that it's okay (indeed, necessary) to have boundaries.

From a coaching session design perspective, respecting boundaries might also mean being mindful of scheduling coaching activities. For instance, if you're planning a multi-hour virtual workshop, avoid scheduling it across the evening for some participants. Or if an unavoidable meeting falls on a colleague's local holiday, acknowledge it and make accommodations (perhaps record the session or offer a makeup discussion). These gestures show respect and prevent the erosion of goodwill that happens when remote workers feel their personal circumstances are ignored.

Lastly, consider emotional boundaries and well-being. Remote work can be isolating, and the boundaries between professional and personal stress can blur. As an Agile coach, you're not a therapist, but you are often a keen observer of team morale and individual well-being. Pay attention to signs of burnout or disengagement. If a usually upbeat team member grows quiet and stops participating, it could be a sign of overwhelm. One intervention could be a private coaching conversation to check in: "I've noticed you seem a bit down lately; how are you coping with the current setup?" Encouraging team members to take time off when needed, or even to declare a "video-free day" occasionally to decompress from screen time, can maintain long-term team health. Many remote teams implement practices like "Drop-off Fridays" (logging off early when workload allows) or meeting-free days to alleviate constant pressure.

In summary, the coach's role in virtual settings extends to helping the team create structure where natural boundaries previously existed. By explicitly addressing working norms, ensuring time zone fairness, and encouraging self-care, you guide the team to sustainable ways of working. This prevents the slow creep of overwork or resentment that can poison a team's spirit. A self-organizing Agile team thrives within healthy constraints, and defining those constraints in a virtual world is a collaborative effort that the coach can facilitate.

Designing Engaging and Effective Virtual Sessions

One of the most practical challenges you'll face when "going virtual" is how to design coaching sessions, workshops, and team meetings that are as engaging and effective as their in-person counterparts. Many coaches new to the virtual format initially attempt to replicate physical sessions exactly via video, only to find that attention wanes, interaction is stilted, and outcomes suffer. The truth is, virtual facilitation is a skill in its own right, and it requires thoughtful design choices. Here we discuss key nuances of virtual session design, from session length and activities to the use of tools and techniques to keep participants involved.

A first principle is shorter, more focused sessions. In person, it might be feasible to keep a team in a room for a half-day workshop (with coffee breaks) and maintain productivity. Online, that would likely court disaster in the form of fatigue and distraction. Virtual team coaching sessions should generally be kept shorter; many experts suggest 90 minutes as an absolute maximum for continuous full-group work. In fact, breaking work into even smaller chunks (with breaks in between) can greatly improve engagement. For example, if you need a three-hour workshop, consider two 90-minute sessions with a break in between or doing the sessions on separate days. Scrum events, such as sprint planning or sprint retrospective, may need to be timeboxed more tightly than their in-person counterparts or split into parts. The idea is to preserve energy and attention. When planning a virtual agenda, ask: *Can any portion of this be completed offline or asynchronously to save live meeting time?* Perhaps status updates or reading materials can be shared beforehand (via email or Confluence) so that the live session is dedicated to discussion and decision making rather than one-way information transfer. Clutterbuck advised that everything that can be done by email beforehand should be done, leaving the precious meeting time for interaction. This might mean team members do a bit more homework, but it maximizes the value of when everyone is together online.

Next, interaction, interaction, interaction. An engaging virtual session involves frequent participant interaction (see Table 10-3) at least every few minutes. In a physical meeting, people are naturally stimulated by being in a shared space. Online, it's easy to become a passive observer (or worse, start checking email on the side) if the format is too lecture-like. Avoid long monologues or slide presentations in virtual sessions—lengthy PowerPoint use is discouraged in favor of interactive dialogue. As a coach, design activities that prompt involvement by using open questions, directing the group into breakout rooms for small-group discussions, or having everyone write ideas on a shared whiteboard simultaneously. The technology actually offers some enhanced interaction modes that can surpass in-person; for example, using real-time polling tools to gauge the team's mood or opinion on an issue. Quick impromptu polls like "On a scale of 1–5, how confident are we in this plan?" can get everyone to contribute, and the anonymity can yield more honest input. Similarly, the chat function allows people to chime in without interrupting the speaker—encourage its use for questions or running commentary. In fact, some shy team members may participate more via chat than they would verbally; as a coach, you can monitor the chat and give voice to good points raised there.

Table 10-3. Interactions for Better Engagement

Technique	Intent/Purpose	When to Use
Silent reflection rounds	Surface deeper thoughts without pressure	Before decision making or after tense moments
Body check-in	Reconnect with physical presence	At session start or transitions
Chat-storming	Capture simultaneous input	For quick consensus or broad input
Breakout retrospectives	Create psychological safety in small groups	When discussing sensitive or emotional topics
On-screen visual metaphors	Make abstract ideas visible	For goals, roles, emotions, or blockers

Variety and creativity are your allies. In a remote session, plan to switch modalities or activities to keep things fresh. For instance, start with a quick icebreaker (like a fun question everyone answers in chat), then move to a group discussion, then perhaps a silent brainstorming where everyone adds sticky notes on a digital board, then regroup and discuss patterns. This changes the pace and taps different engagement channels. Leverage visual aids and metaphors that work online: some coaches use virtual backgrounds or on-screen drawing to illustrate a concept. The rule of thumb is to avoid doing any one thing for too long in the virtual format. Keep a cadence: presentation → interaction → reflection → etc., to maintain engagement.

Establishing clear facilitation norms is another important design aspect. In a room, a lot of facilitation "rules" are understood implicitly (e.g., don't all talk at once, raise your hand lightly, or just catch the facilitator's eye when you want to speak). Online, you need to set those expectations clearly to avoid chaos or disengagement. At the start of a session, it helps to review "how we will work together today." This can include norms such as: *Please mute when you're not speaking (to reduce noise) but stay off mute if you can commit to a quiet background (to increase spontaneity). Use the hand raise button or simply type "stack" in chat to indicate you want to speak next. If you're not speaking, consider keeping your camera on so we can see reactions (if bandwidth allows). And we encourage use of the chat for side comments or questions—the facilitator will keep an eye on it.* These guidelines, agreed upon as part of the virtual contracting, create a smoother session. They align with what we discussed in Chapter 3 about explicit contracting—here applied to meeting behavior. It's also useful to define what happens if we talk over each other ("No problem—I'll act as moderator to call on people, and if two start at once, I will invite one and then the other").

Because virtual sessions are usually shorter, preparation and focus are paramount. Ensure everyone knows the purpose and agenda in advance. Distribute any pre-reading or data ahead of time, and be clear about what outcomes you're driving toward in the meeting. Starting on time is crucial (since remote folks might be juggling back-to-back calls). One technique is to log in a few minutes early and greet people as they join; this also provides a tiny buffer for casual chat or troubleshooting any technical

CHAPTER 10   GOING VIRTUAL

connection issues for individuals. When the session starts, consider doing a quick check-in round to bring everyone into the "virtual room" mentally (e.g., each person shares one word about their current state of mind). This serves both as an engagement tactic and as data for you; if half the team says "tired" or "distracted," you know to perhaps inject an energizer or be gentle with the agenda.

Finally, be ready to adapt on the fly. Virtual environments can be unpredictable—someone's audio may fail, or a planned group activity might not work as intended when everyone is remote. Have a flexible mindset and a toolkit of backup methods. If the video call drops for many participants, consider dialing into a phone conference line instead. If your whiteboard app goes down, resort to a simple round-robin verbal brainstorm. These situations will arise, and your calm, adaptive response sets the tone for the team to persevere rather than give up. Agility in coaching means reading the energy of the virtual room and adjusting. If people look drained, maybe it's time for a five-minute break to stretch (encourage everyone to move away from their screen for those minutes, literally). If conversation is lagging, perhaps shift to a more interactive format or call on individuals with permission.

In sum, designing effective virtual sessions is about maximizing human engagement while minimizing the friction of the medium. It's certainly possible—many teams report that with skilled facilitation, a virtual retrospective or planning meeting can be just as productive as an in-person one, sometimes even more so. As we implement these design choices, we'll see in the next section how they come together as part of best practices and interventions that make virtual Agile coaching successful.

CHAPTER 10 GOING VIRTUAL

Key Practices and Interventions for Successful Virtual Coaching

Having examined the challenges, we now shift to essential practices and interventions that enable Agile coaches and teams to succeed in a virtual environment. These are the strategies and behaviors that directly address the challenges and turn the virtual format into an advantage where possible. We'll explore key practices, starting with virtual-specific contracting and norm setting, then maintaining a strong coach presence and active listening online, and finally fostering team dynamics and accountability in creative ways. Each of these areas supports the others; together, they create a toolbox for effective remote coaching. Many of these practices are extensions of core coaching skills or Agile facilitation techniques you already know, now tailored to the virtual space.

Virtual Contracting

Contracting—the process of establishing clear agreements and expectations is a fundamental step in any coaching engagement (as discussed in Chapter 3). In virtual coaching, contracting takes on even greater importance and often requires additional clauses, so to speak, that we wouldn't need to spell out in person. The mantra here is: Make the implicit explicit. Because remote work removes common situational cues, we cannot assume everyone shares the same understanding of "how we'll work together" unless we talk about it openly.

When kicking off coaching with a virtual Agile team, dedicate time to co-create a virtual working agreement. This is similar to a team charter or team norms, but tuned explicitly for remote collaboration. Include all the usual elements of a coaching contract (scope, goals, roles, confidentiality, etc.), and add virtual specifics such as the following:

- **Communication norms:** Decide on which channels to use for what purpose (e.g., "We'll use Slack for quick daily questions, email for formal announcements, and video calls for retrospectives and reviews"). Agree on expected response times and clarify that, for example, it's okay to not reply to non-urgent messages outside one's working hours. If the team spans time zones, explicitly note overlap hours or core hours, if any, and how to handle urgent issues off-hours (perhaps an on-call rotation or a text message as an exception). This prevents frustration later—no one feels left hanging or pressured around the clock, because you've set expectations together.

- **Presence and availability:** Align on things like camera use. Is the expectation that everyone will have video on during certain meetings to better read each other, or is video optional? Different teams make different choices, but it's key to discuss it. Many coaches encourage video for important coaching conversations to capture non-verbal cues, noting that seeing faces builds connection (unless bandwidth limits prevent it) . Also, talk about what it means to be "fully present." As David Clutterbuck pointed out, being on mute can be a double-edged sword: It preserves audio quality but also makes it easy for people to disengage and do other tasks. In your contracting, you might all agree, "When we are in a coaching session or team meeting, we will treat it with the same focus as if we were in-person. That means minimizing multitasking, and if you must step away or get interrupted, let us know." Essentially, reinforce that listening is an active commitment, not

CHAPTER 10   GOING VIRTUAL

just a passive act of politeness. By stating this, the team holds each other accountable to stay mentally in the room.

- **Participation and turn-taking:** Establish how the team will handle taking turns to speak or contributing ideas. For example, "We will use a round-robin in our retrospectives to ensure each voice is heard" or "We'll default to raising hands in Zoom when a discussion is lively to avoid talking over one another." Also consider how to surface disagreement. Virtually, it may require explicit mechanisms. You could agree on a signal or process: *If you have a different opinion, you can say "I have a different perspective" or put an emoji (like a red dot) in the chat to indicate you want to play devil's advocate.* The contract could state that dissenting views will be welcomed and given space. This preempts the tendency in some cultures or virtual forums for groupthink to take over if no one speaks up. It's essentially a safeguard against silence: Everyone knows that challenging a consensus is not just allowed but encouraged in service of the team's best outcomes.

- **Emotional transparency and trust-building:** Virtual teams risk glossing over feelings because of the medium's lean nature. In your contracting, encourage a norm of openness; for instance, *"We commit to sharing not just progress, but also if we're feeling stuck or frustrated. It's okay to say 'I'm not comfortable with this' or 'I'm upset about how that went'—in fact, it's important."* Clutterbuck notes the tendency of virtual teams to avoid emotional data and the need to explicitly invite it. As a coach, you might add to the

325

agreement that you will routinely conduct check-ins or use techniques to gauge team sentiment, and that everyone will practice candidly expressing not only their thoughts but also their feelings about team issues. By writing this into the working agreement, you legitimize emotional expression as part of work, which can be critical for psychological safety.

- **Logistics and tools:** Decide on things like what platforms are acceptable for everyone (some teams might have access issues or preferences). Agree on backup plans: *"If our video call drops, we will use the dial-in number shared in the invite."* Or *"If someone's audio isn't working, they'll indicate via chat and we'll pause or troubleshoot."* It sounds basic, but under stress, people can forget there was a backup number or option. Having it in your contract or team charter makes it a known and practiced contingency.

Creating these explicit virtual agreements may feel tedious at first, but it pays huge dividends. It brings everyone onto the same page and reduces friction and misunderstandings later. Moreover, involving the team in setting these norms increases their buy-in; it's not the coach dictating rules, but the team defining how they want to work together. The coach's role is to facilitate the conversation, bring up considerations they might overlook (often from your experience or knowledge, such as "Some teams struggle with X; how do we want to handle that if it happens?"), and ensure that the quieter voices contribute to the agreement too.

Once the contract is in place, use it actively. Refer back to it during coaching; e.g., "We all agreed to be fully present—I notice a lot of multitasking today, what's going on?" or "Our norm is to welcome dissenting views; I'm not hearing any disagreement, so either we're all truly aligned or folks might be holding back—remember, it's safe to speak up." These gentle reminders reinforce the norms. As Clutterbuck illustrates with his example, if someone is rambling off-topic and no one interjects, the coach can invoke the contract: "May I remind us of our agreement to be succinct in meetings?" This way, the "rules" are impersonal and collective—it's the team's agreement holding them accountable, not just the coach's personal preference.

In summary, virtual-specific contracting lays the groundwork for everything else. It directly addresses many challenges (miscommunication, disengagement, power imbalances) by setting clear expectations and behaviors. It's an upfront investment in team coherence. Chapter 3 gave you the principles; now, apply them with a virtual twist. The more explicit and agreed-upon the working norms, the smoother your virtual coaching journey will be.

Coach's Presence in the Virtual Space

One of the key qualities of an excellent coach is their presence—that almost-tangible sense of focus, attentiveness, and calmness they bring to a conversation. In a virtual environment, developing and projecting coach presence is both essential and difficult. Without the advantage of physical closeness, eye contact, or a soothing office setting, how do you truly "show up" for your team? Likewise, how do you engage in deep, active listening when digital distractions and physical distance prevail? This section discusses how to adapt the core coaching skill of presence to the online sphere.

First, let's consider your physical and digital environment. Think of your screen as your coaching room—it should feel welcoming, focused, and clutter-free. This means paying attention to your background, lighting, and sound quality. A quiet space, a decent headset or microphone, and a neutral/professional background (or a thoughtfully chosen virtual background) go a long way. If your video is on, ensure your face is well lit and clearly visible; teammates will connect better when they can see your expressions. These might seem like superficial details, but they signal respect and presence. For instance, if you appear in a dark, noisy room glancing away at other monitors, it unconsciously tells the team that you are not fully present. On the contrary, a setup where you appear centered on the screen, making "eye contact" (by looking into the camera at times), nodding and reacting as others speak, conveys that you are right there with them. Coach presence begins before you even speak—it's in how you physically show up on the virtual stage.

Tip   I picked up these tips from Daniel Mezick during a class on teaching in the virtual space, and I've been using them ever since:

- Try positioning yourself slightly off-center on the screen to create space for gestures and to show a bit of your background. Avoid sterile, depersonalized backgrounds; let people connect with you by noticing your surroundings and maybe asking questions like, "I see a guitar, do you play often?"

- Ensure your face is well lit and visible, as people want to see your expressions, which provide helpful cues about your reactions.

Next, minimize your own distractions to model the focus you expect. Close unnecessary windows, mute notifications, and put your phone aside. It's easy to tell when someone's eyes are darting around the screen reading emails—avoid that temptation by removing the cues. Some coaches even put a sticky note on their second screen or over any part of the screen that might lure their attention away, with a reminder like "BE HERE NOW." These little techniques help maintain a focused presence. You might also practice a short centering ritual before a coaching session or meeting: perhaps one minute of deep breathing or setting an intention, such as *"I*

CHAPTER 10   GOING VIRTUAL

am here to listen and serve the team." This echoes what you'd do before an in-person meeting (maybe a calming breath outside the door); it just happens to be at your desk.

Active listening in a virtual environment requires double the effort. Chapter 2's guidance on listening—like truly hearing the words, tone, and noticing what's not said—applies strongly. However, virtually you must compensate for missing body language. Focus intently on the speaker's face (if video) or voice. Notice micro-expressions or changes in vocal pitch. You may have to rely more on verbal feedback to show you're listening: use small verbal acknowledgments ("mmm," "I see," "uh-huh") more than you might in person, since the person can't always see nods if not on video or if they're looking at a shared screen. Paraphrasing and summarizing become invaluable: "So, what I'm hearing is that you're frustrated with the current process because it's causing delays, did I get that right?" This not only confirms understanding but reassures the speaker that you are fully engaged. It also slows the conversation to a thoughtful pace, which is useful online where things can become chaotic if people speak too quickly or over each other.

One subtle aspect of presence is being comfortable with silence, even on a video call. Many people find silence on a conference call extremely awkward and rush to fill it. A skilled virtual coach, however, knows that silence can be a powerful coaching tool (for reflection, for allowing someone to gather thoughts). You might say in advance, "Don't be alarmed by silence; I'm giving us space to think." This primes everyone that silence is not a tech glitch but a conscious choice. It takes confidence and presence to hold silent space remotely; practicing this will differentiate you as a coach who isn't afraid of a few seconds of quiet. It signals you're patiently present, not nervously trying to fill gaps.

Empathy and intuition remain integral to presence, but you may need to adjust how you utilize them. You might not "feel the energy in the room" physically, but you can tune into it by carefully observing the cues available. If several team members have their cameras off and haven't spoken, you might sense disengagement, so run a quick interactive activity to re-engage, or gently ask, "I'd love to hear from those who haven't shared yet—how are you seeing this?" Trust your coaching instincts: If something feels off, it probably is, even if you can't see all the faces. Don't shy away from naming it: "I have a sense that there's some hesitation around this decision. Is anyone feeling uneasy or have concerns we haven't heard?" Such an observation, made from curiosity and care, often brings the issue to light. This is presence in action—being so tuned in that you pick up on undercurrents and bring them to the surface for the team to address.

Leveraging Digital Tools for Engagement and Collaboration

One advantage of coaching in the digital realm is having access to a plethora of tools that can enhance engagement, creativity, and organization. While technology poses challenges (as we discussed earlier), it also presents unique opportunities for virtual coaching. A skilled coach will leverage these tools not for their own sake, but to serve the team's needs and make collaboration smoother and more fun.

Video conferencing platforms (Zoom, Microsoft Teams, Webex, etc.) These are our virtual "rooms," and knowing how to use their features can elevate a session. Most platforms have built-in tools like screen sharing, chat, polls, breakout rooms, reactions (emoji icons), and whiteboards. Use them! For example, if a discussion needs a visual aid, screen share a quick sketch or a relevant chart. If you want quick input from everyone, launch a poll or ask people to drop an icon (thumbs up/down) to gauge consensus. Encourage team members to utilize chat to ask questions or share links without interrupting. When deeper discussion or intimacy is needed in a large team, use breakout rooms to let small groups confer—this can increase participation from those who are quiet in big groups. The idea is to make the virtual experience as interactive as possible, which these features support. As one coach quipped, "Zoom is my new office—I better learn all the tricks to use it effectively."

Digital whiteboards and collaborative documents (Miro, Mural, Google Docs, Confluence, etc.) In Agile coaching, we often use flip charts, sticky notes, or whiteboards in person. Virtual equivalents can actually surpass those in capability. Tools like Miro or Mural allow participants to all write sticky notes simultaneously, group and vote on them, and save the board for later—something hard to do with physical stickies that get thrown away. You can run an entire retrospective or brainstorming session on a digital whiteboard, with sections for "What went well / What to improve" and dot-voting features to prioritize ideas. Many teams find that introverted members appreciate typing their thoughts (which feels less on-the-spot than saying them aloud), and the simultaneous input avoids the bias of one person's ideas dominating early. Leverage anonymity features when appropriate; e.g., in a retrospective, you might allow anonymous notes on the board to encourage candor about sensitive issues. Collaborative documents (such as Google Docs or Sheets) also allow teams to co-create content in real time; for instance, building a definition of done or editing a team norms document together, with everyone's cursors visible. This level of participation can actually be higher than in person, where one person typically writes and others speak. The key for the coach is to be familiar with these tools and integrate them seamlessly into session designs. Don't introduce five new apps at once (overload!), but gradually bring in what adds value.

One must remember, however, that tools are only as effective as their use. It's easy to overwhelm a team with too many platforms or to misuse a tool, turning it into a distraction. The coach's judgment is vital in choosing the right tool for each purpose. Also, consider the learning curve—if your team isn't tech-savvy, introduce new tools gradually and offer guidance. For example, if you plan to use a Miro board for the first time, maybe send a link to a practice board or spend two minutes at the start showing how to add a sticky note. This upfront effort will help the session run more smoothly. Likewise, be patient if glitches happen (they will!). Part of effective tool use is having fallback options; if a fancy polling app fails, you can always resort to "Type your answers in chat" as a simple backup.

Fostering Team Dynamics and Accountability Remotely

A self-organizing Agile team relies on healthy team dynamics—things like trust, mutual respect, constructive conflict, and accountability to each other. When teams go virtual, some of the natural mechanisms that foster these dynamics need reinforcement or substitution. As an Agile coach, part of your role is to stay attuned to team dynamics and design interventions that strengthen the team's cohesion and sense of responsibility, even when they rarely (or never) meet in person.

Building Cohesion and Camaraderie

Earlier, we addressed building trust; here, let's focus on maintaining an ongoing sense of team identity and camaraderie. Remote teams can easily fall into a pattern where interactions become purely task-oriented, which over time erodes the social glue that makes a group gel. To counter this, coaches can facilitate periodic team-building activities suited for a virtual format. These don't have to be elaborate—even a 10-minute game or a casual "show and tell" segment in a meeting can inject some fun and personality. For instance, some teams do a "virtual team coffee" where, once a week, a random pair of teammates is assigned to have a 15-minute non-work chat (many chat platforms have bots that set this up). This helps people who don't normally interact to bond. Another idea is to have a rotating "team DJ" who gets to share their favorite (work-appropriate) music at the start of meetings, or a "photo of the week" contest on Slack (like cutest pet photo, etc.). As a coach, you can suggest these ideas or sponsor them so that the team can adopt and implement them. The aim is to cultivate a sense of belonging. Research from Atlassian emphasizes the importance of personal connection in building trust and morale—the stronger colleagues know each other as human beings, the better they work together. And don't underestimate the value of laughter and informal banter; remote teams that find a way to joke and play a bit tend to weather conflicts and high-pressure periods with more resilience.

Facilitating Inclusive Communication

Good dynamics depend on everyone's having a voice and feeling valued. In virtual settings, strong facilitation (often by the coach or Scrum master) is essential to prevent a few voices from dominating. You might introduce structures in discussions, like "rounds" (each person speaks in turn) for updates or perspectives, which guarantees airtime for everyone. Alternatively, use the chat and then read out contributions from quieter members who wrote instead of speaking. Pay particular attention to newcomers on the team or junior members, as noted earlier, who can feel especially adrift or undervalued when working remotely. Encourage the team to do proper introductions and onboarding for new members ("buddy up" a new hire with a veteran for the first few weeks, via scheduled video calls, to transmit culture and context). A good practice is to hold one-on-one virtual meet-and-greets for a newcomer with each existing member—that helps the new person build relational links across the team quickly, rather than being the awkward stranger on calls.

Managing Conflict

Conflict is natural in any team. In fact, as David Clutterbuck noted, virtual teams are *more likely* to have conflict, potentially worsened by cultural differences. The coach's job is not to eliminate conflict but to make sure it's expressed and resolved in a healthy way. Virtual conflict can be tricky—a minor misunderstanding can spiral if people start assuming tone or intent from a curt email, for example. Coaches should encourage the principle "don't fight via email or chat." If tension is sensed, get people talking live sooner rather than later. Offer to facilitate a frank discussion. Use video so they can see each other's faces, which can re-humanize the interaction compared to cold text. Remind the team of their working agreements. Perhaps you agreed to assume positive intent or address issues directly with the person involved rather than gossiping—now is the time to reinforce those. One intervention is to create a team norm for conflict resolution; e.g., "If something upsets you, speak up within 24 hours either to the person or in the retrospective." Having it as a norm makes it less likely that issues fester unspoken. In a remote context, also be mindful of misunderstanding due to language—encourage folks to ask for clarification: "Could you clarify what you meant by X? I interpreted it as Y, but I want to be sure I understood." This simple practice can defuse a lot of friction.

Promoting Accountability and Self-Organization

Accountability in a co-located team often occurs socially—you see your teammate working hard, you feel pressure to do your part, or someone casually asks in the break room about a task, which nudges you to finish it. Remote teams need to replicate some of that. Agile ceremonies (daily stand-ups, sprint reviews) are already designed to encourage transparency and accountability. As a coach, make sure the team truly leverages these. For example, the daily Scrum in a virtual team might benefit from screen sharing the task board as each person speaks, so everyone sees what's in progress and what's next. If someone is stuck, encourage them to say so, and have someone else volunteer help—just as would happen if they saw a colleague struggling on site. The coach might need to prompt: "I recall you mentioned that bug yesterday, Raj. Any progress, or do you need a hand?" This fosters accountability in a supportive manner. Additionally, consider using "buddy checks"—pairing team members to check in mid-sprint on each other's progress and obstacles, essentially creating a peer accountability system.

Encouraging Leadership at All Levels

In a healthy Agile team, members step up to lead in different areas (facilitating a session, researching a tool, mentoring others, etc.). Remote work can sometimes default leadership back to whoever is loudest or has formal authority, because self-organization feels harder when apart. Coaches can counteract that by deliberately rotating certain responsibilities. For example, rotate the facilitator of the retrospective each sprint (even if you help them prepare, let a team member run it). Or have different people own parts of meetings ("Alice presents the demo for Feature A, Bob for Feature B"). When people actively participate in leading, they feel more accountable to each other and invested in the team's outcomes. Plus, it prevents over-reliance on the coach or Scrum master to drive everything. You might also create space in coaching sessions to discuss team norms around accountability: Ask the team, "How do we want to handle it if someone isn't delivering what they committed? How will we call each other out?" Remote colleagues might shy away from holding each other accountable, fearing it could come off harsher online. By discussing it explicitly, they can agree on a respectful approach (perhaps by assuming a misunderstanding and then clarifying expectations, etc.). This ties back to contracting—include peer accountability in the working agreement.

As a real-world example: Imagine a global software team struggling with late deployments and finger pointing. The Agile coach observed a lack of cohesion—developers in one country rarely spoke on calls, letting others dominate, and when deadlines slipped, those silent members were often blamed indirectly. The coach stepped in by introducing a rotating "demo buddy" system where each feature was paired with a developer from each location to co-demo the work. This encouraged collaboration and communication. They also held an honest retrospective focused on trust and accountability, where the team, guided by the coach, voiced frustrations and agreed on new norms; for instance, no making commitments for others without agreement, and if any member feels a timeline isn't feasible, they must speak up early. Over subsequent iterations, with these changes, the team started to gel; members knew each other better and felt responsible toward each other rather than against. Deliveries improved, along with team morale. This example shows how deliberate interventions can positively change group dynamics.

Conclusion

Adaptability is the cornerstone. Just as we ask Agile teams to inspect and adapt, we as coaches must continuously adapt our approach to fit a virtual world. Challenges like technology glitches, communication gaps, and cultural distances are not insurmountable—they are invitations to innovate in our coaching practice. By being flexible (for instance, adjusting session formats or learning new tools) and maintaining an Agile mindset, coaches can turn potential hindrances into opportunities. The coaches who thrive virtually are those who stay curious and resilient in the face of change, embodying the very agility we cultivate in teams.

Explicit contracting and clarity build trust. One of the strongest through-lines in this chapter is the power of explicit agreements. Whether it's setting ground rules for virtual meetings, clarifying communication norms, or aligning expectations on availability, making things explicit removes ambiguity that can otherwise erode trust. Chapter 3's wisdom on contracting has echoed here: In a virtual context, "say what you mean and agree on how you'll operate." Teams feel safer and more confident when they know the rules of engagement and have had a hand in crafting them. This clarity is a foundational layer upon which all other coaching interventions rest. When in doubt, come back to the contract—is there a new situation to explicitly address? Perhaps the team wants to revise norms after learning something; that's great. Keep the dialogue open. The virtual world changes quickly, and our agreements can evolve in tandem.

Relational skills and human connection are paramount. Technology may mediate our interactions, but it does not change the basic truth that people are at the heart of Agile. In fact, when distance intervenes, *intentionally strengthening human relationships* becomes even more critical. Chapter 2's focus on listening and presence finds renewed importance online. We succeed by listening not just for facts but also for feelings, by being present not just in body but also in full attention and empathy. We've seen how coaches can foster trust, psychological safety, and team cohesion through seemingly small acts: a thoughtful check-in, a moment of shared laughter, a gentle prompt to include a silent member. These "soft" skills produce hard results—teams that are engaged, open, and collaborative will outperform those that are divided or guarded. As coaches, honing our ability to build rapport and address interpersonal dynamics (drawing on insights from Chapter 9 on power and inclusion) is what makes the technical aspects of Agile truly click. In a virtual era flooded with digital noise, the coach's role as a beacon of human-centered leadership is more vital than ever.

In practice, basics still matter—with some twists. Many fundamentals you've learned throughout this book carry over into virtual coaching: the importance of clear goals, iterative improvement, managing power dynamics, etc. The core coaching stances—mentor, teacher, coach, facilitator—are still your toolkit. The difference is primarily in execution. You might mentor a Scrum master via video call instead of in person, or facilitate conflict resolution with webcams and headsets instead of in a meeting room. The tools and environment shift, but the essence remains. We referenced several previous chapters as reminders: contracting (Chapter 3), coaching fundamentals (Chapter 2), and power dynamics (Chapter 9). These concepts are your anchor. Whenever virtual work feels alien or frustrating, revisit those basics and ask, "How do I apply this here and now?" Often it will become clear; e.g., "Oh, we need to revisit our working agreement," or "I should use my listening skills to uncover what's unsaid on these calls." The fundamentals guide the way, just adapted to new terrain.

In closing, "Going Virtual" is not just a chapter title, but also a reality that has transformed how we collaborate. Agile team coaching in virtual environments is indeed challenging, but it is ultimately deeply rewarding. When you witness a once-disconnected remote team become a cohesive, high-performing unit, when you see faces light up in a grid of webcam squares because *they* solved a problem together or had a breakthrough in trust, you realize that distance is just a logistical detail. The essence of what we do as coaches transcends location. It lives in conversations, in insights, in the collective growth of teams, whether in a conference room or a Zoom gallery view.

Reflection Moment

- Consider your own level of comfort with the tools your team uses. How confident are you in troubleshooting a sudden audio or screen-share problem during a session? Identify one action (like learning a new platform shortcut or creating a "Plan B" communication channel) that could improve your technological readiness as a virtual coach.

- Consider a time you *felt* trust in a virtual group and a time you didn't. What contributed to those feelings? How might you recreate the positive factors (e.g., regular personal check-ins, clarity of communication, responsiveness) in the teams you coach now?

- Recall a virtual meeting or workshop that you felt was particularly engaging. What did the facilitator or coach do to create that engagement? How can you incorporate those elements into the next session you design?

- On your next video call, pay attention to your own presence. Are you fully attentive, or are you sneaking peeks at notifications? How is your posture and eye contact on camera? Challenge yourself to eliminate one distraction and add one behaviour (like more frequent nodding or verbal affirmations) that can enhance your virtual presence.

PART IV

Enhancing the Coaching Craft

CHAPTER 11

What If We Don't Need Another Tool to Be Impactful?

Agile team coaches operate in an environment of constant change, high uncertainty, and interdependence. In this dynamic and complex context, simply accumulating more techniques or tools (what we might call growing horizontally) often isn't enough to make a lasting impact. Yes, mastery of Agile practices and solid facilitation skills are essential, but true effectiveness comes from something deeper. Coaches need to evolve in how they think and who they are, not just what they know or do. This is where vertical development comes in—the growth of the coach's internal capacity to navigate complexity and create change at a systemic level, rather than just adding more tools to their toolkit .

Vertical development represents a shift in the coach's being and mindset. It means fundamentally transforming how we make meaning of situations, expanding our ability to handle ambiguity, and seeing the bigger picture within and around the team. A horizontally skilled coach might have a wide array of techniques, but a vertically developed coach has the mental and emotional breadth to know which techniques (if any) to apply and how to adapt when things get complex. In other words, to be truly effective, a coach doesn't necessarily need to keep adding "one

CHAPTER 11   WHAT IF WE DON'T NEED ANOTHER TOOL TO BE IMPACTFUL?

more tool"—they need to grow vertically in their maturity and perspective. When an Agile coach increases their vertical capacity, they are better equipped to guide teams through complexity, uncertainty, and growth. They essentially become a "bigger" person on the inside (Figure 11-1), able to hold and influence more complexity with less overwhelm.

Figure 11-1.   Capacity expansion in vertical development

In this chapter, we will explore what vertical development means for an Agile team coach, why it is essential to coaching effectiveness, and how coaches can actively cultivate this form of growth in themselves. We'll see that coaching impact isn't just about doing more—it's about *being* more. By the end, you should have a practical understanding of why developing yourself "vertically" is perhaps the most important evolution on your journey as an Agile coach, and how it enables you to be truly impactful in today's Agile landscape.

CHAPTER 11   WHAT IF WE DON'T NEED ANOTHER TOOL TO BE IMPACTFUL?

Understanding Vertical Development for the Coach: A Shift in Being

Let's clarify vertical development in the context of a coach's personal and professional growth, and how it differs from the more familiar horizontal development. Horizontal development refers to expanding what you know—acquiring new skills, techniques, and knowledge that enhance your performance in familiar ways . For example, a horizontal growth step might be learning a new retrospective format or studying a new scaling framework. In contrast, vertical development is about how you think, how you interpret the world, and your capacity to handle complexity. It's an upward shift in consciousness or perspective rather than an outward addition of knowledge.

In practical terms, vertical development for a coach involves a transformation in mindset and meaning making. It might manifest as progressing through distinct stages of maturity in how you view yourself, your team, and your environment. Developmental researchers have described successive stages of adult growth; for instance, moving from more egocentric stages (where one's focus might be primarily on personal success or one's own immediate tasks) toward more ecosystemic stages (where one's view encompasses the broader system, interconnections, and collective good). As a coach develops vertically, they experience key shifts in perspective. Early on, a coach might be preoccupied with their own performance or using coaching "by the book." At later stages, that same coach sees themselves as part of a larger system, intuitively understanding how team dynamics, organizational culture, and stakeholder needs interrelate. This mirrors findings in coach maturity models: As coaches mature, they expand from a narrow focus on techniques to a broader awareness of themselves, others, and the surrounding system.

One way to describe the outcome of vertical growth is an increase in the "size of person" the coach has become (internally). With each developmental step, a coach gains a greater capacity to notice nuances

CHAPTER 11   WHAT IF WE DON'T NEED ANOTHER TOOL TO BE IMPACTFUL?

in complex situations, reflect on them, and respond effectively. It's as if their mind and perspective get larger, able to hold more complexity without being overwhelmed. For example, a less-developed coach might see a team's conflict at face value and try a standard conflict-resolution technique. A more vertically developed coach might perceive the conflict's deeper root in unmet needs or systemic pressures and address it at that level. Crucially, vertical development tends to include and transcend horizontal skills; a vertically developed coach still has skills, but now uses them with a wiser, more adaptive mindset. It's been said that vertical growth changes the coach's internal "operating system"; it's not just adding new apps. This upgraded internal operating system is capable of appreciating multiple perspectives, sitting with paradox, and adapting one's approach based on the broader context.

Vertical development often involves moving through established stages of development (sometimes called levels of consciousness or meaning-making stages). Various theorists (e.g., Jane Loevinger, Robert Kegan, Susanne Cook-Greuter, Bill Torbert, and others) have outlined stage models for adult growth. While I won't dive deeply into specific stage definitions here, the key takeaway is that each stage represents a more complex and inclusive way of thinking. As coaches, progressing through these stages might mean evolving from a rule-following, self-oriented mindset to a more autonomous, principle-driven mindset, and eventually to a systemic, interdependent mindset. For instance, an Agile coach might start by rigidly adhering to a framework or methodology (seeing things in black and white, right or wrong). Later, they might evolve to understanding when to flex the approach to serve the team's goals (seeing shades of grey and multiple "right" answers). Later still, they could operate from an ecosystem perspective, balancing the needs of the team, organization, and even society, and helping others develop their own capacity in turn.

CHAPTER 11 WHAT IF WE DON'T NEED ANOTHER TOOL TO BE IMPACTFUL?

At the highest levels of development, coaches are often described as having a kind of wise, fluid adaptability—they can handle unpredictable, high-stakes situations with grace, and their presence alone can influence positive change.

Importantly, vertical development is a shift in being—it changes how a coach shows up. A coach undergoing vertical growth may notice changes in themselves, such as greater self-awareness of their own biases and triggers, a natural ability to empathize with perspectives very different from their own, comfort with uncertainty and not having immediate answers, and an inclination to think longer-term and systemically. They transition from reacting to problems with quick fixes to responding with curiosity and a broader perspective. In essence, vertical development transforms the coach's internal operating system, enabling them to handle greater complexity. It's not about discarding the valuable skills and knowledge (those remain important), but about expanding the container that holds those skills. A more developed coach can thus bring all their tools to bear more effectively.

To summarize, vertical development for an Agile coach means a shift in mindset from *"What tool do I apply?"* to *"How do I sense what's really needed here?"* It's an increase in cognitive, emotional, and relational capacity. It's the journey from doing Agile coaching to being an Agile coach at a higher level of maturity. By growing vertically, coaches unlock the ability to truly meet teams and organizations where they are and help lead them to deeper agility, rather than just operating at the surface level of practices.

Table 11-1 highlights the differences between these forms of growth, horizontal and vertical, showing how each contributes to our effectiveness as coaches.

Table 11-1. Horizontal vs. Vertical Development—Key Differences

Aspect	Horizontal Development	Vertical Development
Focus	Acquiring new skills/tools	Expanding perspective and consciousness
Nature of Growth	Adding knowledge or techniques	Shifting mindset and worldview
Example	Learning a new retrospective format	Increasing comfort with ambiguity and paradox
Outcome	Increased capability within current thinking	Greater adaptability in complex environments

Why the Agile Team Coach's Vertical Development Matters

Why invest time and effort in the coach's vertical development? Simply put, the coach's level of development directly affects their effectiveness and the outcomes they can achieve with teams. Here are several specific reasons why an Agile team coach's vertical growth is so critical.

Navigating Complexity and Ambiguity

Agile environments are often described as VUCA—volatile, uncertain, complex, and ambiguous. A vertically developed coach has an increased capacity to process and make sense of this complexity without being paralyzed by it. As Robert Kegan is an American developmental psychologist noted, there's often a mismatch between the complexity of modern organizational life and a leader's (or coach's) mental complexity. Vertical development helps close that gap. Coaches with higher cognitive complexity can take in multiple streams of information—team dynamics,

CHAPTER 11   WHAT IF WE DON'T NEED ANOTHER TOOL TO BE IMPACTFUL?

organizational politics, market changes—and synthesize an approach in real-time. They can hold paradoxes and navigate ambiguous situations more calmly. Research on leadership has shown that vertical growth equips individuals to handle complexity, ambiguity, and even paradox, in ways that pure skill training cannot. For an Agile coach, this means being able to guide a team through unclear situations (like a sudden shift in business priorities or a clash of departmental cultures) with clarity and confidence. Rather than defaulting to a cookie-cutter solution, the coach can tolerate the uncertainty, inquire deeper, and help the team find a path forward even when the "answer" isn't obvious. This ability to navigate complexity is arguably *the* differentiator between a merely competent Agile coach and an exceptional one.

Working with Systemic Challenges

Agile coaches don't just deal with isolated team practices; they often encounter systemic issues: organizational impediments, cross-team dependencies, cultural obstacles, hidden incentives misaligning behavior, etc. A coach who has developed vertically is better equipped to see and address these systemic challenges. As we grow, we learn to adopt a broader, systems thinking perspective (sometimes called adopting a systemic or ecosystemic perspective). Instead of viewing a team in a vacuum, a mature coach views the team as part of a wider network, influenced by leadership, structure, and even societal factors. This shift from an egocentric to an ecosystemic view greatly enhances a coach's effectiveness. For example, an egocentric approach might lead a coach to blame a team for resistance, whereas an ecosystemic approach would lead the coach to explore how the organization's culture or policies are contributing to that resistance. Coaches with a systemic mindset can identify interdependencies and patterns that less-aware coaches miss. They're able to work with individuals and teams, and can also subtly coach the broader system by liaising with stakeholders, suggesting organizational improvements, and addressing root causes. Being able to integrate multiple perspectives and hold a systemic frame significantly increases a coach's capacity to handle complexity. In short, vertical development enables the coach to transition from "fixing the team" to "improving the whole environment in which the team operates."

Holding the Coaching Space Under Pressure

Agile teams often go through growing pains—conflict, failure, tight deadlines, and organizational pressure. In those moments, how the coach shows up can make all the difference. Vertical development usually involves increases in self-awareness and emotional regulation. A more developed coach has a stronger ability to remain present and non-reactive amid chaos. They can create and hold a safe container for the team's toughest conversations and challenges. For instance, a coach at a higher maturity level is comfortable with not knowing the answer and can sit with the team's tension or strong emotions without rushing to "solve" or escape the discomfort. This creates a space where real issues surface and get addressed. Coaches with less development might inadvertently shut down these uncomfortable but necessary moments, perhaps by changing the topic when conflict arises or by imposing a solution to regain a sense of control. In contrast, a vertically developed coach can empathize, listen deeply, and maintain composure, signaling to the team that it's okay to explore the difficult stuff. Their presence is often described as grounded and attentive. They are aware of their own triggers (for example, noticing "I feel defensive because this discussion is challenging my approach") and manage them so that they don't interfere with the coaching. This ability stems in part from doing their own "inner work" as a coach—a hallmark of vertical growth. The result is a coaching environment where team members feel genuinely heard and supported, even when things get hard. Team psychological safety increases, and deeper learning happens. In essence, the coach's vertical development allows them to hold a larger emotional space for the team.

Managing Multiple Stakeholders and Agendas

Agile team coaches often have to balance the expectations and needs of various parties, including team members, product owners, Scrum masters, line managers, department heads, and possibly an Agile transformation office or HR. These stakeholders may have conflicting agendas or measures of success. A vertically developed coach possesses the ability to take multiple perspectives, understanding and navigating these viewpoints without becoming lost or overly biased. As one leadership development source put it, advancing in vertical development "facilitates a shift from a unilateral, linear perspective to the ability to embrace and manage multiple perspectives simultaneously," which is particularly valuable when incorporating various stakeholder interests. For example, imagine a scenario where a team wants to experiment with a new technical practice that might slow velocity in the short term, while a senior manager is pressuring for immediate results. A mature coach can hold the tension between innovation and efficiency—validating the team's need to learn and the manager's need for outcomes—and help find an approach that addresses both (perhaps by framing the experiment in terms of long-term ROI and setting expectations accordingly). They avoid the trap of seeing it as "pick a side." Instead, they act as a neutral party who seeks alignment and shared understanding. Coaches at earlier stages might struggle here: an ego-driven coach could align with whichever side they personally favor, or feel stressed and get caught in the crossfire. Vertical growth fosters the wisdom and patience necessary to navigate the complexity of stakeholder relations, finding integrative solutions and maintaining trust with all parties. Additionally, a more developed coach is less likely to take things personally; for instance, they won't feel personally insulted if an executive questions the Agile approach. Instead, they'll inquire into the concern and address it professionally. This level of composure and perspective comes from vertical development, where the coach's identity is secure and not constantly threatened by challenges.

Role-modeling Growth and Agility

One often overlooked aspect of coaching is how the coach's own way of being serves as a model (consciously or unconsciously) for the team. Teams learn not just from what the coach says, but from how the coach behaves and what they embody. A coach committed to their own vertical development demonstrates qualities like reflection, openness to feedback, vulnerability about not having all answers, and continuous learning. This can be profoundly influential. When a coach exemplifies these behaviors, it invites the team to do the same. For instance, a coach who openly reflects on a session (*"I noticed I was getting a bit attached to a particular outcome there—I need to remind myself to stay curious. What did you all notice?"*) shows the team that it's okay to admit imperfections and learn from them. This is powerful role modeling for a team learning to be Agile, because agility thrives on inspect-and-adapt, honesty, and courage. If the coach demonstrates comfort with vulnerability and "not knowing," the team is more likely to take interpersonal risks as well (like surfacing a hard truth in a retrospective). Conversely, a coach who is ego-driven always needs to be the expert, or never admits mistakes may inadvertently teach the team to hide weaknesses or avoid challenges, undermining an Agile culture. Thus, as the coach matures vertically and practices what they preach, they become a living example of the growth mindset and emotional intelligence that Agile teams themselves need. Indeed, a common saying is that an organization or team cannot evolve beyond its leadership's level of development. In Agile coaching, you are a leader. As one leadership expert observed: "I, as a leader, cannot take an organization any farther than I can go myself." Coaches who have transformed themselves vertically can catalyze deeper changes in others because they "walk the talk." They've been through the tough journey of growth, so they can empathize and guide others on theirs.

Supporting the Team Leader's Development

In many team coaching scenarios, the Agile coach partners closely with a team leader—typically a manager, a tech lead, or a Scrum master—to help that person develop into an Agile leadership role. A vertically developed coach can more effectively facilitate a leader's growth because they can meet that leader where they are developmentally and gently nudge them forward. If a coach's own stage of development is higher or at least on par with the team leader's, the coach can challenge the leader's assumptions in a productive way and introduce more advanced leadership mindsets when appropriate. However, if a coach is significantly less mature than the team leader, the coach may not be able to understand the leader's perspective or might oversimplify the leader's challenges, creating a mismatch that hinders progress. For example, consider a team leader who is learning to delegate and foster self-management in the team. If the coach still operates with a need for control and clear authority (a more concrete mindset), they might unknowingly reinforce old patterns (*"Well, have you tried enforcing the rules more?"*). A coach at a higher developmental stage, however, might help that leader explore their identity shift, fears of letting go, and new ways to enable shared leadership, because the coach personally understands the journey of moving from controlling to empowering. In essence, the coach's vertical development allows them to hold a developmental partnership with the team leader. They can coach not just on practices, but on the leader's mindset and being—supporting, for instance, a manager's evolution from a directive "boss" to a facilitative servant-leader. Moreover, a mature coach recognizes the potential in the team leader to grow (rather than writing someone off as "not Agile enough"), thus creating a more compassionate and effective coaching relationship.

Enhancing Ethical Maturity and Wisdom

Higher stages of development often correlate with more nuanced ethical reasoning and a stronger internal moral compass. Agile coaches frequently face ethical dilemmas, including confidentiality issues, pressure to deliver at all costs, and concerns about diversity and inclusion. Vertical development contributes to what we might call ethical maturity—the ability to navigate complex moral situations with wisdom, integrity, and care. A coach operating from a developed mindset is better at recognizing ethical issues in the first place (because they see the system and long-term consequences, not just the immediate task). They're also more likely to consult their principles and multiple perspectives when making decisions, rather than defaulting to authority or personal interest. For example, if an organization asks a coach to share confidential team retro notes, a less mature coach might obey out of deference or fear of authority. A more mature coach would pause, consider the ethical implications for psychological safety, perhaps engage the organization in a dialogue about why confidentiality matters, and find a solution that upholds ethical practice. They have the backbone to say "no" when necessary and the wisdom to explain their reasoning in a constructive way. Vertical growth also usually brings greater empathy and a broader sense of responsibility (seeing oneself as a steward for the system and people, not just a hired contractor to please the boss). This means that a coach at a higher maturity level will strive for solutions that serve the whole, not just one faction. It also means they'll be more aware of their own biases and therefore act more justly. The International Coach Federation and other bodies emphasize integrity and ethics; vertical development gives the coach an embodied capability to live those ethics, not just intellectually know the code. Additionally, in tricky situations, a mature coach has the humility to seek supervision or dialogue (rather than thinking they must have all the answers), which often prevents ethical blind spots. In short, as a coach grows vertically, they tend to develop wisdom—a blend of knowledge, experience, and deep principles—that guides them in doing the right thing by their team and organization.

For coaches to be truly "fit for purpose" in today's complex environment, we must achieve a fit between the complexity of the challenges and our own capacity. If the environment grows more complex but we do not, we'll find ourselves out of our depth. But if we invest in our vertical growth, we will elevate our ability to serve teams and organizations in profound ways.

Cultivating the Coach's Vertical Development

Knowing that vertical development is crucial is one thing, but how can Agile team coaches actually foster this growth in themselves? Vertical development tends to require deliberate effort and often support from others. It's a journey of mindset and "self" evolution, which is different from attending a standard skills course. In this section, I will focus on practical pathways and practices (see summary in Table 11-2) that can help an Agile coach cultivate their own vertical development. These are strategies that go beyond simply reading a book; they involve engaging in experiences and reflections that expand your perspective, enhance self-awareness, and challenge you to grow. Think of them as creating the conditions in which vertical development thrives.

Table 11-2. *Practices for Cultivating Vertical Development*

Practice	Description	Benefit (Impact on Coaching)
Coaching supervision	Structured reflection with a qualified supervisor	Increased self-awareness, ethical maturity
Individual coaching	Experiencing personal coaching	Empathy, insight into own biases, vulnerability
Reflective practice	Regular self-analysis of coaching experiences	Enhanced meta-awareness, intentional action
Continuous learning	Studying psychology, systems thinking, etc.	Broader cognitive complexity, informed perspectives
Peer coaching partnerships	Mutual peer support and shared reflection	Diverse perspectives, reduced blind spots
Seeking feedback	Actively obtaining feedback from others	Accurate self-perception, targeted growth areas
Challenging assignments	Engaging with complex or unfamiliar scenarios	Growth through adversity, resilience building
Systemic awareness	Intentionally understanding broader contexts	More strategic interventions, systemic impact

Engaging in Coaching Supervision

If there is one practice highly recommended for coach development, it is receiving regular supervision. Coaching supervision is a structured process where a coach (the supervisee) brings their work experiences to a qualified supervisor (often an experienced coach trained in supervision) for reflection and guidance. Supervision has been called "the coach's secret weapon" for ongoing growth. Why? Because it provides a confidential, supportive space to reflect on client work, gain new perspectives, uncover blind spots, and ensure you're coaching ethically and effectively. In

CHAPTER 11 WHAT IF WE DON'T NEED ANOTHER TOOL TO BE IMPACTFUL?

supervision, you might discuss a challenging team conflict you facilitated last week, and with the supervisor's help you could discover, for example, that you were unconsciously colluding with one strong personality or that you were avoiding a certain topic because it triggered your own fears. This kind of insight is gold for vertical development, as it increases your self-awareness and provides the opportunity to adapt your approach in the future.

The supervisor's role is not to "audit" you, but to support and challenge you in service of your development. They wear multiple hats: a formative function (helping you develop skills and understanding), a normative function (keeping an eye on ethics and standards), and a restorative function (supporting you emotionally). For instance, formative might mean helping you brainstorm ways to handle a resistant stakeholder; normative might mean discussing how to maintain confidentiality in a tricky situation; restorative might mean debriefing the emotional toll a coaching engagement is taking on you and finding ways to replenish. By engaging in these dialogues, you expand your capacity to handle future scenarios. Supervision, especially with a skilled supervisor, also introduces you to systemic thinking. Many supervision approaches (such as the Seven-Eyed Model by Peter Hawkins) explicitly help you look at the coach–client–system relationship from multiple angles. You learn to see how the team's issues might reflect larger organizational patterns, or how your own reactions might be mirroring the client's issue. This systemic lens in supervision greatly aids vertical growth—you start seeing wider and deeper than before.

Additionally, supervision is a safe place to explore ethical dilemmas and ensure you are "fit for purpose." A good supervisor will gently probe you to consider if you're working within your competence and adhering to your principles. If you're ever unsure, "Was it appropriate that I did X with the team? Am I crossing into consulting or therapy?", those conversations in supervision refine your judgment and ethical maturity. Over time, this builds a coach who is both confident and conscientious. There's also the personal support aspect: Coaching can be lonely and sometimes stressful work; knowing you have a supervisor to confide in can itself increase your resilience and capacity to handle difficult assignments. Many coaches report feeling "held" by their supervisor, which frees them to take necessary risks in their client work, knowing they can later process it in supervision.

Receiving Individual Coaching (Being the Coachee)

We often say in the Agile world, "walk the talk." One of the most practical ways to develop yourself is to experience coaching from the other side—that is, get coached by someone. When you act as a client (coachee) in a coaching engagement, you gain invaluable insight into the coaching process and into yourself. Why is this vertically developmental? First, it's a mirror for your own growth areas. A skilled coach will help you uncover your assumptions, limiting beliefs, and growth edges. By working through these with your coach, you're essentially undergoing the kind of mindset shifts we associate with vertical development: You might redefine what leadership means to you, or realize you have a larger capacity than you thought. It's personal transformation, which is vertical growth. Second, being coached increases empathy and understanding for your clients. You remember what it feels like to be vulnerable, to struggle with change, to have someone gently hold you accountable—and that makes you a more compassionate, attuned coach for others. Coaches who regularly have their own coach often report that it keeps them "honest" and grounded. It's hard to ask your team or client to step out of their comfort zone if you're not doing the same somewhere in your life.

There are also very practical learnings. As a coachee, you observe how another coach operates. You'll pick up new coaching techniques, powerful questions, or ways of structuring sessions that you might incorporate (or note what you don't like and avoid that!). It's experiential learning of the coaching craft at a deeper level than any classroom can provide. Importantly, having your own coach helps you refine your "inner coach." One coaching author noted that if you're not being coached yourself, you miss out on perhaps the most powerful means of developing your inner coaching behaviors. The "inner coach" refers to your mindset and presence as a coach, which is exactly what vertical development is about. By working with your own coach on your goals and challenges, you practice openness, humility, and the willingness to change. You also likely will address personal areas (work-life balance, confidence, communication, etc.) that, when improved, will positively influence how you show up with teams. In essence, being coached helps you become the best version of you, which directly translates into a stronger coaching presence.

Many professional coaches consider it best practice always to have a coach. Whether it's a peer coach in a reciprocal arrangement or a hired coach, the relationship ensures you are continuously growing. It "sharpens the saw," keeping your skills fresh and your perspective expanding. It can be humbling at times—you'll experience the discomfort your clients feel when challenged—and that's a good thing. It increases your capacity for empathy and reminds you what a powerful, transformative process coaching can be (renewing your faith in the work we do). In short, if you want to help others develop, never stop developing yourself, and having your own coach is a great way to do that.

Engaging in Reflective Practice

Reflection is the engine of learning from experience. For vertical development, it's essential not only to have new experiences but also to digest and integrate them. Reflective practice means deliberately taking time to think about your coaching experiences—what happened, why you did what you did, what you were feeling, what patterns you notice, what you learned, and what you might do differently. This could take many forms: journaling after coaching sessions, recording yourself and analyzing it, meditation or contemplative practices focusing on your coaching, or even engaging in dialogue with peers about your cases (in a colloquial way, outside of formal supervision). The key is to create a habit of learning from your day-to-day work.

For example, after a team meeting that you coached, you might jot down: "The retrospective went off the rails at one point when topic X came up. I felt a strong urge to intervene but held back—why? In hindsight, was I avoiding something? What was the team needing at that moment?" Such reflections can reveal subtle blind spots (maybe you realize you consistently avoid conflict when it involves a certain leader in the room) or eureka moments (you notice that when you stayed quiet, the team actually resolved it themselves, teaching you the power of silence). These kinds of insights accumulate to form greater self-awareness and coaching wisdom. As two coaching researchers, Tatiana Bachkirova and Elaine Cox, have pointed out, each stage of development enriches a coach's capacity for reflection and nuanced understanding of situations. So it's a virtuous cycle: More development leads to deeper reflection, which leads to more development.

To make reflective practice more effective, having structure and discipline often helps. You might set aside 20 minutes at the end of each week to reflect on key coaching moments. Some coaches use frameworks like Gibbs' Reflective Cycle or Kolb's learning cycle to guide their thinking (e.g., Describe ➤ Feelings ➤ Evaluation ➤ Conclusions ➤ Actions). Others might focus on critical incidents: "What's one thing that was uncomfortable or puzzling this week, and what can I learn from it?" Over time, reflective practice enhances your ability to observe yourself in action. You begin developing a sort of "witness" mindset where part of you can step back, even during coaching, to notice what's happening. This meta-awareness is a strong indicator of vertical development—being able to think about your thinking and sense your own emotions while choosing your response. It results in more intentional, flexible coaching rather than autopilot behavior. More on reflective practice will be presented in the next chapter.

CHAPTER 11   WHAT IF WE DON'T NEED ANOTHER TOOL TO BE IMPACTFUL?

The practical result of continuous reflection is that you become a learning-oriented practitioner. You're less likely to repeat the same mistakes blindly, because you've analyzed them. You're more likely to adapt your style to what each team needs, because you've reflected on past mismatches. And you become more comfortable with complexity, because you've sat with confusing situations after the fact and made some sense of them (rather than just moving on). In essence, reflective practice helps you "connect the dots" between experiences and inner growth. It is an essential habit to cultivate if you aim to keep growing vertically throughout your coaching career.

Continuous Learning (Horizontal Learning with Vertical Benefits)

While we distinguish between horizontal and vertical development, it's not that horizontal learning (skills and knowledge acquisition) is bad; in fact, it can support vertical growth when done wisely. Continuously learning in areas that broaden your perspective can feed your vertical development. For instance, learning about psychology (maybe you read up on motivation theory or group psychology) can give you new lenses to interpret team behavior, thereby enriching your sense-making capacity. Studying systems thinking or complexity science can help you see organizational patterns and cause-and-effect in complex systems, which directly contributes to having a more systemic perspective as a coach. Delving into adult development theory itself (learning about how humans grow through stages) can normalize the challenges you and your clients face and help you identify where someone might be developmentally and how to coach them appropriately. All these domains—psychology, systems theory, organizational development, neuroscience, ethics, etc.—add richness to your mental models.

CHAPTER 11   WHAT IF WE DON'T NEED ANOTHER TOOL TO BE IMPACTFUL?

The key is to approach continuous learning not just as collecting facts, but also as expanding your ways of thinking. If you treat it as *"I'm taking a course on somatics to get a certificate,"* that's horizontal. But if you immerse yourself in learning with curiosity—*"What does this new field show me that I didn't see before?"*—you integrate it into your worldview. For example, after learning about systemic coaching, you might start paying attention to stakeholders who are not in the room but influence the team (like *"What is marketing's relationship with this team? How could we involve their perspective?"*). Or after learning about cognitive biases, you become more vigilant about how confirmation bias might be affecting a team's decision. Each new piece of knowledge can become a scaffold to higher-order thinking if you reflect on it and apply it.

A caution: It's easy to get caught in endless horizontal learning as a form of procrastination (*"I'll be ready to coach that leadership team after I've done advanced training X, Y, Z . . ."*). Vertical development requires that we not only gather but also apply and integrate learning. So as you pursue continuous education, keep relating it back to your current work and how it can deepen your effectiveness. One might say, read widely but reflect deeply. The combination of breadth and depth will support your vertical growth. Many vertically mature coaches are characterized by having a broad "knowledge base," but one held lightly—they aren't rigid in one ideology. They can draw from multiple disciplines as needed.

In practice, you might set a goal to read certain seminal books or attend workshops outside your comfort zone each year. Perhaps take a course on counselling micro-skills, or read about organizational constellations, or join a webinar on developmental coaching. These can all feed your growth. Remember, vertical development is partly about making better meaning—the more perspectives and models you're exposed to, the more complex and nuanced your meaning making can become (provided you synthesize and not just compartmentalize that knowledge). So keep learning—both "hard" skills and theoretical concepts—as fuel for your ever-expanding coaching mindset.

CHAPTER 11   WHAT IF WE DON'T NEED ANOTHER TOOL TO BE IMPACTFUL?

Seeking and Processing Feedback

Feedback is a catalyst for growth—if we're open to receiving it. Actively soliciting feedback from clients (teams, team members, managers you work with), peers, and supervisors provides an outside view of your impact and areas to improve. This is not always comfortable; in fact, it often isn't! But vertical development thrives on disconfirming data that challenges our current self-concept and encourages us to evolve our approach. A coach who never gets feedback can become complacent or self-deluding ("All my teams love me"—well, have you asked them?). By asking for feedback, you model humility and continuous improvement, which again is good role modeling for Agile values.

In practice, you might periodically run a feedback survey or simply ask a client sponsor, "How do you feel the coaching is going? What could I be doing differently to support the team better?" You could ask team members after a quarter, "What about my coaching has been most helpful to you? What has been least helpful?" And importantly, when you get feedback, process it rather than react defensively. Even if you disagree, sit with it and see what nugget of truth might be there. Perhaps a team says, "Sometimes it feels like you push us too hard to adopt practices." That might hurt to hear, but upon reflection, maybe you realize your enthusiasm for agility sometimes overrides meeting the team where they are. That insight could be pivotal in shifting you toward a more pull-based coaching style, a significant developmental leap.

Feedback from stakeholders can also illuminate systemic issues that you, as a coach, need to navigate. For example, a manager might provide feedback, "*I'm not clear what value these coaching sessions provide.*" Instead of justifying on the spot, a mature approach would be to consider how you can better communicate or even adapt to provide value in their eyes—this might deepen your capacity to demonstrate agility's benefits in business terms.

Additionally, consider 360-degree feedback or coaching supervision feedback. In supervision, a supervisor might give you feedback like, "*I notice you often shift to consulting mode and give advice—have you noticed that?*" Such feedback, coming from a place of support, can be a strong prompt to adjust habits that are limiting your effectiveness. It's often said in coaching that we each have our own "signature presence" and also our "signature faults"—those blind spots that we just won't see unless someone points them out. Embrace feedback as a gift. It takes courage to ask for it and even more to truly receive it. But every piece of constructive criticism, every unexpected perspective on your work, can enlarge your understanding of yourself and make you a more versatile coach. Over time, you'll even become better at self-feedback (instantly sensing, "*Oops, there I go again, talking too much. Let me step back*"). This is another sign of vertical growth: the internalization of feedback mechanisms so you become largely self-correcting and self-driven in improvement.

Confronting and Learning from Challenging Assignments

It's often our most difficult coaching assignments that spur the most significant growth. When everything is easy and smooth, we aren't usually forced to stretch. But when we take on a tough scenario—perhaps coaching a team in crisis, or working with an executive team resistant to change, or stepping into a coaching role in an unfamiliar domain—we experience what vertical development literature calls "heat experiences." These are situations that push us beyond our current capacities, creating discomfort and sometimes failure. While challenging, they are fertile ground for development if we approach them with a learning mindset.

For example, you might engage with a team that, despite your usual bag of tricks, isn't improving. Maybe conflict is rampant, and nothing you do seems to help. This could be frustrating, but it might also force you to dig deeper—perhaps you seek out new conflict resolution models, or you

CHAPTER 11   WHAT IF WE DON'T NEED ANOTHER TOOL TO BE IMPACTFUL?

consult a more experienced colleague, or you get really creative and try something entirely out of your previous repertoire. In the struggle, you likely grow. You might have an epiphany about group dynamics or your own presence under pressure (*"I realized I was afraid of their conflict, so I was avoiding it. Once I worked through my own fear, I was able to coach them through theirs."*). That kind of personal breakthrough often only comes because the challenge demanded it of you. Research suggests that such "crucible" experiences or stretch assignments are a primary driver of vertical leadership development; they shake up your habitual way of operating and thus drive you to develop a more complex approach.

Therefore, don't shy away from challenges. Say yes to opportunities a little beyond your comfort zone—maybe coaching a group of senior leaders when you've mostly done team level, or coaching in a different culture, or tackling a transformation effort that requires multi-team coordination. Of course, do so ethically (don't wildly over-promise or take on something wildly beyond your skill without support). But recognize that discomfort is the crucible of growth. When things get tough, rather than immediately thinking "I'm failing" or "This is just impossible," consider reframing to "This is teaching me something new." Afterward, debrief thoroughly (with yourself, your supervisor, etc.) to extract the lessons. Over time, a series of challenging experiences will greatly expand your range as a coach—you'll find fewer and fewer situations "impossible" because you've walked through fire already and emerged with new strengths.

In Agile coaching specifically, this might look like volunteering to coach a team that's historically "difficult" or taking on a dual coaching + facilitation role at a big offsite, or working with a startup one quarter and a Fortune 500 company the next. Each context forces you to adjust and learn. You might fail in some ways (maybe one engagement ends with lukewarm results), but if you reflect, that "failure" can teach you more than any book or successful project could. Many seasoned coaches, when telling their development story, point to the hardest projects as the turning points where they truly stepped up in capability. So, embrace challenges as a key part of your development diet.

CHAPTER 11   WHAT IF WE DON'T NEED ANOTHER TOOL TO BE IMPACTFUL?

Developing Systemic Awareness

A recurring theme in vertical development is widening one's scope of awareness—seeing the system, the context, the interconnectedness of things. Agile team coaches can cultivate this by intentionally focusing on the broader organizational and ecosystem context of their teams. Concretely, this might mean spending time to understand the business domain more deeply, learning about other departments' objectives, being curious about external factors (market changes, customer feedback) that influence the team, and generally avoiding a siloed view. Some practical steps: attend stakeholder meetings beyond the team when possible, read company strategy documents, talk to people in different roles or levels to get their perspectives, or map out the team's network of interactions (suppliers, customers, other teams). The more you understand the system that surrounds the team, the more effectively you can coach the whole system.

Systemic awareness also includes noticing patterns over time. For example, you might observe that every autumn the team's work gets disrupted by budget planning—a cyclical systemic event. With that awareness, you can pre-emptively coach around it next cycle. Or you discern a pattern that new features from Team A often upset Team B's workflow, indicating a system design issue. A vertically developed coach not only helps a team with what's happening internally, but also helps them interface better with the larger system. You might facilitate better stakeholder reviews or align team Objectives and Key Results (OKRs) with organizational goals, etc. This increases your impact beyond the team level.

Moreover, developing systemic awareness changes your internal stance. You start to see issues less as isolated "bad behaviors" and more as emergent phenomena of a system. This mindset can make you less judgmental and more strategic in your interventions. For instance, rather than labeling a team "resistant," you might see how the system incentivizes them to stay the same, leading you to address that incentive structure with leadership. In doing so, you act as a bridge between the team and the wider organization—a hallmark of higher-level coaching. Many Agile coaches eventually evolve into enterprise or systemic coaches precisely by broadening their lens in this way.

One way to practice this is through systems thinking tools: causal loop diagrams, system maps, constellations, etc., which force you to depict all the players and influences. Another way is simply regularly asking yourself, "Who/what is not immediately visible here but is part of this situation?" and "What are the upstream and downstream effects of this issue?" Initially, this might be an intellectual exercise, but over time it becomes a natural mode of perception. You begin to sense the system's presence in every team interaction. That is vertical growth—moving from seeing parts to seeing wholes. And when you help a team become aware of the wider system, you empower them too (teams can fall into silo thinking; a coach with systemic awareness can gently expand their view, making them more effective).

Each of these pathways—supervision, being coached, reflection, continuous learning, peer coaching, feedback, challenges, systemic awareness—can reinforce the others. Together, they create a rich developmental environment for you as a coach. It's often said that vertical development isn't something you can force (one cannot simply decide to jump to a later stage), but you can certainly create the conditions for it. Engaging in these practices provides the fertile ground and stimuli for your vertical growth. Over time, you'll likely notice shifts in how you show up and think as a coach. Others may notice too, perhaps commenting that you seem to handle chaos more calmly, or you ask questions that really make them think, or you exhibit a presence that's notably wiser. These are signs that your investment in self-development is bearing fruit.

Table 11-3 contrasts these differences across key areas of impact. It highlights how vertical development influences coaching practice in tangible ways that teams and organizations can immediately feel.

CHAPTER 11 WHAT IF WE DON'T NEED ANOTHER TOOL TO BE IMPACTFUL?

Table 11-3. *Impact of Coach's Vertical Development on Teams and Systems*

Area of Impact	Less Vertically Developed Coach	More Vertically Developed Coach
Team conversations	Surface-level conversations	Deeper, reflective dialogues
Conflict navigation	Avoids or suppresses conflict	Uses conflict constructively
Stakeholder engagement	Limited or biased perspective	Balances and integrates multiple perspectives
Role-modeling	Maintains expert persona	Demonstrates vulnerability, openness, and curiosity
Ethical maturity	Rule-based, less nuanced	Principle-based, ethically reflective, nuanced
Leader development	Offers tactical advice	Fosters deeper identity and mindset shifts in leaders

Conclusion

Effective Agile coaching transcends simply acquiring more tools or techniques. It requires evolving internally—shifting how you perceive complexity, ambiguity, and relationships within and around teams. This internal growth, known as vertical development, allows coaches to operate from a deeper, more systemic perspective. Rather than merely applying methods or frameworks, vertically developed coaches bring increased emotional intelligence, reflective capability, and a broader cognitive perspective to their practice.

CHAPTER 11   WHAT IF WE DON'T NEED ANOTHER TOOL TO BE IMPACTFUL?

Vertical development expands your capacity to navigate complexity, address systemic challenges, maintain emotional composure under pressure, manage diverse stakeholder expectations, and embody authentic agility. Cultivating vertical development involves practices such as regular coaching supervision, being coached yourself, consistent reflective practice, continuous learning across diverse fields, actively seeking and processing feedback, confronting challenging coaching assignments, and deepening systemic awareness.

By engaging in these pathways, you foster the internal conditions necessary for meaningful and lasting impact. This journey is ongoing and inherently challenging—it demands personal investment, vulnerability, courage, and continual self-awareness. Yet, the rewards are profound. Coaches who grow vertically become catalysts not only for team effectiveness but also for broader organizational agility and resilience. Ultimately, vertical development transforms Agile coaches into leaders who embody the very agility they strive to instill in others.

Reflection Moment

1. When facing complex team situations, what patterns do I notice in my own responses (e.g., avoidance, rescuing, controlling)? What might these reactions reveal about my growth edges?

2. How often do I find myself drawn into problem-solving or giving advice instead of holding space for the team to explore their own solutions? What drives this behavior in me?

3. In what ways do I notice my own ego or identity influencing my coaching decisions or interactions? How might a shift to an ecosystemic perspective change my approach?

4. When tensions or conflicts arise, what emotions surface within me, and how effectively do I manage these emotions to facilitate constructive team dialogue?

5. How open am I truly to receiving feedback, especially critical feedback, from my teams, peers, or supervisors? What internal narratives do I experience when feedback challenges my self-image?

6. Where in my coaching practice am I most resistant to uncertainty or ambiguity? How could greater comfort with "not knowing" enhance my effectiveness as a coach?

7. What role do my personal biases or preferences play in the way I coach different individuals or teams? How might increased awareness of these biases positively impact my coaching presence?

8. Which stakeholder relationships do I find particularly challenging to navigate, and what developmental insights can these challenges offer about my own assumptions or mental models?

9. In situations where ethical boundaries or professional limits were tested, what did my reactions teach me about my level of ethical maturity and wisdom as a coach?

10. Reflecting on my recent coaching experiences, how effectively have I integrated systemic thinking—considering broader organizational dynamics—in my interventions? Where is there room for growth in adopting a more systemic perspective?

CHAPTER 12

Pause, Reflect, Act

In the fast-paced world of Agile coaching, it's easy to get caught up in the next sprint, the next challenge, or the next goal. But effective Agile coaches know the power of hitting the "pause" button. Taking time to reflect—to thoughtfully consider recent experiences, feelings, and outcomes—is not a luxury; it's a necessity.

Reflection is at the heart of the learning process for anyone, but it's especially critical in Agile team coaching. Simply accumulating coaching hours or collecting experiences isn't enough to guarantee competence. What matters is how you integrate those experiences into your practice. Reflective practice enables you to extract lessons and insights from day-to-day coaching experiences, transforming routine events into sources of growth. In fact, reflection is what transforms activity into learning. Without it, even a seasoned Agile coach can repeat the same mistakes or miss opportunities to improve.

Moreover, reflective practice is not just a set of exercises you perform once in a while—it's a foundational attitude toward both life and work. Great coaches approach their work with curiosity and a commitment to learn from every situation. Professional coaching bodies emphasize this; for example, the International Coaching Federation (ICF) explicitly includes ongoing reflective practice as essential for enhancing one's coaching. Similarly, the Chartered Institute of Personnel and Development (CIPD) considers reflective practice the foundation of professional development, noting that it helps turn insights from experience into

CHAPTER 12   PAUSE, REFLECT, ACT

practical strategies for personal growth and organizational impact. In other words, reflection isn't a nicety—it's central to continuously becoming a better coach and making a bigger impact.

Another reason reflection matters is its effect on self-regulation. Coaching Agile teams can be an emotional rollercoaster—there are triumphs, setbacks, team conflicts, deadlines, and everything in between. A reflective mindset helps you notice and regulate your own thoughts, feelings, and actions amid these challenges. For instance, after a tense meeting, a reflective coach might pause to ask, *"What am I feeling right now, and why? How might that be affecting my response to the team?"* This self-awareness is invaluable. It prevents you from reacting on autopilot or letting stress hijack your coaching. Instead, you can select responses that align with your values and the team's needs.

Finally, reflective practice gives Agile coaches the ability to uncover hidden issues and ask the tough questions that might otherwise go unasked. In Agile environments, many challenges are emergent— problems with team dynamics, stakeholder expectations, or processes often lurk beneath the surface. By reflecting critically, you train yourself to see subtle patterns that others might miss. Perhaps you notice certain team members always stay quiet in retrospectives, or you realize you've been avoiding a tough topic with leadership. Recognizing these subtleties is the first step; now you can frame the kind of searching questions that cut to the core of issues. This ability to surface and explore hidden dynamics can be the difference between a team that stagnates and one that truly grows.

Perhaps the most profound reason to practice reflection is its role in continuous personal and professional development. On the journey of being an Agile coach, you don't want to simply "be"—you want to thrive and evolve. Reflective practice is a catalyst for that evolution. By regularly examining your own work, you start to notice subtle areas where you can stretch and grow. For instance, you might realize through journaling that you handle conflict hesitantly, or that you're strongest in technical coaching but need to develop your facilitation skills. These insights become the roadmap for your development, highlighting where to focus next.

Importantly, reflection doesn't just make you a better coach in theory—it actively improves your ability to handle the day-to-day challenges of the role. Agile coaching can be demanding and high-pressure. A strong reflective practice has been shown to enhance a coach's resilience and emotional intelligence. By reflecting, you learn to manage stress more effectively because you understand your triggers and coping strategies. You become more adept at regulating your emotions (critical when, say, a team's frustration might otherwise trigger your own). This translates into better decision making and more productive relationships with your teams and stakeholders. In other words, reflection helps you keep a clear head and a compassionate heart in the thick of Agile chaos.

Another outcome of continuous reflection is heightened self-awareness. Self-awareness is a core element of emotional intelligence and a hallmark of great coaches. As you pause and reflect, you become more conscious of your own coaching style, biases, and impact. You might discover, for example, that you have a tendency to step in and "rescue" the team too quickly when problems arise, rather than allowing them to self-organize. Catching such patterns in yourself is gold, because once you're aware, you can choose to adjust.

Finally, reflective practice helps you identify your learning needs and chart out your ongoing development. In an Agile context, there's always something new to learn, be it a scaling framework, a new facilitation technique, or deeper coaching skills. Through reflection, you might notice gaps in your knowledge or instances where you felt unsure. Instead of ignoring those, a reflective coach takes them as cues for growth. You might decide to seek out training, find a mentor, or experiment with a different approach in the next sprint. In short, reflection ensures that your professional development is intentional and aligned with reality.

CHAPTER 12   PAUSE, REFLECT, ACT

Rather than just collecting certifications or attending workshops at random, you are driven by insights from your own practice about what will make the biggest difference for you and your teams.

Core Concepts of Reflective Practice

Before diving into techniques, let's clarify the term. *Reflective practice* means actively thinking about and analyzing your experiences to learn from them. It's often defined as paying critical attention to the values and theories that guide your everyday actions by examining your practice reflectively (looking back on what happened) and reflexively (examining your own assumptions and responses) to gain insight. In simple terms, it's a habit of asking yourself, *"What happened, why did it happen that way, and what can I learn from it?"* on a regular basis.

Not all reflection is the same. In the context of coaching (and originally in the work of Donald Schön on how professionals learn), it's useful to distinguish between different types of reflection. Each type occurs at a different time relative to the action and serves a different purpose. Let's look at three key types:

1. *Reflection-in-Action:* This is the classic "thinking on your feet." It refers to reflecting in the midst of an activity so that you can adapt in real time. Imagine you're running a team workshop and notice that people are disengaged—perhaps their eyes are drifting or their energy is low. If you pause mentally and ask, *"Hmm, what's going on here? Should I change something right now?"*, you're engaging in reflection-in-action. For an Agile coach, this could mean adjusting a facilitation technique in the middle of a meeting because you sense it's not landing well. Another example might be recognizing

during a sprint planning that the team seems confused about a story, so you decide on the spot to bring out a quick visual aid or analogy. Reflection-in-action is about being present and alert to what's happening, and willing to tweak your approach based on that immediate feedback. It requires a mindset of curiosity even while you're busy doing the work.

2. *Reflection-on-Action:* This type happens after the action is over. It's when you deliberately revisit and evaluate an experience. Most of us have done this informally; for instance, driving home thinking, *"That retrospective was chaotic; what on earth happened?"* By reflecting on action, you give yourself the chance to derive lessons from events once you have the benefit of hindsight. In practice, you might sit down after a sprint or a coaching session and journal about it: What went well? What didn't? How did you feel, and why? This process has been described as "reliving and re-rendering" the experience—mentally walking through it again to bring details into focus. An Agile coach doing reflection-on-action might realize, for example, that a certain team member's comment in the retrospective triggered an emotional reaction in them (the coach), which influenced how they facilitated the discussion. Such insights are incredibly valuable because they often reveal subtle factors you missed in the moment. By analyzing the experience, you can extract meaning and decide what you might do differently when a similar situation arises.

3. *Reflection-for-Action:* This is proactive reflection—essentially thinking ahead to guide future actions. It's the planning and preparation that incorporates what you've learned from past reflections. If you have a challenging event coming up (say, a sprint review with a difficult stakeholder or a team conflict mediation), you engage in reflection-for-action by imagining scenarios and how you might handle them. For example, an Agile coach preparing for a conflict resolution meeting might reflect in advance: *"Last time I had a similar situation, I got defensive. This time, I want to stay calm. What techniques can I use? Maybe I'll prepare some open-ended questions and remind myself to listen more than talk."* Reflection-for-action is like a mental rehearsal grounded in past learning. It boosts your readiness and confidence because you've already thought through strategies and considered your own mindset. Many coaches use this type of reflection to set intentions; e.g., *"In tomorrow's retrospective, if it goes off track, I'll remember to ask the team what they need rather than jumping in with advice."* By reflecting *beforehand*, you prime yourself to act more skillfully when the moment comes.

Deeper Learning: Adult Development and Double-Loop Learning

Reflective practice doesn't exist in a vacuum—it's closely tied to how adults learn and grow, especially in complex roles like coaching. One useful concept here is double-loop learning, a term from theorists Chris Argyris and Donald Schön. In single-loop learning, we might ask, *"Am I doing things right?"* and then make adjustments. Double-loop learning goes a step further and asks, *"Am I doing the right things, and why do I think they're right?"* In other words, it isn't just about fixing the immediate issue (like a team not meeting a commitment); it's about questioning the underlying assumptions (like, *"Why do we commit to this scope in the first place? Is that assumption still valid?"*).

For an Agile coach, practicing reflection in a double-loop way means you regularly challenge your own beliefs and habits. This is sometimes called being reflexive—you're not only reflecting on the external events, but also turning the mirror on yourself. You might question things like, *"What assumptions am I making about this team? What biases might be influencing my coaching?"* This kind of reflective inquiry can feel messy and even uncomfortable. It's not always easy to examine our prejudices or habitual actions under a microscope. In fact, truly deep reflection often involves moments of uncertainty and self-doubt—you may realize that something you took for granted was mistaken. However, it's precisely this willingness to engage with the tough questions that leads to transformative change. (As one witty reminder goes, *"The unconsidered is deeply considerable,"* meaning the things we usually overlook can hold significant insights if we're brave enough to look.)

This level of reflection is what drives vertical development (as opposed to just horizontal skill acquisition). Horizontal development involves acquiring additional knowledge or skills; for example, learning a new Agile tool or technique. Vertical development is about expanding your capacity to think in more complex, systemic, and integrative ways. Reflective practice, especially the critical, double-loop kind, pushes you upward vertically. It forces you to rethink your mental models and expand your perspective beyond the surface. An Agile coach engaging in this kind of reflection might move from a conventional mindset (e.g., "My job is to enforce the process") to a more advanced one ("My job is to foster the right environment, and sometimes that means bending the process"). These shifts are profound and typically arise from grappling with the deeper questions about values, context, and purpose.

It's important to note that this deep reflection is often non-linear and ongoing. It's not a one-time epiphany. Rather, it's an iterative process of questioning and refining your approach. At times, it will feel inconclusive—you might end a reflection session with more questions than answers. That's okay. In fact, it's a sign you're digging into meaningful territory. For example, you might start reflecting on why a particular team irritates you, only to uncover further questions about your own leadership style or your organization's culture. This kind of journey can be unsettling, but it's ultimately what fosters growth. By continuously engaging in double-loop reflection, Agile coaches keep themselves honest and open to change, ensuring they're not accidentally creating the very problems they're trying to solve (like imposing structures that contradict Agile values).

Superficial vs. Transformational Reflection

Not all reflection is equal. There's a big difference between simply going through the motions of reflection and engaging in genuinely transformational reflection. You might have seen, for example, a situation where someone fills out a retrospective document or coaching log just because it's required, jotting down a few observations without much thought. That's what we could call superficial retrospection. It usually remains at the level of description—what happened—or sticks to safe, surface-level analysis. For instance, a superficial reflection entry might say: *"This week I facilitated three meetings and learned I need to improve my time management."* There's nothing wrong with that, but note that it's quite general and technical (and perhaps a bit perfunctory).

Transformational reflection, meanwhile, digs a lot deeper. It's sometimes referred to as critical reflection or reflexivity. It's not just about what happened, but why it happened and how you felt and reacted as it happened. This kind of reflection is often emotive and candid. It connects

CHAPTER 12 PAUSE, REFLECT, ACT

the dots between your thoughts, feelings, and actions in a given situation. Let's say an Agile coach has a tough sprint review where stakeholders were unhappy. A deeper reflective entry might be: *"During the stakeholder Q&A, I felt defensive the conversation came to a point where our adoption of Agile was questioned. I realize I interrupted one of the managers—that was my insecurity talking. Why did I react that way? I think I took the criticism personally, as if I were failing. This highlights how much of my identity I've tied up in being 'the Agile expert.'"* Notice how this reflection isn't comfortable or neat—it's vulnerable and probing. But from that vulnerability comes a deeper sense of "knowing" about oneself and the situation, which is the starting point for meaningful change.

One way to tell you're engaging in transformational reflection is that it often leads to new perspectives or even shifts in your approach. It's like turning over a rock and discovering rich soil (or some bugs!) underneath, whereas superficial reflection is like glancing at the rock and walking on. Deep reflection might lead you to realize that you need to apologize to someone, acknowledge a bias you held, or experiment with a radically different strategy next time. These are what someone might call "radical movements for change"—they fundamentally alter your behavior or mindset going forward. Superficial reflection rarely does that; it's more about minor tweaks or ticking a box.

To avoid the trap of superficiality, it's helpful to approach reflection with curiosity and courage. Be willing to ask yourself hard questions and be honest about the answers. Instead of just listing what happened, push into why it happened, how it affected you, and what it reveals about your own attitudes or skills. If you find yourself writing in a detached, purely analytical way, consider adding sentences that begin with "I felt . . ." or "I realized . . ." or "I wonder if . . ." to connect to the personal dimension. Remember, the goal of reflection in coaching isn't to produce a report for someone else—it's to facilitate your growth. Being genuine and even critical of yourself (in a constructive way) is far more valuable than writing

379

what you think sounds good or what you should say. When you engage at this level, reflective practice truly becomes a transformative force in your development as an Agile coach.

Applying Reflective Practice: Agile Coaching Scenarios

To see how all these ideas come to life, let's explore a few realistic scenarios an Agile coach might face and how reflective practice can help in each.

Scenario: Team Resistance

The situation: You're coaching an Agile team that consistently resists adopting new practices. Every time you introduce a change (such as a new approach to daily Scrum or a different way of estimating), you encounter pushback. Team members insist the old way works fine, or they blame any hiccups on factors outside their control ("Management won't let us" or "This wouldn't be a problem if another team did their job"). Meetings feel like a tug-of-war, and progress is stalling.

Reflective approach: Instead of charging ahead or blaming the team, you decide to pause and reflect on what's really going on. A useful tool here is Brookfield's Four Lenses of critical reflection—looking at the situation through different perspectives. You start with the self-lens, examining your own role and feelings. You ask yourself, *"How might my coaching style be contributing to this resistance?"* and *"What am I feeling when they push back—am I annoyed, defensive, discouraged?"* Maybe you realize that you've been taking the team's resistance personally and responding by pushing even harder (which only increases their defiance).

CHAPTER 12   PAUSE, REFLECT, ACT

Next, you consider the team's perspective (Brookfield calls this the student or "client" lens, which we adapt here to the team lens). How does the world look through their eyes? You might reflect, *"They keep saying management is the problem. Do they feel powerless? Are they afraid Agile is a fad that'll blow over? Perhaps I haven't addressed their underlying concerns."* By empathizing with their viewpoint, you discover that maybe the team is not just stubborn—they could be anxious about their performance or job security in the new way of working. Perhaps they're thinking, *"If we try this new practice and fail, we'll get blamed."* This lens helps you shift from seeing the team as "difficult" to understanding the legitimate fears or context behind their behavior.

You don't stop there. Through the colleague lens, you seek feedback from fellow coaches or a mentor. You might discuss this scenario in a coach's meetup or with a trusted peer: *"Have you ever dealt with a team that's so resistant? What did you do?"* Sometimes another coach can see blind spots that we miss. Let's say your colleague points out, *"Have you noticed you're always the first to speak in meetings? Maybe the team feels railroaded."* Ouch—that feedback might sting, but it's invaluable. It reveals a behavior you hadn't considered: Perhaps in your enthusiasm, you're not giving enough space for the team to voice ideas, leading them to dig in their heels. Your colleague's perspective acts as a mirror, reflecting something important back to you.

Finally, you add a theory lens. Drawing on Agile coaching wisdom, you recall that people often resist change when they don't feel heard or when they fear losing something important. This insight leads you to a new idea: Instead of pushing a practice, use the next retrospective to invite an honest conversation about their concerns. In that meeting, you come in with a different mindset—curious and calm, not combative. You pose a question like, *"What do we fear we might lose by changing how we work?"* That unlocks a real conversation. The team opens up about issues (for example, some fear that adopting new methods might make their jobs harder or less secure). Together, you agree on trying a small experiment rather than

CHAPTER 12   PAUSE, REFLECT, ACT

a forced overhaul. In the end, your reflective approach turns what was a standoff into a collaborative problem-solving session. The resistance starts to soften because the team feels heard and involved, all thanks to the perspectives you gained through reflection.

Scenario: Uncertainty in Facilitating a Difficult Conversation

The situation: You are about to facilitate a session to address a major conflict between two team members (let's call them Alice and Bob). The tension between them has been dragging the whole team down, and it's finally time to address these issues openly. As the day approaches, you find yourself feeling anxious. How will you keep the conversation productive and not let it descend into a blame game? What if emotions run really high—are you equipped to handle that? In short, you're uncertain how to navigate this minefield.

Reflective approach: Start with reflection-for-action, preparing yourself before the big meeting. You acknowledge to yourself, *"I'm nervous about this."* That's okay; it means you care. To channel that nervous energy productively, you decide to adopt a beginner's mindset—almost what Buddhist psychology might call *"being more stupid,"* in the sense of letting go of the need to be the expert with all the answers. Your plan: enter the conversation with curiosity and openness rather than a fixed agenda. Practically, this means coming armed with some open-ended questions and a mindset of deep listening. For example, you might prepare questions like, *"Can each of you share what this situation feels like from your perspective?"* or *"What outcome would you like to see from this discussion?"* These questions are meant to draw out honest communication, not to find a quick fix.

You also anticipate the emotional aspect. One reflective technique you use is visualization: You imagine the meeting getting heated—voices raised or tears shed—and you picture yourself staying calm and centered. Maybe

CHAPTER 12   PAUSE, REFLECT, ACT

you practice a few mindfulness techniques beforehand (like focusing on your breath) to ground yourself. You remind yourself that your role is not to judge or immediately "solve" their conflict, but to create a space where they feel heard and can find a resolution together. This bit of reflection-for-action gives you a sense of preparedness. You've thought through how to react if, say, Alice accuses Bob of not pulling his weight, or Bob shuts down completely. You have a mental game plan: stay curious, ask questions, and resist the urge to take sides or offer premature solutions.

Now, in the moment—during the actual facilitation—you engage in reflection-in-action. Suppose Bob says, "This is pointless, you're just going to side with Alice because she's louder." In that very second, you notice a pang of defensiveness in yourself (whoa, he's questioning my impartiality!). But because you've primed yourself to be reflective, you catch that feeling and choose not to react with anger or a quick rebuttal. Instead, you take a breath and respond with something like, *"It sounds like you're worried I might not be fair. I get that. My goal is to be fair to both of you. Can you tell me what a fair process would look like for you?"* By doing this, you're practicing reflective inquiry—responding with a question that helps Bob reflect on his needs, rather than getting pulled into an argument.

Throughout the meeting, you keep applying this reflective stance. When high emotions swirl, you might say, "Let's pause for a moment. I notice this is really important to both of you. Could we take a deep breath? I'm here to help you both understand each other, not to judge either side." This kind of meta-commentary, born from reflection, helps the participants also step back for a moment and reflect on what's happening. Slowly, the conversation starts yielding understanding: Alice shares that she's been under intense pressure from a client and felt Bob wasn't supporting her; Bob reveals he was unaware of her expectations and felt kept at a distance. They aren't hugging and singing Kumbaya by the end, but there's a palpable shift—they acknowledge each other's feelings and agree on some communication steps moving forward.

Afterward, you reflect on the whole incident (reflection-on-action) to lock in the learning. You note what worked well—for instance, resisting the urge to "fix" the problem for them—and what you could do better next time; maybe you noticed you almost sided with one person due to your own bias. By analyzing these, you prepare yourself to handle future conflicts even more effectively. In sum, by reflecting before, during, and after the difficult conversation, you managed to facilitate it in a way that was calm, fair, and ultimately constructive.

Scenario: Burnout, Ethical Dilemmas, or Identity Conflicts

The situation: Consider a scenario where you, the coach, are the one in distress. Maybe you've been supporting three Agile teams at once, working long hours, and you feel burnt out—mentally and emotionally exhausted. Or perhaps you've encountered an ethical dilemma; for example, an executive asks you to share confidential details from your one-on-one coaching sessions with team members, pressuring you to divulge information that you know should remain private. You might even experience an identity conflict, questioning whether you're really making a difference as a coach or feeling torn between being a coach, a consultant, and an employee of the organization. These are heavy moments, and they can shake your confidence to the core.

Reflective approach: This is where reflective practice becomes not just a professional tool, but also a bit of self-care and survival kit. Start by giving yourself permission to step back and acknowledge what's happening. If you're burnt out, that might mean admitting, *"I'm at the end of my rope; something needs to change."* If you're facing an ethical conflict, it means recognizing, *"I'm really uncomfortable with this request; it clashes with my values."* Sometimes coaches feel they have to be superhuman, but reflection encourages honesty—both with yourself and with others—about your limits and values.

One reflective exercise that can be incredibly supportive in these moments is writing to your "internal mentor" (your wise, ideal self). Find a quiet space and pour your thoughts out in a journal as if writing to a mentor about your situation—all your frustrations, fears, and doubts. Then, switch perspectives and write a response to yourself from the standpoint of a compassionate, wise mentor (imagine the advice *you* would give if you were counseling a friend in the same boat). For example, your internal mentor might remind you that you *"can't pour from an empty cup"*—encouraging you to set boundaries and recharge so you can coach effectively. Or it might affirm that *integrity is your most valuable asset*—nudging you to stand firm on confidentiality and find a principled way to address the executive's request. This exercise often surfaces solutions or at least clarity that was hard to see when you were mired in stress. It taps into your own accumulated knowledge and values, which is empowering.

Another aspect of reflection here is reconnecting with your core values and principles. In an ethical dilemma, explicitly write down or speak out about what values are at stake. For instance: *"I value trust and confidentiality. If I break that, I harm my integrity and the trust the team has in me."* Seeing this in front of you can steel your resolve to handle the situation in alignment with those values—maybe by diplomatically pushing back on the request or finding a compromise that doesn't violate confidentiality (such as sharing generalized progress indicators instead of personal details). For burnout or identity crises, reflect on why you became a coach in the first place. What purpose and passion drive you? Which parts of the work light you up, and which drain you? This might reveal that you've been spending too much time on things outside your "zone of genius," or that you need to negotiate your workload or seek support. Reflection can be a wake-up call: Perhaps you discover that you haven't taken a real day off in months, or that a particular team consistently pushes your boundaries (and you need to address that pattern).

Importantly, reflection in these tough scenarios should also lead to action, often in the form of setting boundaries or seeking help. For example, your reflections might lead you to conclude, *"I need to talk to my manager about reducing my team load,"* or *"I will decline to share those confidential details, even if it's uncomfortable, because it's the right thing to do."* You might even reflect on a question like, *"Would I eventually walk away from this coaching engagement if I felt I could not practice ethically or add real value?"* It's a tough question, but considering it can clarify just how far you're willing to compromise (or not). Sometimes just acknowledging that you have that choice is liberating—you're not trapped; you have agency.

Reflective Tools and Techniques

Journaling Prompts and Exercises for Agile Coaches

One of the most accessible and effective reflective practices is journaling. Writing things down forces you to put vague thoughts and feelings into words, which can lead to new realizations. For Agile coaches, keeping a reflection journal can become a treasured routine—a private space to process the week and plan improvements. Here are some tailored prompts and exercises to consider:

- "Reflections of the Week": Some coaches like to structure their journaling by weekdays, especially if their workflow revolves around weekly sprints. For example:
    - **Monday:** What was the most significant interaction in our sprint planning today? What thoughts or feelings did it evoke in me?

- **Tuesday:** Describe a moment when the team showed either high collaboration or noticeable tension. What did I observe in their behavior or in my own?

- **Wednesday:** Identify an assumption I held about a team member's behavior that might not be true. What made me notice this?

- **Thursday:** How did my facilitation or coaching today impact the team's dynamics? If I rated my effectiveness 1–10, what would it be and why?

- **Friday:** What is a key learning I gained this week about Agile values in practice, and how will I integrate it going forward?

Using a template like this ensures you touch on different facets each day—from team dynamics to personal beliefs to outcomes and improvements.

- General powerful questions: You don't need a fancy format to journal; sometimes just responding to a great question is enough to spur insight. Here are a few versatile ones:

  - What did I observe in this coaching session or Scrum event (facts and feelings)?

  - What are five things that struck me most about this team (or individual) today?

  - What did I learn from the team today that I didn't know before?

  - How could I have done a better job coaching?

- What is another approach or technique I could have tried in this situation?

  These prompts encourage you to go beyond surface recollection and think about alternatives and lessons learned.

- The Six-Minute free-write: When you're short on time (or feeling a bit overwhelmed by an experience), try a quick "six-minute free-write." Set a timer for six minutes and just write continuously about the event or feeling on your mind. Don't stop, don't censor yourself, and don't worry about punctuation or making it sound nice. This stream-of-consciousness exercise often helps unearth thoughts and emotions that a structured approach might miss. For example, after a chaotic meeting, a six-minute free-write might reveal emotions or anxieties you hadn't fully acknowledged. You can always analyze these reflections later—in the moment, the goal is simply to capture them on the page.

Transformational Journaling: Emotions, Assumptions, and Patterns

It's worth emphasizing that reflective writing is inherently emotive and personal. To get the most out of it, don't shy away from feelings—yours or others'. Before you write, take a moment to notice how you're feeling. Are you upset, excited, or confused? Jot that down. As you write, allow those emotions to come through. It's okay to write, "I'm really frustrated with how the retro went" or "I feel proud of how I handled that conflict." This matters because moving the feelings from your heart onto the page helps you process them. Often, once an emotion is acknowledged in writing, you can then dig into why it's there and what it means for your actions.

CHAPTER 12   PAUSE, REFLECT, ACT

Another powerful use of a journal is to identify patterns. A single incident might not reveal a trend, but if you flip back through a month of entries, you might notice, for example, that "Trust issues between Dev and QA" kept coming up, or that you felt exhausted every Tuesday when you had back-to-back meetings. These patterns can be golden nuggets of insight. They shift your reflection from isolated events (micro level) to seeing the system of behaviors and events (macro level). For instance, spotting a pattern that *"whenever I skip my morning prep, the day's meetings feel chaotic"* is a simple but powerful insight; it might prompt you to adjust your routine. In teams, noticing a pattern like *"whenever we have a deadline crunch, pair programming goes out the window"* could lead you to address that trade-off explicitly with the team.

Transformational journaling also means challenging your assumptions. We all carry mental models and biases. Your journal is a safe place to ask, *"What assumptions am I making? What if the opposite were true?"* Suppose you write about a team member who never speaks up, and you assume they are disengaged. You might challenge that: *"Could it be they just process internally or don't feel safe to talk? What evidence do I have either way?"* By questioning your own thought processes, you practice the reflective skill of reflexivity. Sometimes, writing about an event that you initially thought was unimportant (an "unconsidered" or forgotten moment) can reveal an insight—like realizing you consistently overlook quiet team members until conflict arises. As the saying goes, *"the unconsidered is deeply considerable"*—those little moments or assumptions you typically ignore might actually hold the key to breakthroughs.

Don't feel confined to plain text in your reflection journal either. Creativity can unlock deeper reflections. Sketch a diagram of team interactions as you perceive them. Draw a mind map of a problem, with branches for technical issues, people issues, process issues. Maybe create a quick storyboard of a day in the team's life as you experienced it. Some coaches even make collages or use color coding for emotions (e.g., highlighting angry moments in red, successes in green). Why do this? Because sometimes the linear nature of writing sentences can limit our thinking. A doodle might reveal a connection you hadn't articulated, or a metaphor might emerge ("I drew the workflow as a maze ... interesting, I do feel the process is labyrinthine!"). Engaging different modes of expression taps into the right-brain intuition and creativity, complementing the left-brain logical analysis. It helps you access insights that a straightforward written narrative might not surface.

Structured Reflection Frameworks for Coaches

In addition to free-form journaling, there are several structured frameworks that can guide your reflection. These frameworks provide a series of steps or questions that ensure you cover different angles of an experience. Let's look at a few that Agile coaches can adapt:

- Gibbs' reflective cycle (Figure 12-1): This is a classic model by Graham Gibbs (1988) that guides you through six stages of reflection. It's very useful when you want a thorough debrief of an event. In an Agile context, you might apply it to something like a sprint review or a coaching session. The stages are as follows:

    1. Description: What happened, in factual terms? (e.g., *"During the sprint review, two stakeholders started debating a requirement."*) Describe the event in detail, including who was there and what was said or done.

    2. Feelings: What were you thinking and feeling during the experience? (e.g., *"I felt anxious when the debate started, and I noticed the team looked uncomfortable."*) Be honest about your emotional and mental state.

CHAPTER 12   PAUSE, REFLECT, ACT

3. Evaluation: What was good or bad about the experience? Consider both your perspective and the team's. (e.g., *"Good: The stakeholders' concerns came to light. Bad: It derailed the meeting and the team shut down."*) What went well, and what didn't?

4. Analysis: Why do you think it happened that way? Dig into causes and dynamics. (e.g., *"Perhaps I didn't set clear ground rules for the review, so stakeholders felt free to argue. Also, the team might not have felt empowered to intervene."*) Look at the wider context and patterns.

5. Conclusion: What could have been done differently? What insights or conclusions can you draw? (e.g., *"I realize I need to intervene earlier when side debates start. Also, maybe a pre-meeting with feuding stakeholders could help."*) Summarize key learnings.

6. Action Plan: Based on what you learned, what will you do next time? (e.g., *"Next print review, I'll establish Q&A rules at the start and facilitate more actively. I'll also follow up with those two stakeholders separately to address their issue."*) This ties the reflection back to future practice.

CHAPTER 12   PAUSE, REFLECT, ACT

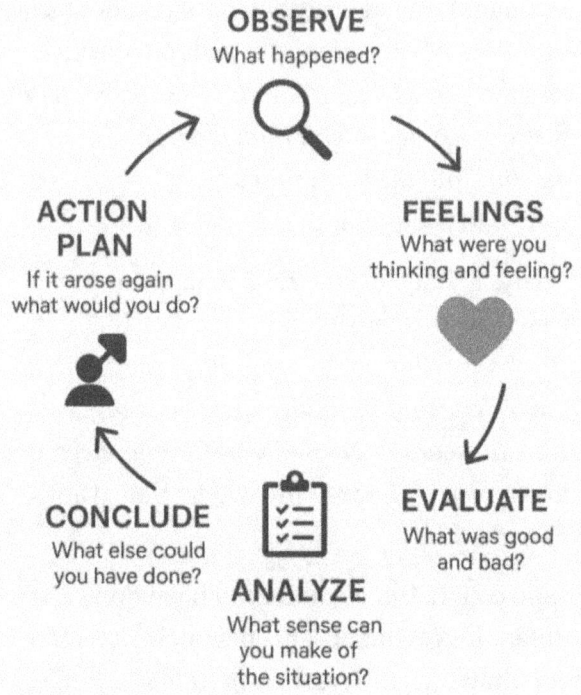

Figure 12-1. Gibb's reflective cycle

Going through these steps ensures you don't skip straight from problem to action without understanding the feelings and root causes in between. It brings rigor to your reflection and can be especially useful after complex or challenging situations.

- The Henley eight questions: Developed at Henley Business School's coaching program, the "Henley Eight" is a set of reflective questions designed to deepen a coach's self-awareness. They are highly relevant to Agile coaches as well (and my favorite too!). In brief, the questions ask the following:

CHAPTER 12   PAUSE, REFLECT, ACT

1. What did I observe? (Describe objectively what happened or what you noticed.)

2. What was my response? (Capture your immediate thoughts, feelings, and actions in that moment.)

3. What does this say about me personally? (What might your response reveal about your beliefs, biases, or tendencies?)

4. What does this tell me about myself as a coach or leader? (Reflect on how your behavior relates to your role.)

5. What strengths does this offer? (How might the traits or actions you noticed be strengths in your coaching practice?)

6. What are the potential pitfalls? (How might those same traits or actions hinder your coaching practice?)

7. What did I learn? (Noting what you can take forward into your practice—insights about yourself, the team, or the situation.)

8. What might I do differently next time? (Committing to applying the learning in the future.)

Working through these questions is like having a guided coaching session with yourself. It forces you not just to recount what happened, but also to consider your internal landscape (your reactions and what they say about you). By the end, you've connected the dots from observation to personal learning to future action. Some coaches incorporate the Henley Eight into their regular journaling routine; for example, picking a particularly puzzling incident of the week and running it through this filter.

- Critical moments reflection: Sometimes, rather than reflecting on an entire event, it can be helpful to zero in on a single critical moment—a point in time that was especially significant, emotional, or revealing. For instance, maybe during a retrospective, one team member said, "I don't trust our velocity numbers," and the room went silent. That was a critical moment. To reflect on it, you might ask the following:

  - *Why was this moment critical?* (What made it stand out? In this case, it touched on trust and transparency—core issues.)

  - *What does my reaction to this moment say about what's important to me as a coach?* (If you felt alarmed, maybe it shows you highly value trust; if you felt relieved that an elephant in the room was named, perhaps you value honesty.)

  - *How can I apply this realization in future coaching?* (If trust is a key issue, you might prioritize trust-building exercises or discuss the topic during team retrospectives.)

CHAPTER 12 PAUSE, REFLECT, ACT

- *What will I do differently when a similar moment arises?* (Maybe next time you won't let the silence linger too long before addressing the statement, or you'll encourage the person to elaborate.)

  By dissecting a high-impact moment, you uncover rich insights that you can apply going forward. It's like focusing the microscope on a single cell to understand the health of the entire organism.

- Using metaphor and imagery: Sometimes our rational mind gets stuck, and a good metaphor can unlock new understanding. Try describing a challenging situation in a metaphor: *"My team is like a tangled ball of yarn,"* or *"Our planning meetings are a game of Tetris,"* or *"I felt like a ship without a rudder in that coaching session."* Then, reflect on why you chose that image. "Tangled yarn" might indicate confusion and interdependency issues; a "Tetris game" might imply things coming at you fast and needing to fit them in; a "rudderless ship" could reveal you felt directionless or unsupported. Metaphors can bypass our logical defenses and reveal how we're truly perceiving a situation. They can also be fun and creative, sparking ideas on how to "untangle the yarn" or "add a rudder" in practical terms. Similarly, encourage your team (or coachees) to use metaphors in retrospectives or coaching conversations. It often leads to fresh insights and a shared understanding of abstract issues.

CHAPTER 12   PAUSE, REFLECT, ACT

Designing a Reflective Practice Routine

Integrating Reflection into Daily, Weekly, and Sprint Rhythms

How do you make reflection a habit instead of an occasional afterthought? The key is to embed it into your regular routine. For an Agile coach, that means leveraging the natural cadences of your work—daily routines, weekly cycles, and sprint cycles—as prompts for reflection:

- Daily micro-reflections: Find a small moment each day to pause and think. This doesn't have to be a huge time sink; even five to ten minutes can do. Some coaches take a few minutes during their commute home or right after the last meeting to ask, *"What went well today? What could have gone better?"* This quick mental scan keeps you aware of your growth on a day-to-day basis. For example, you might realize, *"I handled that surprise production issue calmly (win), but I talked over John in the stand-up (oops)."* By noting these, you carry forward the wins and consider adjustments for the "oopses". Some coaches jot a quick note in a journal or an app daily—like a one-sentence reflection—to capture these thoughts.

- Weekly dedicated time: Set aside a slightly longer block once a week for deeper reflection. It can happen on Friday afternoons or Monday mornings—whenever you can protect a timeslot. Treat it like an important meeting with yourself. During this time, you might review your journal entries or notes from the week, and then write a summary or talk aloud to yourself about patterns. Use structured prompts if you like (for example, the weekly questions template we mentioned earlier). At the weekly level, you can connect the dots between days. Perhaps you'll see that *"Team Alpha was struggling early in the week, but after the mid-week workshop I ran, they picked up. So that intervention seemed to work."* You can also set *personal improvement goals* for the next week based on your reflections, like *"Next week, I will try a different technique to engage quiet team members in discussions."* By making this a routine, you ensure that insights don't slip away in the rush of work.

- Sprint-level or monthly reflection: In Agile, the end of a sprint (or a month) is a natural time to reflect on bigger themes. Consider doing a personal retrospective for yourself as a coach, parallel to the team retrospective. Ask yourself things like, *"Over this sprint, where did I see the team grow? Where did I struggle in helping them?"* Review any notes you've collected and measure them against your goals. This is also a good time to update your professional development plan—maybe you realized you need to learn more about facilitating remote teams, or that you'd like to focus next sprint on improving the team's test automation practices. Integrating coach reflection with the Agile sprint rhythm reinforces the idea that continuous improvement applies to you too, not just the team. Some coaches even write a short "sprint report" for themselves, summarizing what they learned and how they plan to adapt their coaching in the next iteration.

CHAPTER 12   PAUSE, REFLECT, ACT

Common Pitfalls and How to Avoid Them
When Reflection Turns into Rumination

Reflective practice aims to be positive and enlightening, but what if those "reflective" thoughts just spin around in your head and make you feel worse? That's rumination—the unproductive cousin of reflection. Rumination is when you replay mistakes repeatedly or fixate on negative feelings without finding a resolution. It's reflection gone off track; instead of leading to insight and action, it results in self-doubt and stress. For some coaches, especially those new to reflective practice, there can be a fear that delving into mistakes will be *"scary"* or overwhelming—like opening a can of worms that could lead to hopelessness or burnout if they discover too much wrong.

How to avoid this trap: If you notice your reflection session has become a blame session ("I messed up everything . . ." or "I'm a terrible coach"), pause and reframe. One technique is to switch to an action-oriented question: *"Okay, given what happened, what's one small thing I can do next time to improve?"* This gently shifts your mind from dwelling to problem solving (Figure 12-2). Another approach is to talk it out instead of only writing. Sometimes voicing your concerns to a trusted mentor or colleague can break the loop, because they'll likely respond with a more balanced view (*"It's not as bad as you think, here's what I see . . ."*). If you have fears or lack confidence in some area, share those with someone you trust—an outside perspective can reassure you or help you find a constructive path forward.

CHAPTER 12 PAUSE, REFLECT, ACT

Figure 12-2. *From rumination to reflection*

The goal of reflection is learning, not perfection. It's about process, not beating yourself up for outcomes. Keep an eye on your emotional state. If you find yourself feeling worse after reflecting, it may be a sign to step back. Try a different method (maybe a lighter prompt, or focusing on a success before analyzing a failure). Also, schedule reflection at a time when you're not too tired or emotional. Doing a heavy reflection right after a big setback might be too raw. You could start by calming down and reflecting a bit later when the emotion is less intense. And yes, sometimes reflection will uncover uncomfortable truths (*"I think I handled that situation poorly"*). But by immediately pairing that with compassion (*"Everyone slips up sometimes, I'm learning"*) and action (*"Next time I'll do X"*), you ensure it propels you forward rather than dragging you down.

Beyond the Checklist: Authentic Engagement vs. Going Through the Motions

Have you ever filled out a retrospective form just because you had to? Or written a journal entry thinking, *"There, I've done my reflection for the week"* without really meaning it? Reflective practice can become an

CHAPTER 12   PAUSE, REFLECT, ACT

onerous chore if we treat it like a checkbox on a to-do list. This is a pitfall where reflection loses its soul—it becomes superficial. You might find yourself simply describing events (*"Monday: did X, Tuesday: team argued, etc."*) or stating generic goals (*"I'll communicate better"*) without any real introspection. When done this way, reflection doesn't yield much value and can feel like a waste of time, which only reinforces the urge to rush through it next time.

How to avoid this trap: The key is to approach reflection with curiosity and personal interest, rather than obligation. Remind yourself why you're reflecting: It's for your growth and benefit, not because some boss or book said you should. Try to cultivate a questioning mindset: Instead of *"I have to write something,"* think *"What was truly interesting or puzzling about today?"* or *"What's something I really want to understand about myself or my team?"* Making reflection enjoyable can help—if you hate writing long paragraphs, maybe use bullet points, draw a sketch, or record an audio note. Choose methods that feel natural to you, whether it's a colorful mind map or a straightforward list.

Also, connect reflection to your core values and passions. For instance, if you value creativity, reflect on where creativity showed up (or didn't) in your work this week. If helping others drives you, ponder a moment when your coaching truly helped someone, or when it fell short and what that means to you. When you tie reflection to what matters to you personally, it stops being a dry academic exercise and becomes a meaningful conversation with yourself. Some coaches even give their reflective journal a title like "My Agile Journey" or "Lessons Learned Corner" to mentally frame it as a narrative of their professional adventure rather than a report to file.

Finally, be patient and kind with the process. Early on, you might write shallow reflections because you're still getting the hang of it—that's okay. Over time, as you get more comfortable, your reflections will naturally deepen. You can look back at earlier entries and see progress in the way you think and write about experiences. That in itself can be motivating. Remember, quality over quantity: A single genuine insight ("I realized I avoid giving tough feedback because I'm afraid of not being liked") is worth more than three pages of perfunctory chronicle. Aim for authenticity—it's better to be messy and real in your reflection than neat and surface-level. This isn't being graded; it's for you.

Uncovering Blind Spots: Seeing What You Normally Miss

By definition, we can't see our own blind spots . . . at least not without effort. Even the most dedicated Agile coach has biases and habitual ways of thinking that can limit their perception. One common pitfall in reflective practice is avoiding or failing to notice those uncomfortable blind spots—effectively reflecting only on the safe or obvious topics. For example, you might carefully reflect on team processes or skills you want to improve (the "above the surface" topics), but never address deeper issues like your discomfort with confrontation or a bias toward a particular personality type. Similarly, you might focus on dramatic incidents and overlook the subtle patterns in between.

How to avoid this trap: The remedy is reflexivity—making it a habit to question your own attitudes and perspectives. Challenge yourself with questions that probe your thinking: *"What might I be assuming here? What would someone with an opposite viewpoint say about my coaching style?"* It can be helpful to occasionally focus on "non-critical" incidents for reflection—those that *didn't* seem to go clearly right or wrong. Ask, *"What's something I usually wouldn't bother reflecting on?"* and then have a look. You might find, for example, that you always dismiss one quiet team member's lack of input as no big deal. By reflecting on that "untold" story, you may realize that their silence is actually a vital missing voice in decisions. Essentially, treat some of your reflections like detective work—you're searching for clues of issues you haven't already labeled as problems.

CHAPTER 12 PAUSE, REFLECT, ACT

Another tactic is to use the "external lenses" we discussed: colleagues, team feedback, mentors. Proactively ask others to help you see what you might be missing. *"Hey, I notice our retrospectives seem fine, but is there anything you think we're not talking about as a team?"* or *"You've observed my coaching for a while; what's something you think I might not realize about my style?"* Be ready—you might hear something unexpected. But that's the point. It's much better to discover, for instance, that *every time a senior dev speaks, you unconsciously nod more and give them more floor time* (thus others feel lesser)—and to discover it from a colleague's observation—than to never realize it and keep wondering why some team members disengage.

Above all, **"keep it real"** with yourself. Authentic reflection involves acknowledging both the good and the bad, as well as the challenging aspects. If something went wrong, don't write a sanitized version in your journal as if everything was fine. Conversely, don't ignore successes due to false modesty—reflect on what you did well so you can do it again. By being honest and transparent in your reflections, you create a true mirror for self-improvement. The phrase *"the unconsidered is deeply considerable"* serves as a good reminder: The things you are *not* reflecting on might be the very areas where insight is hiding. So each time you reflect, ask: *"What am I not considering here, and what might that reveal?"* It's a question that can keep you humble and continuously learning. And in Agile coaching—a field that thrives on adaptation and inspection—the ability to see yourself and your environment with fresh eyes is a superpower.

Conclusion

In the rush of Agile delivery, it is tempting to measure progress only in features shipped or metrics improved. Yet the deepest progress often comes in the moments when we deliberately pause, reflect, and integrate what we've learned. Reflection transforms activity into insight, and insight into wiser action. Without it, we risk repeating old patterns; with it, we grow both as coaches and as human beings.

This chapter has shown that reflective practice is not an optional add-on to Agile coaching—it is the very mechanism by which we adapt, learn, and stay grounded in complex environments. Whether through quick reflection-in-action during a heated retrospective, a quiet journaling practice after a sprint, or proactive reflection-for-action before a difficult conversation, these pauses give us the perspective to act with clarity and intention.

For Agile team coaches, cultivating reflection is also an act of role-modeling. When teams see their coach examine their own assumptions, learn from missteps, and adjust course, it legitimizes reflection as a team practice. In this way, the coach's habit of pausing and reflecting ripples outward, helping teams embed continuous learning into their own DNA.

Ultimately, to "pause, reflect, act" is to embrace agility at the most personal level. It keeps us aligned with our values, resilient in the face of challenge, and open to the deeper development that enables us to serve teams with integrity. In the long game of coaching, it is not the number of sprints we support but the depth of learning we cultivate—within ourselves and within our teams—that leaves a lasting impact.

Reflection Moment: Reflect on Your Reflective Practice

- Where in my coaching practice do I tend to avoid discomfort, and what might I be protecting by doing so?
- What patterns do I notice in how I respond to tension, silence, or conflict within teams—and how does that impact team dynamics?

CHAPTER 12   PAUSE, REFLECT, ACT

- Which reflective practices (journaling, supervision, peer feedback, silent pause) feel most natural to me—and which ones do I resist or overlook? Why?

- What is one recent moment in coaching that stayed with me emotionally—and what might that moment be trying to teach me?

- If I were to dedicate just 10 minutes this week to pause and reflect, what question would I most need to ask myself—and what space would I need to hear the answer?

CHAPTER 13

The Power of Supervision and Deliberate Practice

Agile team coaching unfolds in a dynamic environment of complex problems, shifting priorities, and multiple stakeholders. The coaching profession itself is relatively young—only about 22 years since it became formally organized as a field—and coaching supervision has an even shorter history. In such a nascent field, there's a premium on maintaining a beginner's mind, staying open to new ideas and disruptions that can improve our practice. Team coaches often find themselves navigating challenging group dynamics. Conventional one-on-one coaching tools aren't always enough. To truly serve Agile teams, coaches must take a systemic perspective, looking beyond individual issues to see the bigger organizational picture that influences team effectiveness. Supervision, along with deliberate practice, becomes vital to helping coaches reflect on these complexities, learn continuously, and develop strategies that fit the living system of an Agile team.

Mastery in Agile coaching is not just about accumulating tools or techniques; it's about developing the coach's presence and depth of understanding. In other words, who you are as a coach and the beliefs and mindset you bring matter as much as what you do. Coaching supervision is often described as focusing less on technical skills and more on the "way of being" of the coach. It encourages coaches to listen to their inner voice and tap into their internal resources and values. By getting to the heart of one's coaching practice (through supervision and reflection), a coach learns to bring their whole self into their work—even if that means embracing uncertainty and vulnerability. In fact, great coaching often happens when the coach can be fully authentic and present with the team. In short, the journey to coaching excellence is as much about personal growth—cultivating compassion, courage, and self-awareness—as it is about skill acquisition.

The Essence of Coaching Supervision

At its core, coaching supervision is a protected and disciplined space for reflection. It's a formal arrangement where a coach (the supervisee) works with a trained supervisor to reflect on their coaching practice, much like coaches work with clients. The aim is to understand better both the client system (e.g., the Agile team and its context) and oneself as part of that system. In this safe, confidential setting, coaches can examine specific situations or dilemmas from their work, including the reactions and patterns these situations evoke in them, and by working through them in supervision, transform their approach for the benefit of their clients. In essence, supervision is a form of guided learning from experience—it's not about "checking up" on a coach, but rather about helping the coach learn and grow from their own practice. It has been described as a collaborative, collegial process rather than a policing role. A good supervision relationship creates mutual trust so the coach feels able to openly explore challenges, ethical dilemmas, or uncertainties in their work.

CHAPTER 13   THE POWER OF SUPERVISION AND DELIBERATE PRACTICE

What Is Coaching Supervision?   In practical terms, coaching supervision can be one-to-one, in groups, or even in peer circles. It is a formal, interpersonal process in which the coach brings real client work into a confidential dialogue with a supervisor. Together, they reflect on what's happening in the coaching, the coach's strategies, the client's needs, and so on, to enhance the coach's competence, insight, and confidence. All parties agree to a clear contract for supervision, just as in coaching, so that expectations and boundaries are explicit. The focus is on creating a supportive learning alliance that ultimately ensures the coach can provide the best possible service to their teams and clients. (Put simply: Coaching supervision is to coaches what coaching is to clients—a dedicated space to grow and challenge oneself, guided by an experienced partner.)

Many Agile practitioners use the terms *mentoring* and *supervision* interchangeably, but they serve different purposes. Mentoring is typically about learning from someone else's experience, while supervision is about stepping back to reflect on your own practice in a structured, supportive way. Both are valuable, yet they play distinct roles in a coach's development.

Table 13-1 highlights the key differences between mentoring and coaching supervision, making clear how each contributes to growth in complementary ways.

CHAPTER 13 THE POWER OF SUPERVISION AND DELIBERATE PRACTICE

Table 13-1. *Mentoring vs. Supervision*

Aspect	Mentoring	Coaching Supervision
Focus	Transfer of experience	Reflection and exploration
Role of seniority	Senior advises junior	Equal partnership with inquiry
Goal	Guidance and tips	Deeper self-awareness and insight
Typical format	Informal conversations	Structured reflective process

Why should an Agile coach engage in supervision? Supervision offers several important benefits, as follows:

- *Enhanced reflection and self-awareness:* Supervision is an invaluable forum for shining light on a coach's "blind spots" and areas for development. No matter how skilled we are, we all have biases or habits we don't fully see. A supervisor, by providing an external perspective, helps "take the blinkers off," revealing things the coach might be missing. This reflective dialogue encourages deep self-discovery—coaches come to understand their own triggers, patterns, and "hot buttons." For example, through supervision, a coach might realize that they consistently avoid addressing conflict in teams because of their own discomfort, or that their cultural background is subtly influencing their coaching approach. Good supervision invites us to examine those personal elements. As one text puts it, "we do this with knowledge of our hot buttons, our patterns, our social, educational and cultural background."—acknowledging how who we are impacts how we coach. With greater self-awareness, an Agile coach can be more intentional and effective.

CHAPTER 13   THE POWER OF SUPERVISION AND DELIBERATE PRACTICE

- *Ethical guidance and professional accountability:* Coaching (and especially team coaching) is often practiced in contexts without strict regulation. Supervision helps maintain high ethical standards and accountability in such an environment. It provides a checkpoint for questions like: *"Am I doing what's best for the team and all stakeholders?"* or *"How do I handle this confidentiality or boundary dilemma?"* The supervisor acts as an ethics partner, ensuring the coach stays aligned with professional guidelines and their own values. This is particularly critical in multi-stakeholder Agile engagements; for instance, when an Agile coach is hired by senior management to help a team, but also has a responsibility to the team members. Conflicting interests or "hidden agendas" can emerge in these situations. Supervision offers a place to unpack these complexities. In fact, supervision can illuminate those under-the-surface agendas and power dynamics so the coach can address them transparently. By discussing supervision cases, coaches demonstrate accountability—they are willing to have their work scrutinized and to learn from mistakes, which ultimately protects clients.

- *Restoration and self-care:* Agile coaches give a lot of themselves to their teams—facilitating tough retrospectives, mediating conflicts, motivating through change. It can be emotionally intense and draining work. Supervision provides a restorative, supportive space for coaches to process their own emotions and stress. In the field of counseling, this has long been seen as one of supervision's primary functions (often called the "restorative" or resourcing function), and it's just as applicable to coaching. Supervision focuses on the well-being of the coach and how their client's work is impacting them. It's a place to offload frustrations, doubts, or even the emotional burdens we carry from particularly challenging coaching sessions. By doing so, we re-energize and "restore" our capacity to coach effectively. For example, an Agile coach might feel disheartened or burned out after several sprints where the team didn't improve. In supervision, they can safely vent those feelings and regain perspective. Research suggests that supervision and other forms of social support significantly reduce the risk of burnout in helping professionals. Additionally, a supervisor can help the coach notice signs of compassion fatigue or over-extension and develop strategies for self-care. This ensures the coach doesn't quit out of exhaustion and can remain present and effective with teams in the long run. In short, supervision is a structured form of self-care for coaches. As one supervisor metaphorically described, it's like a "utility room" where, after doing the "dirty work" in the garden, you come in to wash your face, clean up, and reflect before returning to normal life. In supervision, we wipe off the grime of tough sessions, process the emotions, and emerge refreshed.

- *Developing deeper insight and improving practice:* Perhaps the most significant benefit of supervision is how it helps coaches learn and improve in concrete ways. By reflecting on real coaching situations with a supervisor, a coach can unpack why something

CHAPTER 13 THE POWER OF SUPERVISION AND DELIBERATE PRACTICE

worked or didn't work and gain new insight for next time. For instance, imagine an Agile team session where every retrospective seems to stall because team members won't speak up. In supervision, the coach and supervisor might explore this from multiple angles: What's the team dynamic here? What's the coach's reaction in the moment—frustration, impatience? Is the coach inadvertently contributing to the silence? Through skilled questioning, the supervisor helps the coach see patterns and possibilities that were invisible to them alone. This kind of reflective sense making leads to practical improvements in the coach's craft. In the supervisee–supervisor dialogue, every element of the coaching process is open for examination. The supervisee might role-play a difficult moment or analyze their own internal dialogue during a session (e.g., *"I noticed I got defensive when the product owner questioned my expertise. Why was that, and how did it affect my response?"*). Such exploration often yields "Aha!" moments that directly benefit the coach's clients thereafter. Studies have noted that by examining one's own reactions and assumptions, coaches become more reflective practitioners overall. They also learn to consider how the supervisory relationship itself might mirror the coaching relationship (for example, if a coach feels intimidated by their supervisor, could it be similar to how a team member feels intimidated by the coach's authority?). Nothing is off-limits for inquiry. This level of meta-reflection—reflecting not just on the client, but also on the coach and even on the supervisor–coach dynamic—cultivates a profound level of awareness. As a result, coaches report that supervision helps them notice nuances in their client work that they previously missed, and to be more thoughtful and creative in how they respond going forward. In sum, supervision turns everyday coaching experiences into rich learning opportunities. It's an "engine" for continuous improvement in one's coaching mastery.

Supervision provides a structured space to step back from the day-to-day and examine your coaching practice with fresh eyes. But how do you know what to bring into supervision? Often, it starts with a signal—an inner clue that something in your work deserves closer reflection. These signals might show up as emotions, repeated patterns, or moments of doubt.

Table 13-2 offers examples of common signals and links them to possible themes you might explore in supervision. Think of it as a translation guide: What feels like frustration, confusion, or overload in the moment often points to a deeper area for learning and growth.

Table 13-2. *Signals That Supervision Might Be Needed*

Signal	Possible Theme to Explore in Supervision
Feeling stuck with a team	Coach's internal process (Eye 4)
Frustration with a leader	Wider system dynamics (Eye 7)
Emotional overload after session	Restoration and self-care
Doubts about ethics	Ethical tension and multiple loyalties
Repeating ineffective patterns	Need for deliberate practice and awareness shift

Models and Frameworks in Agile Team Coaching Supervision

The 3 P's: Philosophy, Purpose, Process (PPP)

One useful framework for coaches (and supervisors) to reflect on their practice is the *"3 P's"* model (see Figure 13-1): Philosophy, Purpose, and Process. Articulated originally by coaching scholars Peter Jackson and Tatiana Bachkirova, the 3 P's framework invites you to examine your coaching and supervision on the following three levels:

- *Philosophy:* What are the core beliefs, values, or theoretical perspectives that underpin *why* and *how* you coach? This might include your views on human nature, how people change, what coaching is for, and so on. For example, you might believe that people are inherently resourceful and that the role of a coach is to facilitate their self-discovery—that belief will shape your approach. (It's like the "lens" through which you view your work.)

- *Purpose*: What is the purpose of your coaching or supervision work? In other words, what outcomes are you aiming to achieve for your clients? This could be anything from "helping teams continuously improve their collaboration" to "enabling clients to find their own solutions" or "supporting ethical practice and well-being for coaches" in the case of supervision. Clarifying purpose ensures that your coaching has direction and intention, rather than being ad hoc.

CHAPTER 13   THE POWER OF SUPERVISION AND DELIBERATE PRACTICE

- *Process*: What process do you follow to fulfill that purpose that is consistent with your philosophy? Here you'd describe what you actually do—the methods, techniques, and structures you use in sessions. For instance, you might use certain Agile retrospective formats, or a GROW model for one-on-one coaching, or in supervision you might contract at the start, use a listening technique, etc. Process covers the *how*.

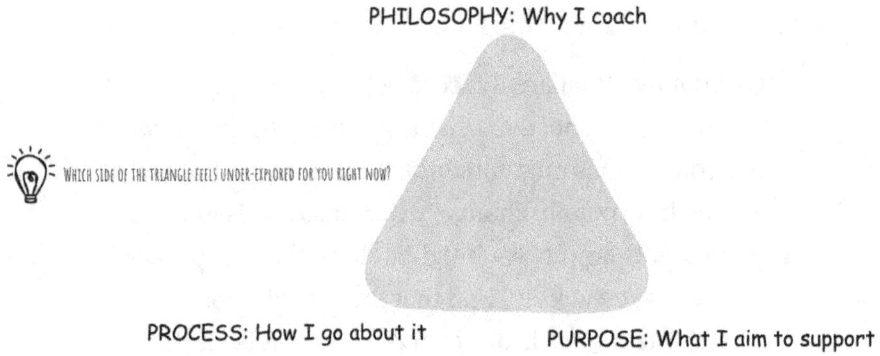

PHILOSOPHY: Why I coach

WHICH SIDE OF THE TRIANGLE FEELS UNDER-EXPLORED FOR YOU RIGHT NOW?

PROCESS: How I go about it   PURPOSE: What I aim to support

Figure 13-1. *3 P's triangle*

According to this model, a coach's or supervisor's practice can be understood and developed by looking at all three of these strands and how they align. By reflecting on the 3 P's, coaches often bring to light their espoused theories versus their theories-in-use; i.e., the difference between what we say we do or believe and what we actually do in practice. It surfaces our assumptions and, crucially, our blind spots. The ultimate aim is to achieve greater coherence in our practice—ensuring that our processes align with our deeper philosophy and that our actions serve our intended purpose. For example, if your philosophy is that "people learn best through experimentation and failure," but your process in team coaching is very prescriptive (not allowing any failure), there's a mismatch to explore. The 3 P's model encourages that kind of introspection.

Reflection Exercise: Take a few minutes to jot down notes about your own philosophy, purpose, and process as an Agile coach. Don't worry about getting it "right," just capture what comes to mind. For instance, philosophy—what do you fundamentally believe about teams and change? Purpose—what do you most want to accomplish for teams? Process—what methods do you rely on? Once you've outlined some points, pick one of these P's to dig deeper. How does that aspect show up in your day-to-day coaching? Do you ever contradict it? This exercise can reveal areas you might want to discuss in supervision or develop further.

Hawkins' Seven-Eyed Model: A Systemic Lens for Agile Contexts

One of the most widely used frameworks in coaching supervision is the Seven-Eyed Model (see Figure 13-2) developed by Peter Hawkins (originally for therapy supervision, later applied to coaching). It's "seven-eyed" because it proposes seven different "eyes" or perspectives through which a supervisor and coach can examine a coaching session or relationship. The idea is to capture the whole system of interactions. Here are the seven eyes (or modes) in brief, tailored to an Agile coaching context:

1. *Eye 1—The client (or team) system:* This eye focuses on the client's content and experience. In Agile coaching, this means looking at what the team is saying and doing. What are the issues the team brings up? How do team members present themselves in coaching sessions? (For example, a team might come into a retrospective visibly frustrated and silent—that's important data about their state.) Eye 1 asks, *"What is happening for*

the team?" and *"How might the team's behavior in coaching reflect their broader patterns?"* For instance, a team that is tense and hurried in the coaching conversation might be tense and rushed in their daily work as well.

2. *Eye 2—The coach's interventions:* This perspective looks at the coach's actions, strategies, and techniques during the session. Here we scrutinize the moves the coach made: the questions asked, exercises used, advice given (if any), etc. The idea is to consider the effectiveness of those interventions. Did the coach use a certain tool repeatedly? How did the team respond? For example, maybe as a coach you notice you always default to the same conflict-resolution exercise. Eye 2 might reveal that you're using a familiar tool even when it's not fitting, or conversely that an intervention was particularly effective (or not) with this team. Key questions: *"What did I (the coach) do, and why?"* and *"What was the impact of my choices on the team?"*

3. *Eye 3—The coaching relationship:* This lens examines the relationship and dynamics between the coach and the client (team). In team coaching, this could include the psychological contract and trust level between you and the team, expectations on both sides, and the "feel" of your interactions. Are you seen as a neutral facilitator, or is the team looking to you as an expert with answers? Is there any tension or over-dependence in the relationship? Hawkins noted that many issues coaches bring to supervision actually relate to the coaching contract

CHAPTER 13   THE POWER OF SUPERVISION AND DELIBERATE PRACTICE

or relationship not being clear enough. For example, if an Agile coach feels like they are "doing all the work" and the team is passive, Eye 3 would explore what assumptions or agreements might be causing that (perhaps the team expects the coach to solve everything, indicating a contracting issue). In supervision, we might ask: *"What's the quality of the coach-team relationship? What expectations are in place, and are they helping or hindering?"* The team's "energy" with the coach and any relational patterns (like a team always deferring to the coach's opinions) are important data here.

4. *Eye 4—The coach's inner feelings and reactions:* This eye turns inward, looking at the coach's own experience during coaching. As coaches, we have emotional and bodily responses in our work; Eye 4 encourages awareness of those. Maybe during a team session, you felt particularly anxious, or a specific team member's behavior irritated you. Those reactions can be full of insight. Perhaps a coach realizes, *"Whenever this team's tech lead crosses his arms and goes quiet, I start feeling insecure and rushing to fill the silence."* Eye 4 is about noticing such internal cues: *"What was happening within me as I coached this team?"* It surfaces any biases or personal triggers; for example, a team member might remind the coach of someone (this is akin to *countertransference* in therapy, where the coach projects feelings because of a similarity). In supervision, exploring Eye 4 helps the coach manage these reactions or even use them as

information. If you feel bored in a team meeting, maybe the team is also bored—that's worth discussing with them! Many times, what *we* feel can be a clue to an unspoken team dynamic. Eye 4 thus improves the coach's self-regulation and use of self as an instrument.

5. *Eye 5—The supervisory relationship:* Now we step into the meta-level—Eye 5 looks at the relationship between the coach (supervisee) and the supervisor. Why is that relevant? Because Hawkins found that often parallel processes occur. The way the coach interacts with their supervisor can unconsciously mirror the way the client interacts with the coach. For example, during a supervision session, a supervisor might notice, *"It feels like you're waiting for me to give you answers."* That could indicate that in the coach's work, their team might be waiting for the coach to give answers (a parallel dynamic of dependency). In Eye 5, the supervisor and coach pay attention to what's happening here and now between them and ask, *"Is this showing us something about the coach–client relationship?"* It's a bit abstract, but very powerful. For instance, if the coach is very defensive when the supervisor gently challenges them, Eye 5 might reveal that the coach is experiencing similar resistance from a team when challenged. Eye 5 basically says: The here-and-now of supervision can provide clues to the there-and-now of coaching. In Agile contexts, since team coaching often has many parallel processes (team

CHAPTER 13   THE POWER OF SUPERVISION AND DELIBERATE PRACTICE

dynamics reflecting organizational dynamics), being alert to parallels in supervision adds a systemic insight.

6. *Eye 6—The supervisor's internal process:* This perspective focuses on what the supervisor themselves feels or experiences while hearing the coach's account. A skilled supervisor may use their own intuition or gut reactions as data. For example, as a coach describes a team situation, the supervisor might begin to feel anxious or sense a "knot in the stomach." If the supervisor shares this observation—*"As you talk about your last sprint review, I notice I'm feeling a bit tense and worried"*—it could turn out that the coach *also* felt that way in the session, or perhaps that's how the team felt. Eye 6 treats the supervisor's embodied responses as potentially reflective of the client system. It requires trust, as the supervisor offers their feelings carefully and without judgment for the coach to consider. For an Agile coach, this might surface issues that aren't obvious logically. For instance, the supervisor might say, *"Hearing you describe the team's debate, I felt an urge to intervene and mediate—like things were about to break down."* That might be exactly what the coach felt but hadn't voiced, or it might highlight the intensity of the team conflict. Using Eye 6, a supervisor acts almost like a tuning fork, resonating with the unspoken tone of the situation. It's another source of insight into the coach–team interaction that pure analysis might miss.

CHAPTER 13   THE POWER OF SUPERVISION AND DELIBERATE PRACTICE

7. *Eye 7—The wider context (wider system):* Finally, Eye 7 directs attention to the broader context in which the coaching is happening. For Agile coaching, this is particularly crucial. The wider system includes the organization's culture, the environment, stakeholder influences, and any larger trends impacting the team. An Agile team does not exist in a vacuum; factors like organizational structure, industry changes, or cross-team dependencies can heavily influence what's happening within the team. Eye 7 asks: *"What's going on in the wider system that might be showing up here?"* For example, if a team isn't following through on action items sprint after sprint, a systemic look (Eye 7) might reveal that the company's culture lacks accountability—nobody follows up on anything in that organization, so the team's behavior is a reflection of a larger norm. Or perhaps power dynamics at the enterprise level (like a re-org or fear of layoffs) are trickling down into the team's interactions. By considering Eye 7, the coach and supervisor ensure they *"zoom out"* and don't mistakenly treat a systemic problem as an individual one. In supervision, an Agile coach might explore questions like: *"How is the broader company culture influencing this team conflict?"* or *"What external pressures (market, leadership, etc.) are at play here?"* One supervisee shared that often the behaviors in a team coaching session mirrored the wider client organization's patterns—*"I have seen reactive, 'drama-driven' behavior exhibited by my client's clients (the end users) being played out in the

CHAPTER 13   THE POWER OF SUPERVISION AND DELIBERATE PRACTICE

culture of the organization and at times within our coaching sessions." Eye 7 encourages these insights. It's a reminder that to coach the system, we must be aware of the system's system!

Figure 13-2. Hawkins' Seven-Eyed model

Using the Seven-Eyed Model, an Agile coach in supervision can methodically work through different "eyes" to gain a comprehensive understanding of a situation. You don't always need to cover all seven in every discussion, but being aware of them prevents blind spots. For instance, if a coach keeps focusing only on what techniques to use (Eye 2), the supervisor might introduce Eyes 4 or 7 to broaden the perspective: *"What were you feeling at that moment?"* or *"What else is happening around the team right now?"* The model is systemic and relational—it recognizes that coaching involves multiple interconnected elements (coach, client, relationships, context). This is why it's so valuable for Agile team coaches, who operate in complex systems.

Applying the Seven-Eyed Model to Agile Team Dynamics

In Agile coaching supervision, Eye 7 (the wider context) often proves especially enlightening. Organizational culture, management decisions, legacy processes, and broader market forces influence Agile teams. By deliberately considering Eye 7, coaches ensure they are not "blaming" a team for issues that are actually systemic. For example, if an Agile team seems resistant to adopting test automation, Eye 7 might reveal that the organization's incentive structure rewards quick-and-dirty delivery over quality, thereby discouraging testing. Similarly, Eye 5 and Eye 6, though subtle, can uncover parallels and patterns. Perhaps the coach realizes that the frustration they feel toward their supervisor in a supervision session ("*Why won't you just tell me the answer?*") is akin to how the Scrum master in the team feels toward the coach ("*Why won't you just tell us the solution?*"). These insights help Agile coaches adjust their stance—maybe they need to be more forthcoming in guidance with the team, or, conversely, to help the team take more ownership. In summary, the Seven-Eyed Model gives Agile coaches and their supervisors a rich map to navigate the full complexity of coaching Agile teams, ensuring that no significant element—be it personal, relational, or systemic—is overlooked in the quest to help teams thrive.

The CLEAR Model for Supervisory Sessions

Many Agile coaches will be familiar with GROW or other coaching models used to structure a conversation. Supervision, too, can benefit from a structured approach. One popular model adapted from coaching for use in supervision is the CLEAR model, originally developed by Peter Hawkins

CHAPTER 13   THE POWER OF SUPERVISION AND DELIBERATE PRACTICE

in the 1980s. "CLEAR" stands for Contract, Listen, Explore, Action, Review. This provides a simple yet effective framework to structure a supervision session (whether one-to-one or group supervision), as follows:

- *Contract:* At the start of the supervision conversation, establish a clear contract for the session. This means agreeing on practicalities (time, confidentiality) and, importantly, the focus or outcomes for that session. Just as an Agile meeting benefits from a stated goal, supervision starts by clarifying *"What would be most useful for us to focus on today?"* The supervisee (coach) might say, for example, "I have an issue with team conflict I'd like to resolve" or "I just need to vent and recover from a tough week." The supervisor and coach collaboratively set the agenda and ground rules (e.g., Is it okay for the supervisor to challenge directly? Are we focusing on one case or multiple?). This contracting stage ensures alignment and psychological safety—both know what the purpose is and how they'll work together. In Agile terms, it's like agreeing on the sprint goal and Definition of Done for the session.

- *Listen:* Next, the supervisor listens while the coach describes the situation or issue. This is an active listening phase, where the coach is encouraged to share freely, and the supervisor may ask clarifying questions, but primarily creates space for the coach's narrative. Often, simply describing the coaching scenario out loud begins the reflection process for the coach. The supervisor listens not just to the content (what happened) but also to the emotional tone and implicit questions or hesitations. They may use cathartic listening—allowing the supervisee to release emotion—and supportive listening, conveying empathy. For example, an Agile coach might outline how their last retrospective went off the rails. The supervisor listens carefully, maybe summarizing: *"So the team lead walked out in the middle, and you're left wondering what to do?"* This attentive listening validates the coach's experience and ensures the supervisor really understands the situation before jumping in. It sets a foundation of trust and clarity.

- *Explore:* Now the conversation explores deeper. In this stage, the supervisor and the coach together analyze and reflect on the issue. The supervisor will ask probing questions, offer observations, and invite the coach to consider alternative perspectives (often using the multiple "eyes" or other frameworks as guides). This is where insights are often generated. They might explore the coach's feelings (Eye 4: *"How did it feel when the team lead walked out?"*), the team perspective (*"What might have caused him to walk out—what was happening for him or the team?"*), the coach's choices (*"What did you do next? What were you thinking at the time?"*), and possible different strategies (*"If you could replay that, what might you try?"*). The exploration should be a creative, open dialogue—brainstorming explanations, examining dynamics, and testing hypotheses. It's not about the supervisor telling the answer, but about jointly reflecting to help the coach reach a new understanding. For instance, through exploration, the coach might realize that the team lead felt unsafe and that perhaps a private one-on-one could complement the group retrospectives.

Or the coach might see the conflict triggered by them and inadvertently escalate it. The supervisor might also share some relevant theory or knowledge ("*This reminds me of the Storming phase in Tuckman's team model—perhaps the team is normalizing conflict*"). In CLEAR, *Explore* is typically the longest and richest phase, akin to the "analysis" or problem-solving part of the session.

- *Action:* After thorough exploration, the focus shifts to action planning—what next steps or actions will the coach take as a result of this session? The idea is to translate insight into practice. The supervisor helps the coach consider various options or solutions that have emerged and choose a way forward. This might involve role-playing a difficult conversation the coach plans to have, or "fast-forward rehearsing" how they will handle the next team meeting differently. For example, if the issue was handling team conflict, the action might be, "*In the next retrospective, I will introduce a team working agreement to foster psychological safety, and I will personally check in with the team lead beforehand.*" The supervisor and coach discuss the feasibility of the action, any support or resources needed, and how success will be recognized. It's important the action is owned by the coach and feels both challenging and achievable. Sometimes the best action is actually inaction—deciding to observe for a while longer or consciously *not* intervening prematurely. The key is that the coach leaves the supervision session with a clear idea of what they will do or experiment with based on the new understanding they've gained.

- *Review:* Finally, the session reviews and closes. In CLEAR, *Review* serves two purposes: (1) to briefly review the actions agreed upon, ensuring clarity and commitment; and (2) to reflect on the supervision process itself. The supervisor might ask, *"Before we finish, let's recap what you're taking away—what actions have you decided on?"* and also, *"How was this session for you? What was helpful or not so helpful?"* This meta-review helps improve the supervision relationship and process. Maybe the coach says, "It helped a lot that you challenged me on my assumption that the team lead was just 'being difficult.' I realize now I was jumping to conclusions." Or they might say, "I felt a bit defensive at one point, but I understand why you asked that." Such feedback allows continuous improvement of supervision itself. It mirrors what we do in Agile teams (retrospecting on the retro, so to speak). In the review stage, any loose ends are also identified if something couldn't be addressed today, note it for next time. And if the session was emotionally heavy, the supervisor makes sure the coach is in a good headspace before leaving (sometimes called "recontracting or resourcing out" if needed, to ensure the coach isn't leaving upset or confused).

The CLEAR model is straightforward but powerful. It ensures that a supervision conversation has a clear beginning, middle, and end, and that it moves from issue to insight to action and learning. Agile coaches might appreciate CLEAR because it's analogous to the structure of an Agile meeting or workshop: set the stage (Contract), gather data (Listen), generate insights (Explore), decide actions (Action), and close/retro (Review). It's a good reminder not to rush straight to problem solving (action) without fully understanding (listen/explore), and conversely, not to end a session with lots of talk but no application (action). Many supervisors use CLEAR or a variant of it to keep supervision on track and productive.

Cultivating Deliberate Practice

Deliberate practice refers to a very specific, focused approach to improving a skill, and it goes well beyond just accumulating experience or attending training courses. The concept, introduced by psychologist Anders Ericsson, is that expertise is built by practicing in a thoughtful, targeted way with feedback, rather than just performing a task over and over on "autopilot." For an Agile coach, engaging in deliberate practice means intentionally working on particular coaching skills or behaviors to refine them and understand why they work, not just that they work.

In traditional learning, a coach might attend a workshop or read a book, then try to apply those ideas in the field. Deliberate practice is more systematic: You identify a specific micro-skill to improve, practice it in a controlled or heightened way (sometimes in role plays or with colleagues), get immediate feedback, and repeat, often pushing your comfort zone. It's the difference between a casual jog and a structured training regimen that includes intervals, sprinting, and technique drills. One might say, experience alone is a great teacher only if combined with reflection and adjustment, which is exactly what deliberate practice enforces.

Why does this matter for Agile team coaches? Team coaching is a complex performance that involves many micro-skills: listening, questioning, facilitating, observing group dynamics, giving feedback, managing energy, etc. We all have our strengths and weaknesses in these areas. Deliberate practice allows us to hone the weaker areas or take good skills to an even higher level. For example, you might be generally good at facilitating, but maybe you realize you're not as adept at intervening when two team members dominate the conversation. Deliberate practice would mean you purposely work on interventions for quieting dominant voices—perhaps by practicing phrases or techniques in a peer coaching practice session—rather than just hoping you'll do better next time by sheer luck.

Another aspect: Deliberate practice is often uncomfortable. It requires coming out of autopilot and really concentrating on how you do something, often under the guidance of a coach, mentor, or supervisor. It's very much an antidote to what can become "mechanistic" coaching or supervision. Deliberate practice reintroduces creativity and conscious improvement. You might deliberately try new approaches in a session to stretch yourself, rather than sticking only to your usual repertoire.

In summary, deliberate practice is about the quality of practice over quantity. Ten years of coaching experience can either be repeating the same year ten times, or it can be ten years of refinement and improvement. Deliberate practice ensures it's the latter. It's a commitment to never stop learning—turning your coaching work itself into a series of learning experiments.

Integrating Deliberate Practice into Agile Coaching Development

How can an Agile team coach actually apply deliberate practice in day-to-day development? Here are a few ways:

- *Focusing on micro-skills and meta-skills:* Start by breaking down the broad competency of "coaching" into smaller micro-skills. In one-on-one coaching, for instance, micro-skills are things like asking open-ended questions, reflecting back what you heard, or summarizing. In team coaching, micro-skills might include encouraging quieter members to speak, reframing a negative comment positively, sensing

CHAPTER 13 THE POWER OF SUPERVISION AND DELIBERATE PRACTICE

the mood of the room, or giving process feedback to the team. Choose one or two micro-skills to work on at a time. For example, you might decide: "I want to get better at clarifying what someone means before I respond, instead of assuming." That's very specific. You can then deliberately practice this by, say, in every meeting for a week, focusing on paraphrasing what people say and asking "Did I get that right?" before moving on. You could ask a colleague (or your supervisor) to observe or listen for that skill and give feedback. In addition to micro-skills, consider meta-skills—a term sometimes used to describe the attitudinal qualities behind skillful practice. Meta-skills are like the tone or energy you bring: examples are patience, curiosity, confidence, empathy and calm presence. A coach could practice a meta-skill by intentionally cultivating a certain quality of being in sessions. Say you realize you often feel anxious, silent, and rush in—you might practice the meta-skill of patience, deliberately allowing more silence and projecting calm. These subtle shifts can significantly change the impact of your coaching. Deliberate practice allows you to isolate and improve these building blocks of mastery, one by one.

- *Drawing from psychotherapeutic practice (e.g., motivational interviewing)*: Deliberate practice has been deeply embraced in fields like psychotherapy. A great example is motivational interviewing (MI). In this counseling approach, practitioners break down counseling into specific behaviors and practice them intensively (often recording sessions, coding

CHAPTER 13   THE POWER OF SUPERVISION AND DELIBERATE PRACTICE

them, and getting detailed feedback). MI trainers have identified core skills (often remembered by the acronym OARS: Open questions, Affirmations, Reflective listening, Summaries), and they do drills to get better at each, much like athletes do drills. Agile coaches can take inspiration from this. For instance, one research study in therapy found that eliciting the client's own observations and evaluations of their behavior—rather than the therapist telling them—was key to effective outcomes. Translating that, an Agile coach might practice prompting the team to assess their own performance (self-observation), evaluate their own adherence to agreements (self-evaluation), and recognize their own improvements (self-reinforcement). These are essentially meta-skills coaches encourage in teams, and coaches can deliberately weave them in. You might deliberately plan that in the next sprint review, before giving any feedback, you will ask the team, "How do you think we did in communicating with stakeholders this sprint? What are you proud of? What would you do differently?"—thus practicing the skill of eliciting self-assessment from the team. There is evidence from organizational research that high-performing teams engage in self-reflection and self-correction more than do average teams. By practicing coaching behaviors that get teams to do this, you not only improve your skill but also directly improve team effectiveness.

CHAPTER 13   THE POWER OF SUPERVISION AND DELIBERATE PRACTICE

- *A deliberate practice exercise:* Let's illustrate a concrete exercise for an Agile coach:

  Step 1: Choose a specific skill. Pick one coaching skill to improve. For example, *"Facilitating conflict constructively during a team meeting."* This is a complex skill, so maybe narrow it to *"Noticing and intervening when two team members start to have a heated argument, in a way that calms things and helps them listen to each other."*

  Step 2: Set a stretch goal. Define what improvement looks like. *"In the next retrospective, if conflict arises, I will intervene within 30 seconds and use a structured technique (like asking each person to state their perspective one at a time) instead of letting it spiral."* The goal should be specific and a bit challenging (out of your comfort zone but attainable).

  Step 3: Visualize and prepare. Before the meeting, visualize yourself executing the skill well. An athlete might mentally rehearse making a free throw; likewise, you can imagine the scenario: Two team members start arguing. You stay calm, you speak in a neutral tone: *"Alex and Sam, I notice tensions are high. Let's pause for a moment. Alex, could you summarize your concern, and then Sam, I'll ask you to summarize what you heard?"* Picture it in detail. This primes your mind to actually do it.

  Step 4: Do it mindfully. During the retrospective, consciously focus on the goal. If conflict erupts, remember your plan and carry it out. (It's like remembering your form during a golf swing—you might even have a little reminder note.) Apply the specific technique or behavior you planned.

Step 5: Immediate reflection. Right after the session (or even during a break), reflect on what happened. Jot a quick note or talk it through with yourself or a colleague: *"They did have a clash. I stepped in early as planned. It seemed to help because they each aired their view. However, I noticed I got a bit nervous and my voice tightened."* The sooner you reflect, the more details you'll retain. This immediate debrief is crucial for learning.

Step 6: Get feedback. If possible, discuss with a supervisor or a peer. *"Here's what I tried, this is where I felt it went well, and here's where I fumbled. What do you think? Any suggestions?"* A supervisor could give you pointers (maybe share how your tone could be more neutral, or validate that the intervention was timely). Or if no one observed, you might at least share the scenario and your approach in your next supervision session to get an external perspective.

Step 7: Refine and repeat. Based on the reflection and feedback, decide what to keep doing and what to adjust. Maybe you realize you did intervene quickly (good), but the method could be tweaked (maybe next time have them write down points first to slow things down). You integrate that and try again in the next opportunity. Over multiple iterations, you will find that your ability to handle conflict in the moment improves significantly—you've essentially trained that skill through deliberate focus.

This kind of cycle can be applied to virtually any aspect of coaching: asking powerful questions, holding silence, giving positive feedback to teams, managing time in meetings, etc. It's helpful to involve your supervisor in identifying skills and measuring progress. They can often notice improvements you might not and keep you accountable to your practice goals.

Practical Application: Scenarios and Structures for Agile Coaches

So far we've discussed the what and why of supervision and deliberate practice. Let's turn to some practical applications: real-world scenarios Agile coaches might face and how supervision helps, as well as how to actually set up your "ecosystem" of support (supervision formats, peer learning, etc.) to embed these practices in your routine.

Navigating Complex Team Dynamics and Conflicting Agendas

Imagine an Agile coach working with a leadership team or a product development team where politics are at play. Perhaps two senior members of the team (or board) have separate, clashing agendas for the team's direction. Meetings are fraught with indirect comments, and the team is stuck. Or consider a scenario where upper management insists "Team A is the problem" when, in fact, systemic issues (like unrealistic deadlines) are the cause; the team is scapegoated unfairly. These kinds of multi-layered dynamics are extremely challenging. In supervision, you can lay out the whole messy picture confidentially. A supervisor provides a safe container to process the complexity: "Here's what person X wants, here's what person Y wants, and here's me in the middle of it." Together, you might map the different stakeholders and their covert agendas. The supervisor, being removed from the situation, can help identify patterns or reframe the problem: *"It sounds like this conflict isn't really about the Agile process at all, but about long-standing power struggles in the organization."* They might ask, *"What's your role in this system? How can you avoid becoming the rope in their tug-of-war?"* By reflecting in supervision, the coach can devise a strategy, such as facilitating a session to surface and align objectives, or practicing neutrality and not taking sides. Moreover, the supervisor can role-play with the coach how to handle a tense meeting or how to push back diplomatically on management's misplaced attribution of blame. Coaches often report that after discussing a convoluted situation in supervision, they feel less alone and more confident in handling it. The previously "swirling" dynamics seem clearer, and they have a game plan. In essence, supervision turns confusion into clarity and action. Without it, a coach in such a bind might either become overwhelmed and withdraw, or take reactive steps that backfire. Supervision helps sort the signal from the noise.

Addressing Ethical Dilemmas in Multi-Stakeholder Environments

Agile coaches frequently operate in a nexus of client relationships; for example, the team is one client, the sponsoring manager or HR is another, and there may even be end users indirectly in view. This can raise tricky ethical questions, especially around confidentiality and divided loyalty. A classic scenario: A manager asks the coach, "Can you tell me what issues the team members have been bringing up to you? I want to know if there are performance problems." The team members, however, share things with the coach, expecting it won't go straight to their boss. What to do? Supervision is an ideal place to thrash out these dilemmas. A supervisor can guide the coach through ethical decision frameworks or share how such issues are handled per professional standards. They'll likely remind the coach that maintaining trust with the team is paramount and help devise a response to the manager that honors confidentiality while addressing the manager's concerns. Hidden agendas can also emerge; for instance, perhaps HR engaged the coach, but the team thinks the coach is an "agent of management," leading to mistrust. Discussing in supervision can help the coach strategize transparency and re-contracting with all parties. Sometimes, supervision might reveal a conflict of interest so serious that the coach decides to withdraw from an engagement. It's much easier to see that with a supervisor's outside perspective. Furthermore, supervision upholds the coach's own ethical posture. Simply knowing you will discuss your decisions with a supervisor creates a kind of ethical feedback loop—you are less likely to make a dubious choice in the moment if you know you'll be reflecting on it later (a bit like knowing you'll be doing a code review; you write cleaner code). In fields like counseling, it's well documented that supervision significantly aids practitioners in navigating confidentiality and other ethical issues. The same holds for coaching. Agile coaches often operate without a formal code of ethics mandated, so supervision is a voluntary but crucial checkpoint to ensure we don't drift into grey areas unchecked. It's the place to bring those "I'm not sure what the right thing to do is here" questions and emerge with greater clarity and conviction about the path that maintains integrity.

Managing the Coach's Emotional Responses and Biases

We touched on this in the benefits, but it's worth emphasizing through a scenario. Agile coaches are human—we will sometimes get triggered or emotionally hooked by situations in teams. Say a team consistently shows up late to every coaching session or retro, and despite all your efforts, it keeps happening. You notice you feel resentful and start thinking, "This team doesn't respect me or this process." If unchecked, in the next session,

CHAPTER 13   THE POWER OF SUPERVISION AND DELIBERATE PRACTICE

you might show irritation or become disengaged (biasing your coaching). Or perhaps one team member reminds you of a difficult colleague from your past; you find yourself always subtly siding against their ideas. These are natural but potentially harmful to our effectiveness. Supervision is like a mirror that helps you notice these internal states and biases before they contaminate the coaching. In a supervision conversation, you might confess, "I have to admit, I'm really frustrated with this team right now." That admission itself is healthy; supervisors often normalize such feelings. Then they'll help you unpack it: *"What's beneath that frustration? What does it say about your expectations or needs?"* Maybe you realize you're taking it personally, or that you're feeling like a failure because the team isn't cooperative, which taps into a personal need for approval. The supervisor can then help you separate yourself from the situation, perhaps reframing it as, "What does the team's lateness say about their environment or stress levels? How could you address it with them constructively?" Instead of silently stewing, you might decide to bring it up with the team candidly yet supportively, or you might realize you need to adjust your own attitude ("They're not disrespecting me; they are overwhelmed—I can help by acknowledging that."). By processing emotions in supervision, you clear them out or harness them beneficially, rather than letting them leak out unconsciously in your coaching. Biases too—maybe you discover in supervision that you've been favoring the engineers in the team discussions because that's your background, inadvertently sidelining QA folks' input. A good supervisor will challenge you: *"Who do you find yourself drawn to or avoiding on the team? Why might that be?"* It can be humbling to realize our blind spots, but it's far better to realize with a supervisor (who's on your side to help) than never to realize and keep repeating the bias. Ultimately, this makes you a more objective and fair coach to the team, and it models the kind of self-awareness we hope team members develop too.

CHAPTER 13 THE POWER OF SUPERVISION AND DELIBERATE PRACTICE

Setting Up Your Supervision and Reflective Practice Ecosystem

Individual Supervision: Finding the Right Fit

Many Agile coaches choose to have one-on-one supervision (just like executive coaches do) with a dedicated supervisor. If you go this route, it's important to find a supervisor who resonates with you. Look for someone who has sufficient experience (especially with team coaching or organizational work if possible) and whose approach or philosophy feels compatible. Often, an initial chemistry meeting helps; you want to feel safe and understood, but also confident that this person will challenge you and not just nod along. It's often recommended to choose a supervisor who also supervises others and who adheres to a code of ethics, because that indicates they are serious about their practice and continuously learning. Ethical maturity is another factor; a supervisor who is savvy about ethics can guide you better. Practicalities matter too: agree on things like frequency (many coaches do a session every 4–6 weeks), length (60–90 minutes), and cancellation policies. All this should go into a supervision contract. The contract will also clarify confidentiality (usually, what's said in supervision stays there, with a few exceptions like an immediate risk of harm) and any note-taking or recording procedures. Since Agile coaches might be employees in an organization, it's worth clarifying whether the supervisor can or cannot report anything back to the organization. In independent coaching, it's almost always totally confidential. The trust in this relationship is paramount; you need to be able to bring your shadow side, your mistakes, your uncertainties without fear of judgment. A good individual supervisor provides a balance of support (being your confidant and advocate) and stretch (pushing you to grow).

CHAPTER 13   THE POWER OF SUPERVISION AND DELIBERATE PRACTICE

Group Supervision: Leveraging Collective Wisdom

Group supervision involves one supervisor with a group of coaches (typically anywhere from three to six or so). It's a popular and cost-effective format that Agile coaches can utilize, and it has unique advantages. In group supervision, coaches take turns bringing cases or topics, and the supervisor facilitates the group in providing reflection and feedback. One benefit is peer learning: You learn not only when you present your own case, but also by listening to others. You might hear a fellow coach's dilemma that you haven't faced yet and learn from it proactively. It builds a sense of community in what can be a lonely profession. For internal Agile coaches in a company, group supervision can function as a community of practice where patterns in the organization become visible across teams. Edna Murdoch (a pioneer in coaching supervision) described group supervision as a "microcosm of the system"—dynamics that unfold in the group often echo the dynamics in the clients' situations. For example, if in the supervision group the conversation keeps drifting off-topic, it might reflect that the coaches' clients (teams) are struggling with focus too. The supervisor can point out these parallels. Additionally, group supervision is often more affordable since the cost is split, and for organizations, it's a scalable way to support many coaches with fewer supervisors. Group supervision does require a climate of trust among participants; confidentiality and respect must be agreed upon by all. Done well, it's incredibly rich: You get multiple viewpoints on your issue (like having several consultants brainstorm on your problem) and a shared sense of not feeling alone in challenges. Coaches often breathe a sigh of relief when a peer says, *"I've had that exact issue with my Scrum team too"*—it normalizes their experience. In Agile contexts, where many coaches might be working in the same company across different teams, a supervision group can surface systemic issues (like "all our teams seem to be struggling with unrealistic deadlines from above"), which can then be escalated appropriately. It gives a systemic lens: *the group format ensures more voices from the system are represented.* The supervisor's role in group supervision is to manage time, ensure everyone learns (not just the person presenting), and maintain psychological safety since sharing can make one feel vulnerable in front of peers. Over time, well-run supervision groups become tight-knit support circles.

Peer Supervision Chains and Communities of Practice

Besides formal supervision with an expert supervisor, Agile coaches can also set up peer supervision or peer coaching arrangements. One model mentioned in the literature is a peer supervision chain, where a group of coaches supervise each other in a rotating manner. For example, Coach A brings a case and Coach B acts as the "supervisor" for that session, and then the roles rotate. The group might also meet without a designated leader and follow a structured process to help whoever has the issue of the day. The Global Supervisors' Network and other bodies often encourage these kinds of peer-learning structures because they foster mutual growth at low cost. The key is that all members need some grounding in how to give constructive feedback and maintain a reflective (not advice-giving or judgmental) stance. Often, peers will use a protocol, such as each person asking one question to the presenter in a round-robin, rather than everyone jumping in with opinions. Communities of Practice (CoPs) for Agile coaches, which many organizations or Agile communities have, can also incorporate a supervision element. For instance, a monthly CoP meeting might include a segment where one coach shares a challenge and others help in a supervision-like discussion. Peer arrangements won't replace the expertise of a trained supervisor, but they are a valuable supplement. They especially shine in providing emotional support and shared identity, knowing "we're in this together." In a peer chain described in *The Heart of Coaching Supervision*, members noted "significant personal and professional development" as a result of exchanging peer supervision over time. They found it *"resourced each member holistically"* and ultimately benefited their clients because the coaches became better. The beauty of peer supervision is its reciprocal nature—as the saying goes, "to give is to receive." When you act as a peer supervisor for someone else, you often learn as much as when you're the one in the hot seat. Explaining your thinking or coaching someone through reflection forces you to articulate approaches you might use implicitly. It's a bit like teaching—it consolidates your own knowledge.

If you want to start a peer supervision group, it's wise to set some ground rules: confidentiality (what's said in the group stays in the group), equal time if possible, no interrupting, and clarifying whether it's okay to challenge each other or if it should stick to supportive inquiry. Some peer groups document their "working agreement" just like Agile teams do. Rotating roles (facilitator, time-keeper, etc.) can be useful. And periodically, peer groups should reflect on their process: *"Is this meeting our needs? How can we improve our peer supervision practice?"*—essentially doing a retro on the peer supervision itself. When done thoughtfully, these peer structures become an essential part of a coach's development *ecosystem*, alongside any formal external supervision.

Action Learning Sets for Collaborative Problem Solving

Action learning is a technique where a small group meets regularly to solve real problems through a structured process of questioning and reflection (pioneered by Reg Revans). While action learning is often used directly with teams (and indeed, some Agile coaches incorporate action learning approaches in communities of practice or cross-team retrospectives), it's also a form of peer group reflection that coaches themselves can use. An action learning set of Agile coaches could form where each coach brings a challenge, and through open questions from peers, they reflect and identify actions. It's similar to peer supervision, with the difference that action learning strictly focuses on questioning (peers typically don't give advice or share their story; they ask questions to help the person think). This can lead to very insightful outcomes because the problem presenter does most of the thinking. For example, a coach might say, "My problem is: my team isn't taking ownership in retrospectives." The group then asks questions like, *"What do you think is causing them not to take ownership?"* or *"What would taking ownership look like, ideally?"* or *"What have you tried so far?"* etc. As the coach answers, they often come to new realizations. Perhaps they conclude, "You know, I realize I haven't actually asked them to design the retro format; I've been spoon-feeding it. I could try handing that over." They then commit to an action (e.g., next retro, have the team facilitate a part). At the next meeting, they report back on the outcome. This cycle continues, embedding continuous learning and action, which aligns perfectly with Agile principles.

Action learning sets can be self-facilitated, or one member can act as a facilitator each time (rotating). They require discipline to stick to questions and reflection rather than conversation (some models allow some suggestion phase at the end, but not until the person has done their own thinking thoroughly). Agile coaches might find this format refreshing since we're often in the role of asking teams powerful questions; here we get to be on the receiving end of questions from peers.

While action learning isn't exactly team coaching (because it's usually an individual's problem being addressed by group questions), the skills overlap heavily with coaching and supervision: deep listening, non-directive questioning, a supportive environment, and a bias toward action and learning. In fact, being part of an action learning set will likely improve your questioning skills, which you can then take back to your teams.

For instance, one might discover a really juicy question used by a peer and think, "I could ask my Scrum master that same question when she comes to me with her problem." It also fosters an equal learning community, echoing the Agile value of shared leadership. There's no single expert; the wisdom is in the group's questions and the individual's reflection.

Some internal Agile coaching programs set up action learning for their coaches as a form of ongoing training. It's like saying that the best way to learn coaching is to experience it repeatedly on real issues. And because it's action-oriented, it ensures that insight leads to experiments in the field, which then yield results to discuss, and so on.

A side benefit: Tackling real problems in such a setting can lead to organizational improvements. Suppose five Agile coaches meet and in successive sessions it turns out three of them have a similar problem (say, "Product wners are disengaged in our sprint reviews"). That might indicate a need to raise that issue to higher management. So, an action learning set can also function as an incubator for organizational change ideas.

If you're new to action learning, it might help to have a brief training or use a coach familiar with it to get started. But fundamentally, it's about harnessing the power of open questions and reflection in a group—something quite in line with an Agile mindset of collaborative inquiry.

Overcoming Challenges in Supervision and Deliberate Practice
Addressing the "Checklist" Mentality

In some environments, especially those that are highly regulated or risk-averse, there's a tendency to turn supervision into a tick-box exercise. In this formal requirement, the richness of reflection is lost. You might find organizations saying, "*Yes, we do supervision—coaches must attend a*

CHAPTER 13   THE POWER OF SUPERVISION AND DELIBERATE PRACTICE

quarterly supervision meeting," but if the culture around it is fearful, those sessions could devolve into a perfunctory check-in or a manager-driven performance review. Similarly, an individual coach might approach supervision with a compliance mindset: *"Okay, I'll bring a case, I'll get some advice, I'll implement it—done."* This mechanistic approach sucks the life out of what should be a creative, human process. When stress and anxiety levels are high, people often seek refuge in structure and protocols, and supervision can revert to checklist approaches that smother reflective practice. For example, a supervisor might rigidly go through a set of questions every time, or a supervisee might present issues only in a sanitized, formulaic way to avoid scrutiny. While structure (like models and checklists) has its place, the real growth in supervision comes from being present to the unique unfolding of each conversation—allowing emergent insights, grappling with uncertainty, even moments of silence or emotion. In other words, when supervisor and coach fully engage in this specific conversation, with curiosity and openness, rather than treating it as one more item on an agenda, that's when magical breakthroughs happen. If you ever find your supervision sessions feeling like rote routines, address it: maybe bring it up with your supervisor (*"Can we try a different approach? I feel like we're going through the motions."*). Or, if you are the supervisor, dare to deviate from the script—perhaps share an intuition or invite a creative exercise. The same caution goes for deliberate practice; it's possible to approach that in a box-checking way ("Did my 10,000 hours, now I'm an expert!"). But if practice is not reflective and is just repetition, you might reinforce bad habits or plateau. Avoid treating practice as just a quota of hours or a strict checklist of sub-skills. Instead, keep the spirit of experimentation and mindfulness. In Agile terms, it's like the difference between doing Scrum events as dead ceremonies versus living the Agile principles. The antidote to a checklist mentality is injecting awareness: Supervision is a space for surprise, not just confirmation.

Indeed, some of the most valuable supervision moments come when a session heads somewhere unanticipated—a tangential comment reveals a core issue, or an emotional moment flips understanding.

Bridging the Gap Between Theory and "Being"

Agile coaches are often quite well-educated in coaching models, Agile frameworks, psychology theories, etc. The challenge is translating all that knowledge into a way of being with teams that is effective and authentic. It's one thing to know about systemic coaching or emotional intelligence; it's another to embody it in the heat of a team conflict. Supervision helps make that translation by repeatedly linking theory to practice through reflection. But coaches can still find themselves frustrated: *"I know the right approach intellectually, but in the moment I didn't do it!"* This is normal—building new habits or mindsets takes time and often deeper personal work. For example, you might thoroughly understand that a coach should be non-judgmental and trust the team's wisdom (philosophy), but if you secretly believe "this team is hopeless without me," your being in the session will radiate some judgment or control, despite your theoretical stance. Overcoming this requires more than knowledge—it requires what some call vertical development (growth in self-awareness, emotional maturity) in addition to horizontal (skills). In supervision, you might work on exactly that: noticing inner beliefs, exploring values, confronting fears (like, *"If I truly let go of control, what am I afraid will happen?"*). It's a more personal journey than just acquiring techniques. Some coaches even pursue therapy or their own personal coaching alongside supervision if they find certain triggers (impostor syndrome, need for approval, etc.) consistently impede their "being fully present." The coherence between what effective coaches do, say, and believe—sometimes called congruence or integrity—is a hallmark of masterful coaching. If you feel a gap, say your style feels forced or you're acting how you think you "should" rather than what feels genuine, bring that to supervision. That space can help you gradually integrate knowledge with authentic self-expression. One might realize, for instance, that they have been imitating a certain famous coach's style that doesn't actually fit their personality; supervision can give permission to drop the act and coach in a way that aligns with their strengths and values. This evolution from "outside-in" coaching (applying models mechanically) to "inside-out" coaching (flowing from your own centered presence with models as resources) is significant. It's often why seasoned coaches seem to operate at a different level—they are not thinking about how to coach, they are simply *being* a coach, fully attentive, and all their knowledge is internalized.

Such coherence doesn't happen overnight. It demands self-reflection and often some humbling encounters with one's own limitations (we all hit moments that show us we aren't as patient or empathetic or skilled as we thought). Supervision provides a safe crucible for this alchemy of turning knowledge into wisdom. Over time, you find that you're not just doing Agile coaching; you're living its principles in the room: collaboration, respect, openness, courage, focus (sounds like Scrum values!).

Conclusion

Achieving a set of competencies (skills, knowledge, techniques) is necessary to be a good coach, but masterful coaching goes beyond that into the realm of presence. Presence is somewhat intangible—it's the quality of being fully here and now with the team, with a calm yet dynamic awareness. It's your authenticity, empathy, intuition, and confidence rolled into a way of relating that the team can feel. Teams often might not articulate it, but they sense when a coach is truly present with them versus when the coach is half-distracted or rigidly following a script. The work you've done—reflecting on beliefs, aligning your philosophy with practice, handling your triggers—all contributes to developing a state of presence.

CHAPTER 13 THE POWER OF SUPERVISION AND DELIBERATE PRACTICE

In the presence, you are not preoccupied by what technique to use next; you are deeply listening and responding to what is, in the moment, drawing from a wealth of experience and knowledge without being a slave to it. This is where creativity in coaching arises. You might, in a present moment, combine methods or say something novel that precisely fits the situation—something no textbook could have dictated—because you are tuned in to the team and trusting yourself. That level of mastery often correlates with what we call "systemic eclectic" coaching: you have a wide toolkit and you've integrated it into your own style.

At this stage, the coach's being indeed becomes a primary instrument of change. Your presence acts almost like a catalyst for the team. If you bring positive energy, clarity, and calm, it influences the team's emotional state (teams have said things like "when you're in the room, we communicate better"—that's presence at work). Of course, the goal is to help the team eventually embody these capacities without you, but to get there, you often model it through your presence.

Supervision and deliberate practice are vital in reaching this level because they ensure self-awareness and continual alignment of your actions with your values. They help you scrub off any rust of complacency. Think of it like a ship's captain keeping the vessel's instrumentation well-calibrated and the hull barnacle-free. Presence is partly a result of having done the inner work (removing inner barriers like fear or bias). Supervision helps with that by giving you a relational mirror. As you progress, supervision might become less about basic skill correction and more about the fine nuances of coaching presence. For instance, conversations might revolve around the coach's intuition (*"I had a hunch to confront the team with a hard truth, but I hesitated—can we explore that?"*) or purpose (*"What's the legacy I want to have as a coach in this organization?"*). These are deep topics that a seasoned supervisor can help you unpack, ensuring your orientation and mindset are as honed as your behaviors.

CHAPTER 13   THE POWER OF SUPERVISION AND DELIBERATE PRACTICE

In this analogy, supervision is the lighthouse that periodically comes into view to help orient you. Every time you engage in supervision, it's like you sail within sight of a lighthouse (someone with a broader view on the coastline) that can signal to you, *"Careful, you're veering a bit off course to the north,"* or *"There are rocks to your east you might not see."* It offers that vital perspective outside of your own immediate experience, helping you avoid hazards (like ethical pitfalls or repeated mistakes) and keep on track toward your destination. The lighthouse doesn't sail your ship for you, but its guidance is lifesaving in fog or storm. Similarly, supervision doesn't do the coaching for you, but it enlightens your journey, especially when things get tricky.

Meanwhile, deliberate practice is akin to the disciplined training of your crew and maintenance of the ship. A wise captain continuously trains the crew in navigation, knot-tying, emergency drills, etc., before the big storm hits. You don't wait for a crisis to learn how to reef a sail. Through practice drills (like your role-plays, reflection exercises, and learning new methods), you and your "crew" of skills are ever more prepared. Deliberate practice also involves checking the ship's condition—patching minor leaks, recalibrating compasses—i.e., improving the small things that, if neglected, could become big issues over time. This is like you fine-tuning micro-skills and addressing little bad habits.

For an Agile coach, supervision serves as a vital control tower in a constantly changing airspace. It provides the elevated perspective to observe the intricate flight patterns of multiple Agile teams, anticipate emergent challenges, and gain real-time feedback on their own "piloting" skills, ensuring both individual resilience and collective mission success in the face of unpredictable winds and turbulent conditions.

CHAPTER 13 THE POWER OF SUPERVISION AND DELIBERATE PRACTICE

Reflection Moment

1. When I reflect on my recent coaching engagements, what patterns—of intervention, reaction, or avoidance—keep surfacing, and what might they reveal about my current development edge?

2. What is one micro-skill or meta-skill I want to improve in the next month deliberately, and how will I track my progress in applying it?

3. In moments of team conflict, silence, or resistance, how do I typically respond—internally and externally—and how could supervision help me explore new options?

4. What part of my own coaching philosophy feels strongest and most aligned with my practice—and what part might be outdated, conflicted, or unconscious?

5. Whom do I turn to for reflection, challenge, and growth in my coaching practice—and how could I strengthen my supervision or peer reflection ecosystem?

6. When was the last time I felt emotionally impacted by a coaching session, and how did I process it? What support structures (like supervision or journaling) helped me stay grounded?

7. What kind of presence do I bring into a coaching session—and how do I know whether it is helpful, distracting, or invisible to the team?

CHAPTER 14

Mastering the Inner Game: Staying Grounded in Chaos

Agile coaches often feel like they're standing in the eye of a storm. One day you might be mediating a heated conflict between team members; the next, you're facing resistance from a senior leader who questions the "new Agile way." The pressure is unique—you sit at the heart of team and organizational dynamics, mediating conflicts, driving change, and facing pushback on all sides. It's not just theoretical stress: You might witness intense arguments in a retrospective or have to convince a skeptical manager to support the team's experiment. These situations can be emotionally charged, even chaotic, testing your composure as much as your coaching skills. Agile frameworks (Scrum, Kanban, etc.) provide practices and processes, but in the heat of the moment—when voices raise or a plan falls apart—it's not a diagram from the Scrum Guide that saves the day. It's you: your inner stability, awareness, and resilience as a coach.

The "inner game" of coaching refers to the internal state and mindset you bring when coaching under pressure. We know external techniques and frameworks are vital, but an Agile coach's effectiveness is profoundly influenced by what's happening inside. If you feel unsure, stressed, or triggered, you might react impulsively rather than respond thoughtfully.

For example, if you're internally seething with anxiety or self-doubt during a conflict, you might snap with a judgmental comment or withdraw at the worst moment. In contrast, if you stay grounded and self-aware, you can choose a response that calms the situation. In other words, losing your grounding can sabotage progress and relationships, despite all your Agile knowledge.

This chapter focuses on helping you cultivate resilience and self-awareness to navigate these inner-game moments. We'll draw on powerful psychological models—notably Acceptance and Commitment Therapy (ACT) and Shirzad Chamine's Positive Intelligence (PQ) framework—to offer practical strategies for staying grounded. These strategies include ways to notice and defuse difficult thoughts, calm your nervous system, reconnect with your coaching purpose, and shift into a more resourceful "Sage" mindset. The goal is to equip you to respond thoughtfully, rather than reacting on autopilot, even in the most intense Agile storms. Think of it as developing your inner agility: the flexibility and strength to remain calm, clear-headed, and aligned with your values as a coach, no matter what chaos is happening around you.

Recognizing Your Internal Signals—The Body, Mind, and Saboteurs

Before you can respond effectively in a turbulent moment, you first need to recognize the early warning signals within yourself. Your body and mind are constantly providing feedback. Tuning into those signals is the first step in interrupting a reactive cycle.

Figure 14-1 illustrates one such process. It illustrates the inner steps a coach can take, progressing from the initial signal of being triggered through grounding, defusing, reconnecting with values, and ultimately choosing a wise and intentional response. Think of it as a roadmap for shifting from autopilot reactivity to conscious action.

CHAPTER 14   MASTERING THE INNER GAME: STAYING GROUNDED IN CHAOS

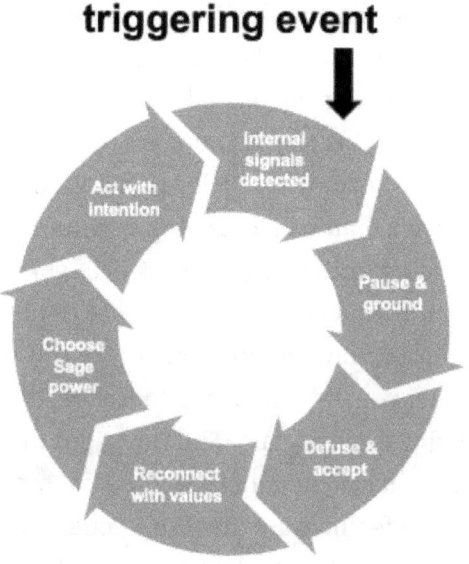

Figure 14-1. *Inner game response flow*

- *Physiological signs of stress and overwhelm:* Pay attention to your body under stress. Do your shoulders tighten up into a knot? Is your heart suddenly racing or your breathing turning shallow? Perhaps you get a sinking feeling in your stomach or a clenched jaw. These physical cues are often the first indicators that the "fight-or-flight" stress response has kicked in. Research on coaching under stress describes this state as being caught "in the vortex"—a whirlwind of physical and mental stress responses. When you're in that vortex, your body may be in high alert: a quicker heart rate, tense muscles, and rapid, shallow breaths are common signs. For an Agile coach, this might happen the moment a team conflict erupts or when a project manager's criticism blindsides you in a meeting. By noticing these sensations early (such as a racing heart or tight shoulders), you have a chance to step out of autopilot reactions.

451

CHAPTER 14   MASTERING THE INNER GAME: STAYING GROUNDED IN CHAOS

- *Cognitive and emotional triggers:* Alongside your body, notice your thoughts and feelings in real-time. What stories is your mind telling when challenges hit? You might catch thoughts like, "This team is hopeless," or "I'm about to fail." Emotions can surge up as well—perhaps anxiety, frustration, anger, or even shame. In coaching, common triggers might include feeling undervalued (spark of anger or hurt), seeing a team ignore your advice (frustration), or hitting a setback in a transformation initiative (anxiety or self-doubt). Rather than judging yourself for having these reactions, simply acknowledge them as data. They are signs that something important is happening. In fact, these uncomfortable thoughts and feelings are often self-generated by your inner Saboteurs—those habitual negative mind patterns that we all have. According to the Positive Intelligence framework, these Saboteurs thrive on generating negative emotions (stress, anger, guilt, shame, etc.) that undermine your effectiveness. Recognizing when this inner commentary flares up is crucial to not being controlled by it.

- *Unmasking your Saboteurs:* Shirzad Chamine's Positive Intelligence (PQ) model identifies ten common Saboteurs—automatic mental habits that "hijack" us into negativity. The master Saboteur is the Judge, who affects everyone. The Judge is that inner voice that criticizes you and others, finds fault in circumstances, and fuels a lot of anxiety and blame. For example, your Judge might berate you with *"You're not a good coach"* or label a team member *"lazy and resistant."* This Saboteur generates self-doubt and a harsh, unhelpful mindset. In addition to the Judge, most of us have a few "accomplice" Saboteurs. Here are some common ones and how they might show up in Agile coaching:

CHAPTER 14   MASTERING THE INNER GAME: STAYING GROUNDED IN CHAOS

- The Avoider: Urges you to avoid difficult or unpleasant tasks and conflicts. As a coach, the Avoider might tempt you to postpone that hard conversation with a team member or gloss over serious team dysfunction in a retrospective, preferring to "keep things positive." This provides short-term comfort but at the cost of long-term problems festering.

- The Controller: Drives an intense need to take charge and control situations. In a coaching context, the Controller Saboteur might manifest as you over-managing a team ceremony or dominating a retrospective because you're anxious about things going "off track." Others may feel steamrolled or disengaged as a result.

- The Victim: Soaks in feelings of helplessness or martyrdom to gain sympathy. As a coach, you might notice Victim thoughts if you catch yourself thinking *"Why do these things always happen to **me**?"* during team chaos, or wanting others to acknowledge how *hard* things are for you. This mindset can sap your energy and resourcefulness.

- The Pleaser: Encourages you to win affection and approval by meeting others' needs, at the expense of your own. A coaching example is bending over backward to accommodate every stakeholder request or never saying no to additional responsibilities. The Pleaser might make you avoid giving tough feedback to a team because you fear displeasing them—ultimately causing more harm by not addressing important issues.

CHAPTER 14   MASTERING THE INNER GAME: STAYING GROUNDED IN CHAOS

- The Hyper-Achiever: Pushes you to define your self-worth through constant achievement and external validation. In Agile coaching, this Saboteur might make you over-prepare for every session, obsess over metrics to "prove" your worth, or work excessive hours to ensure every transformation initiative is perfect. It can lead to burnout and a loss of balance, as you're never satisfied with "good enough."

- The Hyper-Vigilant: Keeps you on high alert, constantly scanning for potential issues. In practice, this could mean you enter a team meeting already bracing for conflict, or you're constantly worried, *"Leadership is going to push back on this, I just know it."* A Hyper-Vigilant coach finds it hard to relax, and that anxiety can be contagious to the team.

These are just a few of the Saboteurs (others include the *Stickler,* who fixates on perfection, the *Restless,* who constantly seeks new stimulation, and the *Hyper-Rational,* who focuses on logic to the exclusion of emotion). The key is to identify which Saboteur voices (see Table 14-1) are at play when a challenging moment strikes. Are you judging someone (Judge) or yourself? Avoiding something uncomfortable (Avoider)? Trying to control the uncontrollable (Controller)? Simply giving a name to these mental habits starts to defuse their power.

Table 14-1. Behaviors of Saboteurs

Saboteur	How It Shows Up in Coaching	Potential Impact
Judge	Harsh inner self-talk; blaming teams	Undermines confidence and relationships
Avoider	Postpones hard conversations	Issues fester; conflict avoidance
Controller	Over-manages ceremonies or decisions	Disempowers teams
Pleaser	Over-accommodates stakeholders or team members	Burnout; avoids constructive challenge
Hyper-Achiever	Ties worth to results and recognition	Perfectionism; fatigue
Hyper-Vigilant	Expects things to go wrong	Anxiety spreads; short-term focus

Scenario Based on a Real Story

Imagine you're facilitating a sprint retrospective and two team members suddenly start arguing loudly, each criticizing the other's work. The room's tension shoots up. In that instant, you notice your jaw clenching and your heart pounding. A thought flashes through your mind: "This team is impossible; they just want to fight." Here, your body is signaling stress (tight jaw, racing heart), and your Judge Saboteur has jumped in with a harsh, all-or-nothing judgment about the team. Recognizing these internal signals—"I'm feeling physical tension and the thought that 'this team is impossible' just popped up"—is your crucial first clue. It tells you that you are getting triggered. This awareness sets the stage for you to take further steps (like pausing or defusing) rather than automatically reacting (e.g.,

CHAPTER 14   MASTERING THE INNER GAME: STAYING GROUNDED IN CHAOS

scolding the team or shutting down the retrospective). In the very act of noting your racing pulse and the Judge's commentary, you've begun to step out of the emotional storm, positioning yourself to coach more effectively.

Instant Grounding—Pausing in the Moment of Challenge

When the pressure is on and your stress responses are firing, one of the most powerful skills you can deploy is grounding yourself in the present moment. In high-pressure situations, our instincts often yell at us to "Do something, quick!"—we feel an urge to react immediately. However, as the saying (often attributed to Victor Frankl) goes: *"Between stimulus and response there is a space. In that space is our power to choose our response."* The first goal is to create that space by pausing, as follows:

- *The power of the pause:* Simply pausing—even for a few seconds—is a game changer. It's a deliberate break in the action that prevents your knee-jerk reaction from spilling out. In Agile coaching, this might mean taking a slow breath before answering a challenging question, or asking the room for a brief silence when emotions run high ("Let's take 10 seconds, everyone, and breathe"). This short circuit gives your rational brain a chance to re-engage. In Acceptance and Commitment Therapy (ACT), this aligns with the practice of cultivating conscious presence, which involves noticing what is happening here and now, rather than getting carried away by worries or anger. A pause might feel counterintuitive ("Won't people think I'm freezing up?"), but in reality, it often has a calming effect on others as well. It shows you're thoughtfully considering your next move instead of reacting impulsively.

- *ACT grounding techniques:* ACT offers a toolbox of quick exercises to ground yourself in the present moment—essentially to get out of your head (where the storm of thoughts rages) and into your direct sensory experience. Here are a couple of techniques you can use on the fly:

    - Notice five things (5-5-5 Senses Exercise): This simple grounding exercise can be done in under a minute. Silently and quickly notice: five things you can see, five things you can hear, and five things you can physically feel right now. For example, *"I see the conference room table, the laptop light, the coffee mug, the clock ticking 3:15, the team Kanban board . . . I hear John's voice, a keyboard clacking, an AC hum, distant laughter in the hallway, my own breathing . . . I feel my feet on the floor, my back against the chair, the sleeve of my shirt on my arm, my cool watch metal on the wrist, the air on my skin."* By actively engaging your senses, you anchor yourself to the immediate here-and-now reality, which has a calming and focusing effect. This helps pull you out of the mental whirlpool. It's a quick way to disrupt panic and regain clarity.

    - Three-minute breathing space: If you have a few minutes (perhaps during a short break or a moment when someone is speaking and you're not on the spot), a brief mindfulness meditation on the breath can center you. You don't need any special posture—sit comfortably and direct your attention to the sensation of breathing. Notice the inhale and exhale, the feeling of air entering your nose or the rise and fall of your chest. Whenever your mind wanders (which it will, especially if you're stressed), gently bring your focus back to the breath. Even doing this for a minute or two can slow your heart rate and quiet the swirl of thoughts. It's like hitting "reset" on your internal state.

- Soothing rhythm breathing: This is a specific breathing technique often used to calm the nervous system. It involves taking slow, deep breaths at a steady rhythm—for instance, inhaling for a count of four, exhaling for a count of six, and repeating. By elongating the exhale, you stimulate the body's relaxation response (the parasympathetic nervous system), which naturally lowers stress arousal. You can do this subtly in a meeting without anyone noticing by breathing a bit deeper and more slowly. After 5–10 breaths, you'll likely notice a shift toward calm. Coaches sometimes teach this technique to teams as a way to collectively cool down a heated discussion.

- *Physical anchors and PQ Brain "activation":* In the Positive Intelligence approach, when you notice your Saboteurs hijacking your mind, one way to shift to your calmer, wiser PQ Brain (the Sage region of the brain) is through a PQ rep—a quick focus on a physical sensation. The idea is to activate a different part of your brain by concentrating on a subtle sensory detail for at least 10 seconds. For example, you might rub your thumb and forefinger together with such intense attention that you can feel the fingerprint ridges on

CHAPTER 14   MASTERING THE INNER GAME: STAYING GROUNDED IN CHAOS

each finger. Alternatively, you might focus on listening for the quietest sound in the room or become acutely aware of the sensation of your feet pressing into the floor. This laser focus on a physical sensation crowds out the negative chatter for a moment and helps shift your brain's gears. Think of it as a mental push-up; each rep strengthens your self-command. If you practice these "PQ reps" regularly (even when not stressed), you'll build the muscle to center yourself when things get tough quickly. Many coaches integrate these micro-techniques into their day—for instance, doing a few reps while waiting for a Zoom meeting to start or during a walk between offices—so that they can use them more easily in a pinch.

Scenario Based on a Real Story (Continued)

Let's return to that escalating team conflict scenario. Two developers are arguing in the retrospective, and you've just noticed your own jaw clenching and the thought "This team is impossible." Now you take action to ground yourself. As one team member continues to vent, you quietly take a deep, subtle breath. You decide to use the "Notice five things" exercise right there in your chair. You glance around: monitor, notepad, the coffee stain on the carpet, the Agile values poster, the pen in my hand . . . You tune into the sounds: Jim's voice, Sara flipping pages, the hum of the projector, faint traffic outside, my breath going in . . . You feel your body: feet flat on the ground, back against the chair, cool air on your hands, ring on your finger, shirt collar on your neck. This barely takes 15 seconds, and no one notices you doing it. But in that brief pause, you've prevented yourself from either freezing or jumping in reactively. You then exhale slowly, feeling your shoulders drop slightly. This short grounding sequence creates a bit of

CHAPTER 14   MASTERING THE INNER GAME: STAYING GROUNDED IN CHAOS

mental space. Now, instead of being swept up in the team's emotion or your own, you have regained a measure of composure. You're ready to respond more intentionally—perhaps by calmly intervening to set some ground rules for the discussion—rather than, say, snapping "Everyone stop it now!" out of sheer overwhelm. Grounding yourself has helped you stay grounded during the storm.

Unhooking from Difficult Thoughts and Feelings—Defusion and Acceptance

Even as you ground yourself in the present, you might still find that difficult thoughts or feelings are clinging to you. Perhaps you calmed your breathing, but that thought "This team is impossible" is still looping in your head. Or a feeling of anxiety is still twisting your stomach. It's normal—we can't just delete thoughts or feelings on command. What we can do is change how we relate to them so they don't dictate our actions. This is where techniques from Acceptance and Commitment Therapy (ACT) are especially useful: unhooking from thoughts (known as cognitive defusion) and making room for feelings (known as acceptance), as follows:

- *Unhooking from mental traps:* When we're distressed, our minds often get **"hooked"** by unhelpful thoughts and beliefs. You might fuse with ideas like "I'm a terrible coach," or "They have no respect for me," or "This whole project is doomed." When fused, we treat these thoughts as literal truths and orders that must be followed, which can lead us to behave in ways that pull us away from who we want to be (ACT calls these "away moves"—actions driven by fear or impulse that stray from our values). The goal in ACT is not to eliminate the thoughts (good luck with that!), but to reduce

CHAPTER 14 MASTERING THE INNER GAME: STAYING GROUNDED IN CHAOS

their power over you. You learn to see them for what they really are: just transient mental content—words and images passing through your mind—rather than objective truths or threats.

- *ACT cognitive defusion techniques: Defusion* means creating a bit of distance or separation ("de-fuse") between you and your thoughts so you're no longer tangled up in them. One classic defusion move is to add a simple phrase in front of the thought: *"I am having the thought that . . ."* For example, instead of *"I'm a failure as a coach,"* you tell yourself: *"I am having the thought that I'm a failure as a coach."* Notice what that does—it turns the thought from a statement of fact ("I am X") into a noticed experience (*"I am observing this thought"*). This subtle linguistic trick reminds you that the thought is just that—a thought, not a concrete reality. It's like shifting from looking *from* your thoughts to looking *at* your thoughts. You become more objective and less entangled. Another defusion technique is to literally name the story your mind is telling—e.g., *"Ah, the 'this team is impossible' story is here."* Or you might imagine the thought in a silly voice or as a caption on a cartoon—anything that helps you see it as just words, not something to believe automatically. The point is not to ridicule your mind, but to observe it with a bit of detachment. As ACT teaches, you have a **"Thinking Self"** (the part of you that produces the stream of thoughts, judgments, memories, etc.) and an **"Observing Self"** (the part of you that is aware and notices experience without judgment). By stepping into your Observing Self, you can watch the internal drama without getting consumed by it.

461

CHAPTER 14   MASTERING THE INNER GAME: STAYING GROUNDED IN CHAOS

In ACT metaphors, you might hear that you are the sky, and your thoughts and feelings are like the weather—sometimes stormy, but always moving through; you are not the storm. Or the "chessboard metaphor": you are the chessboard and your thoughts/feelings are the chess pieces fighting—you can watch the battle without being a piece in it. These images reinforce that you are the container, not the content of your thoughts. By holding this perspective, upsetting thoughts have less bite, and you gain freedom to choose your response.

- *Acceptance and expansion:* Along with defusing from thoughts, we practice acceptance of feelings. Note: Acceptance in ACT doesn't mean liking the feeling or resigning yourself to suffering. It simply means acknowledging and making space for your real feelings, instead of futilely fighting them. If you're feeling anxious, you notice that anxiety in your body and allow it to be present ("I see you, anxiety") rather than desperately trying to suppress it or pretend you're fine. Why do this? Because often the struggle against emotional pain (*"I must not feel anxious; this is bad!"*) just adds another layer of stress (now you're anxious and mad at yourself for it). Instead, ACT suggests we treat feelings like the weather—if it's raining, you can't stop the rain by yelling at the clouds. You can, however, let the rain be and figure out how to still move forward (perhaps with an umbrella or a raincoat). In practice, if you feel a surge of anger or fear during a tense meeting, acceptance might mean quietly name the feeling ("There's anger here"), breathe into it (sometimes I literally imagine breathing around the tight feeling in my chest to give it space), and let it sit there without immediately reacting to it. You might even inwardly say, "It's okay, I can be with this feeling." Paradoxically, when you stop fighting the feeling, it often loses its intensity—like loosening a Chinese finger trap by not pulling so hard. You're not feeding it additional energy through resistance. This frees up attention to focus on what matters next.

- *Reframing Perspectives:* Another tool to handle difficult thoughts is conscious reframing. This is a bit different from ACT defusion (which doesn't challenge the thought's content, just our relationship to it). Reframing is more of a coaching technique where you intentionally choose to interpret the situation in a more constructive way. For example, if your immediate thought is *"This stakeholder is being a pain and blocking us,"* you might reframe it to, *"This stakeholder is really concerned about risk—how can that perspective help us address issues proactively?"* Look for the positive intention behind someone's behavior or the silver lining in a challenge. A "challenging team" can be reframed as *"an opportunity for me to sharpen my conflict facilitation skills."* A project failure might be *"a chance to learn what didn't work and improve for next time."* Be genuine—reframing isn't about sugar-coating reality or blind optimism; it's about finding *useful* and reality-based ways to view the situation. Another reframing approach is to recall exceptions—times when the problem was absent or less severe. If you think *"The team never cooperates,"* challenge that: Was there *ever* a time they did cooperate? What was different then? Such questions open your mind to a more nuanced picture, away from all-or-nothing judgments, and often reveal potential solutions.

CHAPTER 14   MASTERING THE INNER GAME: STAYING GROUNDED IN CHAOS

Scenario Based on a Real Story (Continued)

After grounding yourself in the heated retrospective, you still notice that judgmental thought lingering: "This team is impossible; they just want to fight." Now, consciously, you practice defusion. In your mind, you rephrase it: "I am having the thought that this team is impossible." You might even imagine that sentence in a cartoon bubble or say it in a goofy Homer Simpson voice internally—anything to take it a bit less seriously. This simple step lessens the thought's grip; it's not a truth, it's just your stressed brain barking an opinion. You remind yourself: There's your Thinking Self churning out judgments, and your Observing Self, who can just watch it and say, "Interesting, my mind is throwing labels around." You choose to adopt the Observing Self perspective, almost as if you were a fly on the wall watching the whole scene (including your own inner reactions) with curiosity.

You also acknowledge the feelings in the room (and within you) like weather passing through. "Wow, there's a storm of anger between Jim and Raj, and I feel a knot of anxiety in my stomach . . . This is like a sudden thunderstorm in our retrospective." Instead of seeing these emotions as a threat to your competence or something to panic about, you remind yourself: storms blow in, and they blow out. This particular conflict is intense but temporary. You can't stop the storm by sheer force, but you can navigate through it. Like a sailor in rough seas, you focus on steadying your own ship (your inner state) and charting a course, rather than cursing the waves. By defusing your thoughts and accepting the feelings present (in yourself and the team), you find you're less hooked. The thought "they're impossible" doesn't feel as compelling; it's just one perspective, and you know other perspectives are possible. In fact, you counteract it by reframing: "This team is having a tough conflict right now, but it doesn't mean they're always like this. They've worked well together in the past (I recall last month's smooth release). This conflict might be a sign they care about the project, even if it's messy. My job is to help them channel that energy constructively." This new framing—*conflict as caring*—gives you a more optimistic and purposeful mindset to intervene. You see the "storm" now as something you can guide them through, rather than an omen of doom. With this shift, you feel a surge of determination to coach through the conflict, not just suppress it.

Reconnecting with Your Purpose and Values

When chaos reigns and you feel lost or overwhelmed, one of the most stabilizing things you can do is to reconnect with your deeper purpose and core values as an Agile coach. Think of your values as your internal compass or North Star—they help orient you when external situations are confusing or tough. Values are fundamental to choosing effective, committed actions. They represent what truly matters to you, in the grand scheme of things. By clarifying and remembering your values, you can break out of reactive mode and decide on a response that aligns with the kind of coach (and person) you want to be, as follows:

- *Clarifying your Agile coaching values:* Take some time (outside of crises) to reflect on and write down the core values that drive you as a coach. Ask yourself: "What kind of coach do I aspire to be? What do I want to stand for, especially in difficult moments?" Common coaching values might include trust, collaboration, empathy, courage, respect, learning, empowerment, transparency, psychological safety, and so on. For example, you might identify "I value fostering an environment of trust and safety" or "I value growth and continuous learning for myself and others." These values act like a compass. In a stormy moment, you can pause and ask, "What value do I want to express right now?" If you stand for psychological safety, then in a conflict you'll aim to respond in a way that increases safety (perhaps by ensuring each person is heard respectfully), rather than, say, taking sides or shutting people down. If you value collaboration, you'll try to steer even a nasty disagreement toward a cooperative problem-solving discussion. Writing your values down and even visualizing your best self as a coach can deepen this connection. An exercise might be: write a short description of "what I look like when I'm being the coach I most want to be," or list behaviors that align with each value (e.g., Value = respect; Behaviors = I listen fully without interrupting; I acknowledge people's contributions, even small ones). This preparatory work builds a strong sense of purpose that you can call upon in tough times.

- *Committed action (moving toward values):* Values by themselves are like directions on a compass—they tell you where to go, but you still need to take steps. In ACT, committed action means taking concrete steps guided by your values, especially when it's hard. It's "committed" because it's about pledging to act in line with what truly matters to you, come what may. A key point is that these actions can be small and incremental; in fact, small is often better because it's more achievable under stress. For an Agile coach, a committed action might be as simple as: "In this meeting, I will speak up to ensure the junior developer's voice is included, because I value respect and inclusion," or "I will directly address the tension I sense between the PO and the tech lead, because I value transparency, even though it feels uncomfortable." Living your values often requires courage—doing the right thing rather than the easy thing—and that's why being grounded in purpose helps so much. When you choose a values-driven action, you're making a "towards move" (moving toward what matters to you) even if unpleasant feelings accompany it. This is the essence of ACT: accept the feelings, choose the values-based action. It's okay if your voice shakes or your heart pounds while you do it—that's true courage and growth. Each time you act in accordance with your values, you strengthen your sense of integrity and personal agency, which makes future tough situations easier to navigate.

- *The Sage's guiding light:* In Positive Intelligence terms, this alignment with values and purpose is like tapping into your Sage's Navigate power. The Sage perspective is your inner wise self, and one of its five powers is Navigate, which is all about keeping you aligned with your deeper meaning, mission, and values. When you invoke the Navigate power, you ask questions like, *"What course of action would be most meaningful here?"* or *"Which option aligns best with my core purpose or the team's ultimate goals?"* It's a longer-term, big-picture perspective—like climbing up to see the lighthouse while in a storm so you can recalibrate your direction. In practice, this might involve briefly recalling *why* you became an Agile coach in the first place: maybe to help create workplaces where people thrive, or to enable teams to build products that truly help users, or to transform organizational culture for the better. Connecting to that "why" can cut through the immediate noise and stress, giving you a calming sense of direction. It's like, *"Ah, right, this is why I'm here. I'm here to help this team work better together, so what can I do right now that serves that mission?"* Even in chaos, this clarity of purpose is grounding—it shifts you from a reactive stance to a proactive, values-driven stance.

Scenario Based on a Real Story (Continued)

In our ongoing scenario, you've grounded yourself and defused the initial onslaught of thoughts and feelings. Now the two team members are staring each other down, and the rest of the team is silent and uncomfortable. This is a pivotal moment. You take a quick mental step back and ask yourself, "What is my purpose here as their coach? What do I stand for?" Immediately, you recall that you deeply value healthy team dynamics and open communication. You genuinely want this team not just to deliver software, but to grow in trust and collaboration. This conflict, as messy as it is, presents an opportunity to coach them toward that value—if handled well. You also value courage and truth—meaning you don't want just to sweep this conflict under the rug to make the meeting superficially pleasant; you want to help them address it and learn from it. Internally, you affirm to yourself: "I am here to foster safety and growth. This is uncomfortable, but this is exactly when it matters most to live those values." Reconnecting with that purpose brings a steadiness to you—like an anchor in the storm.

Now, guided by those values, you commit to a course of action: You decide you will intervene to facilitate a resolution. A specific committed action might form in your mind: "I'm going to calmly interrupt, acknowledge the tension, and guide them in finding a better way to discuss this issue." This aligns with your value of improving team communication. You know it might be tough—maybe both individuals will be defensive—

and a part of you feels nervous about stepping in. But because you see it as a move toward what truly matters (instead of just a reaction to make the noise stop), you feel morally fortified. In essence, you choose a purposeful response over a knee-jerk reaction. Instead of, say, admonishing them ("Cut it out, you two!" which might be an impulse from frustration), you might say something like, "Okay, let's pause for a moment. I can sense how strongly both of you feel about this. Our goal isn't to blame; it's to solve this together. Let's remember we're on the same team. Can we try to reset and approach this one step at a time?" You might remind them (and the whole team) of the working agreement or prime directive, if you have one for retrospectives, which often states that we assume everyone did their best and focus on improvement, not blame. By speaking from your values, your tone is firm yet caring, rather than angry. You're effectively serving as the team's "lighthouse," guiding them back on course. And even if it's still a bumpy conversation, you can take pride afterward knowing you acted in alignment with your core coaching purpose.

Shifting to Sage Mode—Leveraging Your Innate Powers

Up to now, we've talked about managing the inner storm—noticing Saboteurs, grounding, defusing, remembering your values. The ultimate aim of all these steps is to help you shift from a negative, distressed state (dominated by Saboteurs) into a more positive, clear-headed state. In Shirzad Chamine's Positive Intelligence terms, that means shifting from Saboteur mode to Sage mode (Table 14-2). Think of Saboteur mode as when your "survival brain" is running the show—you're in fight/flight/freeze, driven by fear, anger, ego, etc., which narrows your perspective and creativity. Sage mode, however, is when your "positive brain" circuits are activated—you feel calmer, centered, and capable of handling challenges with curiosity and empathy. The good news is that the Sage is already

CHAPTER 14   MASTERING THE INNER GAME: STAYING GROUNDED IN CHAOS

within you (it's the part that knows your values, loves coaching, and wants the best for teams). You don't have to invent it; you just need to access it by weakening Saboteurs and strengthening Sage responses.

Table 14-2. *Saboteur vs. Sage*

Saboteur Mode	Sage Mode
Judgmental, reactive, fear-based	Curious, intentional, values-driven
Tight chest, racing thoughts	Centered body, present attention
Blame or avoidance	Exploration and ownership
"I need to fix this now or I've failed"	"What's the opportunity for growth here?"

- *From Saboteur to Sage:* The goal is to gradually make Sage mode your default response, even under stress. This doesn't mean you'll never feel negative emotions (you will, you're human!), but it does mean you recover faster and choose a Sage-powered response more often. It's like building a mental habit: catch the Saboteur, do a quick grounding or reframing, and invite the Sage perspective in. One way to evoke Sage mode is to ask yourself, *"What would my wiser, empathic self do in this situation?"* or *"If I were coaching someone else through this, what would I advise from a place of clear-headed wisdom?"* Sometimes, even imagining a symbol of your Sage (perhaps an image of a calm mentor you admire, or your future self who's an "Agile coaching master") can help you shift gears. It's a proactive stance: You're not just trying to survive the chaos, you're aiming to harness it or transform it into something useful. Chamine suggests that every problem or conflict can be seen as a potential gift or opportunity through the Sage

CHAPTER 14   MASTERING THE INNER GAME: STAYING GROUNDED IN CHAOS

perspective. In practice, shifting to Sage might mean literally taking a brief timeout to do a PQ rep or recall a Sage mantra (for instance, one Sage perspective is curiosity—you might say, "Hmm, I'm curious what is really upsetting Jim right now" instead of "Jim is such a pain"). This mental shift opens up a suite of positive ways to respond.

- *The five Sage powers in action:* The Sage in Positive Intelligence has five key abilities, or "powers," that you can apply in challenging situations. Let's illustrate each of these and how an Agile coach might use them when chaos hits:

    1. Empathize—This is the power of understanding and compassion, directed both at others and yourself. In a conflict or high-stress moment, activating empathy means pausing to see and acknowledge the human emotions truly involved. For instance, with two team members fighting, the Sage's empathetic power would have you think, *"They must both be feeling hurt or frustrated about something important."* Instead of judging them as "difficult," you become curious about their feelings and what's underneath the anger. You might say, *"I can tell you both care a lot about this. It sounds like there's frustration and maybe disappointment here—is that right?"* By naming and validating feelings, you help people feel heard. Empathy power also applies to you as the coach—instead of beating yourself up for "losing control of

the meeting," you give yourself some grace: *"This is tough, and I'm doing my best. It's okay to feel a bit shaken; I can still help from here."* Empathy has a calming effect; it builds trust and de-escalates tension because people sense genuine care. In leadership, showing empathy even toward those resisting change can be transformative—e.g., recognizing that a leader's resistance to Agile might stem from their own fear of losing status or feeling insecure in a new system. By empathizing with that, you approach them as an ally addressing a fear, rather than an enemy in a power struggle.

2. Explore—This power is about curiosity, an open mind, and a beginner's mindset. When you engage Explore, you drop assumptions and really investigate what's going on, asking questions without blame. In our retrospective conflict example, an Explore approach could facilitate a blameless post-mortem of the conflict itself once things cool down: *"Let's understand what happened here, step by step, without blaming. What led up to this? What are each of you concerned about?"* You encourage a *"blameless autopsy"* (as they say in Agile/DevOps) where the goal is to learn, not punish. You might use open-ended questions to dig deeper: *"Jim, what's the core issue for you in this argument? Raj, what do you feel is not being acknowledged?"* By exploring, you turn a conflict into a *process discovery*. This Sage power treats

problems as puzzles or opportunities to gain insight. It's exactly what we do in retrospectives at a larger scale—find the root cause, learn from it. With Explore activated, a coach remains inquisitive rather than accusatory. Even outside conflicts, say a new Agile practice isn't sticking, the Sage approach is to get curious: *"That's interesting—the daily stand-ups are faltering. I wonder why? Let's gather some data or perspectives."* This mindset is the opposite of the Judge Saboteur. It's open and eager to learn, which generally leads to better understanding and creative solutions.

3. Innovate—This is the power of creativity and outside-the-box thinking. After (or during) exploration, the Sage loves to ask, *"What's a completely different way we could approach this?"* In a tense situation, innovating might involve suggesting a novel solution or reframing the problem entirely. For example, in the team conflict, once you've empathized and explored the root issues (perhaps it turns out they're arguing about code quality versus speed of delivery), you might facilitate *brainstorming options* they hadn't considered. Maybe you introduce a new idea like: *"How about we experiment with a pair programming session next sprint to alleviate the code quality concerns?"* or *"Could we establish a short-term quality gate that satisfies both of you?"* Innovate means you don't bind yourself to the usual

solutions. You encourage creativity in how the team resolves issues—perhaps using a game or metaphor to help them see things from a different perspective (e.g., *"Let's imagine this problem from the customer's perspective"* or *"If this conflict were a story, how might we rewrite the ending?"*). By tapping Innovate, you help the team break out of rigid thinking or win-lose frames. For an Agile coach personally, innovating in the moment might also mean using a surprising coaching move to shift energy—maybe you draw a quick diagram on the whiteboard to illustrate the impasse, or propose a fun retrospective activity to address tension indirectly. The spirit of Innovate is playful and inventive, which can diffuse heaviness and open new possibilities free from the Saboteurs' tunnel vision.

4. Navigate—As mentioned, Navigate is about aligning with what's truly important in the big picture (your values, your purpose, the team's overarching goals). In action, the Navigate power might prompt you to ask the team to step back momentarily and consider the long-term vision or common purpose. For instance, in the conflict, you might remind everyone: *"We all want this project to succeed, and we all care about quality and hitting our deadlines. Let's remember we're on the same side trying to achieve the same outcome."* This helps shift the perspective from one another to the problem,

CHAPTER 14   MASTERING THE INNER GAME: STAYING GROUNDED IN CHAOS

realigning them as collaborators. Navigate can also mean helping individuals connect a difficult task to a bigger personal purpose. For instance, if a team member is very resistant to test automation, you as a coach might help them see how learning this skill could advance their career or reduce late-night stress in releases, tying it to something they value. In your internal dialogue, Navigate might involve asking, *"What action here would best serve the organization's Agile journey?"* or *"What would future me be proud that I did in this scenario?"* It provides direction when you're at a fork in the road. Teams often struggle in chaos because they lose sight of their North Star; the coach's Sage uses Navigate to shine a light on that North Star again so decisions can be made in service of it.

5. Activate—This is the power to move into *decisive action* with clarity and focus once the other powers have informed a path. It's about avoiding analysis paralysis or endless processing. In Sage mode, Activate means you take clear, positive action untainted by the Saboteurs' second-guessing or emotional hijacking. Continuing our vignette, an Activate moment might be when you conclude the conflict mediation by saying: *"Alright, here's what we'll do: Jim and Raj, you will pair tomorrow morning to review the code in question together and come up with a joint improvement*

475

plan. I'll sit in for the first 15 minutes to help facilitate. Additionally, we'll briefly discuss this in the next stand-up to ensure transparency with the team. Are we all agreed on this course of action?" You lay out a concrete next step that embodies what was discussed. You do this calmly and confidently—that's Sage's influence. Activate isn't a rushed, panicky action (that would be Saboteur-driven); it's purposeful. It's like a surgeon making the precise incision after careful diagnosis, rather than a flustered reaction. In a broader sense, Activate for an Agile coach could be deciding on any next small step to improve things: maybe scheduling an off-site team bonding if morale is low, or directly asking a silent team member for their input to activate inclusion. The key is, it's action born from a quiet, focused mind. When you're in Sage mode, you can commit to action without those nagging doubts because you've engaged empathy, explored options, aligned to values, and now it's just time to move forward.

Scenario Based on a Real Story (Conclusion)

You've decided to shift into Sage mode to handle the retrospective conflict fully. First, you silently infuse yourself with Empathize power: You look at the two arguing team members and genuinely acknowledge to yourself, "They both care and are feeling threatened/frustrated. They're human, like me." This softens your attitude from irritation to compassion. Then you Explore out loud; you say, "Let's understand what's really at the heart of this. Jim, what's the main concern you're raising?" and then, "Raj, how do

CHAPTER 14   MASTERING THE INNER GAME: STAYING GROUNDED IN CHAOS

you see it?" You listen actively to each, perhaps using coaching techniques to ensure they each feel heard (e.g., paraphrasing their points). It turns out Jim is worried that rushing features is causing poor quality, and Raj feels pressure from leadership to deliver faster and thinks quality issues are being exaggerated. Now you Innovate by suggesting a creative solution: "It seems we have a quality-versus-speed dilemma. What if we did a one-sprint experiment: pair programming on critical tasks to boost quality without slowing velocity too much? Maybe we can satisfy both aims." The team considers this, and it's a novel idea they hadn't tried—their tension eases as they shift to problem solving. You help them Navigate by reminding them of the shared goal: "Ultimately, we all want to deliver a product we're proud of and meet the business needs. Let's keep that in mind—we're finding a way to do both." This re-focuses them on collaborative success rather than personal point-scoring. Finally, you Activate by clearly outlining the next steps: You set up the pairing experiment for the next sprint and schedule a follow-up to evaluate it. The formerly warring team members agree to this plan. You might even have them shake hands or verbally acknowledge each other's good intent before closing the retrospective.

As the meeting comes to a close, you reflect on what has happened. By accessing your Sage powers, you transformed what could have been a disastrous meeting into a productive turning point. Instead of leaving with more profound resentment, the team leaves with an action plan and perhaps a newfound respect for how conflicts can be handled. This is the power of mastering your inner game—you not only stayed grounded yourself, but also helped the team as a whole find its grounding again. Over time, as you repeat this pattern, you'll notice your default response to chaos becomes less about stress and more about "Which Sage power do I need now?"—a far more empowering stance.

CHAPTER 14   MASTERING THE INNER GAME: STAYING GROUNDED IN CHAOS

Integration and Continuous Practice—Your Coach's Toolbox

Mastering the inner game isn't a one-and-done achievement. It's an ongoing practice, much like agility itself—a continuous journey of inspection and adaptation, applied inward. In this final section, let's discuss how you can integrate these techniques into daily coaching life and build habits that strengthen your resilience over time. I'd like to offer a few practical "tools" for your toolbox for in-the-moment coaching challenges.

- *Developing a sustainable practice:* Just as teams conduct retrospectives to continually improve, Agile coaches benefit from regular self-reflection and practice to reinforce their inner skills. Consider establishing a simple routine, such as a daily reflective practice. This could be 5–10 minutes at the end of each day to mentally replay and assess your coaching interactions: *What went well today? Where did I get triggered or feel off-center? How did I respond, and how might I want to respond differently next time?* You might keep a small journal of these notes. By reviewing these, patterns might emerge (e.g., "*I tend to lose grounding when the CTO questions me in meetings*"), which gives you specific areas to work on. Additionally, do weekly or monthly check-ins with yourself. For example, each Friday afternoon, step away to a quiet spot and evaluate your week: *Where did I demonstrate the inner game mastery I aspire to? Where did I slip? What did I learn?* You can even set a small improvement goal for the next week (e.g., "Practice at least one grounding exercise each day," or "If conflict arises, remember to pause and use at least one Sage power"). Treat it as your

CHAPTER 14   MASTERING THE INNER GAME: STAYING GROUNDED IN CHAOS

personal Kaizen. If you have a mentor or fellow coach, discussing these reflections can add accountability and insight. The key is consistency—the more regularly you practice these mental and emotional skills, the more natural they will become under pressure.

- *Go-to practices for in-the-moment coaching:* It helps to have a few quick tools or phrases at the ready for those trigger moments. We've covered many (breathing, sensing, defusion, etc.), but here are a few more "in the moment" tricks:

  - Stress inoculation phrases: These are short, calming phrases you say to yourself when you feel triggered—a form of positive self-talk to counter the Saboteurs. They work like a mental vaccine against stress. Examples: *"I've handled tough situations before; I can handle this too."* Or *"This is temporary; I will get through it."* Or even a simple *"Breathe . . . stay present . . . it's okay."* Find a phrase that resonates and practice using it. Some coaches write them on a sticky note as a reminder. Over time, your brain begins to accept these assurances, reducing the panic response. It's like having your internal coach always with you—giving you a pep talk when needed.

  - "Ask-Tell-Ask" communication: When you need to provide feedback or intervene, a helpful structure is Ask-Tell-Ask, which comes from coaching and medical communication models. First, Ask the person for their perspective (*"How do you feel the sprint is going so far?"*). This engages them and shows respect. Then Tell—share your observation or feedback (*"I noticed in the retrospective there were a lot of interruptions during discussion, which might be a sign people don't feel heard."*). Keep it factual and neutral. Finally, Ask again—invite their thoughts or an action plan (*"What are your thoughts on that? Anything we could try to improve listening next time?"*). This approach turns feedback into a two-way conversation. It can be especially useful if you're nervous about giving direct feedback—it keeps things collaborative and less confrontational.

- Constructive challenging (with permission): Sometimes, as a coach, you need to challenge a team or an individual—perhaps calling out a contradiction (*"You say quality is important, but you skipped writing tests again"*) or pushing them to confront an uncomfortable issue. Doing this skilfully is an art. One tip is to ask for permission first, which can create psychological safety. For example: *"I'd like to challenge us on something I'm observing—would that be okay?"* or to a client, *"Would you be open to a tough question about what you just said?"* If they consent (they almost always do, because curiosity is piqued), they're psychologically bracing and ready, instead of feeling blindsided. Then deliver the challenge in a non-personal way, focusing on behavior or discrepancy, not character; e.g., *"You shared that you value open communication, yet I notice in stand-ups you often avoid mentioning blockers.*

How does that fit?" Challenging with care can lead to breakthroughs, and by seeking permission, you show respect and partnership.

- *Reflection prompts for deeper learning:* In your personal retrospectives or even when stuck in a moment, asking yourself powerful coaching questions can unlock new insights. Here are some prompts to use on yourself:

  - *"What assumptions am I making right now?"*—Perhaps you're assuming a leader is just being obstinate, when maybe they have pressures you're unaware of. Challenging your assumptions can reveal new approaches.

  - *"What does this situation tell me about my own beliefs or values in action?"*—For instance, feeling very upset in a conflict might reveal how much you value harmony or respect. It can highlight what's non-negotiable for you.

  - *"How can I maintain resilience here?"*—This reminds you to consider your self-care or inner tactics. The answer might be, "I need to take a short walk after this meeting to clear my head," or "I should reach out to my peer coach for a debrief later." Identifying what keeps you resilient ensures you don't neglect those resources.

  - *"What support might I need?"*—Coaches need coaching too. Maybe you realize, "I'm pretty affected by this team's conflict; perhaps I'll discuss it with my supervisor or a mentor to get a perspective." There's strength in knowing when to seek help or at least a sounding board.

CHAPTER 14 MASTERING THE INNER GAME: STAYING GROUNDED IN CHAOS

- *"What is the client's (or team's) preferred future?"*—This is a solution-focused question. It shifts attention to a vision of success: "If this conflict or issue were resolved in the best possible way, what would that look like?" Picturing that can reduce anxiety and also guide your next steps (you can then try to work backward from that envisioned outcome).

Scenario Based on a Real Story (Final)

Let's fast-forward. It's the end of a particularly draining week. You coached through that big conflict and a few other smaller fires. Maybe there was also resistance from a senior manager about the team's new approach, which took a lot of diplomatic effort on your part. By Friday, you're feeling a bit exhausted. Here's how integration and continuous practice come into play: You decide to dedicate the last hour of your work week to personal reflection and reset. You find a quiet corner or maybe a nearby park bench. With journal in hand, you reflect on the week: You write down the high points (the conflict got resolved, the team actually thanked you for facilitating it) and the low points (you notice you felt especially triggered when the manager implied the timeline issues were due to "this Agile nonsense"—that really got under your skin). You realize that comment spiked your Judge Saboteur, which led you to feel defensive. You jot, "Assumption check—I assumed he was dismissing my competence; maybe he's just under pressure." You consider how you might handle it next time: perhaps by using Empathize (acknowledging his pressure) and Explore (asking him to share his concerns more fully) rather than getting tense.

Next, you revisit your core values list that you had created earlier. You ask: "Did I live these values this week?" For example, if one value is collaboration, you might note, "Yes, especially when I involved the team in brainstorming solutions to their conflict." If another value is calm leadership, you might admit, "I lost my calm a bit in that meeting with the manager—something to work on." You then identify two small committed actions for next week to realign or grow: one, each morning you'll do a five-minute mindfulness practice to start centered; two, you plan to practice "ask-tell-ask" with the team when giving them some feedback about meeting etiquette. You also write a stress inoculation phrase at the top of next week's planner: "Remember, focus on purpose, not pressure." Finally, you close your journal with a short note of self-compassion: "This was hard, and I handled a lot. It's okay to rest now." Perhaps you even do a quick three-minute breathing meditation to symbolically let go of the week's stress.

By intentionally reflecting and planning in this way, you are reinforcing your inner game muscles. You walk away from this personal retrospective feeling a bit lighter and more confident. You know you have a plan for maintaining your grounding, and you've learned from the week's experiences instead of carrying them as baggage. This continuous practice ensures that, over time, chaos rattles you less and less. Just like an Agile team improves with each sprint, you, as an Agile coach, improve your inner agility with each reflection cycle. You'll find yourself more frequently in that centred Sage zone by default, which not only makes you more effective but also makes this work more joyful and sustainable.

Conclusion

Staying grounded in chaos is an essential skill for an Agile team coach, and it's entirely learnable. By listening to your body's signals, naming your Saboteurs, grounding your mind, unhooking from thought traps, and reconnecting with your purpose, you create the space to choose your best response. Then, leveraging empathy, curiosity, creativity, values-guidance, and decisive action—those Sage powers—you can turn even the fiercest storm into an opportunity for growth and connection. It's the inner game

CHAPTER 14   MASTERING THE INNER GAME: STAYING GROUNDED IN CHAOS

mastery that complements your outer game of Agile practices. As you cultivate this inner resilience through continuous practice, you'll find that not only do you weather the storms better, but you might even start to appreciate the storms for all the rich learning and transformation they invite, in both your teams and you as a coach.

Remember, you are the coach *in* the storm, but you don't have to be the coach *consumed by* the storm. With these tools, you can be the calm, guiding lighthouse that stays steady, helping everyone navigate to safe harbor. That is the true art of Agile coaching when things get chaotic—mastering your inner game so you can master the moment.

Reflection Moment

1. What are the earliest physical or emotional signs that tell me I'm becoming triggered or reactive?
2. Which inner voices or thought patterns tend to dominate when I'm under pressure?
3. When was the last time I paused instead of reacting? What did that shift make possible?
4. Which grounding technique helps me return to presence most effectively?
5. What thoughts regularly "hook" me in stressful coaching situations?
6. How do I typically respond to uncomfortable emotions during conflicts or tense situations?
7. What personal values do I most want to embody when coaching under stress?

CHAPTER 14 MASTERING THE INNER GAME: STAYING GROUNDED IN CHAOS

8. Which inner resource or mindset do I want to strengthen for handling chaos?

9. What did a recent challenging moment reveal about my inner state or habits?

10. What small practice could I commit to this week to build my inner resilience?

EPILOGUE

The Long Game: Beyond Frameworks to Living Systems

The Coach's Journey Home

Two years after our last retrospective, I found myself walking back into TechCo's sprawling campus. The invitation had come unexpectedly—not from leadership this time, but from Team Atlas itself. "We want to show you something," their message read. No crisis. No intervention needed. Just . . . come see.

What I witnessed that afternoon would have seemed impossible during our early sessions, when they couldn't even agree on a Definition of Done without my facilitation. The team was mid-sprint, dealing with what would have once been a crisis: Their product owner had just resigned, a critical integration was failing, and the CEO had requested a complete pivot in priorities. Yet there I sat, essentially invisible, watching them navigate these storms with a quality I can only describe as graceful coherence.

They didn't need me anymore. And that, I realized, was the whole point.

EPILOGUE   THE LONG GAME: BEYOND FRAMEWORKS TO LIVING SYSTEMS

This moment of recognition—when a team no longer needs their coach—isn't an ending but a revelation. After 20 years in this work, through the rise and fall of countless frameworks, through Agile transformations that transformed nothing and others that changed everything, I've come to understand that self-organization was never about the methodology. It was never about perfect Scrum events or pristine Kanban boards.

The real work, the work you've journeyed through in these pages, happens in the invisible spaces: the psychological distances we navigate, the hidden contracts we surface, the Drama Triangles we gently dismantle, the supervision conversations that keep us honest. The real work is helping teams see their own patterns, honor their resistance as information, and build structures that enable rather than constrain their collective intelligence.

As you close this book and return to your teams—whether they're struggling with their first sprint or navigating complex organizational dynamics—remember that you're not trying to create perfectly Agile teams. You're cultivating living systems capable of continuous adaptation. The shift from "doing Agile" to "being Agile" isn't semantic; it's the difference between compliance and transformation.

Beyond the Fatigue: Seven Durable Principles

We live in an era of Agile fatigue. Teams roll their eyes at another framework, another certification, another transformation initiative. They've been through SAFe, LeSS, Spotify Model variations, and homebrew combinations that promised salvation but delivered only new forms of confusion. Yet beneath this exhaustion lies opportunity—the chance to return to principles that transcend any particular methodology.

EPILOGUE   THE LONG GAME: BEYOND FRAMEWORKS TO LIVING SYSTEMS

Through thousands of hours with teams, through supervision sessions that challenged my assumptions, through the humbling moments when my interventions backfired spectacularly, seven principles have emerged as constellation points for navigation. These aren't rules but living tensions to hold:

1. **Contact before contract — always.** Before any agreement, methodology, or intervention comes a human connection. Teams don't resist change; they resist being changed by strangers. Whether you're introducing a new practice or confronting dysfunction, establish genuine contact first. See the humans before the roles, the anxiety beneath the resistance, the hope hiding behind the cynicism.

2. **The system holds the pattern.** Individual behavior is usually system behavior in disguise. That "difficult" team member? They're likely expressing something that needs to be said but can't be voiced directly. That recurring conflict between teams? Look for the organizational structure and create it. As we discovered, the exploration of power dynamics reveals that the pattern isn't personal—it's systemic. Your intervention point isn't the individual but the system that shapes them.

3. **Resistance is information, not opposition.** To turn resistance into resilience, we must first receive it as data. When a team resists your coaching, they're not rejecting you—they're protecting something vital. Perhaps it's their last vestige of autonomy in an over-managed organization. Perhaps it's a survival mechanism developed through past

betrayals. Listen to resistance with curiosity rather than frustration. It will teach you what the team truly needs.

4. **Supervision is safety, not surveillance.** The radical difference bears repeating: supervision isn't about monitoring performance, but about creating a reflective space for the coach's development. In an industry that valorizes lone heroes and natural talent, admitting you need supervision feels like weakness. It's not. It's the professional maturity to recognize that holding space for others requires someone to hold space for you.

5. **Teams have secret lives—respect them.** Beneath the visible layer of stand-ups and story points exists what we call the team's "secret life"—unspoken alliances, hidden contracts, psychological games played below consciousness. You can't eliminate these dynamics, nor should you try. But you can surface them gently, name them respectfully, and help teams choose which patterns serve them and which sabotage them.

6. **Power dynamics never disappear, only transform.** The egalitarian promise of self-organization doesn't erase power differentials; it reshapes them. The senior developer's technical authority, the product owner's market knowledge, the Scrum master's process expertise—these create invisible hierarchies that influence every interaction. As we learned through our exploration of psychological distance and Drama Triangles, pretending

power doesn't exist only drives it underground. Better to acknowledge it, map it, and work with it consciously.

7. **Self-organization requires structure, not chaos.**
   This paradox threads through every chapter: genuine autonomy needs clear boundaries. Working agreements, Definition of Done, sprint cadences—these aren't constraints on self-organization, but an essential scaffolding. Like the banks of a river that enable flow by providing definition, structure channels team energy toward value creation rather than endless negotiation about basics.

These principles form a constellation—distinct stars that together create a pattern for navigation. When you're lost in the complexity of a coaching engagement, when the methodologies fail and the team dynamics confound, return to these lights. They won't give you answers, but they'll orient you toward useful questions.

The Emerging Landscape: AI, Ethics, and Systems Leadership

The landscape of team coaching is shifting beneath our feet. As I write this, AI tools are already participating in daily stand-ups, generating user stories, and even attempting to facilitate retrospectives. The question isn't whether AI will impact our work—it's how we'll integrate it while preserving what makes teams essentially human.

AI as Thinking Partner, Not Replacement

The temptation to use AI for efficiency—faster story writing, automated meeting summaries, instant retrospective themes—misses the deeper opportunity. As we noted in the introduction, the risk isn't that AI will replace coaches but that teams will bypass the collaborative conversations that create shared understanding.

The path forward isn't resistance but conscious integration. Use AI as a thinking partner that surfaces patterns humans might miss. Let it analyze communication patterns to reveal hidden dynamics. Have it generate provocative questions that push teams beyond their usual thinking. But never let it replace the messy, inefficient, profoundly human work of building trust and navigating conflict together.

From Team Coaching to Ecosystem Orchestration

The boundaries of "team" are dissolving. Modern work happens across fluid networks of contributors—full-time employees, contractors, AI agents, external partners. The neat Scrum team of 7±2 people is becoming the exception.

This demands evolution from team coach to ecosystem orchestrator. You're no longer coaching a bounded team but facilitating collaboration across a constellation of interdependencies. The skills remain relevant—contracting, surfacing dynamics, building psychological safety—but applied across more complex topologies.

Responsible Metrics: Measuring Transformation, Not Velocity

The metrics that dominate Agile—velocity, burn-down rates, cycle time—measure activity, not progress. As coaches, we must promote metrics that reflect real transformation: How often do teams identify and resolve conflicts on their own? How quickly do they adjust to unexpected changes? How safe do members feel to voice dissent openly?

These are not easy to measure, which is exactly why they are important. The vital work—building trust, developing resilience, fostering innovation—resists simple measurement. Our role includes helping organizations value what truly matters beyond what can be measured.

Your 90-Day Practice Architecture

Knowledge without application remains philosophy. As you return to your teams, you need more than inspiration—you need architecture for practice. This 90-day progression isn't prescriptive but suggestive, a scaffold you can adapt to your context.

Week 0: Foundation Audit

Before beginning, map your current reality. For each team you coach, draw the triangle of team–coach–sponsor. Where are the psychological distances? Who's too close, creating a collision? Who's too distant, creating disconnection?

List the hidden contracts you sense but haven't surfaced. Note the recurring conflicts that might signal Drama Triangle dynamics. This isn't judgment but observation—seeing clearly what is before attempting to change it.

EPILOGUE THE LONG GAME: BEYOND FRAMEWORKS TO LIVING SYSTEMS

Days 1–30: Establishing Your Supervision Architecture

The first month focuses on creating your reflective support system. This isn't optional—it's the foundation that enables everything else.

Week 1: Research supervision options. Contact three potential supervisors or peer groups. Don't just consider convenience—seek challenge and growth.

Week 2: Attend your first supervision session. Bring your messiest situation, your most confounding team. Vulnerability in supervision models vulnerability with teams.

Week 3: Establish your supervision contract. Frequency, boundaries, confidentiality—make it explicit. Practice what you preach about contracting.

Week 4: Complete your first reflective cycle using the Seven-Eyed Model from Chapter 13. Work through each lens systematically. What do you see differently?

Signal of Progress: You've established a supervision arrangement that feels both supportive and challenging. You're no longer coaching alone.

Days 31–60: Surfacing Hidden Dynamics

Month two turns toward your teams, applying your developing awareness to surface what's been hidden.

Weeks 5–6: Use the Five Questions tool with each team. Who does the team work with? Why now? What do they want? Who am I invited to be? What are the structural considerations? The answers reveal the invisible forces shaping visible behavior.

Week 7: Map Drama Triangle patterns in your most challenging team. Who plays Victim? Rescuer? Persecutor? How do roles shift? Share observations gently—awareness precedes choice.

Week 8: Facilitate a psychological safety assessment with each team—not a survey but a conversation. What can't be said here? What questions can't be asked? The silences speak volumes.

Signal of Progress: Each team has named at least one previously hidden dynamic. The unspeakable has become discussable.

Days 61–90: Building Resilience Infrastructure

The final month shifts from revelation to construction—building structures that sustain transformation.

Weeks 9–10: Co-create team resilience agreements. Not rules imposed but principles discovered. What helps this specific team bounce back? What patterns support their recovery from setbacks?

Week 11: Introduce reflective practice rituals to teams. Perhaps a Monday morning check-in using metaphors, or a Friday afternoon appreciation circle. Small rituals create large changes.

Week 12: Facilitate a "learning from resistance" retrospective. Celebrate the times the team pushed back wisely. What were they protecting? How did resistance serve them?

Signal of Progress: Teams begin self-facilitating difficult conversations. They catch their own Drama Triangle patterns. They no longer wait for you to name the elephant in the room.

EPILOGUE   THE LONG GAME: BEYOND FRAMEWORKS TO LIVING SYSTEMS

The Daily Five

Beyond the 90-day architecture, establish a daily reflective practice—five minutes that compound into transformation:

1. **What patterns did I notice today?** In myself, the team, the system.
2. **What triggered me?** Irritation, impatience, and anxiety are diagnostic data about my own edges.
3. **Where did I collude?** With whom did I unconsciously align against whom?
4. **What wants to emerge?** Beyond problems to solve, what's trying to be born?
5. **How did I stay present?** When did I drift into autopilot versus conscious choice?

These questions, asked consistently, develop the reflective muscle that distinguishes masterful coaches from competent ones.

A Personal Note: On Staying True

I need to tell you something I rarely share. Three years into my coaching career, I nearly quit. Not because teams weren't improving—they were. Not because I lacked skills—I had certificates aplenty. I nearly quit because I was drowning in the gap between who I was and who I pretended to be.

In team sessions, I projected confidence while feeling fraudulent. I preached psychological safety while fearing judgment. I facilitated vulnerability while armoring my own. The performance was exhausting.

EPILOGUE   THE LONG GAME: BEYOND FRAMEWORKS TO LIVING SYSTEMS

Then I found supervision—not the evaluative kind but the reflective, compassionate, challenging kind we've explored in this book. In that safe space, I could finally admit: I don't always know what to do. Sometimes teams trigger my own unresolved conflicts. Occasionally, I make things worse.

These admissions didn't diminish me—they freed me. I stopped pretending to be the expert with answers and became a fellow human with questions. Paradoxically, this made me a far better coach.

You will face this choice repeatedly: perform invulnerability or practice authenticity. The teams don't need your perfection—they need your presence. They don't require your answers—they benefit from your curiosity. They don't demand your heroics—they flourish through your humanity.

This doesn't mean abandoning professionalism or boundaries. It means what Christine Thornton calls "professional love"—bringing your whole self to service while maintaining the container that enables transformation.

The path ahead isn't easy. You'll facilitate sessions that fall flat. You'll misread dynamics and intervene clumsily. You'll watch teams regress despite your best efforts. You'll question whether any of this makes a difference.

In those moments, remember: The work isn't about you. It's about creating conditions where teams can discover their own capacity. Your role isn't to have answers but to hold space for questions. Your expertise isn't in knowing but in not-knowing with skillful curiosity.

Find your supervision. Build your peer community. Develop your reflective practice. Not because you're deficient but because the work demands it. The teams entrust you with their dynamics, their conflicts, their potential. That trust requires that someone holds you while you hold them.

EPILOGUE THE LONG GAME: BEYOND FRAMEWORKS TO LIVING SYSTEMS

The Quiet Revolution

As I finish writing this book, I'm aware of a paradox. The Agile revolution was loud—manifestos, movements, massive transformations. But the real revolution, the one you're part of, is quiet. It happens in the moment you help a team see its own pattern. It occurs when you choose curiosity over judgment. It unfolds as teams discover they can navigate complexity without heroes or hierarchies.

This quiet revolution doesn't make headlines. It won't trend on LinkedIn. But team by team, coach by coach, supervision session by supervision session, we're creating workplaces where humans can bring their full intelligence, creativity, and humanity to collective challenges.

The journey to self-organization isn't a destination but a continuous becoming. Teams don't achieve self-organization once and maintain it forever. Like health or wisdom, it requires constant attention, adjustment, and renewal. Your role is to tend this becoming—not as an outside expert but as a committed companion on the journey.

Twenty years ago, when I began this work, I believed my job was to create self-organizing teams. Now I understand differently. Teams don't need to be created—they need to be uncovered. Beneath the dysfunction, politics, and learned helplessness, the capacity for self-organization already exists. Our work is excavation, not construction. We remove obstacles, surface dynamics, and provide structures that enable what's already present to emerge.

This shift—from creator to enabler, from expert to facilitator, from hero to companion—represents the maturation not just of individual coaches but of our entire field. We're moving beyond the mechanistic application of frameworks toward the cultivation of living systems capable of continuous adaptation.

EPILOGUE   THE LONG GAME: BEYOND FRAMEWORKS TO LIVING SYSTEMS

Closing: The Coach Who Wasn't There

Let me return to Team Atlas, the team that no longer needed me. As I sat in their team space that afternoon, watching them navigate multiple crises with fluid competence, I noticed something remarkable. They were using every principle we'd explored together—contracting clearly with stakeholders, surfacing hidden dynamics, catching themselves in Drama Triangles, holding productive conflict—but they weren't thinking about it. The principles had become embodied, as natural as breathing.

At the retrospective's end, they turned to me. "Any observations?" they asked.

I had many. I could see refinements they might make, edges they could explore, dynamics they hadn't yet noticed. But I also saw something more important: a team that had developed its own capacity for seeing. They didn't need my observations—they needed to trust their own.

"Just one," I said. "You don't need me anymore. And that's perfect."

The highest achievement of a coach isn't indispensability but irrelevance. When teams no longer need us, we haven't failed—we've succeeded. They've internalized not our expertise but their own capacity. They've discovered not our answers but their questions.

This is the art of creating self-organizing teams: not imposing organization but revealing the self-organizing capacity that was always there, waiting to be trusted, waiting to emerge, waiting to transform the very nature of work from obligation to expression, from compliance to creation, from management to mastery.

The teams are ready. The principles endure. The supervision awaits. The quiet revolution continues.

EPILOGUE THE LONG GAME: BEYOND FRAMEWORKS TO LIVING SYSTEMS

Your part in it begins now.

While the formal acknowledgments follow, I must pause here to honor every team that let me witness their journey from compliance to true self-organization—you taught me more than any certification ever could. To my supervisors who held space for my doubts and discoveries, and to the community of coaches who remind me daily that this work is too important to do alone—thank you for showing me that vulnerability is not weakness but the gateway to authentic service.

APPENDIX A

TA Cheatsheet for Agile Coaches

How to Use This Appendix

The book refers to some ideas and concepts from Transactional Analysis that have been used in the book, and it would be helpful to provide an extended description in case you feel lost or confused.

Ego States

In plain words: Think of ego states as the "voices" or modes we all have. In TA, each of us can operate from a Parent, Adult, or Child state. The *Parent* voice mimics what we learned from authority figures (it can be critical or caring). The *Child* voice is our emotional, reactive side (playful, curious, or defensive). The *Adult* voice stays present and objective, focused on facts and solutions. We all shift between these states—sometimes even within the same meeting!

Why it matters in Agile teams:

- Adult-to-Adult communication = better collaboration & decisions.
- Under stress, people slip into Parent/Child modes that derail conversations.

- Recognizing ego states can de-dramatize conflict and build empathy—you see a "harsh" comment as someone's Parent or Child mode, not a personal attack.
- Making *Adult* tone the norm supports respectful dialogue and clear problem solving (fostering self-organization).

How it shows up:

- A developer in a code review barks, "This is completely wrong—who wrote this?" (Critical Parent).
- Team members wait for a manager to direct them instead of taking initiative (Child-like dependence).
- Someone blurts "This isn't fair!" or throws up their hands in a retro (Child state).
- A team lead gives advice in a warm, "I've been there" way (Nurturing Parent).
- Two colleagues calmly examine a bug together, asking, "What are our options?" (Adult-to-Adult problem solving).

One-liner metaphor: It's like having three radio channels: Parent, Adult, Child. Tune into the Adult station for the clearest team communication.

Life Positions

In plain words: *Life positions* are basic attitudes about self and others. The healthiest is "I'm OK, You're OK," meaning you respect yourself and others as capable and worthy. Other positions include "I'm OK, You're not OK" (seeing others as the problem), "I'm not OK, You're OK" (seeing yourself as the problem), and "I'm not OK, You're not OK" (a hopeless view of everyone). These mindsets can color how team members approach collaboration, especially under stress.

Why it matters in Agile teams:

- Trust & safety baseline: "I'm OK, You're OK" fosters mutual trust and psychological safety, crucial for collaboration and self-organization.
- Low-trust signals: The other positions signal trouble. Constant blame (*I'm OK, you're not OK*) poisons team cohesion; constant self-doubt (*I'm not OK*) silences voices.
- Confidence and voice: If someone feels not OK, they may hold back ideas or defer to others, and the team loses valuable input.

How it shows up:

- A team member often says, "This team never gets it right" or "I'm surrounded by idiots!"—a clear *I'm OK, you're not OK* stance.
- Another frequently downplays their own ideas: "This might be stupid, but . . ." —a sign of *I'm not OK, you're OK*.
- The team avoids bringing up issues because "it won't matter"—drifting into *I'm not OK, you're not OK* pessimism.
- In a pairing session, both people listen and build on each other's ideas—an *OK-OK* interaction.
- After a mistake, the team says "We're all human. Let's learn and fix it," instead of finger-pointing—*OK-OK* under pressure.

One-liner metaphor: Life positions are like glasses; "I'm OK, You're OK" is the clear lens. Other positions are like distorted lenses that skew how we see each other.

Scripts and Injunctions

In plain words: A *script* is like an invisible life plan or set of rules we subconsciously follow, often formed in childhood. *Injunctions* are the big "Don't" or "Do" messages that shape those scripts (e.g., "Don't make mistakes," "Always be perfect"). In team life, these show up as personal unwritten rules that can limit behavior. Think of a script as an old story you're acting out even when it doesn't fit the current situation.

Why it matters in Agile teams:

- Unspoken team rules: Sometimes a whole team operates under a hidden mandate (e.g., "Don't question the boss" or "We must appear busy at all times"). Identifying these can prevent groupthink and burnout.

- Hidden personal blockers: Individual scripts like "Don't ask for help" or "I must be perfect" stop team members from collaborating, raising risks, or admitting issues.

- Adapting norms: Surfacing and questioning these assumptions ("Why do we always do it this way?") lets the team update habits to fit reality.

- Understanding resistance: If someone resists a change, they might be following an old rule ("Don't trust anyone," "Don't fail"). Knowing this, you can coach with empathy instead of frustration.

How it shows up:

- Despite an "open door" culture, one engineer never asks for help—likely their inner rule is "Don't be needy."

- The team consistently avoids conflict in retros, as if everyone shares "Don't make waves."

- A high performer refuses to delegate tasks, driven by "If you want it done right, do it yourself" (a perfectionist script).

- Team members downplay or ignore praise; perhaps they carry a "Don't brag" or "Don't stand out" rule.

- A new hire seeks approval for every step, echoing "Don't do anything without permission."

One-liner metaphor: Scripts are like old software running in the background—sometimes you need to update the code to work better today.

Symbiosis

In plain words: In TA, *symbiosis* means two people functioning as if they're one. One person does the thinking or deciding (taking the "Parent" or "Adult" role for both), and the other person just goes along (sticking to the "Child" role). It can feel comfortable because each avoids what the other handles, but it stunts growth. In a team, symbiosis appears as over-helping or over-relying: one person takes on responsibilities that others should share.

Why it matters in Agile teams:

- Collective ownership: Agile thrives on shared responsibility. If one leader always decides and the team just follows, true self-organization and learning can't happen.

- Single point of failure: Over-reliance on one key member is risky – if they're absent, everything stalls.

- Burnout & stagnation: The over-functioning person can burn out, while others under-function and don't develop their skills.

- Balanced team = growth: Breaking a symbiotic pattern creates a more balanced Adult–Adult dynamic. Dependent members gain confidence, and the overloaded leader can step back, making the team more resilient and creative.

How it shows up:

- The product owner writes every detail and calls every shot, while the team quietly implements—a PO/team symbiosis.

- A senior dev "saves" the team on every tough task, so others stop trying and just wait for rescue.

- In meetings, one voice (maybe a manager or a tech lead) speaks for everyone, and the rest just nod along.

- The Scrum master ends up tracking all tasks and solving all impediments for the team, effectively doing their thinking for them.

One-liner metaphor: Symbiosis in a team is like a three-legged race—two people tied together can move, but not as freely as when everyone runs on their own two feet.

Positive Strokes

In plain words: A "*stroke*" in TA means a unit of recognition—basically, any act of acknowledging someone. Positive strokes are the warm fuzzies: thank-yous, praise, a high-five, a thumbs-up. Negative strokes (criticism, scolding) count as recognition too (they're attention), but they hurt. Everyone needs strokes like plants need sunlight; we all crave to feel seen and appreciated. On an Agile team, giving genuine positive strokes fuels morale and connection.

Why it matters in Agile teams:

- Motivation and habits: When people feel valued, they're motivated to do their best and to repeat the helpful behaviors that earned praise.

- Trust and safety: A team that shares appreciation freely tends to have higher psychological safety. People know their efforts are noticed (not just their mistakes).

- Prevent "stroke hunger": If positive strokes are rare, team members might even seek negative attention (criticism) just to feel acknowledged. Keeping a healthy flow of praise prevents that and keeps focus on constructive behavior.

How it shows up:

- Teammates regularly say "Nice job on X!" or give shout-outs in retrospectives, a culture rich in positive strokes.

- A team member who only hears from others when something's wrong may start to disengage or get defensive (sign of stroke deprivation).

- Silence around good work ("no news is good news")—an environment where recognition is scarce.

- One person gets all the kudos while others' contributions are ignored—an imbalance in strokes that can breed resentment.

- The team uses a "kudos" Slack channel or does fun awards each sprint—signs that positive recognition is a norm.

One-liner metaphor: Positive strokes are the team's emotional fuel; keep the tank filled and the engine will run smoothly.

Drama Triangle

In plain words: The Drama Triangle describes three roles people slip into during conflict: Victim, Rescuer, and Persecutor. In *Victim* mode, a person feels powerless ("Poor me"). The *Rescuer* jumps in to save others (whether or not anyone asked), and the *Persecutor* blames or attacks others. It's like a bad drama where everyone has a role, and they often rotate roles without resolving the actual problem. The only way out is for someone to "step off" the triangle by moving to honest, Adult behavior; for example, by taking responsibility (instead of Victim), setting boundaries or making a clear request (instead of playing Rescuer or Persecutor).

Why it matters in Agile teams:

- Wasted energy: When a team gets caught in Victim/Rescuer/Persecutor dynamics, they spend more time in personal drama than solving the issue at hand.

- Erodes trust: These roles create one-up/one-down power dynamics (Persecutor over Victim, Rescuer over Victim). That undermines the equal, trusting environment that Agile teams need.

- Accountability lost: In the triangle, Victims deny their power, Persecutors deny their faults, Rescuers overstep boundaries. By recognizing the pattern, a coach can help the team regain personal accountability and a solution focus.

- Faster conflict resolution: The quicker someone (coach or team member) sees the drama pattern and shifts to Adult-to-Adult communication, the quicker the team can defuse conflict and find a way forward.

How it shows up:

- Victim stance: "This isn't my fault, there's nothing I can do!" or a team member who frequently looks defeated and withdraws at signs of trouble.

- Rescuer behavior: One person always tries to "fix" others' problems or protect someone from consequences: "Don't worry, I'll do your tasks too." They mean well but may foster dependency (and burn themselves out).

- Persecutor actions: Harsh blame or criticism: "Who screwed this up?!" or a cutting, sarcastic comment that makes someone feel attacked.

- Recurring patterns: Often the same drama plays out whenever there's a crisis—and people might even switch roles midstream. (Yesterday's Victim might become today's finger-pointing Persecutor.) The telltale sign is a lot of blaming or martyrdom, and not much progress on the actual problem.

APPENDIX A   TA CHEATSHEET FOR AGILE COACHES

One-liner metaphor: The Drama Triangle is like a game of hot potato—blame and helplessness get passed around until someone puts it down and addresses the real issue.

Games

In plain words: In TA, a *game* is a recurring, negative interaction pattern with a hidden payoff. It's not fun—it's more like a trap. A classic example is the "Yes, but . . ." game: one person asks for ideas, others offer help, but the person deflects every solution ("Yes, but that won't work because . . ."). The hidden payoff might be attention or avoiding change. Games often leave people feeling frustrated or guilty, and nothing really gets solved, yet the pattern repeats until someone breaks it.

Why it matters in Agile teams:

- Wasted time and frustration: Games suck up time and energy with no progress, leaving everyone cynical ("Here we go again . . ."). Morale drops when the same unproductive discussion repeats.

- Hidden problems stay hidden: Games persist because an underlying issue isn't being addressed openly (e.g., the "Yes, but" person might actually fear the proposed changes). Until the pattern is broken, the real concern remains unresolved.

- Transparency and improvement: Agile teams value openness. Spotting a game and naming it (tactfully) brings the real issue to light, so the team can tackle it and improve their process.

- Better teamwork: Breaking out of a game replaces finger-pointing or wheel-spinning with honest communication and action, moving the team forward and restoring trust.

How it shows up:

- "Yes, but..." loop: In a retro, Pat says, "We need to improve X." Team suggests ideas; Pat replies "Yes, but..." to everyone. The discussion circles until everyone gives up.
- Blame ping-pong: Two teams or colleagues keep passing blame: "We're late because *they* didn't clarify requirements"; "Well, we're late because *they* developed too slowly." The argument repeats every project with no change in process.
- One-upmanship: Team meetings turn into a contest of who has the bigger problem: "You think that's bad? Wait till you hear this..." It bonds people in commiseration, but no solution comes; a game of sharing woes instead of solving them.
- Déjà vu conversations: The team groans, "We're stuck in this conversation again." Everyone senses they've been through this exact debate or conflict multiple times (and they have).

One-liner metaphor: Games are like a team *Groundhog Day*—the same bad scene keeps replaying until someone says, "Let's try something different this time."

APPENDIX B

Techniques and Methods for Group Imago Coaching for Self-Organization

How to Use This Appendix

Chapter 5, "The Self-Organization Toolkit," describes a framework and tools for coaching, leveraging the idea of group imago development. This appendix provides a quick recap list of key techniques introduced, organized by each framework step, for easy reference:

- Step 1: Contract & Context
    - *Three-Level Contract Map:* Document administrative, professional (goals), and psychological (relational) agreements.
    - *Sponsor Alignment Checklist:* Ensure management supports team autonomy (no hidden agendas).

APPENDIX B TECHNIQUES AND METHODS FOR GROUP IMAGO COACHING FOR SELF-ORGANIZATION

- *Team Kickoff & Expectations Exercise:* Co-create ground rules and surface hopes/fears to align on how we'll work together.

- *Ethics & Boundaries Discussion:* Clarify confidentiality and the coach's role (not a decider, but a facilitator).

- Step 2: Elicit Individual Imagoes

  - *Imago Drawing:* Members draw team-at-best vs. team-at-worst to reveal internal images (share and discuss themes).

  - *Relational Genogram of Work:* Timeline of past team experiences and roles to connect past to present.

  - *Imago Interview Guide:* 10 prompts ("Who decides?", "Unsafe to say?", "Leaders must . . .", etc.) to articulate assumptions.

  - *Anonymous Assumption Poll:* Use sticky notes or digital tools to collect candid answers (e.g., "The real leader in a team is ____.").

  - *Group Reflection:* Highlight differences and commonalities in these imagos, setting stage for next step.

- Step 3: Create the Shared Team Image

  - *Team Image Canvas:* Fill out Purpose, Boundaries, Roles, Decision Rights, Power Norms, Team Norms, Conflict/Repair rituals on one page.

APPENDIX B TECHNIQUES AND METHODS FOR GROUP IMAGO COACHING FOR SELF-ORGANIZATION

- *Phantoms Sweep:* Acknowledge any lingering "ghosts" of past members or rules; ceremonially let them go.
- *Authority Ladder Exercise:* Place various decisions on spectrum from manager-led to team-delegated to visualize shifts.
- *Consensus on Norms:* Through discussion or voting, agree on key behaviors (e.g., "We challenge ideas, not persons").
- *Sign-Off:* Team members literally sign the canvas or give verbal commitment—marking a shared agreement.

- Step 4: Calibrate Roles, Authority, and Power
  - *Role Clarity Chart:* List each role (PO, SM, Dev, etc.) with responsibilities and name(s). Fill any gaps or overlaps.
  - *Responsibility Matrix (RACI/RCR):* Define who Recommends, who must Agree/Commit, who is Consulted or Informed for major workflows.
  - *Power Mapping:* Plot formal versus informal influence; discuss adjustments (ensure hidden leaders are recognized, silent voices empowered).
  - *BART Quick Scan:* Quick check of Boundaries, Authority, Role, Task clarity; e.g., "Do we all know our decision domain?"
  - *Team Leadership Task Allocation:* Identify leadership functions (boundary setting, mediating, etc.) and confirm the team has them covered (perhaps shared by roles or rotating).

APPENDIX B   TECHNIQUES AND METHODS FOR GROUP IMAGO COACHING FOR SELF-ORGANIZATION

- Step 5: Operating System for Self-Organization

    - *Decision Protocol Cheat-Sheets:* Reference cards for Consent (no objections = move forward) and Advice Process (seek input then decide).

    - *Working Agreement Draft:* Document specifics: meeting cadences, WIP limits, interrupt handling, communication norms (Slack/email usage), etc.

    - *WIP Limit Agreement:* Set and visualize WIP limits on task board; plan to review impact.

    - *Interrupt Policy:* Agree on procedure for urgent issues (on-call rotation, etc.) to protect focus.

    - *Retrospective Structure:* Decide retro frequency and include "team process" in agenda to regularly reflect on the OS itself.

    - *Peer Coaching Dojo:* Schedule periodic session where team members practice coaching each other on any issue—builds internal coaching muscle.

- Step 6: Run Bounded Experiments

    - Safe-to-Try Cards: Write experiments with hypothesis: If we do X, then Y will happen, evidenced by Z.

    - Time-box Experiments: Typically 1–4 weeks. Use an Experiment Board to track.

    - Rotate Roles Trials: e.g., rotate facilitation for daily Scrum as an experiment to increase engagement.

    - Advice Process Pilot: Select one domain (like choosing a tool) to try full advice process and evaluate.

APPENDIX B TECHNIQUES AND METHODS FOR GROUP IMAGO COACHING FOR SELF-ORGANIZATION

- Metrics for Experiments: Decide how to measure success (surveys, counts, time saved, etc.).

- Review in Retro: At experiment's end, discuss results: Adopt, Adjust, or Abandon?

- Step 7: Repair and Re-imprint

    - *Boundary Reset Ritual:* When an external or internal boundary is crossed, explicitly call it out and re-affirm the agreed boundary (perhaps literally re-drawing it or signing off again).

    - *Reparative Pair Dialogue:* Structured format for two members to reconcile after conflict (Acknowledge – Impact – Value – Request – Commit).

    - *Team Conflict Protocol:* Perhaps establish: "If conflict arises, first 1:1 discuss; if unresolved bring to team or coach," so issues are addressed, not buried.

    - *Phantom Farewell:* Name and symbolically remove influences of departed members or past norms (e.g., take down the old org chart on the wall).

    - *Highlight Successes:* Reinforce new imago by celebrating when team handles something well that they struggled with before ("Look, we solved this without any manager input, great job!").

    - *Coach's Imago Check:* As coach, be mindful not to impose your own ideal; seek supervision or peer coach on your involvement to avoid contamination of team with your biases.

APPENDIX B   TECHNIQUES AND METHODS FOR GROUP IMAGO COACHING FOR SELF-ORGANIZATION

- Step 8: Measure, Reflect, Sustain

  - *Self-Org Health Indicators:* Track metrics like % decisions made internally, decision throughput time, team empowerment survey results, etc., and share with team.

  - *Imago Shift Markers:* Observe language changes ("we" vs. "they"), independence level, phantom mentions; discuss these in retros as qualitative signs.

  - *Periodic Team Health Retro:* Every few months, dedicate a retro to team dynamics and self-management status, not just product/process.

  - *Continuous Learning:* Encourage reading, training, or visiting other Agile teams; maybe maintain a team journal of their journey.

  - *Peer Coaching Rotation:* Continue peer coaching sessions to address new challenges, keeping the team adaptive.

  - *Onboarding Guide:* Use the Team Image Canvas and OS as an onboarding tool for newcomers, possibly assigning a buddy to indoctrinate new members in the team's self-organizing culture.

  - *Celebrate Milestones:* Acknowledge anniversaries or big wins of being self-organizing (e.g., "one year since we took charge of our own backlog—pizza party!"). This positive reinforcement binds the team.

This collection of tools and exercises forms a toolkit you can draw from depending on the team's needs at each stage. They are ready to drop into workshops or day-to-day coaching as needed, much like a chef's set of knives—choose the one apt for the recipe at hand.

APPENDIX C

References

Chapter 2: Mastering the Fundamentals

- International Coaching Federation – Team Coaching Competencies (https://coachingfederation.org/resource/icf-team-coaching-competencies/)
- Agile Manifesto (2001) https://agilemanifesto.org/

Chapter 3: Sealing the Deal: Effective Contracting

- Hawkins, P. (2021). Leadership team coaching: Developing collective transformational leadership, 4th Edition
- Clutterbuck, D. (2020). Coaching the team at work, 2nd Edition.
- Turner, E., and Hawkins, P. (2016). Multi-stakeholder contracting in executive/business coaching: An analysis of practice and recommendations for gaining maximum value. *International Journal of Evidence-Based Coaching and Mentoring*
- Hawkins, P., and Smith, N. (2013) Coaching, Mentoring and Organizational Consultancy: Supervision and development, 2nd Edition.
- Thornton, C. (2024). Group and team coaching, 3rd Edition.

APPENDIX C REFERENCES

Chapter 4: Rewriting the Team Imago
On Group Imago and TA:

- Berne, E. (1963). The Structure and dynamics of organizations and groups.
- Tudor, K. (2011). Understanding group imago.
- Hay, J. (2009). Working it out at work: Understanding attitudes and building relationships.
- van Poelje, S. (2020). "Team coaching with transactional analysis."
- Napper, R., & Newton, T. (2014). Tactics: Transactional analysis concepts for all trainers

On Self-Organization:

- Hackman, J.R. (2002). Leading teams: Setting the stage for great performances.
- Laloux, F. (2014). Reinventing organizations,
- Eoyang, G., & Holladay, R. (2013). Adaptive action: Leveraging uncertainty in your organization.

Chapter 5: The Self-Organization Toolkit

- Berne, E. (1963). The structure and dynamics of organizations and groups.
- Gibb, J. (1961). Defensive communication. *Journal of Communication*, 11(3), 141-8.
- Gersick, C. J. G. (1988). Time and transition in work teams: Toward a new model of group development. *Academy of Management Journal*, 31(1), 9-41.

- Van Poijle, S. (2019). Team coaching with transactional analysis. Amsterdam: Intact Academy.
- Edmondson, A. C. (1999). Psychological safety and learning behavior in work teams. *Administrative Science Quarterly,* 44(2), 350-83.

Chapter 6: Clearing the Roadblocks: Overcoming Issues with Contracting

- Berne, E. (1964). Games people play: The psychology of human relationships.
- Micholt, N. (1992). Psychological distance and group intervention.
- Thornton, C. (2019). The art and science of working together.

Chapter 7: Power Plays and Hidden Agendas Revealed

- Thornton, C. (2024). Group and team coaching (Essential coaching skills and knowledge), 3rd Edition.
- Berne, E. (1964). Games people play: The psychology of human relationships.
- Van Poelje, S. (2020). Back to basics executive coaching series—how to get out of psychological games.

Chapter 8: Turning Resistance into Resilience

- Argyris, C. (1990). Overcoming organizational defenses: Facilitating organizational learning.
- Kegan, R., & Lahey, L. L. (2009). Immunity to change.
- Dweck, C. (2006). Mindset: The new psychology of success.

APPENDIX C REFERENCES

- Edmondson, A. C. (2018). The fearless organization.
- Google re:Work (Project Aristotle). "Guide: Understand team effectiveness."

Chapter 9: Staying True

- Code of Ethical Conduct for Agile Coaching https://agilealliance.org/agile-coaching-code-of-ethical-conduct/
- ICF Code of Ethics https://coachingfederation.org/credentialing/coaching-ethics/icf-code-of-ethics/
- Clarkson, P. (1993). Bystander games. *Transactional Analysis Journal* 23(3).
- Clarkson, P. (1987). The bystander role. *Transactional Analysis Journal* 17(3).

Chapter 10: Going Virtual

- Dumitru, C. (2021). Building virtual teams.
- Micholt, N. (1992). Psychological distance and group intervention.
- Clutterbuck, D., et al. (2019). The practitioner's handbook of team coaching.

Chapter 11: What If We Don't Need Another Tool to Be Impactful?

- Hawkins, P. (2021). Leadership team coaching: Developing collective transformational leadership, 4th Edition.
- Kegan, R. (1982). The evolving self: Problem and process in human development. Harvard University Press.

- Center for Creative Leadership (2025). Vertical vs. horizontal development: Why your leaders need both (https://www.ccl.org/articles/leading-effectively-articles/developing-talent-youre-probably-missing-vertical-development)
- Cox, E., Bachkirova, T., & Clutterbuck, D. (Eds). (2014). The complete handbook of coaching.
- Wageman, R., Nunes, D. A., Burruss, J. A., & Hackman, J. R. (2008). Senior leadership teams: What it takes to make them great.
- Ellis, K., & Boston, R. (2019). Upgrade: Building your capacity for complexity.
- Bluckert, P., & Thorp, A. (2019). A comprehensive guide to vertical development.

Chapter 12: Pause, Reflect, Act

- Schon, D. (1983). The reflective practitioner: How professionals think in action.
- Cox, E. (2013). Coaching and learning: Integrating reflective practice into coaching.
- Van Nieuwerburgh, C., & Love, D. (2024). Your essential guide to effective reflective practice: Improving practice through self-reflection and writing.
- Johns, C. (2022). Becoming a reflective practitioner, 6th Edition.

Chapter 13: The Power of Supervision and Deliberate Practice

- Turner, E., & Palmer, S. (2018). The heart of coaching supervision: Working with reflection and self-care.

APPENDIX C REFERENCES

- Hawkins, P. (2021). Leadership team coaching developing collective transformational leadership.

- Passmore, J. (ed.). (2021). Succeeding as a coach: Insights from the experts.

- Rousmaniere, T. (2024). Deliberate practice for psychotherapists: A guide to improving clinical effectiveness.

- de Haan, E., & Regouin-van Leeuwen, W. (2022). Being supervised: A guide for supervisees.

Chapter 14: Mastering the Inner Game: Staying Grounded in Chaos

- Shirzad, C. (2012). Positive intelligence: Why only 20% of teams and individuals achieve their true potential AND HOW YOU CAN ACHIEVE YOURS.

- World Health Organization. (2020). Doing what matters in times of stress: An illustrated guide.

- Forman, C., & Bryan, U. (2019). The practice of self-management: A handbook for walking the path from reactivity to presence and connection.

- Harris, R. (2019). ACT made simple: An easy-to-read primer on acceptance and commitment therapy.

Index

A

Accelerating learning, 30
Acceptance, 460, 462
Acceptance and Commitment Therapy (ACT), 450, 456, 460
    acceptance and expansion, 462, 463
    cognitive defusion techniques, 461
    metaphors, 462
    real story scenario, 464, 465
    reframing perspectives, 463
    unhooking from mental traps, 460
Accomplice Saboteurs, 452
Accountability, 334
ACT, *see* Acceptance and Commitment Therapy (ACT)
ACT cognitive defusion techniques, 461
ACT defusion, 463
ACT grounding techniques, 457
Action learning, 440–442
Activate, 475, 476
Active listening, 33–35, 43, 315, 329

Adaptability, 336
Adapted imago, 88
Adaptive system, 85
Administrative contracting, 63
Adult development, 376–378
Advice process, 145
Agency, 268
Agent of management, 435
Agile, 244
Agile Alliance, 283
Agile coach, 10–13, 16
    detective, 246
    effectiveness, 449
    journaling, 386–388
    progressing, 450
    resistance (*see* Resistance)
    role, 241
    structured reflection frameworks, 390–395
    team, 241
    team conflict, 451
Agile coaches
Agile coaching, 295, 302, 303, 305, 381
Agile fatigue, 488
Agile frameworks, 449
Agile philosophy, 265

INDEX

Agile practices, 343
Agile revolution, 498
Agile's "Five Whys", root-cause analysis, 269
Agile team coach, 483
Agile teams
    resilience (*see* Resilience, Agile team)
    resistance (*see* Resistance)
Agile transformations, 488
Agility, 352, 353
Anxiety/self-doubt, 450
"Ask-Tell-Ask" communication, 479, 480
Assertiveness, 298
Authentic engagement *vs.* going through the motions, 399–401
Authentic reflection, 402
Authority, 97, 139
Authority ladder, 136, 137

B

BART, *see* Boundary, authority, role, task (BART)
Behavioral agreements, 28
Behaviors of Saboteurs, 454, 455
Blind spots, 401, 402
Body language, 15, 186
Boundary, authority, role, task (BART), 141
Boundary drift, 159, 160
Boundary spanning, 218

Bystander behavior
    ethical considerations, 294
Bystander effect, 291
Bystander stance, 291, 294, 299

C

Catching, 373
CDE, *see* Containers, differences and exchanges (CDE)
Challenging assignments, 364, 365
Challenging team, 463
Chartered Institute of Personnel and Development (CIPD), 371
Chessboard metaphor, 462
CIPD, *see* Chartered Institute of Personnel and Development (CIPD)
Clarified imago, 90, 91
Clear contracting, 286, 293, 294
CLEAR model
    action, 425
    Agile meeting/workshop, 426
    contract, 423
    explore, 424, 425
    framework, 423
    listen, 423, 424
    review, 426
    supervision conversation, 426
Client relationships, 434
Coaching engagement, 261, 285
Coaching supervision, 300, 356–358

action learning, 440–442
checklist mentality, 442–444
CLEAR model, 422–427
description, 406
developing deeper insight and improving practice, 410–412
enhanced reflection and self-awareness, 408
ethical guidance, 409
field—and, 405
group supervision, 438, 439
guided learning, 406
individual supervision, 437
vs. mentoring, 407, 408
mutual trust, 406
one-to-one, 407
peer supervision/peer coaching, 439, 440
practical application
  emotional responses and biases, 435, 436
  ethical dilemmas in multi-stakeholder environments, 434, 435
  team dynamics and agendas, 433, 434
professional accountability, 409
restoration, 409, 410
self-care, 409, 410
seven-eyed model, 415–422
signals and links, 412
teams and clients, 407
theory and "being", 444, 445
"3 P's" model, 413–415
tools/techniques, 405
work with clients, 406
Coaching techniques, 7
Coach's resilience, 373
Coach's responses, 31
Coach supervision sessions
  principles, navigation
    contact before contract, 489
    power dynamics, 490
    resistance, 489
    self-organization, 491
    supervision, 490
    system holds pattern, 489
    team's "secret life", 490
Coach's vertical development
  Agile coach, 347
  agility, 352, 353
  "by the book", 345
  complexity and ambiguity, 348, 349
  cultivating (*see* Cultivating vertical development)
  ethical maturity and wisdom, 354, 355
  vs. horizontal, 347, 348
  and horizontal development, 345
  operating system, 346, 347
  personal and professional growth, 345
  researchers, 345
  role-modeling growth, 352, 353
  self-awareness, 347

INDEX

Coach's vertical development (*cont.*)
  "size of person", 345
  space under pressure, 350, 351
  stages, 346
  stakeholders and agendas, 351, 352
  systemic challenges, 349, 350
  team leader's development, 353, 354
  team's goals, 346
  theorists, 346
  transformation in mindset and meaning, 345
Code of Ethics, 285
Cognitive defusion, 460
Collaborative documents, 331
Collective efficacy, 267
Committed action, 466, 467
Common coaching values, 465
Communities of Practice (CoPs), 169, 439
Competencies
  active listening, 33–35
  client growth, 37–39
  coaching mindset, 25, 27
  establishing and maintaining agreements, 27–29
  ethical practice, 24, 25
  evoking awareness, 35–37
  maintaining presence, 31, 32
  overview, 23, 24
  professional standards, 21
  trust and safety, 29, 30
Confidentiality, 20, 285–289

Conflict, 333
Conflict avoidance, 215
Conflict coaching, 14
Conflicting agendas, 247, 248, 258–260
Conflict of interest, 288
  coaching contract, 289
  defined, 288
  ethical practice, 289
  professional integrity, 289
  role duality, 288
Congruence/integrity, 444
Conscious design, 139
Constructive challenging, 480
Contact
  conditions, 59, 60
  defined, 58
  elements, 58, 59
  manipulative/defensive behaviors, 58
  narrative, 61
Containers, differences and exchanges (CDE), 85, 86
Continual learning, 301
Continuous improvement, 9, 26, 37, 43, 194
Continuous learning, 361, 362
Continuously learning, 437
Continuous reflection, 373
Contracting, 260, 288, 293, 297
Contracts, 173
  alliance, 52–55
  coaching, 71
  contact, 57–62

context, 119–121
difficulties, 49–51
flow, 52
levels, 62, 63, 77
   administrative, 63
   professional, 63
   psychological (*see* Psychological contracting)
meeting sponsors, 55–57
negative goals, 76
omitted sponsor, 74
organizational goals, 47
purposes, 47
rebalancing, 189
safety, 48
team coaching *vs.* skills transfer, 72, 73
vagueness, 75
Contractual engagement, 295
CoPs, *see* Communities of Practice (CoPs)
COVID-19 pandemic, 305
Crafting agreements, 28
Critical moments reflection, 394, 395
Cultivating vertical development
   challenging assignments, 364, 365
   coaching supervision, 356–358
   continuous learning, 361, 362
   individual coaching, 358, 359
   peer coaching partnerships, 359, 360, 363, 367
   practices, 355, 356
   reflective practice, 359–361
   seeking and processing feedback, 363, 364
   self" evolution, 355
   systemic awareness, 366, 367
   teams and organizations, 367, 368
Cultural sensitivity, 312
"Culture of silence", 243
Customer collaboration, 28, 34, 39

D

Daily micro-reflections, 396
Decision-making, 40, 81, 145, 211
Decisive action, 475
Deeper learning, 376–378
Deep listening, 34
Defensive behaviors, 245
Defusion, 461
Deliberate practice, 447
   autopilot, 428
   checklist mentality, 442–444
   coaching skills/behaviors, 427
   in day-to-day development, 428
   dominant voices—perhaps, 428
   experience/training courses, 427
   focus on goal, 431
   get feedback, 432
   immediate reflection, 432
   mechanistic coaching/supervision, 428

Deliberate practice (*cont.*)
   micro-skills and meta-skills, 428, 429
   psychotherapeutic practice, 429–434
   refine and repeat, 432
   specific skill, 431
   stretch goal, 431
   team coaching, 427
   theory and "being", 444, 445
   traditional learning, 427
   visualize and prepare, 431
Depth *vs.* surface, 42
Developmental researchers, 345
Difficult behaviors, 256–258
Difficult conversation, 382–384
Digital fatigue, 309
Digital whiteboards, 331
Dot voting, 137
Double-loop learning, 270, 376–378
Double-loop reflection, 378
Drama Triangles, 488, 490, 493, 495, 508–510

E

Ectoplasm, 93
Effective communication, 313
Emotional aspect, 382
Emotional cues, 186
Emotional intelligence, 373
Emotional self-management, 250
Emotions, 452

Empathic and neutral coaching stance, 250, 251
Empathize, 471
Empathy, 298, 312, 317, 329, 337, 472
Empathy power, 471
Empowerment, 97, 229
Escalation path, 146
Ethical agility, 299
Ethical competencies, 302
Ethical dilemmas, 384–386
   in multi-stakeholder environments, 434, 435
Ethical maturity, 299, 300, 302, 354, 355
Ethical team coaching, 291
Ethical vigilance, 295
Ethics, 283
Explore, 472, 473
External lenses, 402

F

Face-to-face conversation, 32, 305
Facilitation, 6, 12, 13, 31
Facilitation *vs.* coaching, 6, 40–42
Family constellation, 92
Fear of change, 242, 243
Feedback, 450
"Fight-or-flight" stress response, 451
Formal power, 97, 143
Framing—conflict, 465
Free-form journaling, 390

INDEX

G

Genogram, 123
Gestalt theory, 251
Gibbs' reflective cycle, 390–392
GICSO, *see* Group-Imago Coaching for Self-Organization (GICSO)
Global Supervisors' Network, 439
Group coaching models, 246
Group functioning, 156
Group-Imago Coaching for Self-Organization (GICSO)
  bounded experiments, 152–158
  contract and context, 119–121
  individual imagos, 121–128
  measure, reflect, sustain, 165–172
  OS, self-organization, 144–152
  repair and re-imprint, 158–165
  roles, authority and power, 138–144
  shared working, 128–138
  steps, 117, 118
Group imago development
  calibrate roles, authority and power, 515
  contract & context, 513, 514
  create shared team image, 514, 515
  elicit individual imagoes, 514
  measure, reflect, sustain, 518
  operating system for self-organization, 516
  repair and re-imprint, 517
  run bounded experiments, 516, 517
Group maturity process, 95
Group supervision, 438, 439
Growth mindset, 265
Growth mindset behaviors, 266
Growth mindset culture, 266
Guiding lighthouse, 469, 484

H

Hawthorne effect of observation, 170
Henley eight questions, 392–394
Hidden dynamics, 197
  addressing, 209
  challenges
    agendas and unspoken goals, 212–214
    conflicts and tensions, 214–216
    power imbalances and authority, 210, 211
    role ambiguity and boundary issues, 216–219
  concepts, 201
  continuous development, 237
  cultural shift, 237
  diagnostics, 207, 208
  dysfunctional pattern, 236
  high-maturity team, 237
  secret life
    alliances and cliques, 205
    defensive routines, 203

531

INDEX

Hidden dynamics (*cont.*)
    emotional undercurrents, 205
    factors, 202
    groupthink and
      conformity, 206
    hidden agendas, 204
    power dynamics and status
      differences, 204
    psychological safety, 203
    unspoken expectations and
      norms, 204
Hidden group dynamics, 246
Historical imago, 91
Horizontal development, 345
Humble inquiry, 215
Hyper-Rational, 454
Hyper-Vigilant coach, 454

I

ICF, *see* International Coaching
    Federation (ICF)
Identity conflicts, 384–386
Imago
    assumptions, 113
    boundaries, roles, authority and
      power, 95–103
    concept, 81
    defined, 87
    discovery phase, 121
    drawing exercise, 122
    ethical considerations
      autonomy and adult ego
        state, 111
      continuous consent, 111
      cultural changes, 112
      cultural sensitivity, 110
      dual roles confusion, 110
    group fantasy, 91
    group template, 92
    insights, 127
    internal models, 94
    interviewing, 124–128
    leader figures, 93
    operating manual, 94
    organizational shift, 114
    phantoms, 93
    relational team genogram, 123
    secondarily operative and
      historical, 91
    self-organization, 82–87
    self-reinforcement, 113
    shift markers, 167, 168
    stages
      adapted, 88
      clarified, 90
      operative, 89
      provisional, 88
      secondarily adjusted, 89
    team pictures, 82
    traps, 104–111
    unconscious processes, 91
Immune system, 245
Implicit team, 202
Individual coaching, 358, 359
Individual (one-on-one)
    coaching, 5
Individual supervision, 437

Influence paths, 143
Informal power, 97, 143
Information flow, 187
Inner game response flow, 451
   cognitive and emotional triggers, 452
   physiological signs of stress and overwhelm, 451
   real story scenario, 455, 456
   The Avoider, 453
   The Controller, 453
   The Hyper-Achiever, 454
   The Hyper-Vigilant, 454
   The Pleaser, 453
   The Victim, 453
   Unmasking your Saboteurs, 452
Inner Saboteurs, 452
Innovate, 473, 474
Instant grounding
   ACT, 457
   notice five things, 457
   physical anchors and PQ Brain "activation", 458, 459
   The power of the pause, 456
   real story scenario, 459, 460
   soothing rhythm breathing, 458
   three-minute breathing space, 457, 458
Integration and continuous practice
   "Ask-Tell-Ask" communication, 479, 480
   constructive challenging, 480
   developing a sustainable practice, 478, 479
   go-to practices for in-the-moment coaching, 479
   real story scenario, 482, 483
   reflection prompts for deeper learning, 481, 482
   stress inoculation phrases, 479
Internal mentor, 385
Internal team conflicts, conflicting agendas, 259
International Coaching Federation (ICF), 4, 23, 184, 371
Interpersonal conflicts, 30, 160, 161
In the vortex, 451

J

Journaling, 386–388
   free-form, 390
   transformational, 388–390

K

Knowledge acquisition, 73

L

Landscape, team coaching, 491
   to ecosystem orchestration, 492
   responsible metrics, 493
   use AI, 492

INDEX

Leadership, 335, 454
Leadership development, 19
Leadership task, 93, 143
Legacy *vs.* emerging imago, 164
Levels of consciousness, 346
Logistical agreements, 27

M

Manager-driven performance review, 443
Meaning-making stages, 346
Mechanistic approach, 443
Meta-commentary, 383
Metaphors, 37
MI, *see* Motivational interviewing (MI)
Micromanagement, 86
Micro-resets, 163
Mindful communication, 32
Mindset, 25, 27, 43
Miro, 331
Misunderstanding, 310, 313, 314, 326, 333–335
Model team resilience, 263, 264
Motivational interviewing (MI), 429, 430
Multi-hour virtual workshop, 317
Multi-layered dynamics, 433
Multiple agendas, 288
Multi-stakeholder contracting, 56
Multi-stakeholder environments ethical dilemmas, 434, 435
Mural, 331

N

Navigate, 474, 475
90-day practice architecture
 build resilience infrastructure, 495
 daily reflective practice-five minutes, 496
 establish supervision architecture, 494
 foundation audit, 493
 surfacing hidden dynamics, 494, 495
Nonviolent communication (NVC), 14, 254
Norms/behavior patterns, 14
Notice five things (5-5-5 Senses Exercise), 457
NVC, *see* Nonviolent communication (NVC)

O

Observing Self, 461, 464
One-and-done achievement, 478
Operating system (OS)
 components
  decision protocols, 145–147
  feedback loops, 148, 149
  WIP and work rules, 147, 148
 defined, 144
 intentional, 144
 team working agreement, 149, 150

INDEX

techniques, 150, 152
Operative imago, 89
Organizational dynamics, 449
OS, *see* Operating system (OS)
Ownership, 54

P

Pause button, 371
Peer coaching, 169, 170
Peer coaching partnerships, 359, 360, 363, 367
Peer supervision/peer coaching, 439, 440
Perceived loss of control, 244, 245
Personal conflict, 96
Personal vindication, 232
Philosophy, purpose, process (PPP), 413–415
Physical anchors and PQ Brain "activation", 458, 459
Positive Intelligence approach, 458
Positive Intelligence framework, 452
Positive Intelligence (PQ), 450, 452
Positive reinforcement, 258
"Post-traumatic growth", psychology, 271
Power dynamics, 97
Power mapping, 139
Power shifts, 143
PPP, *see* Philosophy, purpose, process (PPP)
PQ, *see* Positive Intelligence (PQ)

Present-moment intervention, 251–253
Preventive action, 257
Proactivity, 268
Product priorities, 130
Professional coaching, 11, 20, 371
Professional contracting, 64
Professionalism, 497
Provisional imago, 88
Psychodynamic interventions, 103
Psychological contracting
    administrative considerations, 67
    agreements, 65
    client growth, 66
    coaching content and boundaries, 67
    ethical practice, 65
    evoking awareness, 66
    group dynamics, 64
    relational agreements, 69
    setting context, 70
    themes, 67, 68
    trust and safety, 66
Psychological distance
    balancing empathy and accountability, 188
    coach–client–sponsor relationship, 178
    concept, 177
    configurations, 179
    diagnosis, 185–188
    hidden contracts, 198
    interventions, 189–194
    patterns, 182–184

INDEX

Psychological distance (*cont.*)
  questions tool, 195–198
  three-party coaching contract, 178
  type A contract, 178
  type B contract, 179
  type C contract, 180
  type D contract, 181
Psychological games
  Ain't It Awful, 230–235
  defined, 219
  Drama Triangle, 219
  formula, 220
  If It Weren't For You, 226–230
  I'm Only Trying to Help You, 223–226
  Why Don't You/Yes, But, 220–223
Psychological safety, 14, 20, 29, 30, 61, 75, 203, 215, 233, 243, 244, 248, 253, 256, 257, 264
Psychological safety assessment, 495, 496
Psychology, 97
Psychotherapeutic practice, 429, 430

Q

Quiet revolution, 498

R

RACI, *see* Responsible, accountable, consulted, informed (RACI)

RACI adaptations, 146
RAPID, *see* Recommend, Agree, Perform, Input, Decide (RAPID)
RAR, *see* Recommend-Agree-Request (RAR)
RCR, *see* Recommend–Commit–Request (RCR)
Reality-testing questions, 229
Recommend, Agree, Perform, Input, Decide (RAPID), 146
Recommend-Agree-Request (RAR), 139
Recommend–Commit–Request (RCR), 139, 146
Reconnecting with purpose and values
  clarifying Agile coaching values, 465, 466
  committed action, 466, 467
  external situations, 465
  ongoing scenario, 468, 469
  Sage's guiding light, 467, 468
Reflection, 269, 271
Reflection exercise, 415
Reflection-for-action, 376, 382, 383
Reflection-in-action, 374, 375, 383
Reflection-on-action, 375, 384
Reflection prompts for deeper learning, 481, 482
Reflective approach, 380, 384
Reflective exercise, 385
Reflective practice, 359–361

INDEX

Agile coaches, 372
   in Agile team coaching, 371
   authentic engagement *vs.* going through the motions, 399–401
   blind spots, 401, 402
   burnout, 384–386
   catching, 373
   coaching, 374
   continuous personal and professional development, 372
   continuous reflection, 373
   deeper learning, 376–378
   designing, 396, 397
   difficult conversation, 382–384
   ethical dilemma, 384–386
   facilitation skills, 373
   identity conflicts, 384–386
   journaling, 386–388
   professional coaching, 371
   reflection-for-action, 376
   reflection-in-action, 374, 375
   reflection-on-action, 375
   rumination, 398, 399
   scaling framework, 373
   self-awareness, 372, 373
   self-regulation, 372
   structured reflection frameworks, 390–395
   superficial *vs.* transformational reflection, 378–380
   team resistance, 380–382
   tense meeting, 372
   transformational journaling, 388–390
Reframing, 229, 464
Remote communication tools, 311
Remote work, 318
Reparative pair dialogue format, 131
Resilience, 241, 450
Resilience, Agile team
   adaptation, 269–271
   aligning changes, 274
   define, 263, 264
   foster team agency, 267–269
   growth mindset (embrace uncertainty), 265, 266
   internal storms, 263
   leveraging strengths, 272–274
   model team resilience, 263, 264
   ownership, 267–269
   purpose, 272–274
   reflection, 269–271
Resistance, 241
   root causes
      coach's missteps, 248, 249
      conflicting agendas, 247, 248
      contribution, 248, 249
      fear of change, 242, 243
      group dynamics, 245, 246
      habitual patterns, 245, 246
      lack of trust, 243, 244
      perceived loss of control, 244, 245
      psychological safety, 243, 244

Resistance (*cont.*)
    real-world example, 246
    systemic and hidden, 246
  strategies
    address and reframe
      patterns/stories, 255, 256
    conflicting agendas, 258–260
    contracting, 260, 262
    empathic and neutral
      coaching stance, 250, 251
    facilitate open dialogue,
      253, 254
    manage difficult
      behaviors, 256–258
    non-defensive listening, 253
    present-moment
      intervention, 251–253
    re-contracting, 260–262
Resistance Radar, 275, 277
Respect, 75
Responsible, accountable,
    consulted, informed
    (RACI), 18, 146
Retrospective exercises, 37
Return on expectations (ROE), 19
Return on investment (ROI), 18, 19
ROE, *see* Return on
    expectations (ROE)
ROI, *see* Return on
    investment (ROI)
Role-modeling growth, 352, 353
Role-playing, 37
Round-robin sharing, 30
R→R Flywheel, 275, 276

recognize, 276
recognize, Resistance
    Radar, 277
re-contract, 276, 278
reframe, 276, 278
reinforce, 277, 279
Rumination, 398, 399

S

Saboteur mode, 469
Saboteurs, 454
Saboteur *vs.* Sage, 470
Safe-to-try cards, 153
Scrum events, 443
Scrum Guide, 449
Scrum master, 241, 243, 251
Secondarily adjusted imago, 89
Secondarily operative
    imago, 91
Seeking and processing feedback,
    363, 364
Self-assessment, 430
Self-awareness, 17, 372, 373, 408,
    436, 450
Self-awareness and emotional
    regulation, 350
Self-care for coaches, 410
Self-correction, 430
Self-evaluation, 430
Self-expression, 445
Self-management, 81, 82, 102,
    153, 170
Self-observation, 430

INDEX

Self-organization, 7, 8, 335, 488, 491, 498, 500
- authority, 97
- boundaries, 95
- consultant, 95
- diagnostics, 101
- explicit structure, 98
- formal/informal power, 97
- fundamentals, 98
- hidden leader, 98
- multi-level scan, 102
- OS, 144–152
- psychodynamic (intrapsychic) level, 100
- psychodynamic issues, 102
- psychodynamic work, 103
- relational (interpersonal) level, 100
- roles, 96
- scaffolding, 95
- shape conditions, 86
- structural level, 99
- teams, 82–87

Self-Organization Toolkit, 513
Self-organizing teams, 498, 499
Self-reflection, 430, 445, 478
Self-regulation, 372
Self-reinforcement, 430
Seven-eyed model
- Agile coaching context, 415
- client (or team) system, 415, 416
- coaching relationship, 416, 417
- coaching session/relationship, 415
- coach's inner feelings and reactions, 417, 418
- coach's interventions, 416
- legacy processes, 422
- management decisions, 422
- multiple interconnected elements, 421
- organizational culture, 422
- parallels and patterns, 422
- supervisor's internal process, 419
- supervisory relationship, 418, 419
- techniques to use, 421
- wider context, 420, 421

Shifting to Sage mode
- activate, 475, 476
- empathize, 471, 472
- explore, 472, 473
- innovate, 473, 474
- navigate, 474, 475
- positive brain circuits, 469, 470
- real story scenario, 476, 477
- from Saboteur to Sage, 470, 471
- Shirzad Chamine's Positive Intelligence, 469
- *The five Sage powers in action*, 471

Single-loop learning, 376
Situational awareness, 16
Six-minute free-write, 388
Skilled virtual coach, 329
Social camaraderie, 232
Soothing rhythm breathing, 458

INDEX

Sponsor alignment, 52, 53
Sponsor meetings, 55–57
Sprint-level or monthly reflection, 397
Stress inoculation phrases, 479, 483
Stress responses, 456
Structured round-robin, 254
Superficiality, 379
Superficial reflection, 379
Superficial *vs.* transformational reflection, 378–380
Supervisee-supervisor dialogue, 411
Sustainable agility, 43
Sustainable development, 37
Swirling dynamics, 434
Systemic awareness, 366, 367
Systemic eclectic coaching, 446
Systemic/ecosystemic perspective, 349

T

Task-focused team, 202
TDD, *see* Test-driven development (TDD)
Team building, 5
Team charter, 293
Team charter *vs.* image, 137
Team coaching
   vs. Agile facilitation, 40–42
   Agile landscape and needs, 3–5
   challenges
      balancing, 16, 17
      coach development, 20, 21
      embedding, 22
      resistance, 19, 20
      ROI, 18, 19
      Scrum masters, 17, 18
   cohesive client, 284
   competencies (*see* Competencies)
   primary client, 284
   principles
      change and complexity, 10
      collaboration and communication, 8
      continuous improvement, 9
      self-organizing teams, 7, 8
   psychological games, 219–235
   vs. team development practices, 5–7
Team coaching *vs.* skills transfer, 72, 73
Team conversation, 54
Team development
   modalities, 41
   stakeholder, 55
Team dynamics, 13–16, 28, 33, 52
Team health champion, 168
Team health retrospectives, 15
Team image canvas, 128–138, 172
Team leader's development, 353, 354
Team mapping, 61
Team member interviews, 53
Team performance, 43
Team process improvement, 168

Team resistance, 380–382
Teams, 245
Team's perspective, 381
Team *vs.* management responsibilities, 84
Test-driven development (TDD), 265
Textbook approach, 268
The Avoider, 453
The coach's secret weapon, 356
The Controller, 453
The Controller Saboteur, 453
The Hyper-Achiever, 454
The Hyper-Vigilant, 454
The "inner game" of coaching, 449
The Pleaser, 453
The Restless, 454
The Sage's guiding light, 467, 468
The Victim, 453
Thinking Self, 461, 464
Three-minute breathing space, 457, 458
3 P's triangle, 414
Transactional Analysis (TA), 58, 87, 178, 219, 246, 292, 296, 297
   Drama Triangles, 508–510
   ego states, 501, 502
   games, 510, 511
   life positions, 502–504
   positive strokes, 507, 508
   scripts and injunctions, 504, 505
   symbiosis, 505–507
Transformational journaling, 388–390
Transformational reflection, 378, 379
Transformation initiative, 452
Trust, 310, 312
Trust-building, 311
Type A contract, 178
Type B contract, 179
Type C contract, 180
Type D contract, 181

U

Unspoken issues, 13

V

Vertical development
   capacity, 344
   coach's (*see* Coach's vertical development)
   coach's being and mindset, 343
   coach's internal capacity to navigate complexity, 343
   complexity, 344
   mental and emotional breadth, 343
Video conferencing, 308, 330
Virtual coaching, 306, 309, 310, 323, 330, 337
   active listening, 315
   challenges, 306, 307
   design coaching sessions, 318–320
   vs. in-person, 306

INDEX

Virtual coaching (*cont.*)
   PowerPoint use, 319
   practices and interventions, 306, 323
      build cohesion and camaraderie, 332, 333
      coach's presence, 327–330
      contracting (*see* Virtual contracting)
      encourage leadership, 335, 336
      inclusive communication, 333
      leverage digital tools, 330–332
      manage conflict, 333, 334
      promote accountability and self-organization, 334, 335
   virtual sessions, 321, 322
Virtual communication gaps, 313
Virtual conflict, 333
Virtual contracting, 323
   communication norms, 324
   emotional transparency and trust-building, 325, 326
   logistics and tools, 326
   presence and availability, 324, 325
Virtual facilitation, 318
Virtual-specific contracting, 323, 327
Virtual team coaching sessions, 319
Volatile, uncertain, complex, and ambiguous (VUCA), 348
Voting, 137

W, X, Y

Weekly dedicated time, 396
WIP, *see* Work-in-process (WIP)
Working agreement, 440
Working agreement/prime directive, 469
Work-in-process (WIP), 147, 148, 155

Z

Zone of genius, 385
Zoom fatigue, 306, 309

GPSR Compliance

The European Union's (EU) General Product Safety Regulation (GPSR) is a set of rules that requires consumer products to be safe and our obligations to ensure this.

If you have any concerns about our products, you can contact us on

ProductSafety@springernature.com

In case Publisher is established outside the EU, the EU authorized representative is:

Springer Nature Customer Service Center GmbH
Europaplatz 3
69115 Heidelberg, Germany

www.ingramcontent.com/pod-product-compliance
Lightning Source LLC
LaVergne TN
LVHW021954060526
838201LV00048B/1574